A Modern Guide to Creative Economies

ELGAR MODERN GUIDES

Elgar Modern Guides offer a carefully curated review of a selected topic, edited or authored by a leading scholar in the field. They survey the significant trends and issues of contemporary research for both advanced students and academic researchers.

The books provide an invaluable appraisal and stimulating guide to the current research landscape, offering state-of-the-art discussions and selective overviews covering the critical matters of interest alongside recent developments. Combining incisive insight with a rigorous and thoughtful perspective on the essential issues, the books are designed to offer an inspiring introduction and unique guide to the diversity of modern debates.

Elgar Modern Guides will become an essential go-to companion for researchers and graduate students but will also prove stimulating for a wider academic audience interested in the subject matter. They will be invaluable to anyone who wants to understand as well as simply learn.

Titles in the series include:

A Modern Guide to the Digitalization of Infrastructure
Edited by Juan Montero and Matthias Finger

A Modern Guide to Sports Economics
Edited by Ruud H. Koning and Stefan Kesenne

A Modern Guide to Labour and the Platform Economy
Edited by Jan Drahokoupil and Kurt Vandaele

A Modern Guide to Financial Shocks and Crises
Edited by Giovanni Ferri and Vincenzo D'Apice

A Modern Guide to Local and Regional Politics
Edited by Colin Copus, Richard Kerley and Alistair Jones

A Modern Guide to Food Economics
Edited by Jutta Roosen and Jill E. Hobbs

A Modern Guide to Post-Keynesian Institutional Economics
Edited by Charles J. Whalen

A Modern Guide to Creative Economies
Edited by Roberta Comunian, Alessandra Faggian, Jarna Heinonen and Nick Wilson

A Modern Guide to Creative Economies

Edited by

Roberta Comunian

King's College London, UK

Alessandra Faggian

Gran Sasso Science Institute, Italy

Jarna Heinonen

University of Turku, Finland

Nick Wilson

King's College London, UK

ELGAR MODERN GUIDES

Edward Elgar
PUBLISHING

Cheltenham, UK • Northampton, MA, USA

Published by
Edward Elgar Publishing Limited
The Lypiatts
15 Lansdown Road
Cheltenham
Glos GL50 2JA
UK

Edward Elgar Publishing, Inc.
William Pratt House
9 Dewey Court
Northampton
Massachusetts 01060
USA

A catalogue record for this book
is available from the British Library

Library of Congress Control Number: 2022938908

This book is available electronically in the **Elgar**online
Geography, Planning and Tourism subject collection
http://dx.doi.org/10.4337/9781789905496

ISBN 978 1 78990 548 9 (cased)
ISBN 978 1 78990 549 6 (eBook)

Printed and bound by CPI Group (UK) Ltd, Croydon, CR0 4YY

We would like to dedicate this book to all the citizens of Europe and their incredible diversity and creativity. In an increasingly divided world, the European Union and its funding programmes have brought us together to work on a project that aims to develop inclusive and sustainable creative economies. We are grateful for this opportunity and for the richness of culture, creativity and care that we can find across Europe.

RC, AF, JH and NW

Contents

Figures

Tables

Contributors

Mark Banks, Professor of Cultural Economy at the School of Culture and Creative Arts, University of Glasgow (United Kingdom).

Ruth Bridgstock, Director of Employability at Swinburne University of Technology (Australia).

Scott Brook, Associate Professor of Communication at the School of Media and Communication, RMIT University (Australia).

Chiara Burlina, Assistant Professor of Applied Economics at the 'Marco Fanno' Department of Economics and Management, University of Padova (Italy).

Roberta Comunian, Reader in Creative Economy at the Department for Culture, Media and Creative Industries, King's College London (United Kingdom).

Alessandro Crociata, Associate Professor of Applied Economics at the Department of Social Sciences, Gran Sasso Science Institute (Italy).

Manfredi de Bernard, PhD candidate at the Department for Culture, Media and Creative Industries, King's College London (United Kingdom).

Tamsyn Dent, Lecturer in Cultural Work at the Department for Culture, Media and Creative Industries, King's College London (United Kingdom).

Lauren England, Lecturer in Creative Economies at the Department for Culture, Media and Creative Industries, King's College London (United Kingdom).

Alessandra Faggian, Professor of Applied Economics, Director of Social Sciences and Deputy Rector at the Gran Sasso Science Institute, L'Aquila (Italy).

Jonathan Gross, Lecturer in Creative and Cultural Industries, at the Department for Culture, Media and Creative Industries, King's College London (United Kingdom).

Jarna Heinonen, Professor of Entrepreneurship at Turku School of Economics, University of Turku (Finland).

Silvie Jacobi, Director of the London School of Mosaic, a not-for-profit education and cultural hub in London (United Kingdom).

Arja Lemmetyinen, Research Fellow at the Turku School of Economics, University of Turku, Pori Unit (Finland).

Lorenzo Mizzau, Assistant Professor of Organization Studies at the Department of Economics and Business Studies, University of Genoa (Italy).

Fabrizio Montanari, Associate Professor of Organization Studies at the Department of Communication and Economics, University of Modena and Reggio Emilia (Italy).

Annette Naudin, Associate Professor in Learning and Teaching at Birmingham Institute for Media and English, Birmingham City University (United Kingdom).

Lenita Nieminen, Researcher at the Turku School of Economics, University of Turku, Pori Unit (Finland).

Damiano Razzoli, Assistant Professor, Department of Communication and Economics, University of Modena and Reggio Emilia (Italy).

Stefano Rodighiero, PhD candidate at the Department of Management, University of Bologna (Italy).

Jon Swords, Senior Research Fellow at the Department of Theatre, Film, Television and Interactive Media, University of York (United Kingdom).

Jessica Tanghetti, Postdoctoral Research Fellow at the Department of Management, Alma Mater Studiorum University of Bologna (Italy).

Federica Viganò, Researcher at the Faculty of Education, Free University of Bozen (Italy).

Nick Wilson, Professor of Culture and Creativity, at the Department for Culture, Media and Creative Industries, King's College London (United Kingdom).

Acknowledgements

First of all, we are very grateful for the financial support provided by the European Union (grant agreement No 822314) through the Horizon 2020 project 'Developing Inclusive and Sustainable Creative Economies' (DISCE). The DISCE project has allowed the authors to meet, discuss and work together for three years, creating a wonderful opportunity for collaboration, creative idea generation and the development of this book. While this collection does not include specific outcomes or data from the DISCE project per se, it does include many reflections that have fed and supported our thinking across the research.

We would like to thank our very supportive colleagues across our institutions (King's College London, Gran Sasso Science Institute and the University of Turku) for contributing to the book and for supporting the project in many different ways.

A Modern Guide to Creative Economies has been written across 2020 and 2021; an immensely difficult and challenging time for so many. Individually and collectively, all the authors have, of course, been affected by Covid-19. At a time when both the challenges and opportunities of connection with others have been brought so sharply into focus, we would particularly like to acknowledge the sustaining support of our families, our friends and our respective local communities. You have connected with us (often virtually), given us time, care and support, and allowed each of us to contribute to this shared endeavour. Thank you!

1. Introduction to *A Modern Guide to Creative Economies*

Roberta Comunian, Alessandra Faggian, Jarna Heinonen and Nick Wilson

1.1 WHY A 'MODERN GUIDE' TO CREATIVE ECONOMIES? AND WHY NOW?

The proposal and initial idea behind *A Modern Guide to Creative Economies* coincided with the start of a new project for the four editors. In 2019 we received a Horizon 2020 European award[1] titled 'Developing Inclusive and Sustainable Creative Economies' (DISCE). From the offset, it was clear that while much research has been undertaken and published in the last 20 years on the creative economy, there were still many challenges in defining, understanding and supporting the sector. The two most visible challenges identified through extensive literature reviews during the project (Comunian et al., 2020; Wilson et al., 2020; Dent et al., 2020) were that the creative economy was often not inclusive and sustainable. Inclusivity and sustainability were identified as the joint focus of the research project, but also a way in which the project was tasked to contribute to a new perspective on growth – beyond gross domestic product (GDP) – for the future of the European creative economy (see Gross, Chapter 14 in this book). While the DISCE project is still ongoing and the findings will be disseminated later in 2022, this *Modern Guide* edited collection has provided an invaluable instrument for the editors to reflect and critically engage with our understanding and approaches to this field of research.

During the project, it was clear our understanding of the 'creative economy' – that is, creativity and cultural activities as a sector of the economy – was not enough. We opted for the use of the plural term 'creative economies'. This builds on the view presented by the United Nations Development Programme and United Nations Educational, Scientific and Cultural Organization (UNDP and UNESCO, 2013: 12) that the 'creative economy is not a single superhighway, but a multitude of different local trajectories found in cities and regions in developing countries'. While the UNDP and UNESCO (2013) here are trying to address concerns of inclusivity in relation to developing contexts, from our perspective the same level of inclusivity is also required within developed economies and societies. Furthermore, as also articulated by Comunian et al. (2021: 6), it is vital to acknowledge that there is 'not one single creative economy but a multiplicity of creative economies which can feature overlapping and diverging agendas'. It is crucial to account for the range of business models and objectives which often extend to the social sphere (Comunian et al., 2020), as well as for new possibilities emerging from the connection between creativity and cultural development (Wilson et al., 2020; De Beukelaer, 2015).

The other important dimension highlighted by this book is the need to look at creative economies from a range of scales and perspectives (Comunian, 2019). The plurality of data, sources and voices that this multidisciplinary collection includes empowers further interdisciplinarity and opportunities for dialogue across researchers that are key to more inclusive approaches. Another critical dimension of this *Modern Guide* is that it gives voice to many young and emerging researchers who have recently contributed to the creative economies debate with new methods and approaches.

The creative economies have now been studied for more than two decades.[2] However, the need to update, expand and question our understanding has never been more needed and essential, due to the impact of Covid-19 on our society, economies and communities. While the contributions and research in this book pre-date the pandemic and could not reflect on its impact (Comunian and England, 2020), the importance of reflecting on the role and value of creative economies in our lives and society has never felt more important.

1.2   CURRENT CHALLENGES TO OUR UNDERSTANDING OF CREATIVE ECONOMIES

Overall, across 15 chapters, the book engages with some key current challenges and limitations of our knowledge of creative economies. In particular, we identify here eight areas where the book contributes, but also where overall more research is needed and should be expanded in the next decade.

Defining and Quantifying Creative Economies

One of the key challenges in understanding creative economies is to define their value and potential beyond the economic sphere, to include their societal contribution and network formation. This requires an interdisciplinary approach, and identifying a common language and framework. Much of the debate around a proper definition of the 'creative economies' relates to whether the definition should be based on a set of firms belonging to specific sectors (the so-called creative and cultural industries, CCIs) or on the skills of individuals and their talent (Comunian et al., 2010; Comunian et al., 2022).

Given how central these sectors have been to policy in recent years, policy is not neutral in shaping our understanding of the creative economies. One good example of this is the historical account of the emergence of the creative industries definition and policy in the United Kingdom (UK) in 1998 (Gross, 2020). Adding to this already complicated scenario is the role of policy in directly funding and contributing to some of the sectors and activities that are part of creative economies. Another important role is played by international policy organisations trying to harmonise definitions and data across countries, either at the European level (Wiesand and Söndermann, 2005) or internationally (UNDP and UNESCO, 2013). The relationship between public, private and non-profit activities varies across countries and shapes not only their trajectory but also the inclusiveness and sustainability of some of the sectors included in these complex ecologies (de Bernard et al., 2021; Wilson and Gross, 2017). It is essential to highlight the ecological nature of the creative economies, which are made up of complex relationships and interdependencies between more informal activities characterised precisely by not being explicitly recognised or directly supported, and more formal and visible ones. Capturing the complexity and ecological nature of the creative economies is fundamental to devising better policies and making them more inclusive and sustainable in the long term (Wilson et al., 2020).

New and Old Methodologies

One of the significant challenges in our understanding of creative economies in the last 20 years has been that, while there is interest from a range of disciplines to contribute, there is very little dialogue across disciplines on how to better capture the working and dynamics of the sector. This book is an attempt to make this wide range of disciplines talk to each other in a fruitful way, hence contributing to building a better picture of creative economies. In this attempt, the dialogue between different methodologies is also key. In fact, while quantitative methods are key and important to identify trends and macro-dynamics (Higgs et al., 2008), other more qualitative methods are also needed to explore rationales, motivations, and push and pull factors in the development of the sector and, above all, its impact on society. As highlighted in this book, ecological and network-based approaches have been very promising in breaking some of the silos in which our understanding of creative economies has been confined in the past 20 years (Dovey et al., 2016; de Bernard et al., 2021). Another important contribution comes from new and old approaches to mapping and contextualising the value of creative economies in space, from local communities to regional economies and national and international profiles (Bakhshi et al., 2013; Brennan-Horley et al., 2010). Finally, creative and co-participatory methods are also critical to allow a range of voices and experiences to be heard (Greene et al., 2013; Hargreaves and Hartley, 2016) within creative economies, and have yet to be fully explored.

Diversity in Entrepreneurship

Entrepreneurship is presented as a key factor in economic growth and innovation as well as a solution to many societal challenges locally and globally. Given that much of the research in entrepreneurship deals with the 'exceptional' high-growth gazelles and unicorns which represent only a small fraction of all entrepreneurs, there is a need to understand better the majority of entrepreneurship, that is, 'everyday entrepreneurship' which portrays the diversity in entrepreneurship (Welter et al., 2017; Dodd et al., 2021). Similarly, Naudin (2018) argues that entrepreneurship research ignores a contextualised understanding of the phenomenon taking place in a variety of structural and cultural conditions, and most importantly it does not capture the injustices and inequalities that impact on culture and those who work in the field (Naudin, 2018: 2). Investigating cultural and creative entrepreneurs challenges understanding on entrepreneurship. Heroic and even mythical stories about high-growth entrepreneurship and entrepreneurs found in Silicon Valley turn to stories of more mundane and everyday entrepreneurship when we look at the entrepreneurial actors in the creative economies. Investigating entrepreneurship in creative economies does not imply diluting the power or impact of entrepreneurship, but rather widening its scope to capture entrepreneurial behaviour also in other contexts. It means widening our understanding of diversity in entrepreneurship and challenging the 'elite' ideal type of an entrepreneur (Dodd et al., 2021). Furthermore, it challenges us to consider entrepreneurship, education and cultural policies from a new perspective.

Entrepreneurship Education in Higher Education

Entrepreneurship scholars have debated whether entrepreneurship can be taught or not, and particularly whether higher education institutions have a role to play here. Often entrepreneurship is associated with practice, whereas university education is based on academic research and scholarly knowledge aiming to develop the students' theoretical and critical thinking. These approaches seem highly different from each other, posing a challenge to entrepreneurship education in higher education (Heinonen and Hytti, 2010). This challenge is equally relevant when considering whether and how to connect entrepreneurship education to creative degrees. Furthermore, there is an additional challenge of balancing between the commercial notion of entrepreneurship and the non-commercial notion of art. How to cope with the tension between artistic ambition and economic profit goals? This is a highly topical question as it is acknowledged that working as an entrepreneur or freelancer is very common in creative economies (Ball et al., 2010). The question is relevant for policymakers, educators and entrepreneurs themselves. In any educational setting, there is a need to understand and define: (1) the context in which entrepreneurship education is taking place (institutional, university-specific context); (2) the content to be taught and learnt (themes, topics and concepts); and (3) the learning environment in which learning occurs (physical spaces and pedagogical aspects of learning); which all impact on (4) learning outcomes to be achieved (Ilonen, 2020). This is also something that needs to be considered when planning how to make entrepreneurship education accessible to creative degree students.

Understanding Networks and Ecologies and Place

In the last 20 years, there has been increased attention to the role of networks and ecologies in creative economies research, as mapped by de Bernard et al. (2021). However, these studies still struggle to capture and evidence the broader connections of creative economies within our social and cultural life, beyond economic supply chains. Current research has also acknowledged the tension between urban (core) versus regional (peripheral) creative economies. There is evidence of strong urban concentration. Capital cities typically dominate, while significant concentrations are also found in secondary or medium-sized cities, which have been the focus of the DISCE project as case studies (Gross et al., 2019). The creative economy and its benefits are distributed geographically unevenly, but the mobility of creative workers is also important to think about in more sustainable versions of creative economies. This is a core–periphery relation, where metropolitan centres benefit and are the sources of cultural jobs. At the same time, regional cities and local clusters have found it difficult to thrive and sustain themselves. However, focusing on a better understanding of the network and ecologies that inhabit each place and city allows for a more distinctive and grounded approach to the value they create and how they can become more sustainable or inclusive. Ecological perspectives are also becoming increasingly central to how policy can engage with the sector (Gross et al., 2020). In particular, it is essential to question who has the power to shape creative economies and their policies. Research conducted by members of the DISCE team demonstrates the need – and emerging possibilities – for more participatory approaches to leadership and governance within creative economies, which can be based on more participatory and inclusive processes of data collection, but also policy deliberation in cities and communities (Wilson and Gross, 2017; Gross and Wilson, 2018; Brokalaki and Comunian, 2021).

Place, Mobility and Education: Opportunities for Creative Development

Within broader networks and ecologies, the role played by education in connecting creatives and communities to place, and creating opportunities for mobility and exchange, is pivotal. As discussed by Comunian et al. (2022), higher education can play multiple roles in supporting local creative economies and their development. This also has broader implications in connection to ideas of inclusivity and sustainability. Wilson and Gross (2017) highlight three overarching concerns that re-think 'inclusive and sustainable growth' from the perspective of a human development approach (Sen, 2001; Nussbaum, 2011), and which have important implications for our understanding of employment and skills development in the CCI sector beyond human capital and talent (Comunian and England, 2018; Comunian et al., 2020). Firstly, the pipeline for those working in the sector is determined, in part, by the cultural opportunity, freedom or 'capability' each and every person actually has (or does not) to give form and value to their experiences and to co-create culture. This is an opportunity, freedom or 'capability' (Sen, 2001; Nussbaum, 2011) that is by no means universal. Secondly, this freedom is supported at a collective level (across families, friendships, networks, organisations and industries) by the level of cultural care or 'solidarity' available from others to develop the interests, skills and behaviours required for professional practice. Thirdly, given the ecological nature of the sector, employment and relevant skills development is contingent on the cultural connectivity that characterises any local, regional or national cultural ecosystems. This is important for widening notions of 'creative careers' beyond those in full- or part-time employment in the CCIs (Brook et al., 2020; Brook and Comunian, 2018).

Ideas of Growth, Development and Value

Recent research has focused on the relationship between culture and development. The relationship between culture and development needs to be put under scrutiny: some commentators focus on culture for development, others culture in development, and others still, culture as development (Dessein et al., 2015). Wilson et al. (2020) identify three underlying conceptual and methodological 'needs' in furthering our knowledge of inclusive and sustainable creative economies and their relationship with cultural development: (1) to develop new understandings of the 'economy', the 'creative economy' and 'sustainable' economic development in the context of increased attention, globally, towards development, sustainability, prosperity, climate change and human use of finite natural resources; (2) to question how values are recognised at the collective level, and how this recognition impacts upon – and is impacted upon by – people's experiences of value; specifically, questioning what gets valued, by whom and what kinds of (overlapping) systems of value recognition are in place at local, regional, national and international levels; and (3) to take an ecological/systemic and 'inclusive' approach to the creative economy.

While the notion of cultural development is used in specific ways by some researchers and policymakers, the overall discursive space of culture and development is exceptionally fuzzy, with different actors relating culture and development in quite different (and often conceptually hazy) ways. By drawing attention to processes of valuation – including the experience of value – as integral to what culture comprises, Wilson et al. (2020) aim to provide a new way of understanding what cultural development consists of, that can go some way towards cutting through the current thicket of terms. Wilson (2019) argues that culture can best be understood as involving both the systems we collectively put in place for recognising value, and our experiencing value(s) for ourselves. As well as moving the focus beyond the unhelpful polarisation of culture as arts and heritage, or as our 'entire way of life', this theorisation challenges the dominant focus on the narrative of cultural values, and suggests the need to turn our attention instead towards processes of valuing.

The Emerging Importance of Care in Creative Economies

Within recent academic work (Wilson, 2018; Gross, 2018), attention is directed towards care as a promising alternative analytical lens through which to understand how inclusive and sustainable creative economies could be developed in practice. Wilson et al. (2020) argue that it is important to take due account of the reality of how people actually live their lives, that is, with diverse caring responsibilities, which pull in competing directions, and which are largely invisiblised; and how creative economies function, in part, via practices of care. Central to the politics of care are questions of its distribution and visibility. Who undertakes the labour of care? How is this labour made visible (and invisible)? What kinds of value are afforded to care? By whom? Within DISCE we are examining these questions in the specific contexts of the creative economy. How, why and with what consequences does care operate within creative economies? Tronto characterises care as 'a reaching out to something other than self ... lead[ing] to some type of action' (Tronto, 1993: 102). Tronto provides a framework that can be applied to all social relations. As Tronto's work exemplifies, care ethics highlights ontological connectedness – humans, in their very being, are relational animals – in direct contrast to the accounts of the individuated, 'rational' subject that underpin many liberal theories. Eva Feder Kittay (2015) uses the term 'inevitable dependency' to illustrate the ubiquitous relevance of care need and care-giving. The care literature suggests that there is also a wider socio-economic argument to be made for establishing greater visibility for care as a matter of public policy. Some of the implications of these debates regarding care within creative economies are discussed in the final chapters of this book.

1.3   ABOUT THIS BOOK

The book contains 15 chapters from a multidisciplinary network involving academics from a range of disciplines and geographical contexts. Their contributions provide an engaging platform to unpack a range of critical issues in relation to the development of creative economies. The book is structured in four parts.

The first part, 'Creative economies: challenging definitions and exploring new methods', explores criticalities and challenges in defining the creative economies, both from a quantitative statistical perspective but also as an area of policy interest. Furthermore, it proposes a reflection on new methodologies and approaches to research in the field that might open up opportunities to capture the complex cultural and creative ecosystems (de Bernard et al., 2021) that we study.

The second part, 'Creative economies and entrepreneurship: re-thinking inclusivity and business models', discusses a variety of ways in which entrepreneurship is present and visible in creative economies. By doing so, it expands the understanding of how entrepreneurship is connected with creative economies and how this could be better reflected in policies, particularly in cultural and educational policies, in order to make the sector more sustainable and inclusive to entrepreneurial endeavours.

The third part, 'Creative economies: focus on networks, place and mobilities', explores more closely the role of networks, place and mobility. It challenges current assumptions and explores dynamics of attachment to a specific location in relation to creative careers and higher education (Comunian and Gilmore, 2016). It explores how higher education has become a hub (Ashton and Comunian, 2019). The focus moves on to networks, collaboration and the importance of places, but also the importance of reflecting on creative work from a range of perspectives, from the statistical (Dent et al., 2020) to the self-reflective experience of individuals in the sector (Dent, 2020; Jacobi and Comunian, 2015; Scharff, 2016).

The final part, 'Creative economies re-imagined', offers insights on the possibility to re-imagine creative economies to be more inclusive and sustainable. It builds on recent literature exploring an alternative understanding of growth against prevailing accounts that limit its understanding to 'economic success'. According to Wilson et al. (2020), there are important interconnections to be made with opportunities for human development and cultural development (Sen, 2001), cultural democracy and freedom (Wilson and Gross, 2017), and care and hope (Wilson, 2019; Gross, 2021).

Part I: Creative Economies: Challenging Definitions and Exploring New Methods

The first part of the book includes four chapters that reflect on the definitional challenges in capturing creative economies. It also introduces new quantitative tools to investigate them with a spatial focus. Although these chapters highlight the specificities of different methods, policies and countries, they all agree on the importance of an inclusive definition and place-specific understanding of creative economies.

In Chapter 2, 'Modular solutions and creative coding', Scott Brook focuses on the development of CCIs in Australia within a policy and a statistical mapping framework. He argues that the new statistical framework has brought the creative economy into existence as an experimental policy object. Within the broad framework, it was important that specific challenging economic concepts were included in the discussion: on one side, the vision of creativity as a form of human capital able to foreground the importance of innovation and automation-resistant human skills; on the other side, the fact that cultural activities can be framed as goods and services that are outputs to a publicly valued industry. However, within the policy 'success' of this newly estab-lished framework in Australia, Brook highlights the disconnect between the CCIs discourse and statistical measures and higher education policies; in particular, the challenges of connecting courses to labour market outcomes and the overall role that higher education can and should play in developing CCIs.

In Chapter 3, 'On GIS and the creative economy', Manfredi de Bernard, Roberta Comunian and Federica Viganò reflect on the use of geographic information systems (GIS) in relation to the creative economy. They map past research and reflections on the value of GIS approaches to the creative economy field, assessing opportunities and challenges. By conducting a sys-tematic and critical literature review to map the main approaches and contri-butions to this method in connection with the study of the creative economy, they prove the increased interest in exploring spatiality and spatial dynamics. In addition, they use a small research project mapping the craft economies of a rural mountain valley (Val Gardena, Italy) to consider the implications of doing GIS research in practice. The literature review, together with the results of a small project, highlights the distinctive value of GIS methods but also the value of integrating it with other research methods.

In Chapter 4, 'Using social network analysis', Jon Swords examines how social network analysis (SNA) can be used to understand the creative indus-tries. It highlights how networks are crucial to the effective functioning of the CCIs. Decades of research have highlighted this importance for activities across the value chain. SNA offers the opportunity to schematically and vis-ually explore connections between different agents in the CCIs. It can also help to analyse and understand how networks are formed, relationships between individuals and other groups of nodes, and statistically identify connected communities. The chapter explores the different ways in which SNA has been applied to the study of CCIs by reviewing current academic and grey literature. A more detailed application of SNA research is provided that uses data on UK creative companies to explore how they define their activities using Standard Industrial Classification codes. In so doing, the chapter highlights some of the challenges and limitations of applying SNA to the CCIs.

In the final chapter, Chapter 5, 'Measuring creative and cultural industries', Alessandro Crociata and Chiara Burlina explore the challenging issue in measuring creative economy by means of cultural and creative industries. They argue that it is essential to develop a more comprehensive and systematic understanding of CCIs within a taxonomies background with mobile definitional boundaries. A key step towards this direction is providing robust evidence about CCIs' definitions and measurement by using available statistical information concerning the European creative economy. In the chapter, different sources are used to consider information on CCIs at the country level. Some data are also present at regional (NUTS2) and province (NUTS3) level. At the city level it is difficult to make finer-grained observations and there is a lack of proper monitoring tools in this spatial unit of analysis. A scholarly debate on composite indices is articulated. The authors also consider new challenges presented by impact metrics, as they become more and more relevant in terms of re-thinking inclusive and sustainable growth for the creative economy. Some composite indices have already been built and discussed, but given the complexity of cultural production and consumption processes and the heterogeneity of players involved, suitable and comparable data are still missing.

Part II: Creative Economies and Entrepreneurship: Re-thinking Inclusivity and Business Models

Narrowing down from the definitional and statistical issues of creative economics, the second part of the book includes three chapters that focus on the phenomenon of entrepreneurship in creative economies. In creative economies, it is common to work as a freelancer or an entrepreneur (Ball et al., 2010). Creative entrepreneurs often work on a small scale and on a part-time basis (Kohn and Wewel, 2018), combining self-employment with paid employment simultaneously (Hennekam and Bennett, 2016). However, profit-seeking behaviour may be remote for creative entrepreneurs, who rather focus on their meaningful and creative work beyond its economic rationale (Brown et al., 2010). There is no one or right way to 'do' entrepreneurship and earn one's living in creative economies, but the variety of examples discussed in the three chapters demonstrate the diversity of the phenomenon of entrepreneurship, particularly in creative economies.

Nuancing existing studies which focus on creative entrepreneurship, in Chapter 6, 'Experiences of belonging to the creative economy', Lenita Nieminen and Arja Lemmetyinen explore how creative and cultural micro-entrepreneurs experience belonging to the local creative economy, or whether they identify more with the creative place brand. The study focuses specifically on the micro-entrepreneurs' social embeddedness in the entrepreneurial process, comprising social structures and entrepreneurial networks. Using phenomenological interviews with four entrepreneurs in the areas of heritage, art, design and creative services, the study applies Wenger's community of practice approach as a lens in the narrative analysis. From the research, it emerges that entrepreneurship as such was not the primary feature defining their identity, but the micro-entrepreneurs described themselves as artists or art lovers. Furthermore, they did not associate themselves or their enterprises with the creative place brand. The studied micro-entrepreneurs represent a typical mundane or everyday entrepreneurship with a variety of motivations other than the economic.

In Chapter 7, 'Cultural entrepreneurship', Annette Naudin asserts the need to study cultural entrepreneurship and related policies in an environment with high levels of population diversity. By drawing on a series of policy interventions aimed at cultural entrepreneurs from diverse ethnic backgrounds, the study focuses on the challenges and opportunities for policymakers who seek to address inequalities in the cultural workforce. There is growing evidence of injustices in arts, media and cultural work in the UK, which point to systemic inequalities (O'Brien and Oakley, 2015) and poor representation within cultural labour markets (Saha, 2017). The case study reflects on a series of localised cultural policy initiatives that highlight: (1) the role of cultural intermediaries; (2) place and the hyperlocal context; and (3) problems with using terms such as 'diverse' to describe inequalities. Naudin highlights that cultural entrepreneurs do not operate in a vacuum, and local policymakers need to appreciate the connections between super-diverse communities, locality, structure and the values which underpin these relationships.

In Chapter 8, 'Creative entrepreneurship in 2021 and beyond', Ruth Bridgstock builds upon her earlier conceptual article 'Not a dirty word: arts entrepreneurship and higher education' (Bridgstock, 2013), which highlighted that all creative practitioners are entrepreneurs, and creative entrepreneurship can be understood in a way which is congruent with the creative ethos. Bridgstock takes the 2013 article as a base and explores how thinking and practice in creative entrepreneurship have changed and developed over the last decade due to networks and the fourth industrial age, and what implications the changes have for creative education. The study presents the ways in which entrepreneurship is a central part of creative practice: namely enterprise, new venture creation and career self-management. It also highlights that successful creative entrepreneurship is nuanced and individualised, and develops and changes over time through experience. Therefore, Bridgstock argues that a challenge for creative entrepreneurship educators in the twenty-first century is currency and relevance. In addition, she suggests that it is equally important to foster creative entrepreneurship literacy and thus support learners to make informed and value-congruent choices about their creative careers

Part III: Creative Economies: Focus on Networks, Place and Mobilities

Broadening the focus from individual entrepreneurs, the four chapters in the third part consider the complex and integrated nature of creative work and the networks and ecology that take place in different locations. Here creative workers (or aspiring creatives) are identified and understood with respect to how they contribute to multiple and overlapping networks and ecologies. While they cultivate a career and work, they also develop opportunities for cultural production, creative intermediation and local creative ecologies that facilitate further collaboration but also shape specific geographical context as supportive to future creative workers and creative economies. Beyond being containers or landscapes of creativity, specific spaces are able to support, encourage as well as provide opportunities for development for creative economies. The chapters in this part of the book illustrate the importance of specificity and scale, and contribute perspectives from a range of geographical contexts and experiences.

In Chapter 9, 'This must be the place', Fabrizio Montanari, Lorenzo Mizzau, Damiano Razzoli and Stefano Rodighiero question the connections between place and creative workers, using the case study of Reggio Emilia in Italy. They explore what features of the specific urban contexts are seen by the local creative workers as enabling factors, and which ones are perceived as inhibiting their work. The chapter uses qualitative interviews with creative workers to illustrate how the life of individual creatives and their work interact within the context of the city, and how the important dimensions of quality of life, place-based identity and local networks add to the attachment and subjective connections of creative workers with their city. The authors highlight how this could be also particularly important for creatives as they start their careers in a specific location, and for which the need of support and belonging in local networks might be more important. They also suggest that this might also have implications in consideration of the impact of Covid-19 on cities, and potential movements and mobility of creatives between metropolitan and non-metropolitan areas.

Further nuancing our understanding of early stages of creative careers is Chapter 10, 'Crafting professionals', by Lauren England. England provides a interesting reflection on how spatial and social dynamics can influence the higher education (HE) experience and professional development, focusing specifically on crafts students. She analyses the literature on networks in creative career development and the role of place in educational contexts, and draws from interviews with crafts educators and students from four HE providers in England conducted between 2016 and 2018. England considers place and educators to be the two key and connected mediators of networks within craft HE. She discusses opportunities and challenges for professional network development, and argues that educators' role as network brokers and mediators, combined with geographical exposure, influences students' identification of potential career pathways. The chapter concludes with reflections on the role of networks in early craft career development and the implications of their spatial and social mediation, including the potential for regional socio-economic inequalities and barriers to accessing craft careers to be reinforced.

In Chapter 11, 'Emerging spatial relations of artists and art scenes', Silvie Jacobi explores further the connections between education and place. She focuses explicitly on the location choice, place engagements and mobility dynamics of art school students and graduates in the cities of Manchester and Leipzig. The chapter firstly highlights the importance of place within creative industries research as interconnected and relational phenomena, and questions the reliance on talent attraction and sector clusters to make a successful creative city. Secondly, Jacobi considers what practices are developed in understanding the formation of a sense of place and spatial relations in the art world. Key literature is introduced to allow for better positioning of the research question and subject area of contemporary art and the art world within the field of creative cities and regions, after which place concepts and theories are introduced to detail from what theoretical perspective the empirical findings were analysed. After outlining the case study contexts, Jacobi discusses in the empirical section similarities and differences between the cases of Manchester and Leipzig and their respective art schools, with the aim to summarise key findings and analyse their significance for understanding geographical dynamics of the art world as an example of mobilities in creative work and networks.

In Chapter 12, 'Exploring contemporary visual arts careers in Italy', Jessica Tanghetti considers the case study of contemporary visual artists in Italy. She explores patterns within the early stages of their career. Careers in the creative sector have been widely investigated for their peculiarities and unstable structures. However, the work of contemporary visual artists has not received much attention. Careers in contemporary visual arts (CVA) are the result of a multitude of social, personal and professional factors, including country of origin, education, networks and mobility. Based on the existing literature and previous work done in the field, the study builds on a longitudinal analysis of the career pathways of emerging contemporary visual artists in Italy. More specifically, the study analyses the relation between the curricula vitae (CVs) of artists and career progress, considering together education, professional experiences, networks and mobility. In doing so, attention is also placed on the role played by gender and geographical and mobility aspects in providing opportunities for contemporary visual artists at the start of their careers.

Part IV: Creative Economies Re-imagined

The four chapters that comprise Part IV offer various complementary takes on the need to re-imagine creative economies to be more inclusive and sustainable.

In Chapter 13, 'Re-futuring creative economies', Mark Banks argues that the capitalist foundations of economic life remain the foundational premises of current 'creative economy' policy. Moreover, such policy lacks any explicitly environmental or (wider) ecological priorities or perspectives. As he observes, in an era of unfolding and urgent crises, 'such a lack seems – to say the least – both inadequate and inappropriate'. Banks laments how orthodox narratives of creative economy have come to fix a set of banal utopian imaginaries across political and civic institutions. Such imaginaries secure existing arrangements of power and inequality, and close down the possibilities of other more progressive forms of creative economy coming into being. For Banks, the most orthodox imaginaries of the creative economy appear to be instrumentally and artificially narrowing the range of possible ways of thinking about culture, economy, technology and ways of being human. As he puts it, they are in danger of 'de-futuring the future'. But there is some hope. In the face of de-futuring we must look to re-future: rejecting the authority of the already prescribed future-present in order to re-think the fundamental categories we live by. In this respect, Banks suggests that the creative economies of tomorrow might serve us better if they drew more on heterodox, feminist and ecological social and economic thought.

In Chapter 14, 'Growth of what? New narratives for the creative economy, beyond GDP', Jonathan Gross asks, 'How do we know when creative economies are doing well?' He provides a historical overview of the creative industries and their young sibling, the creative economy, in the UK, and how these have been defined and measured. The story that the creative economy has sought to enable is one of growth: the growth of the creative industries. As Gross explores, however, many difficulties with this ensue. In keeping with Banks's call for re-futuring creative economy discourse, Gross suggests that interventions can usefully be made 'upstream', by challenging the problems of GDP and its position within prevailing neoliberal economic discourse, and by asking questions of growth: 'Growth of what?' One answer to this question that Gross draws the reader's attention to is Kate Raworth's 'doughnut economics'. Another is Amartya Sen's alternative economic narrative framework: 'development as freedom'. Sen's capability approach to human development is introduced as a compelling underpinning to a new way to think about and position cultural policy. The chapter introduces Gross's research in the DISCE project that uses the capability approach to reconceptualise accounts of cultural opportunity (implicit and explicit) within existing cultural policy. It is argued that real-world experiments in developing alternative narratives for public policy will be crucial if research offering new ways to understand the 'success' of creative economies is going to make a sustained difference at scale. In short: we need new stories.

This is a cue taken up in Chapter 15, 'Inclusive solidarity', in which Tamsyn Dent focuses on forms of inclusive solidarity and collective mobilisation that emerge as forms of resistance within the UK creative economy. We move from 'bad dreams' to the very real lived experience of working in the UK creative economy, and groups of creative workers' responses to the labour conditions they face in the neoliberal economy. Here processes of re-imagining are being undertaken by and through creative workers working in solidarity with each other. The processes of resistance reported on constitute a vital part of what any inclusive and sustainable creative economy is. They respond to questions of inequality that are inclusive and holistic, and which transcend individual personal experience. The model of mutual aid and changemaking introduced in this chapter draws particular attention to the 'dissonance' between a politically celebrated economically resilient creative economy and precarious 'harmful' nature of the creative labour people actually do. The transformative role of the participants that Dent interviews as part of the DISCE research project is cast as being different from other forms of 'activism': they are not process-oriented; they identify as organisers, not activists; they are themselves precariously positioned. What is highlighted here is the resistance and solidarity of 'changemakers' acting from within the workforce.

In the final chapter, Chapter 16, Nick Wilson takes up this challenge by first asking the rather awkward question: 'What is the creative economy – really?' As a spur for looking forwards, and an exercise in re-imagination, he suggests we do not actually know what it is now. At the same time, and in keeping with the book's overall theme of offering a 'modern guide to creative economies' Wilson situates his argument within the *longue durée* of historical time; this sets up a critique of the limited ways in which 'creativity' has become commoditised. Instead of focusing on a blinkered commoditisation of creativity, Wilson's re-imagined creative economy is one where we manage the resources required to enable 'cultural capability': the freedom to recognise what we have reason to value. Attention is drawn to experiential, artful and axiological capabilities that are essential in developing our freedoms to undertake practices of valuing. These are central constituents of a cultural development framework being developed within the DISCE project.

Each of the contributors to this last part of the book would agree that the job of those involved in re-imagining creative economies, be they critical, creative economy scholars, policymakers, activists, organisers or creative workers, is not simply to make alternative and better futures apparent, but to contribute positively to their progressive imagining and building. With so many major crises in the world, it might be easy to see why re-imaginging creative economies is not at the top of policymakers' 'to do' lists. But the job of re-futuring highlighted here is urgent and pressing. As a wise person once said: 'there is no time'; the future is now.

NOTES

1.   The editors would like to acknowledge the European Union Horizon 2020-funded project DISCE (Developing Inclusive and Sustainable Creative Economies), grant agreement N. 822314, for the opportunity to develop further some of the ideas presented in this introductory chapter, and in general for the opportunity it offered for international exchange and collaboration between the editors. We also acknowledge the exchanges and input of the project teams across the three institutions with which the editors are affiliated, namely King's College London (United Kingdom), Gran Sasso Science Institute (Italy) and University of Turku (Finland).
2.   Here we consider specifically the start of the debate about the economic value of creative industries as coinciding with the first DCMS (Department for Culture, Media and Sport) 'Creative Industries Mapping Document' launched in 1998 in the UK. However, we acknowledge that similar and connected research was also pre-existing under the umbrella term of 'cultural industries'.

REFERENCES

Ashton, D., and Comunian, R. (2019). Universities as Creative Hubs: Modes and Practices in the UK Context. In R. Gill, A. Pratt, and T. Virani (Eds.), *Creative Hubs in Question: Place, Space and Work in the Creative Economy*. Palgrave, pp. 359–379.

Bakhshi, H., Freeman, A., and Higgs, P. (2013). *A dynamic mapping of the UK's creative industries*. London: NESTA.

Ball, L., Pollard, E., and Stanley, N. (2010). *Creative Graduates, Creative Futures*. London: Council for Higher Education in Art and Design.

Brennan-Horley, C., Luckman, S., Gibson, C., and Willoughby-Smith, J. (2010). GIS, ethnography, and cultural research: putting maps back into ethnographic mapping. *Information Society*, 26(2), 92–103.

Bridgstock, R. (2013). Not a dirty word: arts entrepreneurship and higher education. *Arts and Humanities in Higher Education*, 12(2–3), 122–137.

Brokalaki, Z., and Comunian, R. (2021). Beyond the hype: art and the city in economic crisis. *City*, 25(3–4), 396–418.

Brook, S., and Comunian, R. (2018). 'Dropping out and working': the vocational narratives of creative graduates. In L. Martin and N. Wilson (Eds.), *The Palgrave Handbook of Creativity at Work*. Cham: Palgrave Macmillan, pp. 125–141.

Brook, S., Comunian, R., Jewell, S., and Lee, J.Y. (2020). More than a day job, a fair job: music graduate employment in education. *Music Education Research*, 22(5), 541–554.

Brown, J., Nadler, R., and Meczynski, M. (2010). Working on the edge? Creative jobs in Birmingham, Leipzig and Poznan. In S. Musterd and A. Murie (Eds.), *Making Competitive Cities*. Oxford: Wiley-Blackwell, pp. 208–232.

Comunian, R. (2019). Complexity thinking as a coordinating theoretical framework for creative industries research. In S. Cunningham and T. Flew (Eds.), *A Research Agenda for Creative Industries*. Cheltenham, UK and Northampton, MA, USA: Edward Elgar Publishing, pp. 39–57.

Comunian, R., and England, L.E. (2018). Creative regions: from creative place-making to creative human capital. In A. Paasi, J. Harrison and M. Jones (Eds.), *Handbook on the Geographies of Regions and Territories* (Research Handbooks in Geography series). Cheltenham, UK and Northampton, MA, USA: Edward Elgar Publishing, pp. 169–181.

Comunian, R., and England, L. (2020). Creative and cultural work without filters: Covid-19 and exposed precarity in the creative economy. *Cultural Trends*, 29(2), 112–128.

Comunian, R., and Gilmore, A. (2016). *Higher Education and the Creative Economy*. London: Taylor & Francis.

Comunian, R., Faggian, A., and Li, Q.C. (2010). Unrewarded careers in the creative class: the strange case of bohemian graduates. *Papers in Regional Science*, 89(2), 389–410.

Comunian, R., Hracs, B.J., and England, L. (eds) (2020). *Higher Education and Policy for Creative Economies in Africa: Developing Creative Economies*. Abingdon: Routledge.

Comunian, R., Hracs, B.J., and England, L. (2021). *Understanding and Supporting Creative Economies in Africa: Education, Networks and Policy: a Policy Report*. King's College, London. Available at: https://kclpure.kcl.ac.uk/portal/files/159173745/Understanding_Supporting_Creative_Economies_Africa.pdf.

Comunian, R., England, L., Faggian, A., and Mellander, C. (2022). *The Economics of Talent*. Cham: Springer.

DCMS. (1998). *Creative Industries Mapping Document*. London: DCMS.

de Bernard, M., Comunian, R., and Gross, J. (2021). Cultural and creative ecosystems: a review of theories and methods, towards a new research agenda. *Cultural Trends*. DOI: 10.1080/09548963.2021.2004073.

De Beukelaer, C. (2015). *Developing Cultural Industries: Learning from the Palimpsest of Practice*. European Cultural Foundation.

Dent, T. (2020). Devalued women, valued men: motherhood, class and neoliberal feminism in the creative media industries. *Media, Culture and Society*, 42(4), 537–553.

Dent, T., Comunian, R., Conor, B., Pica, V., Wilson, N., and Burlina, C. (2020). *Creative and Cultural Workforce in Europe Statistics Report*. DISCE Publications. Available at: https://disce.eu/wp-content/uploads/2020/05/ DISCE-Report-D3.2.b.pdf.

Dessein, J., Soini, K., Fairclough, G., Horlings, L., Battaglini, E., et al. (2015). *Culture in, for and as Sustainable Development: Conclusions from the COST Action IS1007 Investigating Cultural Sustainability*. University of Jyväskylä.

Dodd, S., Anderson, A., and Jack, S. (2021). Let them not make me a stone – repositioning entrepreneurship. *Journal of Small Business Management*. doi:10.1080/00472778.2020.1867734.

Dovey, J., Moreton, S., Sparke, S., and Sharpe, B. (2016). The practice of cultural ecology: network connectivity in the creative economy. *Cultural Trends*, 25(2), 87–103.

Greene, C., Ramster, G., Alexiou, K., Zamenopoulos, T., Alevizou, G., Outten, A., and Gorzanelli, C. (2013). Creative communities, creative assets: Exploring methods of mapping community assets. *Nordes*, 1(5).

Gross, J.D. (2018). Creativity off the clock: re-conceptualizing creative careers. In L. Martin and N. Wilson (Eds.), *The Palgrave Handbook of Creativity at Work*. Palgrave Macmillan, pp. 501–522. https://doi.org/10.1007/978-3-319-77350-6_24.

Gross, J.D. (2020). *The Birth of the Creative Industries Revisited: an Oral History of the 1998 DCMS Mapping Document*. Available at: https://kclpure.kcl.ac.uk/portal/files/125010567/Gross_J._2020_The_Birth_of_the_Creative_Industries_Revisited.pdf.

Gross, J. (2021). Practices of hope: care, narrative and cultural democracy. *International Journal of Cultural Policy*, 27(1), 1–15.

Gross, J., and Wilson, N. (2018). Cultural democracy: an ecological and capabilities approach. *International Journal of Cultural Policy*. Available at: https://doi.org/10.1080/10286632.2018.1538363.

Gross, J., Comunian, R., Conor, B., Dent, T., Heinonen, J., et al. (2019). *DISCE Case Study Framework*. DISCE Publications. Available at: https://disce.eu/ wp-content/uploads/2019/12/DISCE-Report-D3.1-D4.1-D5.1.pdf.

Gross, J., Heinonen, J., Burlina, C., Comunian, R., Conor, B., Crociata, A., Dent, T., Guardans, I., Hytti, U., Hytönen, K., Pica, V., Pukkinen, T., Renders, M., Stenholm, P., and Wilson, N. (2020). *Managing Creative Economies as Cultural Ecosystems*. DISCE Publications. Available at: https://disce.eu/wp-content/uploads/2020/07/DISCE-Policy-Brief-1.pdf.

Hargreaves, I., and Hartley, J. (2016). *The Creative Citizen Unbound: How Social Media and DIY Culture Contribute to Democracy, Communities and the Creative Economy*. Bristol: Policy Press.

Heinonen, J., and Hytti, U. (2010). Back to basics: the role of teaching in developing the entrepreneurial university. *The International Journal of Entrepreneurship and Innovation*, 11(4), 283–292.

Hennekam, S., and Bennett, D. (2016). Self-management of work in the creative industries in the Netherlands. *International Journal of Arts Management*, 19(1), 31–41.

Higgs, P., Cunningham, S., and Bakhshi, H. (2008). *Beyond the Creative Industries: Mapping the Creative Economy in the United Kingdom*. London: NESTA.

Ilonen, S. (2020). *Entrepreneurial Learning in Entrepreneurship Education in Higher Education*. Painosalama: Turku, Finland.

Jacobi, S., and Comunian, R. (2015). Resilience, creative careers and creative spaces: bridging vulnerable artist's livelihoods and adaptive urban change. In H. Pinto (Ed.), *Resilient Territories: Innovation and Creativity for New Modes of Regional Development*. Cambridge Scholar Press, pp. 151–166.

Kittay, E.F. (2015). Centring justice on dependency and recovering freedom. *Hypatia*, 30(1), 285–291.

Kohn, K., and Wewel, S. (2018). Skills, scope and success: an empirical look at the start-up process in creative industries in Germany. *Creativity and Innovation Management*, 27(3), 295–318.

Naudin, A. (2018). *Cultural Entrepreneurship: The Cultural Worker's Experience of Entrepreneurship*. Routledge Studies in Entrepreneurship. London and New York: Routledge Taylor & Francis Group.

Nussbaum, M.C. (2011). *Creating Capabilities*. Boston, MA: Harvard University Press.

O'Brien, D., and Oakley, K. (2015). *Cultural Value and Inequality: a Critical Literature Review*. Available at: https://ahrc.ukri.org/documents/project-reports-and-reviews/cultural-value-and-inequality-a-critical-literature-review/.

Saha, Anamik (2017). *Race and the Cultural Industries*. Cambridge: Polity Press.

Scharff, C. (2016). The psychic life of neoliberalism: mapping the contours of entrepreneurial subjectivity. *Theory, Culture and Society*, 33(6), 107–122.

Sen, A. (2001). *Development as Freedom*. Oxford: Oxford University Press.

Tronto, J. (1993). *Moral Boundaries: A Political Argument for an Ethic of Care*. New York: Routledge.

UNDP and UNESCO (2013). *Creative Economy Report: Widening Local Development Pathways*. Paris: UNDP/UNESCO.

Welter, F., Baker, T., Audretsch, D.B., and Gartner, W.B. (2017). Everyday entrepreneurship – a call for entrepreneurship research to embrace entrepreneurial diversity. *Entrepreneurship Theory and Practice*, 3(41), 311–321.

Wiesand, A.J., and Söndermann, M. (2005). *The 'Creative Sector': an Engine for Diversity, Growth, and Jobs in Europe*. European Cultural Foundation.

Wilson, N. (2018). Creativity at work: who cares? Towards an ethics of creativity. In L. Martin and N. Wilson (Eds.), *The Palgrave Handbook of Creativity at Work*. London: Palgrave Macmillan, Chapter 30.

Wilson, N. (2019). *The Space that Separates: A Realist Theory of Art* (Routledge Studies in Critical Realism). Routledge. https://doi.org/10.4324/9781315692128.

Wilson, N., and Gross, J. (2017). *Caring for Cultural Freedom: An Ecological Approach to Supporting Young People's Cultural Learning*. London: A New Direction.

Wilson, N., Gross, J., Dent, T., Connor, B., and Comunian, R. (2020). *Rethinking Inclusive and Sustainable Growth for the Creative Economy: A Literature Review*. Available at: https://disce.eu/wp-content/uploads/2020/01/DISCEReport-D5.2.pdf.

PART I

Creative economies: challenging definitions and exploring new methods

2. Modular solutions and creative coding: the success of the creative and cultural industries in Australia

Scott Brook

INTRODUCTION

The last two decades of debate about how to classify the creative economy have provided a striking example of the key point of cultural economy studies: namely, that 'the economic' is never simply given, but entangled with the cultural and the social (du Gay and Pryke 2002; Bennett et al. 2008). This is to say that the positivity of phenomena that come to be defined as 'economic' is the outcome of complex and intersecting social and symbolic systems. These include the state policies and legal frameworks that recognise particular identities, relationships and activities for purposes of support, regulation and planning, as well as the statistical agencies and methods for the collection and coding of surveys that represent such phenomena at the level of populations. It is through such organised activities that economic phenomena are 'tabled', in both senses: for policy consideration and action, as well as critical debate and contestation (Miller and Rose 1990: 4–7). That is, they can be tabulated and quantified, and therefore brought 'to the table' of political processes. It follows that although there may be economic theories of the creative and cultural sector, such as one based on creativity as a skills input for innovation, or a social outcome of skills underemployment (see Cunningham 2013 for an example of the former; Brook 2015 for an example of the latter), such accounts themselves are embedded in larger knowledge assemblages that draw together the sector as an economic object (an identified industry) through its classifications and visualisations (Latour 1990). To adopt this approach to the creative economy is to do away with the idea that creativity somehow reveals 'the truth' of human productivity in the post-industrial era, one whose untapped potential awaits emancipation from current classifications.

This chapter hence does not describe Australia's Creative and Cultural Industries (CCIs) in terms of the documented economic phenomena – exports, productivity, employment, intellectual property (IP) – that might support a claim to the success of this sector (see BCAR 2019 for a recent example of this). Rather, it focuses on the development of government statistical coding frames that have sought to table the existence of the sector, and which have sought to integrate asymmetrical economic concepts of 'cultural value' and 'creativity' into a common schema that can work for a variety of stakeholders. It is the success of these coding frames that is the topic of this chapter. For convenience, the chapter's argument can be summarised in terms of two key points.

First, the success of the CCIs model in Australia rests on a modular coding structure that accommodates two asymmetric economic concepts whose prevalence in the CCIs literature has to date been unacknowledged; namely 'creativity' as human capital economic input ('innovation' as human skill or intellectual orientation towards activity), and 'the cultural' as economic outputs ('goods and services') that have publicly agreed value. These concepts appear asymmetric, as a close reading of attempts by the Australian Bureau of Statistics (ABS) to describe their relationship reveals that 'the creative' introduces a division that lies within the cultural as part of its definition, but also sits 'without', as an object that lies beyond the remit of cultural value. That the creative industries agenda is essentially a human capital argument has consequences for the sector that are barely acknowledged in policy debate.

Second, the need for a statistical model that could accommodate these asymmetric concepts dates from the initial coding of Australia's 'cultural industries' undertaken by the Cultural Ministers Council Statistical Advisory Group (CMCSAG) during the late 1980s (CMCSAG 1990). As such, the creative human capital agenda has always supplemented, rather than replaced, an agenda focused on publicly valued cultural goods and services. While a creative skills agenda would hence appear wedded to the origins of Australian cultural policy narratives since the 1980s, it is nevertheless conceptually and statistically separable from a broader and more traditional public policy purpose.

The reference to 'modular solutions' in the chapter title seeks to describe the pragmatic conditions of this policy success in Australia. Implicit here is an assumption that the lack of intellectual agreement is not necessarily an obstacle to policy development, as classification systems are designed to be robust enough to accommodate diverse uses over time, and to a great extent are a process of stakeholder management as much as intellectual clarification.

It is widely acknowledged that the lack of consensus concerning the industrial framework for the study of creative and cultural activity since the advent of the United Kingdom (UK) creative industries policy has provided the occasion for a continuing dispute based on first principles of analysis; namely, whether researchers should focus on 'creativity' as a skills input, where creative skills are defined by their capacity for innovation and, increasingly, intrinsic resistance to automation (Bakshi et al. 2013; BCAR 2019); and 'culture' as goods and services that are publicly valued (Garnham 2005), and hence in need of government support. This has led to a certain amount of shadow boxing in the literature. As shown in the work of Camilla Nelson and Ian Hunter, the two objects have distinct genealogies in the modern industrial era (Nelson 2015, 2018; Hunter 1988), and their current entanglement finds its roots in nineteenth-century Romantic aesthetics which was influenced as much by Kantian theories of the natural sublime, with its capacity for creative destruction, as that of Arnoldian arguments for culture as a civilising mission. As such, they tend towards different styles of policy intervention concerning the state and its relation to the market, such as a neo-Schumpeterian innovation economics (e.g. Potts 2012), and orthodox cultural economics (e.g. Throsby 1999). Where the former looks to the state as an enabler of research and development (R&D) in a leading industrial sector for innovation economies powered by forces of technological distruption, the latter posits the state as the key enabler of an essential public amenity for liberal social democracies that is characterised by market failure. The phrase 'creative and cultural industries' (CCIs) signals less that some sort of détente has been achieved between these competing models, and more that the disagreement itself is increasingly unproductive. This is especially true for those government agencies, such as federal and state arts and culture departments, that are key stakeholders in sector research, and for which such economic debates are not the primary object of policy and such principled positions on the meaning of culture vis-à-vis 'the economic' present an unnecessary choice.

Such an agonistic relation is not new to cultural policy. This ambivalence about the relationship of cultural value to various domains of industry activity, such as commercial television, video games or popular music, are fundamental to cultural policy, once posing problems for the inclusion of modern broadcasting technologies, and continuing to provide conundrums for arts funding bodies, routinely by way of questions of value that become acute in relation to genres of activity that are worthy of the title 'cultural'. Indeed, these structures of cultural value were once a target for creative industries critique (Hartley and Cunningham 2001), and in Australia at least ensured that advocates could draw strength from the reformist politics of Cultural Studies. The commercial populism of John Hartley and Stuart Cunningham's flagship address to the Australian university sector was pitched against the re-assertion of the civic importance of values and cultural expertise under way in Australian Cultural Studies at the time (e.g. Frow 1995), and it is this critical position-taking that was seminal to the legibility of their proposal. This appealed to Keating-era media and communication scholars who saw a happy coincidence of technological revolution and cultural egalitarianism.

While any claim of success may be controversial and premature in Australia, given that the CCIs have never been adopted at the level of federal government policy, the discursive field of Australian cultural policy now routinely accepts the CCIs, with many key agents and stakeholders drawing on its concepts, codings and empirical findings in order to discuss and debate the sector. Two recent Australian surveys of the field show that despite various understandings of what the creative industries refer to, the term is generally accepted by stakeholders across the nation, with policy rationales, metrics and nomenclature being adopted for a variety of purposes across all state government strategies for the cultural sector (Daniel 2017; Flew 2019: 15–17). While it is well known that the ARC Centre for Excellence in Creative Industries and Innovation research at Queensland University of Technology was a key agent for developing and promoting creative industries mapping in Australia, drawing on and contributing to UK policy developments, this chapter focuses on policy work that occurred both after and prior to that period. It foregrounds the 'pick up' of key elements of the CCIs agenda by the ABS and the Department of Communication and the Arts in the 2000s, as well as the appearance of signature CCIs concepts in Australia's first cultural industries policies of the late 1980s. While the Australian CCIs policy push did not proceed from any specific government policy, as it did in the UK, it is similarly not reducible to a critical position-taking within the field of academic policy debate. It has proceeded, intermittently and along multiple paths, by way of coding frames and their stated rationales, a process that has brought the creative economy into existence as an experimental policy object. The genealogy of the creative economy in Australian statistical mapping documents is far more eclectic, bureaucratic and historically long-standing than some of the rhetorical positioning of its advocates and critics would suggest.

CREATIVE AND CULTURAL ACTIVITY, SERVICES AND PRODUCTION: THE BINARY MODELS OF AUSTRALIA'S CREATIVE AND CULTURAL INDUSTRIES

In 2014 the ABS published the outcome of its experimental measures of the economic contribution of creative and cultural activity based on the 2008/09 financial year (ABS 2014). This satellite account visualised creative and cultural activity as two separate but overlapping sectors. It showed that that while the CCIs as a whole contributed 6.9 per cent of gross domestic product (GDP) ($86 billion), the contribution of 'creative' activity was far greater, mainly due to this segment including computer system design, and the wholesaling, manufacture and retailing of clothing and footwear (see Figure 2.1).

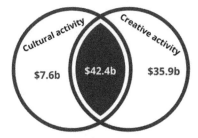

Source: Data sourced from ABS (2014: 6).

Figure 2.1   Creative and cultural activity GDP – national accounts basis, 2008/09

The Venn diagram used to illustrate the data in the report showed the creative and the cultural as two overlapping sets; although the economic size of the occupations and industry codes that were coded to both was significant ($42.4 billion), the economic footprint of their exclusive codes were also significant, if clearly different in scale; the contribution of discrete creative activity was over four and half times that of the cultural. In 2017 this ABS methodology was reapplied by the Commonwealth Department of Communication and the Arts, which showed that in 2016/17 the total value of cultural activity had increased to $63.5 billion, and creative activity to $99.7 billion. The overlap between these – that is, activities coded both creative and cultural – was again substantial, accounting for $51 billion (BCAR 2018: Figure 1, p. 7).

This binary approach to the satellite account was based on a 2013 discussion paper released by the ABS which reviewed a wide range of classifications used in international policy and research. In the absence of an international standard for creative and cultural satellite accounts, its primary purpose was to clarify statistical needs and provide a practical framework. Of signal importance was the proposal of a binary model that might enable separating out the creative and cultural as two distinct, if overlapping, sets of occupational codes. While clearly influenced by the creative industries agenda, the model owed as much if not more to David Throsby's 'concentric circles' model in which a core of culture-producing domains (the arts) were encapsulated by outer rings of service, design and technology industries, and which proposed that the share of creative and cultural content decreased in the goods and services supplied as it moved away from the centre, with the most commercial domains, such as advertising, computer systems and design, occupying the outermost orbit (ABS 2013: 8). As such, it rests on a familiar theoretical dichotomy between symbolic and commercial value that is highly developed in sociology, for instance in Pierre Bourdieu's economic model of symbolic and economic capital in organising the field of cultural production (Bourdieu 1993).

At the core of the distinction, industries and occupations would be coded as:

> 'cultural' in that they communicate symbolic meaning (e.g. beliefs, values, traditions), require human creativity as an input, and potentially contain intellectual property; or are 'creative' in that human creativity is a significant and identifiable input. (ABS 2013: 8)

A key reference here is to creativity as an input. While creative activity is to be distinguished from 'the cultural' in that it enables a non-cultural domain of creative activity, such as software, to be included, at the same time it is a distinction that partly lies within the 'cultural', insofar as cultural activities are also defined by creativity. Despite the logical difficulties this raises – given the above sets, the creative appears as that which lacks the cultural, but not vice versa – the reference to human creativity as an input is an important conceptual clarification as regards economic metrics. We might propose that 'the cultural' refers us to 'culturally valued goods and services' as industry outputs, with an implied scale of value as to what is culturally most valued. Meanwhile, 'the creative' refers to a special type of human capital, 'creativity', potentially spread across all domains as economic input.

The creative and cultural hence appear in an asymmetric relation, referring to distinct objects of measurement. While creativity may be concentrated in the cultural sector (its presence partly defines that sector, but it is not a sufficient criterion), it also exceeds the sector, insofar as it is applied to other goods and services that are not culturally valued.

The ABS focus on skills input was consistent with the development in the UK of a revised model of the creative industries in which the CCIs was to be identified by a workforce rather than an industry sector, through the methodology of mapping 'creative intensity'. This dynamic approach to modelling the sector through its human capital was developed in a National Endowment for the Sciences, Technology and the Arts (Nesta) report that proposed a five-point definition of creative activity as the basis of identifying occupations that require creative skills, which could then be used to identify industries based on a threshold of occupations within that industry (Bakshi et al. 2013). This model of creative skills was scrupulously 'non-cultural', insofar as it made no reference to culturally valued skills (whether in terms of aesthetic, heritage or any other model of cultural value), but rather focused on the role of human novelty and judgement in the creative process (Bakshi et al. 2013: 24–25). This was subsequently applied to the Australian case by Queensland University of Technology researchers Peter Higgs and Sasha Lennon (2014), from which

Table 2.1   *The dynamic model of Australia's CCIs*

Segment	Subgroup	Description
Creative Services	Advertising and Marketing	'Creative services enterprises and creative entrepreneurs provide inputs that are central to businesses across many industries, from manufacturing and construction to retailing and entertainment'
	Architecture and Design	
	Software and Digital Content	
Cultural Production	Film, TV and Radio	'Arts and cultural assets as contributors to quality of life and community well-being and as important contributors to economic activity and development in their own right'
	Music, Visual and Performing Arts	
	Publishing	

Source: Adapted from Higgs and Lennon (2014: pp. 11–12).

another binary model of Australia's CCIs was proposed that involved six segments allocated to 'creative services' and 'cultural production' (see Table 2.1).

Higgs and Lennon's model was far more empirical than the ABS coding of the creative and cultural, insofar as it was based on the Nesta criteria for identifying the creative skills content of occupations, and used this to determine the intensity of creative activity within an industry. However, its real merit lay in its two segments of 'creative services' and 'cultural production', within which six subgroups are proposed, and which are based on stakeholder domains. The six subgroups break down into a further 12 groupings around even more specific domains that cohere around established discrete sectors of activity and infrastructure, such as radio, performing arts, film and television, and advertising.

Although not determined by the methodology, which as noted makes no claims to cultural value, this distinction between 'cultural production', 'creative services' and the proposed subsections makes the model amenable to stakeholders with no interest in the conceptual underpinnings of the classification. For instance, the subgroups of 'cultural production' neatly identify specific domains of public value where most state and federal government investment occurs through dedicated agencies and infrastructure, such as the Australia Council for the Arts, Screen Australia, the Australian Broadcasting Commission, Special Broadcasting Services, and the major cultural infrastructure of galleries, museums and concert halls. With the notable exception of 'design', it also well aligned with the Australian Standard Classification of Education (ASCED), where the field of 'creative arts' matches occupations represented in the 'cultural production' list. While there is no segment for what is sometimes described as the 'GLAM' sector (galleries, libraries and museums), relevant occupations are in fact covered by the 'publishing' (archivists, curators and librarians) and 'visual arts' (conservators, and gallery and museum curators) segments.

As such, the classification is quite capable of mapping a domain of activity that responds to a range of policy rationales. As with the ABS model, users may 'bracket out' segments that do not service their data needs in order to speak more directly to sector interests. This modularity is the result of two properties: the classification system is decomposable into segments that reflect the needs of diverse stakeholders (those in discrete industry segments); and networked via its use of authoritative classification systems maintained by collecting agencies (such as the ABS) that provide a stream of data that is comparable across time.

PROJECTING A CREATIVE ECONOMY: *CREATIVE NATION* (1994) AND *THE AUSTRALIAN CULTURAL INDUSTRY* (1990)

The notion that Australian cultural policy might leverage the value of creative skills via new technologies in order to benefit the broader economy was made explicit in the nation's first framework for cultural statistics developed in the late 1980s. Known as 'The Australian Cultural Industry', this framework was developed by the Ministerial Statistical Working Party and was crucial for the preparation of the Creative Nation policy of the Keating government. A closer reading of these two documents reveals that this new object for cultural policy was not simply a case of 'economic rationalism', but also drew on 'culturalist' understandings of creativity as a valued way of life related to a new period of rapid technological change.

As is well known, the 1994 'Creative Nation' policy of the late Keating government, Australia's first national cultural policy produced by the Department of Communication and the Arts (DCA 1994), anticipated the 1997 UK creative industries policy agendas in many key regards (Luckman 2012: 11). Its explicit references to the economic significance of the cultural sector, the importance of 'copyright industries', 'content industries' and signature emphasis on information technologies, all spoke to a new governmental vision for what it described as 'Cultural Production in the Information Age':

> Information technology, and all that it now offers, has crossed the technical rubicon into the realm of consciousness, to the realm of culture ... This is why the imperatives of the information age and some of its opportunities are addressed here in the context of creative and cultural policy. (DCA 1994: n.p.)

It was for this reason the policy called for more 'interaction between traditional content producers and the software experts' and 'creative and software communities', and saw it 'as imperative ... that we accelerate the integration between them', announcing a series of funded national industry forums and the departmental merger of the arts and communication portfolios. The turn to information technologies in Creative Nation did not signal an attempt to increase the economic size or importance of the cultural sector, but rather proposed to engineer a convergence in order to leverage the value of this sector for broader economic goals. This epochal description of information technology crossing 'the technical rubicon into the realm of consciousness, to the realm of culture', was directly influenced by 1970s and 1980s new media theory, including a revived interest in the work of Marshall McCluhan (1964), which had become influential in the cultural sector during the 1970s and 1980s. Popular works of postmodern culture, such as David Cronenberg's (1983) feature film *Videodrome* and Don DeLillo's (1984) novel *White Noise* (to name two prominent examples), provided contemporary visions of the profound shift in culture and consciousness felt to be under way, and a platform for the academic literature of new media theory.

Key research for Creative Nation was produced by the CMCSAG, which in 1990 published several key reports on what it called 'The Australian Cultural Industry'. Composed of federal- and state-level ministers with cultural portfolios, the Cultural Ministers Council was formed in 1984 and set to addressing the lack of any statistical framework in Australia for assessing the size or significance of the sector. The Ministerial Council established the Statistical Advisory Group (now known as the Statistical Working Group) which conducted stakeholder meetings and engaged a corporate consultancy to develop Australia's first statistical framework for national cultural and leisure data collection, which was released in 1989.

This framework, which has been maintained by the ABS ever since, enabled the first national economic account of the sector, showing that in the 1987/88 financial year, the 'Cultural Industry' contributed $7.6 billion to national GDP, more than base metals, and almost as much as food, beverages and tobacco (CMCSAG 1990). The largest sub-sector of the cultural industry was publishing and printing. The classification was comprehensive for its time, including domains of popular culture, such as television and radio, as well as established domains, such as film, adult education in the arts, festivals, natural environment, the GLAM sector, performing and visual arts, publishing, heritage and community arts. While sport and recreation were included in the statistical framework, it was bracketed out for the purpose of cultural industry accounts.

Apart from the classifications, which produced the impressive economic data that could be cited in Creative Nation, the Statistical Advisory Group attached a novel economic importance to the cultural sector, insofar as it might disseminate the value of innovation throughout the workforce:

> The cultural industry is itself important for the Australian economy, as shown in this [report]. Of greater importance to national economic survival is the existence of a flourishing creative community which can inject imaginative and innovative concepts into all aspects of the environment and the goods and services created for consumption in Australia and for export. (CMCSAG 1990: 'Rationale': 2)

> Such outcomes happen through the transfer of artistic values of creativity, imagination and innovation into every aspect of social, political and economic life. There is an obvious impact on both the quality of life and economic performance of a nation whose managers, bureaucrats, tradespeople and workers embrace artistic values of creativity, innovation, and striving for excellence. (CMCSAG 1990: 'Rationale': 2)

This would appear to be the first coding frame for cultural statistics in Australia to explicitly cite the value of creativity and innovation for the general economy in its rationale. Such 'blue sky' economic thinking – informed by the canon of mid-twentieth-century creativity-for-innovation management writing – reaches far beyond the classifications it presides over to announce a rationale for cultural policy ('national economic survival') that is strikingly new. The 'information revolution' discussed in Creative Nation needs to be read in the context of this new socio-economic mission for culture.

While the rationale is new, this remains a culturalist argument for creativity, insofar as it concerns community-specific concepts and values that need to be 'transferred' and 'injected' (today we would say 'embedded') in the general workforce. As I have argued elsewhere, the enduring pedagogic mission of the creative industries is the promotion of this economic rationale for 'exemplary' ways of working: the innovation economy is a cultural project. As such, it inherits a very traditional governmental project for culture in terms of the formation of a modern liberal citizenry (Brook 2016).

CONCLUSION: HIGHER EDUCATION AND THE LIMITS OF CLASSIFICATION

A recent success for the Australian CCIs came in 2020, with the release of a new classificatory system for fields of research following a review by the ABS (2020). The creation of a dedicated six-digit research classification 'Creative and cultural industries' will draw together a notoriously interdisciplinary field of research expertise as a subdomain of Cultural Studies, thus supporting the visibility of this object in research funding, industry engagement and research impact evaluations.

Higher education (HE) remains a key agent in the visibility of the CCIs in Australia; however, it is in HE policy that we can see a key limit of creative industries policy to date. Given the centrality of creative skills to the creative industries agendas, it is notable that recent reviews and policy proposals for the reform of HE funding have not engaged with the notion of a creative economy. While the Department of Education, Skills and Employment's (DESE) Performance Based Funding Scheme proposes to steer government funding towards areas with strong graduate employment (DESE 2019), it is less clear that the most recent proposed restructure of HE funding will achieve this, as opposed to simply increasing the costs of study for a range of arts and humanities disciplines (DESE 2020). With its focus on the economic resilience of a sector made up of 'protean' workers who can reinvent themselves according to labour market needs (Bridgstock 2005), it should be the case that the CCIs argument is well placed to make a case for the value of creative degrees.

There are two related obstacles to this. The first concerns the granularity of CCIs codings, which create problems of translatability. Fields of study that are cognate to CCIs fields of employment are highly disparate within the Australian statistical framework. This is a problem, as although employment outcomes are collected at a detailed six-digit level, government funding decisions about fields of education have historically been made in relation to 'broad' and 'narrow' fields of education, and this continues to be the case with the release of recent proposals for funding (DESE 2020). According to a recent study already cited, the CCIs are located across no less than six of the 11 available broad fields of Education: 01 Natural and Physical Sciences, 02 Information Technology, 04 Architecture and Building, 08 Management and Commerce, 09 Society and Culture and 10 Creative Arts (BCAR 2019: 24). The problem is not simply that creativity as economically valued input is spread too broadly, as a comparable translation of the United Nations Educational, Scientific and Cultural Organization (UNESCO) framework according to 'domains of cultural activity' (rather than economic sectors) would seek to include the remaining four of the remaining five broad fields of education (03 Engineering, 05 Agriculture and Environment, 06 Health and 07 Education) in order to capture those fields of study in crafts, natural heritage, traditional medicines and education that underpin UNESCO's model of the CCIs (UNESCO 2009: 24–30).

Second, HE codings are not structured around industry segments, but around domains of educational activity whose historically long-standing and highly evolved internal distinctions are not derived from labour market classifications. While training for professional occupations has always been a key rationale for many academic fields, such as law and medicine, and the dissolution of the binary systems of HE in both countries has expanded the employability agenda across all areas of HE study, the framework itself is not based on labour market codings. The stakeholders for the ASCED framework exist in many sectors of the education system, from primary schools to post-graduate studies, and entertain a range of purposes. Furthermore, the school system reproduces a population (students) whose intellectual development is routinely invested in educational fields that do not relate to the labour market, and who translate these interests into university enrolment decisions.

This is especially true of creative and cultural fields of education. As noted earlier, the modularity of the CCIs distinction between creative services and cultural production does produce a set of occupations across the arts and media industries that, with the exception of design disciplines, are well aligned with the broad field of education '10 Creative Arts'. However, the use of government funding mechanisms to steer student choices away from areas of poor employment presents a very real problem for the CCIs project in relation to this segment. While there are few areas of university education that are articulated to professions through the mediation of professional bodies and accreditation systems, many fields of creative study are not conceptually aligned with occupational outcomes in the CCIs, for the simple reason that the forms of training they provide are not structured according to the human capital needs of specific labour markets.

While the mismatch between HE and creative labour markets has been well documented, there has been little acknowledgement of why this might be the case and, more importantly, what this tells us about the creative economy. Fields of creative and cultural education are structured more like domains of cognate activity (which we might variously describe as 'fields' (Bourdieu 1993), 'worlds' (Becker 1982) or 'social network markets' (Potts et al. 2008), rather than industrial sectors of employment or market activity. While the forms of professional cultural identity they inculcate overlap with employment and other economically significant phenomena (creative services, markets for content), they are formally independent of them insofar as they reflect socially recognised 'vocations' that are conceptually independent of commercial value. It is for this reason that the ABS can measure high levels of both paid and unpaid cultural activity across all occupational groupings (not simply cultural professionals), and why there can be very high levels of both for the unemployed and those outside the labour market.

This is not simply an ironic reflection but concerns the significance of the 'creative turn' during a historical period of growing un(der)employment. The emergence of creativity is related to an account of how the social is changing under current technological transformations, one that promotes entrepreneurial modes of sociality that are significant for work and the economy, and whose value lies beyond any industry framework (Potts et al. 2008). It is because such vocations survive despite their distance from the formal economy that they can be regarded as exemplary for the current historical period (Brook 2016). Given this, the 'creative' appears to be as every bit as relational, social and dependent on domains of human-nominated value as the erstwhile notion of 'culture'.

In this context, arguments for the creative economy would best sit in terms of an account of the public value of HE, rather than in terms of private returns to graduates from specific areas of study. While the former argument would be in line with the blue sky economic thinking that has defined CCIs policy discussions around the knowledge economy, the latter argument could only place stress on the integrity of the concept in the first instance, as the fields in which core creative skills are taught would appear more or less economic than others, at least insofar as measurable graduate labour market outcomes are concerned. As such, they might continue to make a qualitative and values-based case for the economy as a particular kind of socio-economic project, rather than object; one that would seem well positioned to address the problems associated with the current economic downturn.

REFERENCES

Australian Bureau of Statistics (ABS) (2013) 'Discussion Paper: Cultural and Creative Activity Satellite Accounts', Commonwealth of Australia, Canberra. Available online at: https://www.abs.gov.au/AUSSTATS/abs@.nsf/DetailsPage/5271.0.55 .0012013?OpenDocument.

Australian Bureau of Statistics (ABS) (2014) 'Australian National Accounts' Cultural and Creative Activity Satellite Accounts, Experimental', Commonwealth of Australia, Canberra. Available online at: https://www.abs.gov.au/AUSSTATS/abs@ .nsf/DetailsPage/5271.02008-9?Open Document.

Australian Bureau of Statistics (ABS) (2020) 'Australia and New Zealand Standard Classification of Research 2020', Commonwealth of Australia, Canberra. Available online at: https://www.abs.gov.au/AUSSTATS/abs@.nsf/Lookup/1297.0Main+ Features12020? OpenDocument.

Bakshi, H., Freeman, A., and Higgs, P. (2013) *A Dynamic Mapping of the UK's Creative Industries*. London: Nesta.

Becker, H. (1982) *Art Worlds*. Berkeley and Los Angeles, CA: University of California Press.

Bennett, T., McFall, L., and Pryke, M. (2008) 'Culture/Economy/Social', *Journal of Cultural Economy* 1(1), 1–7.

Bourdieu, P. (1993) *The Field of Cultural Production: Essays on Art and Literature*. London: Polity.

Bridgstock, R. (2005) 'Australian Artists, Starving and Well-Nourished: What Can We Learn from the Prototypical Protean Career?', *Australian Journal of Career Management* 14(3), 40–48.

Brook, S. (2015) 'Creative Vocations and Cultural Value', in K. Oakley and J. O'Connor (eds), *The Routledge Companion to the Cultural Industries*. London and New York: Routledge, 296–304.

Brook, S. (2016) 'The Exemplary Economy: A Hunterian reading of the Creative Industries as educative project', *International Journal of Cultural Policy* 22(1), 27–40.

Bureau of Communications and Arts Research (BCAR) (2018) 'Cultural and Creative Activity in Australia 2008–09 to 2016–17', Commonwealth of Australia, Canberra.

Available online at: https://www.communications.gov.au/departmental-news/ economic-value-cultural-and-creative-activity.

Bureau of Communications and Arts Research (BCAR) (2019) 'Creative Skills for the Future Economy', Working Paper, Department of Communication and the Arts, Commonwealth of Australia, Canberra.

Cronenberg, D. (Director/Writer) (1983) *Videodrome*. Produced by Pierre David and Claude Heroux. Filmplan International and Guardian Trust Co. Stars James Woods and Debbie Harry.

Cultural Ministers Council Statistical Advisory Group (CMCSAG) (1990) *The Australian Cultural Industry: Available Data and Sources*. Canberra: Australian Government Publishing Service.

Cunningham, S. (2013) *Hidden Innovation: Policy, Industry and the Creative Sector*. St Lucia: University of Queensland Press.

Daniel, R. (2017) 'The Creative Industries Concept: Stakeholder Reflections on Its Relevance and Potential in Australia', *Journal of Australian Studies* 41(2), 252–266.

DeLillo, D. (1984) *White Noise*. New York: Viking Penguin.

Department of Communication and the Arts (DCA) (1994) *Creative Nation: Commonwealth Cultural Policy*. Commonwealth Government, Canberra. Available online at: https://apo.org.au/node/29704.

Department of Skills, Education and Employment (DESE) (2019) 'Final Report for the Performance-Based Funding for the Commonwealth Grants Scheme', Commonwealth of Australia, Canberra. Available online at: https://www.education .gov.au/performance-based-funding-commonwealth-grant-scheme.

Department of Skills, Education and Employment (DESE) (2020) 'Job-Ready Graduates: Higher Education Reform Package', Commonwealth of Australia, Canberra. Available online at: https://www.dese.gov.au/document/job-ready -graduates-discussion-paper.

Du Gay, P., and Pryke, M. (2002) 'Cultural Economy: An Introduction', in P. du Gay and M. Pryke (eds), *Cultural Economy: Cultural Analysis and Commercial Life*. London, UK; Thousand Oaks, CA, USA; New Delhi, India: SAGE Publications, pp. 1–19.

Flew, T. (2019) 'Cultural and Creative Industries – Case for a New Field of Research (FOR) Code – And Creative Economy as a New Socio-Economic Objective (SEO)', submission to the Australian and New Zealand Standard Research Classification Review (ANZSCR). Available online from the ANZSCR page at: https://www.arc .gov.au/anzsrc-review/anzsrc-consultation.

Frow, J. (1995) *Cultural Studies and Cultural Value*. Oxford and New York: Oxford University Press.

Garnham, Nicholas (2005) 'From Cultural to Creative Industries: An Analysis of the Implications of the "Creative Industries" Approach to Arts and Media Policy Making in the United Kingdom', *International Journal of Cultural Policy* 11(1), 15–29.

Hartley, J., and Cunningham, S. (2001) 'Creative Industries: From Blue Poles to Fat Pipes (Case Study 1)', in Malcolm Gillies, Mark Carroll and John Dash (eds), *Humanities and Social Sciences Futures*. Canberra: Department of Employment, Education and Science, pp. 16–26.

Higgs, P., and Lennon, S. (2014) 'Australian Creative Employment in 2011 – Applying the Nesta Mapping Definition Methodology to Australian Classifications', Queensland University of Technology. Available online at: https://eprints.qut.edu .au/92726/.

Hunter, I. (1988) *Culture and Government: The Emergence of Literary Education.* London: Macmillan.

Latour, B. (1990) 'Drawing Things Together', in M. Lynch and S. Woolgar (eds), *Representation in Scientific Practice.* Cambridge, MA: MIT Press, pp. 19–68.

Luckman, S. (2012) *Locating Cultural Work: The Politics and Poetics of Rural, Regional and Remote Creativity.* Basingstoke: Palgrave Macmillan.

McCluhan, M. (1964) *Understanding Media: The Extensions of Man.* McGraw Hill, New York.

Miller, P., and Rose, N. (1990) 'Governing Economic Life', *Economy and Society* 19(1), 1–31.

Nelson, C. (2015) 'Discourses of Creativity', in Rodney H. Jones (ed.), *The Routledge Handbook of Language and Creativity.* London and New York: Routledge, pp. 170–187.

Nelson, C. (2018) 'Beyond Prometheus: Creativity, Discourse, Ideology and the Anthropocene', *Knowledge Cultures* 6(2), 111–131.

Potts, J. (2012) *Creative Industries and Economic Evolution.* Cheltenham, UK and Northampton, MA, USA: Edward Elgar Publishing.

Potts, J., Cunningham, S., Hartley, J., and Ormerod, P. (2008) 'Social Network Markets: A New Definition of the Creative Industries', *Journal of Cultural Economics* 32(3), 167–185.

Throsby, D. (1999) 'Cultural Capital', *Journal of Cultural Economics* 23, 3–12.

UNESCO (2009) '2009 UNESCO Framework for Cultural Statistics', UNESCO Institute for Statistics, Quebec, Montreal. Available online at: http://uis.unesco.org/sites/default/files/documents/unesco-framework-for-cultural-statistics-2009-en_0.pdf.

3. On GIS and the creative economy: opportunities and challenges

Manfredi de Bernard, Roberta Comunian and Federica Viganò

3.1 INTRODUCTION

This chapter aims to bring together past research and reflections on the value and applicability of geographic information system (GIS) approaches to the creative economy field and assess the opportunities and challenges that it might present to research using this method. First, it is important to clarify what GIS is and how it has developed as a methodology in the past 40 years. Its applicability extends from physical geography to military applications, from demography to emotions mapping. For the purpose of this chapter, we specifically focus on how GIS has been used as a method in connections with the creative economy: from archaeology to cultural planning, from creative industries mapping to tourism and heritage routes. We conduct a systematic literature review to show how there has been a growing interest in this method in connection with the study of the creative economy (including cultural and creative industries). Focusing more narrowly on the interconnection between GIS, mapping the creative economy and its geographical dynamics, we review the literature, approaches and contributions available. We then reflect on a small research project mapping the creative economy (precisely, craft economies) of a rural mountain valley (Val Gardena, Italy) using GIS data, and explore its implications. Finally, discussing our small project, we consider the advantages and opportunities of bringing together GIS with other research methods. We also conclude by addressing some of the challenges and limitations.

3.2 GIS: DEFINITIONS AND OBJECTIVES

What is GIS?

The use of GIS has been flourishing since the 1980s in the research industry and academia due to the development and diffusion of new information and communication technologies (Walford 1999). Scholars and practitioners have produced many definitions over time (Maguire 1991; Parker 1988), most of which highlight similar concerns and core aspects of GIS, with minor differences remaining the focus of academic exchanges. Chang's recent definition captures the essential elements involved: 'A geographic information system (GIS) is a computer system for capturing, storing, querying, analysing, and displaying geospatial data. Geospatial data describe both the location and the attributes of spatial feature' (Chang 2019: 1). More broadly, what is essential to any GIS definition are three underlying principles: 'GIS focuses on the cartographic display of complex information; that GIS is a sophisticated database system, and that GIS is a set of procedures and tools for fostering spatial analysis' (Maguire et al. 1991: 13–14). Hence, to understand the potential and workings of GIS, it is essential to define what type of data it uses and how they are managed.

GIS is a computer system specialised in handling geospatial data, these are:

> data about objects, events, or phenomena that have a location on the surface of the earth, including location information (usually coordinates on the earth), attribute information (the characteristics of the object, event, or phenomena concerned), and often also temporal information (the time or life span at which the location and attributes exist). (Stock and Guesgen 2015: 171)

The locations are identified through a coordinate system, such as longitude and latitude, in a geographic coordinate system, or through x, y coordinates in a projected coordinate system, or through surrogate spatial reference such as postcodes or addresses (Bahaire and Elliott-White 1999). On the other hand, attribute and temporal information are statistical and non-locational data associated with spatial entities.

Geospatial data can be furtherly grouped into raster and vector data (see Mitchell 2001: 15). The two kinds of data differently represent spatial features: the first use grid and grid cells – a single cell is a point, a sequence of neighbouring cells is a line, a collection of adjacent cells is a polygon – and are mainly used for continuous features such as elevation and precipitations. The second use points, lines and polygons – each of them is assigned an identification (ID) that can be associated with its attributes – with a precise spatial location and boundary and are ideal for discrete features: streams, roads, lakes and forests. Common GIS operations with geospatial data are data acquisition, data management, data query, vector data analysis, raster data analysis and data display (Chang 2019). We will not comment further on vector and raster data analysis here, as they are outside the chapter's scope; information on these are found in the many manuals and guides available about the extensive range of tools offered by GIS to arrange and display geospatial data (Mitchell 2001,

2005, 2012). On the other hand, the other elements deserve consideration for the following discussion.

First, data acquisition occurs in two main ways: (1) accessing governmental (such as Data.gov for the United States or INSPIRE for the European Union) or non-governmental (such as DIVA-GIS or OpenStreetMap) public databases; and (2) digitalising new geospatial data from a range of sources, including satellite images, Global Positioning System (GPS) data, survey data, geotagged data, street address and text files. Second, concerning data management, a database management system (DBMS) is generally included in GIS software to handle attributes of vector data. This is commonly undergone through the feature–attribute table, in which rows represent spatial features and columns their attributes. Thus, every table's cell indicates a single attribute (for example, height) of one spatial feature (for example, one building). Third, in connection with data query, given that data in GIS are managed through a DBMS, close inspection of them is operationalised through SQL (structured query language) with almost no difference from a generic database query. In contrast, the unique element of GIS is spatial data query. It allows users to select a feature based on its spatial relationships rather than its attributes, for example, individuating a building within x kilometres from a second building or finding all forest parcels intersecting with a river. This kind of query combines two kinds of data: 'finding schools within a county that have over 500 students' presents spatial data in the first part, and attribute in the second (Chang 2019: 4). The last and most intuitive use of GIS is that of data display, through which vector layers on raster data on the same coordinate system are superimposed to produce one map where several characteristics of a geographical area are well represented.

What is GIS for?

GIS has many applications, from telecommunications (Fry 1999) to environmental modelling (Brimicombe 2009), emergency management (Cova 1999), urban planning (Parrott and Stutz 1991) and marketing (Viswanathan 2011).

Additionally, GIS has recently seen unconventional applications. In these, the software traditionally applied within a positivist epistemological framework is used to give spatiality to ephemeral phenomena, such as emotions (Nold 2007). These new applications are possible thanks to technological innovations, specifically GPS and Web 2.0, and Critical GIS scholars' perspectives, a cluster of scholarly researchers aiming to problematise the socio-cultural context in which GIS developed and found significant applications, and the risk of a dominant, biased positivist epistemology. Given that the sources and subject of this chapter share methods and normative positions with the Critical GIS area, we proceed by briefly reviewing their arguments.

When GIS started to emerge as a tool and area of research, its disruptive potential for change was immediately evident in the discipline of geography. Dobson (1983) indeed predicted the growing importance of GIS and quantitative spatial modelling that made geographers influential actors among decision-makers in administration and politics in the following decades. The scholar was sure that such technologies would become a central element in the discipline, and a catalyst for debate.

This rapidly generated concerns among humanistic and cultural geographers, worried that one quantitative data-driven epistemological framework would rapidly dominate the field (O'Sullivan 2006). Their reflections on the social implications of an acritical adoption of GIS were collected in the seminal *Ground Truth* (Pickles 1995). In the book, Goodchild wrote that 'a geography that accept GIS too readily will become a discipline dominated by facts rather than by understanding' (Goodchild 1995: 36), and Taylor and Johnston (1995) raised questions about by whom and how data were acquired, in fear of the emergence of panoptic state geography. Other authors commented on the risk of the development of a 'masculine' technology (Roberts and Schein 1995: 183–84), and on the ethical inconsistency of a neat fracture between the analyser and the analysed, and the consequent worrying possibility of social surveillance and private life monitoring systems (Curry 1995). Severe doubts also arose about the possibility of one hierarchy of ontologies, 'whether the logic of GIS, as result of design decisions ... privileges certain views of the world over others' (Sheppard 1995: 1027).

Afterwards, Critical GIS perspectives moved from an antagonistic position to a collaborative one, actively engaging with the challenges set by conventional, quantitative use of GIS. One of the most concerning issues to be addressed was the unbalanced access to data production. In this regard, it led to the emergence of public participatory GIS (PPGIS), aiming to expand conventional top-down, national sources of geospatial data by favouring a bottom-up approach, which would somehow democratise production and control of geographical information (Dunn 2007). This bottom-up approach was further boosted when GPS and Web 2.0 technologies became accessible to everyone, mainly via mobile technologies. Although this raised new issues regarding access to data and 'apparent surveillance implications' (Pickles 2006: 766), it offered new tools for widening data sources.

This brief review of Critical GIS (for more, see Ferretti 2007) offers context for the following discussion of GIS and the creative economy. Even if spatiality has indeed been crucial in the creative economy field of research, especially concerning creative clusters (Chapain and Sagot-Duvauroux 2020) and creative cities (Evans 2009), GIS has found limited applications so far.

3.3   GIS AND THE CREATIVE ECONOMY

GIS Use in Creative Economy: The Growth Over Time

The use of GIS in connection with creative economy research is relatively recent, with initial contributions emerging in the early 2000s, especially in connection with mapping leisure and cultural activities (Almer and Nischelwitzer 2000; Feeney and Feeney 2003) across a range of approaches and sub-fields.

Following Petticrew and Roberts (2008), we conducted a systematic literature review[1] (SLR) across the creative economy subject areas on Scopus. We considered academic sources that engage with the interaction between three areas under the creative economy umbrella ('creative econom*', 'cultur* industr*' and 'creative industr*') and GIS.[2] Figure 3.1 reveals the trend of these interactions, showing how they started in the early 2000s and emerged more significantly in the last decade. 'Cultur* industr*' was the first to be paired with GIS in academic research, with the trend starting several years before the other two. All three trends have grown steadily over time. The interest in the creative economy concerning GIS remains the lowest overall. The other two fought for primacy for several years, until the creative industries' steep increase in the last few years.

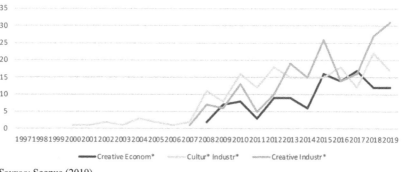

Source: Scopus (2019).

*Figure 3.1   The growing connection between GIS and the creative
economy research area*

The use of GIS in connection with creative economy research spreads across a range of approaches and sub-fields: from its application to cultural heritage mapping and archaeological research, to its use in mapping cultural participation of audiences and communities, to its use in connection with cultural planning at city level.

The earliest usages of GIS in the sector occurred in archaeology (Kvamme 1983), cultural participation analysis (Stern and Seifert 1998) and music industry clustering (Gibson 2002), with quantitative data-only methods. On the other hand, qualitative data and mental mappings have seen few applications in recent times (Brennan-Horley 2015). In many ways, we can argue that the development of GIS within the creative economy field might have followed a similar pattern to the development of GIS in general: from the initial emphasis on data mapping, to a more comprehensive application of data to understand context and people's behaviours and attitudes in relation to place.

In order to succinctly reflect on the existing literature, we have identified six foci of research, connected by the specific focus of interest, yet acknowledging the complexity of the field and the range of scale at which research on the creative economy operates (Comunian 2019). These six foci, emerging from our review, are represented in Figure 3.2. They are not entirely distinct. At times they overlap, and are studied in a connected manner. In the next section, we unpack Figure 3.2 and address how GIS research engages with these different dimensions of the creative economy.

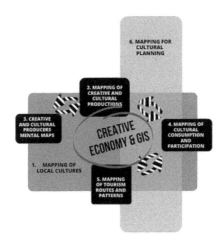

Figure 3.2   *Interconnected layers and foci of research in GIS and the creative economy*

Applications, Research and Reflection

First, the broader focus of research relates to how GIS is used to map local cultures, often with a spatial anthropology perspective. The research of Roberts and Cohen on Liverpool musical and cinematographic heritage gives a brilliant example of how mapping, in this case, a GIS–participatory approach, can provide an instrument to develop spatial historiography and anthropology of a place, adding the human layer on the geographical materiality (Roberts and Cohen 2015). Also, presenting two previous mapping experiences of Liverpool, the authors trace the line between one descriptive and deep mapping meant as inquiry, and one largely instrumental aimed at mere branding and place-marketing. Not far from their mapping exercise is Long and Collins's (2012) on the soundscape of Birmingham, in which the sense of place of the city of the West Midlands is described.

Second, a narrow, creative and cultural industries (CCIs) perspective relies on GIS to map the location and distribution of CCIs, often in connection to a creative and cultural clusters approach. These applications range from conventional uses of GIS, in which the software is adopted to visualise geographic data on a map, to complex implementation such as spatial modelling, in which the evolution of spatial phenomena is partially addressed. Exemplifying the former, He and Gebhardt (2014) and Drummond and Snowball (2021) rely on GIS to locate creative firms and their clustering in Shanghai and in the Sarah Baartman district, South Africa, respectively. It is also worth mentioning the Americans for the Arts (AFTA) report which relies on this kind of mapping to leverage political influence (AFTA 2017). Among the complex applications, Liu et al. (2016) adopt and update an existing internal urban change simulation model and use GIS to forecast changes in land use and spatial distribution of creative firms in Jiading district, Shangai.

Third, connected to creative and cultural production, many studies focus on creatives' experiences and spatial practice. To address this dimension, Brennan-Horley (2015) applies GIS to mental mapping to investigate artistic supply lines between towns, and movements between work sites within them, in the sparsely populated area of Central Darling Shire in Australia. This kind of method highlights the everyday, mundane movements of creative workers, challenging conventional spatial theories in the field (Brennan-Horley 2010). Mental mapping results were geolocated, individuating the distribution of sites, and then the relationship between them was given a magnitude resulting from the aggregation of respondents' answers. Further work using GIS shows areas of Darwin, Australia in which the interviewees draw inspiration, again joined with mental mapping (Brennan-Horley et al. 2010). The answers are indicated as single locations or as areas of the city and aggregated through the software and then visualised, both in 2D and 3D.

Fourth, on the other end of the spectrum, studies aim to map patterns of cultural consumption or participation. A pioneer in applying GIS to cultural dynamics is the Social Impact of the Arts Project (SIAP) (Stern and Seifert 1998). Here, GIS is used to integrate data on culture with other socio-economic data, always contextualised in the geographical location analysed. Recent development of the SIAP method employs the Cultural Asset Index, that synthesises quantitative data from cultural participants, resident artists, non-profit cultural organisations and commercial cultural firms at a census block group level (Stern and Seifert 2017). Evidence on cultural assets is then linked to a geographic database, allowing considerations on their spatial distribution across one area, as with approach 2, and highlighting eventual correlations between the presence (or absence) of cultural assets and other socio-economic factors in the geographical unit chosen.

Fifth, connected to patterns of consumption and cultural participation, and more explicitly concerning place consumption, is the connection between the study of tourism and its patterns and GIS. Inside the creative economy, GIS has found significant applications in tourism. Aside from the intuitive digital map-making use of the software (Wei 2012), GIS shines as a support for decision-making in tourism management (Bahaire and Elliott-White 1999). In tourism planning, Bahaire and Elliott-White illustrate the potential benefit of GIS adoption to address Butler's 'problems of tourism', or the lack of information regarding tourism's actual or potential presence (Butler 1992). The difficulty in assessing the latter's impact, or in individuating adequate areas of development, is addressed through simulation and modelling, analysis of trends or systematic inventorying and monitoring of natural and cultural resources, all of which become feasible through the use of GIS (Bahaire and Elliott-White 1999). The second major group of GIS technologies applications in tourism is related to tourists' movement pattern analysis (McKercher et al. 2012). This kind of investigation has seen the use of GIS combined with several methods of data acquisition: trip diaries (van der Knaap 1999), GPS (McKercher et al. 2012) or geotagged photography (García-Palomares et al. 2015). To conclude, although tracking technologies are not free of issues (see Shoval and Isaacson 2007), they produce accurate data which are easily managed and processed through GIS software (McKercher et al. 2012)

Sixth and finally, the last focus connects GIS to policymaking in the creative economy, specifically through cultural planning. Informing the public using accessible language, and providing empirical facts, are two critical elements in building effective dialogic communication. However, even if traditional means of inclusion in governance processes, such as face-to-face forums, focus groups and surveys, are further expanded through online/digital tools, they still 'require a merely reactive involvement of the public' (Redaelli 2012: 647). Redaelli demonstrates the potential of GIS in addressing issues of participation in cultural planning, as it facilitates 'an understanding of the place by providing a spatial explanation of governance, population, and cultural assets' (ibid.: 649). In other words, besides expanding the number and quality of data sources, GIS possesses a strong communicative power due to its unique ability in managing geospatial data; data organisation and visualisation in GIS hence allowing a straightforward interpretation by the public, reducing technical barriers that could hamper genuine discussion.

3.4   CASE STUDY: MAPPING VAL GARDENA CREATIVE (CRAFT) ECONOMY THROUGH GIS

Val Gardena: Creative Economies on the Mountain and Their Development

Val Gardena is a mountain valley located in the north-western Dolomites of South Tyrol, Italy (Figure 3.3), one of the most attractive and touristic areas, visited all year round for mountaineering and sport activities, trekking and biking in summer, and skiing and cross-country skiing in winter. In 2009, the Dolomites were awarded United Nations Educational, Scientific and Cultural Organization (UNESCO) World Heritage status. While tourism has taken over as the primary source of business for Val Gardena in recent decades, the valley is also celebrated for its traditional culture and local artists and artisans (Mabry 2011). The whole Province of South Tyrol is a bilingual area (Italian and German), but Val Gardena also lies in the Ladin area, where a distinct dialect is spoken and taught in schools. Ladin culture and traditions (that is, traditional garments, folk music) are still alive and cherished by the local population (Valentin 2018).

Figure 3.3   *Val Gardena Location in Northern Italy*

In Val Gardena, one of the most developed traditional sectors is wood carving, located in the district of Ortisei which specialises in the manufacture of artistic crafts and wood products. Most of the district's companies are owned by individual artisans who identify as a 'woodcarver'. There is a 400-year-old tradition of wood carving sculptures and figures of sacred art, which gave rise to an export market known worldwide. Every year, Unika takes place, an art fair of woodcarvings, paintings, bronze sculptures and wood products. Val Gardena is perceived as a very specialised artistic hub, with two sides: the contemporary art featured by the Doris Ghetta contemporary art gallery, and the historical and sacred art housed in the Gherdeina Local Heritage Museum (Museum Gherdëina), situated in the centre of Ortisei. Given the strong link between the traditional sector of wood and the creative economy, the growth of creative new businesses and strategies for local tourism development (Eurac Research 2017) need to be connected.

Connecting Val Gardena Craft Economy and Tourism

The relationship between the creative economy and tourism is quite a contested area of research (Long and Morpeth 2016; Richards 2011). On the one hand, their interconnection has become a new interest in academia, especially for its potential for local economic development, ranging from urban tourism (Ooi 2007; Rogerson 2006) to development (Rogerson 2007). On the other hand, the two sectors remain very different, especially considering workforce composition and value creation. Many argue that they should not be clustered together, especially in mapping one local creative economy, as the larger component of creative and cultural tourism can be reconnected to the service sector. More recently, others have tried to isolate the more specifically 'creative' sub-component of tourism with the new term 'creative tourism' (Richards and Raymond 2000), such as the engaging of visitors in participative activities (such as courses or learning experiences) and offering opportunities for the creative development of individuals, as well as closer contact between visitors and creative and cultural producers.

Within the broader framework of creative tourism many highlight the important role and potential of craft, in terms of both craft making as well as craft skills and experiences (Fillis 2008; Tan et al. 2013). Building on Richards's (2019) reflections on creative development's potential for small communities, it should be of specific interest for a rural location such as Val Gardena and the kind of touristic activities it attracts. In many ways, understanding the potential connection between tourism (and touristic routes) and the presence of creative activities and creative producers is an interesting question that researchers are not currently addressing. However, here we question whether this is an interesting example of an area where, from a research and policy/planning perspective, GIS could contribute to a more systematic understanding of the context and provide some initial insights before qualitative research or policy interventions occur. Therefore, as explained in more details in the methodology section, we use this case study to investigate how creative craft activities and producers spatially interact or interconnect with main tourism patterns in Val Gardena.

Methodology

The method adopted relies on the essential functions of GIS as typical in tourism management (McAdam 1999), investigating the (eventual) coordination of the creative economy and tourism in their spatial dimension in Val Gardena, Italy. Such an approach is positioned somewhere between the second and fifth foci of the above model. The tourism dimension is represented through two main categories, on which data are drawn from Sentres,[3] an online tourism portal that centres on Sud Tirol, the Italian region where Val Gardena is located: general tourism (which includes the accommodations, eating and drinking, and culture categories) and hiking, skiing, climbing and biking routes. While this is a limited dataset, especially considering the very localised nature of the data and limited reach of the region under analysis, it remains valuable to reflect on the connection between local craft economies and touristic routes. The routes are readily available in a geolocated format (.gpx) on Sentres, while we drew the coordinates of the other locations from their address in Google Maps. Figure 3.4 shows the data imported from Sentres. We then plotted the locations of these activities on the OpenStreetMap's database, choosing different symbols, as shown in the legend, to differentiate them.

The creative economy in Val Gardena is mainly related to wood crafting and wood sculpting. To address these dimensions, the local creative economy has been divided into four categories, production (art studios, craft workshops), consumption (galleries, craft shops, markets and fairs), support (education, business support, guilds or associations) and promotion (museums, exhibitions and archives), gathered through the Italian Chamber of Commerce database and through Unika,[4] 'a platform for local and regional artists to showcase their sculptures, paintings and photography', which is also involved in planning two major arts fairs that centre on wood crafting. This second group of data were plotted and indicated with symbols. In order to individuate a second layer, it was then superimposed on the previous figure to highlight the presence (or absence) of any spatial pattern and overlapping (see Figure 3.5).

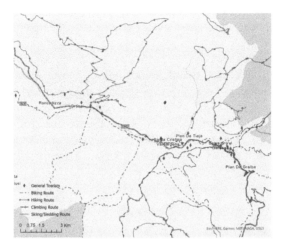

Figure 3.4   Val Gardena tourism routes and services from Sentres

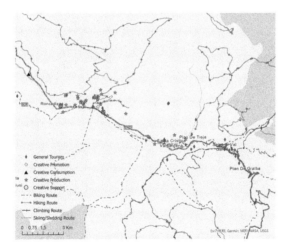

Figure 3.5   Val Gardena with both tourism and craft economy dimension

Data and Discussion

Through the use of GIS, we have been able to visualise and overlay the main touristic routes in Val Gardena and visualise their potential overlap with the presence of craft producers. As visible in Figure 3.5, the tourist routes connected with mountain activities such as hiking or climbing tend to be located remotely and close to the natural landscape and remote mountain locations.

The focus of Val Gardena on natural and sport tourism seems to hinder the opportunity for local tourism to even cross paths with creative and cultural producers.

If we focus more closely on the centres for creative production or consumption (Figure 3.6), it is clear that their location is urban; as far as urban can be found in Val Gardena. They thrive on the human connection and interaction in production, exchange and materials, and potentially interact with tourists who are driving by rather than those visiting the surroundings. There is little overlap: some craft locations might be close to the start or endpoint of a hike or bike route, but generally those two markets and groups – the nature/sport tourism and the creative activities – never meet.

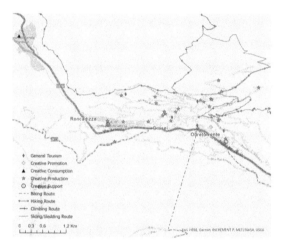

Figure 3.6   Connections in Ortisei between craft economy and touristic routes

This exercise, although small-scale, shows the value of GIS in making visible the patterns (as well as crossings and distance) between creative craft activities and tourism in Val Gardena. Of course, this initial mapping could be integrated with further qualitative data collection, as argued by Kwan and Ding (2008). Alternatively, we could improve the granularity of data using TripAdvisor geotagged photos of the area.

However, even with these initial maps, some interesting learning points can be considered, both from the creative practitioners and from tourism and policy organisations in Val Gardena. For example, if a craft practitioner was thinking of relocating, they might consider how to best attract existing visitors by looking at where tourist routes might give them an opportunity to access customers. Local policies trying to maximise the value brought to the locality by visitors might consider creating new routes (or moving the start of a route) closer to crafters' studios that might provide opportunities for craft production and consumption to interact with existing visitors; similarly, the craft production could be marketed on Val Gardena's tourism brochures and websites and be advertised close to the starting points and endpoints of routes. Lastly, given the stark disproportion between creative production on the one hand, and promotion and consumption on the other, local planners and policymakers could reflect on the latter's role in creating a bridge with the tourism dimension.

3.5   CONCLUSIONS

The chapter has tried to reflect on GIS potential and actual contributions to advancing our knowledge of the creative economy. It has done so by reviewing existing literature and using a small case study to reflect on the practicalities and implications of using GIS. Specific to Val Gardena, we have uncovered a weak connection between existing touristic routes and the presence of craft production and consumption. This might have practical and policy implications but, crucially, highlights how the creative economy is an ecosystem with many layers, which was also discussed in our literature review and illustrated in Figure 3.2, requiring critical mapping and connecting (see also de Bernard and Comunian, 2021). Far from considering our investigation of Val Gardena as the endpoint, we argue that this exercise could provide a very interesting opportunity for exchanges with the local producers and the visitors taking those routes.

Through the literature review, it has emerged that GIS offers research a whole new set of knowledge in terms of how culture, creativity and spatiality interconnect and interact, which other conventional approaches, such as the creative clusters and cities research, do not capture. The latter's uncritical, superficial and top-down investigation of spatiality indeed struggles to provide insights across the different components and stakeholders involved in the sector. Sampling decisions are often taken a priori and not connected to the sector's practices (Wilson et al. 2020), and led by global policy frameworks that offer very little consideration to place specificity; and that consequently leads to a severe underrepresentation of off-the-radar (or out-of-the-market) elements of the creative economy (de Bernard et al. 2021).

Crucially, these limits are not dissimilar from those stressed by Critical GIS scholars, who advocate for the contextualisation of GIS technologies and for its critical employment. We thus argue, first, for a deeper addressing of spatiality in the creative economy through GIS; and second, for such future investigations to be conscious of the perspectives given by the Critical GIS tradition. There is a stark need for research that is sensible to the context and the object of analysis and that is able to adequately add non-quantitative data and methods to the already strong empirical capabilities of GIS.

NOTES

1. The SLR allows us to critically integrate a large body of research to consider the research trends in this area. We choose Scopus as a 'source-neutral' bibliographic database, that is curated by a board of 'independent subject matter experts' (Scopus 2019), hence limiting research bias to a certain degree.
2. We queried for (GIS AND 'creative econom*', GIS AND 'cultur* industr*' and GIS AND 'creative industr*'). We included in the search all the publications fields. We considered only documents in English, published from 1997 till 2019 (last complete year), and found 352 documents between articles (204), books (74) and book chapters (39) and others (35). We limited the search to four subject areas: arts and humanities (67), business, management and accounting (69), economics, econometrics and finance (52), and social sciences (291), with some documents classified as belonging to more than one subject area.
3. https://www.sentres.com/en/val-gardenagroeden.
4. https://www.unika.org/en/about-us/.

REFERENCES

AFTA (2017), 'The Creative Industries in the United States'. https://www.americansforthearts.org/by-program/reports-and-data/research-studies-publications/creative-industries (accessed 3 May 2022).

Almer, A. and Nischelwitzer, A.K. (2000), '3D-visualisation of leisure & tourism information based on remote sensing data', *International Archives of the Photogrammetry, Remote Sensing and Spatial Information Sciences – ISPRS Archives* 33, 4–11.

Bahaire, Tim and Elliott-White, Martin (1999), 'The application of geographical information systems (GIS) in sustainable tourism planning: a review', *Journal of Sustainable Tourism*, 7 (2), 159–174.

Brennan-Horley, Chris (2010), 'Multiple work sites and city-wide networks: a topological approach to understanding creative work', *Australian Geographer*, 41 (1), 39–56.

Brennan-Horley, Chris (2015), 'Mapping methods: Using GIS for regional and remote cultural planning', in C. Gibson, R. Gibson and P. Ashton (eds), *By-roads and Hidden Treasures: Mapping Cultural Assets in Regional Australia*, Crawley: UWA Publishing, pp. 53–70.

Brennan-Horley, Chris, et al. (2010), 'GIS, ethnography, and cultural research: putting maps back into ethnographic mapping', *Information Society*, 26 (2), 92–103.

Brimicombe, Allan (2009), *GIS, Environmental Modeling and Engineering*, 2nd edn, Boca Raton, FL: CRC Press.

Butler, Richard (1992), 'Alternative tourism: the thin edge of the wedge', in L. Smith Valene and R. Eadington William (eds), *Tourism Alternatives: Potentials and Problems in the Development of Tourism*, Philidelphia, PA: University of Pennsylvania Press, pp. 31–46.

Chang, Kang-Tsung (2019), 'Geographic Information System', *International Encyclopedia of Geography*, Wiley, pp. 1–10.

Chapain, Caroline and Sagot-Duvauroux, Dominique (2020), 'Cultural and creative clusters – a systematic literature review and a renewed research agenda', *Urban Research and Practice*, 13 (3), 300–329.

Comunian, R. (2019), 'Complexity thinking as a coordinating theoretical framework for creative industries research', in S. Cunningham and T. Flew (eds), *A Research Agenda for Creative Industries*, Cheltenham, UK and Northampton, MA, USA: Edward Elgar Publishing, pp. 39–57.

Cova, Thomas (1999), 'GIS in emergency management', *Geographical information systems*, 2, 845–858.

Curry, M.R. (1995), 'Geographic information systems and the inevitability of ethical inconsistency', in John Pickles (ed.), *Ground Truth: The Social Implications of Geographic Information Systems*, New York: Guildford, pp. 68–87.

de Bernard, M. and Comunian, R. (2021), 'Creative and cultural ecosystems: visual models and visualisation challenges'. https://www.creative-cultural-ecologies.eu/ research-blog/creative-and-cultural-ecosystems-visual-models-and-visualisation -challenges.

de Bernard, Manfredi, Comunian, Roberta and Gross, Jonathan (2021), 'Cultural and creative ecosystems: a review of theories and methods, towards a new research agenda', *Cultural Trends*. https://doi.org/10.1080/09548963.2021.2004073.

Dobson, Jerome E. (1983), 'Automated geography', *Professional Geographer*, 35 (2), 135–143.

Drummond, Fiona and Snowball, Jen (2021), 'Rural cultural and creative industry clustering: the Sarah Baartman district, South Africa', in B.J. Hracs, R. Comunian and L. England (eds), *Developing Creative Economies in Africa*, London: Routledge, pp. 115–132.

Dunn, Christine E. (2007), 'Participatory GIS – a people's GIS?', *Progress in Human Geography*, 31 (5), 616–637.

Eurac Research (2017), 'Il futuro del turismo in Alto Adige 2030'. http://www.hk-cciaa .bz.it/sites/default/files/uploaded_files/IRE_ricerca_economica/Pubblicazioni/ 170526_Report_IT_.pdf.

Evans, Graeme (2009), *Creative Spaces and the Art of Urban Living*. Routledge.

Feeney, A.E. and Feeney, T.P. (2003), 'Pennsylvania's drive-in movies: the business of preserving a cultural icon', *Pennsylvania Geographer*, 41 (2), 95–112.

Ferretti, Federico (2007), 'La verità del suolo: breve storia del Critical GIS (1983–2007)', *Storicamente*, 3. http://www.storicamente.org/02_tecnostoria/strumen-.

Fillis, Ian (2008), 'Entrepreneurial crafts and the tourism industry', in J. Ateljevic and S.J. Page (eds), *Tourism and Entrepreneurship*, London: Routledge, pp. 133–147.

Fry, Carolyn (1999), 'GIS in telecommunications', *Geographic Information Systems: Principles, Techniques, Applications and Management*, 2, 819–826.

García-Palomares, Juan Carlos, Gutiérrez, Javier and Mínguez, Carmen (2015), 'Identification of tourist hot spots based on social networks: a comparative analysis of European metropolises using photo-sharing services and GIS', *Applied Geography*, 63, 408–417.

Gibson, Chris (2002), 'Rural transformation and cultural industries: popular music on the New South Wales Far North Coast', *Australian Geographical Studies*, 40 (3), 337–356.

Goodchild, Michael F. (1995), 'Geographic information systems and geographic research', in J. Pickles (ed.), *Ground Truth: The Social Implications of Geographic Information Systems*, New York: Guildford, pp. 31–50.

He, Jin-Liao and Gebhardt, Hans (2014), 'Space of creative industries: a case study of spatial characteristics of creative clusters in Shanghai', *European Planning Studies*, 22 (11), 2351–2368.

Kvamme, Kenneth L. (1983), 'Computer processing techniques for regional modeling of archaeological site locations', *Advances in Computer Archaeology*, 1 (1), 26–52.

Kwan, Mei Po and Ding, Guoxiang (2008), 'Geo-narrative: extending geographic information systems for narrative analysis in qualitative and mixed-method research', *Professional Geographer*, 60 (4), 443–465.

Liu, Helin, Silva, Elisabete A. and Wang, Qian (2016), 'Incorporating GIS data into an agent-based model to support planning policy making for the development of creative industries', *Journal of Geographical Systems*, 18 (3), 205–228.

Long, Paul and Collins, Jez (2012), 'Mapping the soundscapes of popular music heritage', in L. Roberts (ed.), *Mapping Cultures: Place, Practice, Performance*, Basingstoke: Palgrave Macmillan, pp. 144–159.

Long, Philip and Morpeth, Nigel D. (2016), *Tourism and the Creative Industries: Theories, Policies and Practice*. Routledge.

Mabry, Wolfgang (2011), 'Giving voice to wood', *Sculpture Review*, 60 (2), 24–33.

Maguire, David J. (1991), 'An overview and definition of GIS', *Geographical Information Systems: Principles and Applications*, 1, 9–20.

Maguire, David J., Goodchild, Michael F. and Rhind, David W. (1991), *Geographical Information Systems Vol. 1, Principles*. Longman Scientific & Technical.

McAdam, David (1999), 'The value and scope of geographical information systems in tourism management', *Journal of Sustainable Tourism*, 7 (1), 77–92.

McKercher, Bob, et al. (2012), 'First and repeat visitor behaviour: GPS tracking and GIS analysis in Hong Kong', *Tourism Geographies*, 14 (1), 147–161.

Mitchell, Andy (2001), *The ESRI Guide to GIS Analysis, Volume 1: Geographic Patterns and Relationships*, Redlands: ESRI Press.

Mitchell, Andy (2005), *The ESRI Guide to GIS Analysis, Volume 2: Spatial Measurements and Statistics*, Redlands: ESRI Press.

Mitchell, Andy (2012), *The ESRI Guide to GIS Analysis, Volume 3: Modeling Sustainability, Movement, and Interaction*, Redlands: ESRI Press.

Nold, Christian (2007), 'San Francisco Emotion Map', http://www.sf.biomapping.net/ (accessed 3 May 2022).

O'Sullivan, David (2006), 'Geographical information science: critical GIS', *Progress in Human Geography*, 30 (6), 783–791.

Ooi, Can-Seng (2007), '16 Creative industries and tourism in Singapore', in J. Wilson and G. Richards (eds), *Tourism, Creativity and Development*, London: Routledge, pp. 240–251.

Parker, H.D. (1988), 'The unique qualities of a Geographic Information System: a commentary', *Photogrammetric Engineering and Remote Sensing*, 54 (11), 1547–1549.

Parrott, R. and Stutz, F.P. (1991), 'Urban GIS Applications', in David J. Maguire, Michael F. Goodchild and David W. Rhind (eds), *Geographical Information Systems: Principles and Applications* (Volume 1), New York: John Wiley & Sons, pp. 247–260.

Petticrew, Mark and Roberts, Helen (2008), *Systematic Reviews in the Social Sciences: A Practical Guide*. John Wiley & Sons.

Pickles, J. (1995), *Ground Truth: The Social Implications of Geographic Information Systems*, New York: Guilford Press.

Pickles, John (2006), 'Ground Truth 1995–2005', *Transactions in GIS*, 10 (5), 763–772.

Redaelli, Eleonora (2012), 'Cultural planning in the United States: toward authentic participation using GIS', *Urban Affairs Review,* 48 (5), 642–669.

Richards, Greg (2011), 'Creativity and tourism: the state of the art', *Annals of Tourism Research*, 38 (4), 1225–1253.

Richards, G. (2019), 'Creative tourism: opportunities for smaller places?', *Tourism and Management Studies*, 15, 7–10.

Richards, Greg and Raymond, Crispin (2000), 'Creative tourism', *ATLAS News*, 23 (8), 16–20.

Roberts, Les and Cohen, Sara (2015), 'Mapping cultures: spatial anthropology and popular cultural memory', in D. MacLennan, N. Duxbury and W.F. Garrett-Petts (eds), *Cultural Mapping as Cultural Inquiry*, Routledge, pp. 170–192.

Roberts, Susan M. and Schein, Richard H. (1995), 'Earth shattering', in J. Pickels (ed.), *Ground Truth: The Social Implications of Geographic Information Systems*, New York: Guildford, pp. 171–195.

Rogerson, Christian M. (2006), 'Creative industries and urban tourism: South African perspectives', *Urban Forum*, 17 (2), 149–166.

Rogerson, Christian (2007), 'Creative industries and tourism in the developing world: the example of South Africa', in G. Richards and J. Wilson (eds), *Tourism, Creativity and Development: Contemporary Geographies of Leisure, Tourism and Mobility*, London: Routledge, pp. 219–251.

Scopus (2019), 'Scopus: Data | Curated. Connected. Complete', Scopus database, Elsevier B.V.

Sheppard, Eric (1995), 'Sleeping with the enemy, or keeping the conversation going?', *Environment and Planning A*, 27 (7), 1026–1028.

Shoval, Noam and Isaacson, Michal (2007), 'Tracking tourists in the digital age', *Annals of Tourism Research*, 34 (1), 141–159.

Stern, Mark J. and Seifert, Susan C. (1998), 'Community revitalization and the arts in Philadelphia', Social Impact of the Arts Project (SIAP), https://repository.upenn .edu/siap/ (accessed 20 June 2020).

Stern, Mark and Seifert, Susan (2017), 'The social wellbeing of New York City's neighborhoods: the contribution of culture and the arts', Social Impact of the Arts Project, University of Pennsylvania, Philadelphia. https://repository.upenn.edu/siap _culture_nyc/1/ (accessed 3 May 2022).

Stock, Kristin and Guesgen, Hans (2015), 'Geospatial reasoning with open data', in L. Robert and P. Watters (eds), *Automating Open Source Intelligence: Algorithms for OSINT*, London: Elsevier, pp. 171–204.

Tan, Siow-Kian, Kung, Shiann-Far and Luh, Ding-Bang (2013), 'A model of "creative experience" in creative tourism', *Annals of Tourism Research*, 41, 153–174.

Taylor, P.J. and Johnston, R.J. (1995), 'Geographic Information Systems and Geography', in J. Pickels (ed.), *Geographic Information Systems and Geography*, New York: Guilford, pp. 51–67.

Valentin, Emanuel (2018), 'Approaches to participative identification of (Ladin) heritage in the Dolomites', in C.L. Salvatore (ed.), *Cultural Heritage Care and Management: Theory and Practice*, Washington, DC: Rowman & Littlefield Publishers, pp. 219–232.

van der Knaap, Wim G.M. (1999), 'Analyse par système d'information géographique des modèles touristiques spatio-temporels pour soutenir le développement touris-tique durable', *Tourism Geographies,* 1 (1), 56–69.

Viswanathan, Nanda K. (2011), 'GIS in marketing', in J. Pick (ed.), *Geographic Information Systems in Business*, Hershey: IGI Global, pp. 236–259.

Walford, Nigel (1999), '"Making more of maps": geography and Geographical Information Systems', *Geography*, 84 (2), 129–138.

Wei, Wei (2012), 'Research on the application of Geographic Information System in tourism management', *Procedia Environmental Sciences*, 12, 1104–1109.

Wilson, N., et al. (2020), 'Re-thinking inclusive and sustainable growth for the creative economy: a literature review', DISCE Publications. https://disce.eu/wp-content/uploads/2020/01/DISCE-Report-D5.2.pdf (accessed 17 April 2020).

4. Using social network analysis to understand the creative and cultural industries

Jon Swords

4.1 INTRODUCTION

This chapter explores the ways in which social network analysis (SNA) can be used to understand the creative and cultural industries (CCIs). SNA allows researchers to schematically trace connections between different agents and understand the characteristics of networks through statistical and visual analysis. Networks are crucial to the effective functioning of the CCIs and decades of research have highlighted this importance for activities across the value chain. Networks are conceptualised in two broad ways in this work. First, they are discussed in general terms, to describe: the social and business networks through which people find work (Bielby and Bielby, 1996); how networks are used to create, and emerge from project teams (Grabher, 2002); how firms are embedded in local/regional networks forming agglomerations (Crewe, 1996); and the role of global production networks in transnational creative economies (Wu, 2017), amongst others.

The second way in which networks are conceptualised is to trace linkages schematically to allow systematic analysis and exploration. This involves generating datasets of network actors and connections between them, and then visualising and/or testing the network statistically. In the CCIs, this might be transactional data in supply chains or employment records. Most often this is done using SNA, which is the approach that this chapter focuses on, by undertaking analysis of companies in the United Kingdom (UK) which are defined as part of the creative industries. SNA is done on a dataset of almost 450 000 enterprises and their connections to the Standard Industrial Classification (SIC) codes that they select when submitting yearly accounts. SNA allows communities of companies which undertake similar activities to be identified, and reveals the work they do which is not defined as part of the creative industries by the UK's Department for Digital, Culture, Media and Sport (DCMS).[1]

This chapter therefore highlights the blurriness of the boundary between the CCIs and the rest of the economy, and the limitations of the SIC system used to identify and focus policy on creative enterprises, and highlights areas for further research.

After this introduction, the chapter begins by outlining the origins of SNA in mathematics and sociology before providing some ways to ensure that it is used appropriately and in a way that does not overstate the results it produces (section 4.2). Section 4.3 outlines the range of ways that SNA has been applied to the CCIs by reviewing a range of literature which reports its use. In section 4.4 a more detailed application of social network is provided that uses data on UK creative companies to explore how they define their activities using SIC codes. This research highlights the work that creative industries companies do outside the standard UK definition of the creative industries, and critiques the way the UK's DCMS defines work in this sector.

4.2   SOCIAL NETWORK ANALYSIS

For Carrington et al. (2005) the origins of SNA can be traced back to the 1930s, but its use took off rapidly in the 1990s.[2] Since this time SNA has been applied to a huge range of social and scientific contexts where networks form. The field has developed, drawing insights from areas as diverse as physics, organisational studies, economics, epidemiology, sociology and geography.

At the heart of SNA, however, is graph theory. Graph theory is a field of mathematics which studies linkages (also called edges or lines) between nodes (also called vertices or points) which form a graph or, in more common parlance, a network (Gera et al., 2018). Nodes can represent many things, including people, organisations, documents, events, media products, animals, diseases and places. The connection between them might indicate collaborations, buyer–supplier relations, employment, citations in documents, involvement or attendance at events, ownership and so on (Sucar, 2015). Graph theory provides mathematical approaches for defining networks and their characteristics by analysing elements such as their size, distance between nodes and how completely connected a network is. More sophisticated analyses provide ways of generating insights about a network's characteristics and prompting further questions for investigation. For example, tests of modularity allow the statistical detection of modules or communities within networks based on shared connections and the identification of divisions between groups of nodes (Newman, 2006). Measures of centrality provide indications of which nodes are most 'important' based on how well connected they are (see Scott, 2017 for an overview).

Drawing on these approaches, SNA emerged from sociology as people's lives were translated into network models to 'understand how individual actions turn into an emergent behaviour of society as a whole' (Zweig, 2016: 27). For Zweig (2016) this was an important moment because it allowed social action to be quantified, but the fundamentals of graph theory are to abstract entities into mathematical formulae. The field has therefore been criticised for overlooking qualitative factors that cannot be abstracted into quantitative form or simplified into vertices and edges (see Knox et al., 2006 for more). Nevertheless, SNA can provide a useful starting point to understand the nature of networks, particularly when they are very large. For instance, it can help to identify communities or groupings for deeper analysis using modularity tests (see below), and tests for centrality can help to highlight significant nodes to concentrate on (for example, highly cited documents, or people connected to many projects).

Getting the Most from SNA

For statistical approaches to work best, the bigger the network you can build, the better. With the rise of big data, and online platforms which harness huge datasets about their users, there has been a tendency for people to search for an 'n = all' approach in SNA, where researchers try to capture entire populations rather than samples, because size is seen as a way to overcome some of the shortcomings of abstracted data (see also Comunian, 2011). In such applications the results which can be gleaned from graph theory allow data-rich platforms to perfect their algorithms, particularly where they lead to recommendations. For instance, SNA analysis can help to identify similarly connected people on Twitter or Facebook to make suggestions about who else to follow or 'friend'. On media platforms, SNA data can be used to recommend what else to watch or listen to next, based on people's overlapping watch histories. The biggest drawbacks with using SNA in this way, however, are the quality of the data you begin with, and the assumptions you make about it. In the context of media platforms, Gerlitz and Helmond (2013: 1358) highlight that simply watching something online, 'liking' something or being connected to another person hides 'a variety of affective responses such as excitement, agreement, compassion, understanding, but also ironic and parodist liking'. The abstraction required for SNA misses these things.

We must therefore be careful and reflexive in the way we generate datasets for SNA and the analysis we undertake. For example, whether drawing on primary or secondary data, it is crucial that classifications and sampling methods are understood so that existing abstractions are clear before further ones are made. For example, using LinkedIn data to trace business networks needs to acknowledge that 'connections' may not reflect real business relationships. Or if a web platform such as Crunchbase adds characteristics to company profiles, it is important to understand the reliability of this data and potential errors. Understanding the underlying assumptions, data collection methods and coding will help to produce robust insights from any SNA done using this data. For primary data, automated collection is often the most straightforward way to quickly build large datasets, and many organisations offer application programming interfaces (APIs) to facilitate this. When APIs are not available or data is not straightforwardly accessible, data scraping can be used to gather it. Here, we must be clear about how data is coded, and ethical considerations are central to these methods to ensure that data is collected, analysed and disseminated in responsible ways so as not to cause harm. As Fiesler and Proferes (2018) have argued, just because data is public in some way does not mean that it can or should be straightforwardly used for research purposes.

If data has been pseudonymised, SNA may remove some of that anonymity by revealing associations that identify actors in a network. Users need to be careful to avoid unintentionally revealing more about the data than is necessary. Finally, when presenting findings from SNA, it is important to be clear about the data collection, the shortcomings of this and any caveats which come with the results. Being careful and reflexive in undertaking SNA provides ways to avoid the pitfall of implied authority which comes from 'scientific' and quantitative approaches and the relative ontological stability these fields denote (Swords and Liu, 2015). As Knox et al. (2006: 116) put it, '[mathematical] methodological expertise has made it possible for SNA writers to claim a monopoly on "scientific" network thinking, by providing them with a means of going beyond "loose", metaphorical approaches to networks, and providing a range of formal tools for "precisely" mapping networks'.

4.3   SOCIAL NETWORK AND THE CREATIVE AND CULTURAL INDUSTRIES

There is a small but growing field of research which uses SNA to understand the CCIs, which this section explores; some of which focuses on people and organisations, while other work concentrates on documents, artifacts and socio-technical devices. Relating to the first area, Taylor (2019) has used information about trustees and directors of cultural and creative organisations to examine the make-up of boards of national portfolio organisations funded by Arts Council England. His analysis reveals the dominance of male decision-makers on these boards, and the interconnections between boards through their members. Similar work has been undertaken by Mould and Joel (2010) on board members of London-based advertising companies. By graphing the networks, they reveal key gatekeepers through whom knowledge is transferred and companies are connected together. As these authors acknowledge, the SNA models can only reveal so much, and the complex manifestation of power within the networks they examine needs qualitative research to be better understood.

Granger and Hamilton (2010) have examined relationships between key individuals and organisations in the creative economy of Coventry, UK. They argue that relational mapping such as this offers a 'richer, more nuanced way of research and developing policy for the creative industries' (ibid.: 57). A similar application is used by Morelli and Gunes (2012) in their analysis of the video games industry. Using data about which developers and publishers work together to produce games over five generations of major games consoles, they highlight the variance in publishing communities around different consoles, and decreasing volatility over time as the video games industry's structure stabilised. In film, cast and crew directories can be graphed to highlight the connections and reconnections throughout people's careers. Senekal and Stemmet (2014) have used SNA to trace the central role of director Jamie Uys in the Afrikaans film industry, highlighting the films through which other celebrated film personnel collaborated. Miller (2011) uses a similar methodology, but connecting studios which have collaborated on different types of film. They examine networks around high-grossing and highly lauded productions to understand more about the outcomes of co-productions. Miller argues that the structural differences in networks of production offer different ways to organise how studios and production companies might collaborate. These examples, again, illustrate useful insights, but the level of abstraction to individual actors (whether companies or individuals) leaves further questions about the nature of relationships unanswered. These questions should be seen as opportunities, however, not drawbacks; and ways of iterating research questions as scholars move from extensive to intensive approaches.

The second approach is to examine linkages between a broader range of objects, artefacts, documents and agents. Joel (2009) has used SNA to map connections between design firms and other parts of the creative industries. They did this using a sample of companies from which further information was gathered to allow linkages to creative sub-sectors to be drawn. This is similar to the work presented in section 4.4 below, but the sample used here is much larger and a wider range of SNA tools were used in the analysis. In the heritage field, SNA has been used to help catalogue cultural heritage artefacts, documents and other objects (Hampson et al., 2012). De Miguel Molina et al. (2016) have used SNA to explore the study of gastronomy in work on intangible heritages. All this work provides useful insights about its subjects, but it recognises that abstraction means some details can be lost along the way.

4.4   USING SOCIAL NETWORK ANALYSIS TO UNDERSTAND CREATIVE INDUSTRIES DEFINITIONS

In this section I present a more in-depth application of SNA to understand the differences between how the UK's DCMS delineates enterprises in the creative industries and how enterprises define themselves. In so doing I try to follow the advice in section 4.2 to be clear about the limits of such an approach. The term 'creative industries' came into popular usage at the end of the 1990s under the influence of the New Labour Government and its economic development policy (for a longer history, see O'Connor, 2011). The DCMS's definition and mapping of the newly labelled creative industries marked an important shift in policy for arts and culture, placing it centre stage for a new government seeking to think differently about the economic value of cultural activities (see Smith, 1998 for insights from the time). For O'Connor (2011) this different approach can be traced back to the work of the Great London Council (Garnham, 1990) and the United Nations Educational, Scientific and Cultural Organization (UNESCO) (Girard, 1982) in the 1980s, while Luckman (2019) and Granger and Hamilton (2010) have argued Australia's Department of Communications and the Arts 'Creative Nation' report is an important precursor to the DCMS work (Department of Communications and the Arts, 1994). Nevertheless, the DCMS's 1998 and 2001 mapping documents, and subsequent policy, have become the epoch-making interventions which cemented the creative industries as key economic activities in the UK and beyond. We can see this as such approaches spread around the world (Fahmi et al., 2015; Kong et al., 2006; Restrepo and Márquez, 2013).

The original 1998 DCMS definition of creative industries focused on 13 sets of core activities: advertising; art and antiques markets; architecture; crafts; design; fashion; film; leisure software (that is, computer games); music; performing arts; publishing; software; TV and radio. The UK definition has changed over the last 20 years, in part due to continued critique of original definitions from academics, practitioners, policymakers and industry groups. There is not sufficient space here to interrogate each of these critiques to a level which does them justice.

Since the early DCMS work, its approach to defining which sectors are included in its creative industries economic estimates, and therefore policy, has shifted in two key ways. First, it now highlights overlaps with other sectors under the Department's remit. Second, it combines data on enterprises, using SIC codes, with data on occupations, using Standard Occupational Classification (SOC) codes, to highlight areas of the economy with the greatest 'creative intensity'. Creative intensity is '[t]he proportion of creative jobs for

each industry was calculated (creative intensity)', and '[i]ndustries with creative intensity above a specified threshold are considered Creative Industries'
(DCMS, 2016: 21). The current threshold for an industry to be included is
a minimum of 6000 jobs; more than 30 per cent are defined as creative (see
Bakhshi et al., 2013, for more on the origins of the creative intensity approach
and a critique). Using this approach, the DCMS acknowledges that creative
workers are found across the economy.

These definitions are used to calculate the size of the creative industries
using various measures. The current definitions used by the DCMS stem from
the latest calculations of creative intensity, and are shown in Table 4.1.

There are, however, a series of drawbacks to this approach. Both SOC and
SIC codes are amended about every ten years, but as soon as the codes are
released they are out of date, and new economic activities are not accurately
captured. There is also an issue with reporting, as enterprises are required to
select codes when they register accounts with Companies House, but misre-
porting is a problem. This could be the result of rolling over outdated codes
from previous accounts, not understanding the coding system, or not considering accuracy a priority. Typos can also have an impact, with a number of
enterprises sampled here appearing to have a digit missing.

Correct reporting also relies on the interpretation of enterprises, account-
ants and statisticians to capture activities as best possible, but some codes
are difficult to differentiate. For instance, in the current UK set of creative
industries SIC codes, organisations classified as '91020 – Museum activities'
are included, but those classified as '91030 – Operation of historical sites and
buildings and similar visitor attractions' are left out, even though many activities of the latter overlap with the former. This is partly a result of the DCMS
approach starting with occupations (SOC codes) to determine sectors (SIC
codes), rather than focusing on whether the products and services an enterprise
produces are 'creative'. This means that some of the multi- and interdisciplinary work in the creative industries is captured, but other work is obscured in
reporting. This is seen in the division of sub-sectors and the aggregation of
these sub-sectors into groupings which may not resemble connected activities
in the economy (seen in the left column of Table 4.1). Moreover, no account
is taken of the other activities that these enterprises undertake outside of the
creative industries.

The remainder of this chapter focuses on these latter critiques to explore
how SNA can reveal more about the CCIs. It does so by taking into account
the multifaceted activities of enterprises working in this and related sectors. In
what follows I argue that using SNA can achieve two things:

Table 4.1   *DCMS creative industries definition*

Creative industries sub-sector	4-digit SIC code	4-digit SOC code
Advertising and marketing	7021 Public relations and communication activities	1132 Marketing and sales directors
	7311 Advertising agencies	1134 Advertising and public relations directors
	7312 Media representation	3543 Marketing associate professionals
		2472 Public relations professionals
		2473 Advertising accounts managers and creative directors
Architecture	7111 Architectural activities	2431 Architects
		2432 Town planning officers
		2435 Chartered architectural technologists
		3121 Architectural and town planning technicians
Crafts	3212 Manufacture of jewellery and related articles	5211 Smiths and forge workers
		5411 Weavers and knitters
		5441 Glass and ceramics makers, decorators and finishers
		5442 Furniture makers and other craft woodworkers
		5449 Other skilled trades n.e.c.
Design: product, graphic and fashion design	7410 Specialised design activities	3421 Graphic designers
		3422 Product, clothing and related designers
Film, TV, video, radio and photography	6010 Radio broadcasting	3416 Arts officers, producers and directors
	6020 Television programming and broadcasting activities	3417 Photographers, audio-visual and broadcasting equipment operators
	7420 Photographic activities	
	5911 Motion picture, video and television programme production activities	

Creative industries sub-sector	4-digit SIC code	4-digit SOC code
Film, TV, video, radio and photography	5912 Motion picture, video and television programme post-production activities	3417 Photographers, audio-visual and broadcasting equipment operators
	5913 Motion picture, video and television programme distribution activities	
	5914 Motion picture projection activities	
IT, software and computer services	6201 Computer programming activities	2135 IT business analysts, architects and systems designers
	6202 Computer consultancy activities	1136 Information technology and telecommunications directors
	5821 Publishing of computer games	2136 Programmers and software development professionals
	5829 Other software publishing	2137 Web design and development professionals
Museums, galleries and libraries	9101 Library and archive activities	2451 Librarians
	9102 Museum activities	2452 Archivists and curators
Music, performing and visual arts	5920 Sound recording and music publishing activities	3411 Artists
	8552 Cultural education	3413 Actors, entertainers and presenters
	9001 Performing arts	3414 Dancers and choreographers
	9002 Support activities to performing arts	3415 Musicians
	9003 Artistic creation	
	9004 Operation of arts facilities	
Publishing	5811 Book publishing	2471 Journalists, newspaper and periodical editors
	5812 Publishing of directories and mailing lists	3412 Authors, writers and translators
	5813 Publishing of newspapers	
	5814 Publishing of journals and periodicals	
	5819 Other publishing activities	
	7430 Translation and interpretation activities	

Source: DCMS (2019).

- help to better understand communities of activity within the CCIs;
- help to identify areas of activity which are complementary to and supporting of CCIs activities.

In so doing, the DCMS groupings are unpicked to provide a more nuanced approach to CCIs activities based on self-selected SIC codes.

Methodology

For this research, data from the Financial Analysis Made Easy (FAME) database was used. The database draws from UK Companies House returns made by enterprises and includes a range of information about a company's financials. It includes some charities and community interest companies, but not all. It also includes some freelancers who work as a limited company, but by no means all do this. Data was downloaded by selecting enterprises which had at least one creative industries SIC code and are based in the UK. The data presented below was downloaded in early 2020, so includes data from returns made in 2018 and 2019. A wide range of company characteristics was gathered to allow analysis beyond what is presented below. As well as SIC codes, the data download included information about a company's establishment date, gender of directors, location information, turnover, employee numbers and legal status. The data was cleaned and coded for use in Gephi, a SNA program. Cleaning the data was necessary to remove data entry errors left over from Companies House submissions, FAME's own data entry or Excel misformatting data which limited the type of analysis which could be undertaken; for example, incorrect characters on company names, removing duplicates and correcting date formats. A random sample of companies was checked to identify potential miscoding of SIC codes at some point from entry to the download. This was done by comparing information about companies online with data from FAME, and helped to identify common mistakes which were then corrected throughout the whole dataset. This also identified issues that I mistakenly believed to be errors, but were interesting insights into what creative companies do. This is discussed further below.

The data was also coded to allow comparisons between regions, analyse the limited gender data in the database and examine the types of companies (for example, limited versus community interest companies; see Butt et al., 2017 for an example), but mainly to prepare it for use in Gephi. This involved creating two new datasets:

1. A list of nodes consisting of: (a) 449 945 companies, their characteristics and unique identifiers; and (b) 652 SIC codes associated with the companies.
2. A list of edges indicating connections between companies and SIC codes.

These new datasets allowed Gephi to understand and graph the companies and their connections to SIC codes. Once in Gephi a series of functions were applied to produce the network in Figure 4.1. First, the number of connections for each node was calculated and this information was used to change the size of nodes. The larger the node, the more connections it has going into it. Second, a modularity calculation was performed to detect communities within the network based on the connectedness of nodes and the detection of divisions between groups of nodes. Nodes with similar sets of connections are identified as within the same community and this information was represented with colours (not shown here). Finally, the network layout was determined using an algorithm called ForceAtlas 2 (Jacomy et al., 2014), which simulates a kind of 'gravity' based on shared connections. Nodes (for example, companies) with the same connections to other nodes (for example, SIC codes) are attracted to one another. The same analysis was done for just companies registered in the Yorkshire and the Humber region in northern England for a different project, and this allowed some sub-national comparison (Swords, forthcoming).

The network shown in Figure 4.1 consists of 449 945 enterprises connected to the 652 different five-digit SIC codes they list to reflect the activities they

Figure 4.1   *Social network analysis of the UK's creative industries (edges removed for ease of viewing)*

undertake, including the 42 creative industries codes defined by the DCMS. In total the network contains 625 744 edges between nodes which is the number of SIC codes against companies in the dataset. There is a 1.39 average degree of connection. The dataset is for the UK as a whole and the regional distribution of the dataset represents what we know from other mapping exercises about the distribution of the CCIs in the UK (Butt et al., 2017; DCMS, 2019; Siepel et al., 2020).

Results

The network shown here consists of 449 945 enterprises connected to the 652 different five-digit SIC codes they list to reflect the activities they undertake, including the 42 creative industries codes defined by the DCME. In total the network contains 625 744 edges between nodes which is the number of SIC codes against companies in the dataset. There is a 1.39 average degree of connection. The dataset is for the UK as a whole, with more than 50 per cent of companies having a registered address in London or the South East. The regional distribution of the dataset represents what we know from other mapping exercises about the distribution of the CCIs in the UK (Butt et al., 2017; Siepel et al., 2020).

Table 4.2 shows the SIC codes with the most connections, that is, the most frequently listed codes by the companies in the dataset. The top 30 account for 82.6 per cent of all connections with information technology (IT) and software-related activities (both those in the DCMS list of creative industries companies and those outside it), accounting for 36.8 per cent of the total.

SNA communities versus DCMS groupings

The SNA test of modularity identifies 16 different communities in the network. These groupings vary in size, with large variances in the number of enterprise nodes and SIC code nodes they contain. The character of each community can be determined by examining the activities that enterprises undertake and the SIC code nodes with the highest number of connections. This examination was used to produce the necessarily broad labels in Figure 4.1 and used in the table below. The variety of SIC codes found in each community also varies, with the *IT Consultancy* community only containing five different codes while *Specialised Design* has 119 different SIC codes. These ranges are dependent on the likelihood of an enterprise selecting more than one SIC code, which in itself is an indication of how well the codes represent what a business does. For example, there are numerous and highly detailed SIC codes for manufacturing activities, but very few for artists and craft practitioners.

The communities resemble many of the DCMS groupings but there is important divergence. Table 4.3 illustrates where there is alignment, or otherwise,

Table 4.2   *Connections to the top 30 SIC codes*

Rank	SIC code description	%	Count	Rank	SIC code description	%	Count
1	Information technology consultancy activities	22.76	142 697	16	Management consultancy activities other than financial management	1.84	11 560
2	Business and domestic software development	7.79	48 837	17	Photographic activities not elsewhere classified	1.75	10 948
3	Artistic creation	5.25	32 893	18	Operation of arts facilities	1.38	8656
4	Specialised design activities	5.09	31 923	19	Media representation services	1.36	8496
5	Advertising agencies	3.96	24 853	20	Book publishing	1.17	7343
6	Architectural activities	3.41	21 394	21	Other software publishing	0.94	5923
7	Motion picture production activities	2.44	15 288	22	Ready-made interactive leisure and entertainment software development	0.92	5761
8	Performing arts	2.44	15 272	23	Cultural education	0.91	5702
9	Other information technology service activities	2.34	14 691	24	Other specialist photography	0.85	5348
10	Video production activities	2.27	14 227	25	Motion picture, video and television programme post-production activities	0.78	4905
11	Television programme production activities	2.03	12 750	26	Other business support service activities n.e.c.	0.72	4529
12	Sound recording and music publishing activities	1.99	12 447	27	Data processing, hosting and related activities	0.69	4309
13	Support activities to performing arts	1.97	12 333	28	Other service activities n.e.c.	0.61	3834
14	Public relations and communications activities	1.87	11 730	29	Web portals	0.60	3756
15	Other publishing activities	1.85	11 578	30	Translation and interpretation activities	0.56	3534

Table 4.3   DCMS creative industries sub-sectors and SIC code
groupings

DCMS category	5-digit SIC code description	Community identified in SNA
Advertising and Marketing	Advertising agencies	Advertising & media rep
	Media representation	Advertising & media rep
	Public relations and communication activities	PR & management consultancy
Architecture	Architectural activities	Architecture
	Urban planning and landscape architectural activities	Architecture
Crafts	Manufacture of jewellery and related articles	Jewellery
Design: product, graphic and fashion design	Specialised design activities	Specialised design
Film, TV, video, radio and photography	Film processing	Photography
	Motion picture distribution activities	Film & TV production and distribution
	Motion picture production activities	Film & TV production and distribution
	Motion picture projection activities	Film & TV production and distribution
	Motion picture, video and television programme post-production activities	Film & TV production and distribution
	Other photographic activities (not including portrait and other specialist photography and film processing) n.e.c.	Photography
	Other specialist photography (not including portrait photography)	Photography
	Portrait photographic activities	Photography
	Radio broadcasting	TV & radio broadcasting
Film, TV, video, radio and photography	Television programme distribution activities	Film & TV production and distribution
	Television programme production activities	Film & TV production and distribution
	Television programming and broadcasting activities	TV & radio broadcasting
	Video distribution activities	Film & TV production and distribution
	Video production activities	Film & TV production and distribution

DCMS category	5-digit SIC code description	Community identified in SNA
IT, software and computer services	Business and domestic software development	Software
	Information technology consultancy activities	IT consultancy
	Other software publishing	Software
	Publishing of computer games	Computer games
	Ready-made interactive leisure and entertainment software development	Computer games
Museums, galleries and libraries	Archive activities	Libraries, museums & archives
	Library activities	Libraries, museums & archives
	Museum activities	Libraries, museums & archives
Music, performing and visual arts	Artistic creation	Art & craft
	Cultural education	Performing arts
	Operation of arts facilities	Art & craft
	Performing arts	Performing arts
	Sound recording and music publishing activities	Music & recording services
	Support activities to performing arts	Performing arts
Publishing	Book publishing	Publishing
	Other publishing activities	Publishing
	Publishing of consumer, business and professional journals and periodicals	Publishing
	Publishing of directories and mailing lists	Publishing
	Publishing of learned journals	Publishing
	Publishing of newspapers	Publishing
	Translation and interpretation activities	PR & management consultancy

between the communities identified in the SNA and DCMS groupings. There is complete alignment for 'architecture', 'crafts' (renamed as *Jewellery* here to more accurately reflect the activities undertaken by firms in this community), 'specialised design' and the 'museums, galleries and archives' grouping is consistent, although relabelled to highlight many galleries are found in the *Art and Craft* community. With the exception of 'translation and interpretation activities', the DCMS 'publishing' grouping is consistent with what was found in the SNA. The DCMS grouping of 'advertising and marketing' splits into two communities: *PR & Management Consultancy* and *Advertising & Media Representation*. Public relations activities join with 'translation and interpretation activities' to form a community where we also find a relatively high number of management consultancy enterprises (not a DCMS creative industries sub-sector). The latter accounts for 13.3 per cent of enterprises in this community, and 67.6 per cent of all management consultancy firms in the dataset are found here.

As one might expect, the DCMS grouping of 'film, TV, video, radio and photography' splits to reflect differences in specialism, production processes and markets for this range of activity. Photographic activities come together into one community (*Photography*) and broadcasting of TV and radio form another (*TV & Radio Broadcasting*). The rest of this grouping is found in a community which encompasses *Film and TV production and distribution activities* that encompasses activities along this value chain except broadcasting.

The DCMS groups together 'IT, software and computer services' but this splits three ways: *IT consultancy activities* is a very distinct community; a second community is made up of activities relating to the production of *Computer Games*; while the third is general *Software*.

Finally, the DCMS grouping of 'music, performing and visual arts' splits into three, as one might have predicted. 'Artistic creation' and the 'operation of arts facilities' are together in the SNA community labelled *Art and Craft*. This community also includes many craft activities found within 'artistic creation' itself, plus 'specialised design activities' and 'other manufacturing n.e.c.'. Music-related activities form their own community, along with SIC codes from outside the DCMS definition which reflect the business models of music businesses: 'retail sale via mail order houses or via Internet' and 'other retail sale not in stores, stalls or markets'. The final community from this grouping is *Performing arts*, which includes 80 per cent of connections to the 'cultural education' SIC code from the DCMS list, but also 81 per cent of the connections to 'other human health activities'. This provides an indication of the range of activities performing arts organisations do, a point I return to below.

Discussion

In this section the key findings from the SNA are discussed, and areas for further research are highlighted. This analysis brings into question the usefulness of the DCMS groupings. On one level it may not seem important, but the discursive work these groupings do can feed into how policymakers and others understand the CCIs. A more accurate picture of how different activities relate to each other, or do not, is important for targeted and effective policy interventions. Understanding this detail is crucial at the national scale as well as regional and local levels, as the groupings diverge in different ways in different places. In Yorkshire and the Humber, for example, all the codes in the DCMS groupings of 'museums, galleries and libraries' and 'music, performing and visual arts' are found in a single community, except 'sound recording' and 'music publishing activities' which forms a community on its own. This is different to the UK-wide picture, but separation is, again, unsurprising given the technical and organisational specialisms required to produce music and take it to market. The amalgamation of the other codes is likely due to a series of interconnected factors which operate differently at the local and regional scales compared to the nation's creative economy. For example, enterprises involved in the performance arts, performance of music, exhibition of visual arts and museum operations are similarly organised, often share facilities, receive funding from allied sources and may have historic connections. Much of the activity undertaken by these organisations (perhaps with the exception of museums) is best captured under the 'artistic creation' SIC code which is very broad and overlaps with a lot of similar activity. At a regional level there may not be the diversity of other connected activities to create separation into distinct communities in the SNA. Moreover, many enterprises in this field undertake 'cultural education' activities as part of career and organisational development and as part of outreach activities which links them. There are likely other local reasons, such as the evolution of the arts sectors in the major cities in Yorkshire and the Humber through the impact of previous policy and/ or funding interventions, governance of the arts sector, the presence of key institutions and long-running festivals, amongst others. These factors will differ across the UK and are worthy of further study.

One of the reasons for the new set of groupings created by the SNA is that 652 different five-digit SIC codes are included and only 6 per cent of them are creative industries codes. The other codes are shared by enterprises and are a major factor in the new communities which form. These figures also demonstrate that the activities undertaken by companies which we could define as part of the creative industries is wide and varied. Examining the breadth of work undertaken by enterprises which we could define as part of the CCIs is worthy of further research, but too large a task for this chapter, so instead some interesting insights are highlighted which illustrate that the boundary between the CCIs and the rest of the economy is not as clear as the DCMS approach might suggest.

We can see the blurring of the boundary at different scales. At the sub-sector level, for example, the SIC code for 'other human health activities' has a relatively small number of connections to it (c. 1100), but 81 per cent of these are concentrated in the *Performing Arts* community. Enterprises identifying as undertaking this code are most frequently also doing 'artistic creation' and 'cultural education', suggesting that there is a crossover between performing arts activities and health benefits. We can see this with increasing recognition of the benefits of social prescribing, where health agencies can refer patients for activities which will benefit their health, including engaging with cultural events and institutions (Romer, 2018).

Looking at the company scale, we can identify businesses whose work bridges across the CCIs and the rest of the economy. For example, there is a company in Leeds registered as 'non-scheduled passenger air transport' and 'support activities to performing arts'; based on its website this does not appear to be a misfiling because it is a music management company which also organises tours for its artists. In Ripon there is a charity which is registered as 'cultural education' and 'plant propagation'. Again, this does not appear to be a mistake as it is a garden and sculpture park with a purpose to provide education. There is a company in London which builds ships but also undertakes IT consultancy because it handles the electronics as well as the superstructure and interior design of boats. There is an international corporation whose activities include 'pre-primary education' and 'child day-care activities' as well as 'business and domestic software' and 'leasing of intellectual property and similar products'. This is because it runs nurseries which include bespoke coding classes. Around the country there are hotels and bed and breakfasts (B&Bs) included because they offer art-based retreats. Toy companies appear in the network because they also publish books. Call centre companies are included because they undertake advertising and marketing work. We can also identify companies using old SIC codes for new activities. For example, there are enterprises producing and publishing computer games which also register as 'other sports activities' which reflects the rise of e-sports.

At the individual scale, there is evidence of the other work that people do alongside activities defined as being in the creative industries. This comes through for sole traders who put primary and secondary jobs under the same limited company. Interesting combinations include, 'freight rail transport' and 'sound recording and music publishing'; 'butter and cheese production' and 'information technology consultancy activities'; 'buying and selling real estate' and 'artistic creation'; 'specialist medical practice activities' and 'artistic creation'. Understanding the ways in which these non-CCIs activities complement, supplement and/or constrain creative work is a further area which needs deeper appreciation by policymakers.

These examples from the SNA help to illustrate the diversity of work undertaken by creative industries companies and creative practitioners, which are not captured in the headlines about the sector. The boundary between the creative industries and the rest of the economy is porous and the interdependencies are strong. It is important that researchers and policymakers do not overlook these connections in the formation of interventions, as they vary between places, and because these connections highlight where skillsets are complementary and where learning and cross-sector innovation might occur.

4.5 CONCLUSIONS

This chapter has sought to explore the ways in which SNA can be used to understand the CCIs. In so doing it has highlighted some of the drawbacks inherent in such work. The level of abstraction required for SNA, for example, requires information about nodes to be stripped out and actors treated in a way which cannot acknowledge their complexity. This limits the detail which can be gleaned from SNA and necessitates further work to be undertaken to triangulate findings, to delve deeper into the nature of relationships within networks, and to understand how broader factors contribute to a node's position in its ecology. This is especially important when using SNA to research the CCIs, as they are characterised by a range of long-standing exclusions and exploitations which need to be highlighted and addressed.

This chapter has revealed the connections that CCIs enterprises have with other companies and work which is not defined as part of the creative industries by the UK's DCMS. The blurriness of the boundary between the CCIs and the rest of the economy, together with the limitations of the SIC system used to identify and focus policy on creative enterprises, highlights areas for further research. Moreover, the blurriness has implications for policy, which needs to better appreciate the interconnections between the CCIs and activities which fall into different spheres of economic, social and cultural development policy.

NOTES

1. In July 1997 the Department was named as the Department for Culture, Media and Sport (DCMS); in July 2017 the Department was renamed as the Department for Digital, Culture, Media and Sport.
2. For the avoidance of doubt, while SNA can be used to understand connections manifest on social network platforms such as Twitter and Facebook, the term pre-dates them by decades.

REFERENCES

Bakhshi, H., Freeman, A., and Higgs, P. (2013). *A Dynamic Mapping of the UK Creative Industries*. London: Nesta.

Bielby, D.D., and Bielby, W.T. (1996). Women and men in film: gender inequality among writers in a culture industry. *Gender and Society*, *10*(3), 248–270. www.jstor.org/stable/189696.

Butt, M., Cross, E., Holliman, N., Kempton, L., Legget, J., Mackenzie, E., Ross, H., Sapsed, J., Swords, J., Vallance, P., and Whitehurst, F. (2017). *Creative FUSE Initial Report*. Newcastle upon Tyne: Creative FUSE North East.

Carrington, P.J., Scott, J., and Wasserman, S. (2005). *Models and Methods in Social Network Analysis*. Cambridge: Cambridge University Press.

Comunian, R. (2011). Social network analysis. *Regions*, *2*(2), 3.

Crewe, L. (1996). Material culture: embedded firms, organizational networks and the local economic development of a fashion quarter. *Regional Studies*, *30*(3), 257–272. doi:10.1080/00343409612331349618.

Department of Communications and the Arts (1994). *Creative Nation: Commonwealth Cultural Policy*. Department of Communications and the Arts, Australia.

DCMS (2016). *Creative Industries Economic Estimates*. London: DCMS.

DCMS (2019). *DCMS Sector Economic Estimates*. London: DCMS.

de Miguel Molina, M., de Miguel Molina, B., Santamarina Campos, V., and del Val Segarra Oña, M. (2016). Intangible heritage and gastronomy: the impact of UNESCO gastronomy elements. *Journal of Culinary Science and Technology*, *14*(4), 293–310. doi:10.1080/15428052.2015.1129008.

Fahmi, F.Z., McCann, P., and Koster, S. (2015). Creative economy policy in developing countries: the case of Indonesia. *Urban Studies*, *54*(6), 1367–1384. doi:10.1177/0042098015620529.

Fiesler, C., and Proferes, N. (2018). 'Participant' perceptions of Twitter research ethics. *Social Media + Society*, *4*(1), 1–14, 2056305118763366. doi:10.1177/2056305118763366.

Garnham, N. (1990). *Capitalism and Communication: Global Culture and the Economics of Information*. London: SAGE.

Gera, R., Haynes, T.W., and Hedetniemi, S.T. (2018). *Graph Theory: Favorite Conjectures and Open Problems – 2*. Cham: Springer.

Gerlitz, C., and Helmond, A. (2013). The like economy: Social buttons and the data-intensive web. *New Media and Society*, *15*(8), 1348–1365. doi:10.1177/1461444812472322.

Girard, A. (1982). Cultural industries: a handicap or a new opportunity for cultural development? In UNESCO (ed.), *Cultural Industries: A Challenge for the Future of Culture*. Paris: UNESCO.

Grabher, G. (2002). The project ecology of advertising: tasks, talents and teams. *Regional Studies*, *36*(3), 245–262. doi:10.1080/00343400220122052.

Granger, R.C., and Hamilton, C. (2010). Re-spatializing the creative industries: a relational examination of underground scenes, and professional and organizational lock-in. *Creative Industries Journal*, *3*(1), 47–60. doi:10.1386/cij.3.1.47_1.

Hampson, C., Lawless, S., Bailey, E., Yogev, S., Zwerdling, N., Carmel, D., Conlan, O., O'Connor, A., and Wade, V. (2012). CULTURA: A metadata-rich environment to support the enhanced interrogation of cultural collections. Paper presented at the Metadata and Semantics Research, Berlin, Heidelberg.

Jacomy, M., Venturini, T., Heymann, S., and Bastian, M. (2014). ForceAtlas2, a continuous graph layout algorithm for handy network visualization designed for the Gephi software. *PLOS ONE*, *9*(6), e98679. doi:10.1371/journal.pone.0098679.

Joel, S. (2009). A social network analysis approach to a social model of the creative industries: the design sub-sector. *Creative Industries Journal*, *2*(2), 191–201. doi:10.1386/cij.2.2.191/1.

Knox, H., Savage, M., and Harvey, P. (2006). Social networks and the study of relations: networks as method, metaphor and form. *Economy and Society*, *35*(1), 113–140. doi:10.1080/03085140500465899.

Kong, L., Gibson, C., Khoo, L.-M., and Semple, A.-L. (2006). Knowledges of the creative economy: towards a relational geography of diffusion and adaptation in Asia. *Asia Pacific Viewpoint*, *47*(2), 173–194. doi:10.1111/j.1467-8373.2006.00313.x.

Luckman, S. (2019). Craft entrepreneurialism and sustainable scale: resistance to and disavowal of the creative industries as champions of capitalist growth. Paper presented at the CAMEo Conference – Re-Futuring Creative Economies, Leicester, UK.

Miller, J. (2011). Producing quality: a social network analysis of coproduction relationships in high grossing versus highly lauded films in the US Market. *International Journal of Communication*, *5*, 1014–1033.

Morelli, T., and Gunes, M.H. (2012, 26–29 August). Video game industry as a social network. Paper presented at the 2012 IEEE/ACM International Conference on Advances in Social Networks Analysis and Mining.

Mould, O., and Joel, S. (2010). Knowledge networks of 'buzz' in London's advertising industry: a social network analysis approach. *Area*, *42*(3), 281–292. www.jstor.org/stable/40890882.

Newman, M.E.J. (2006). Modularity and community structure in networks. *Proceedings of the National Academy of Sciences*, *103*(23), 8577.

O'Connor, J. (2011). The cultural and creative industries: a critical history. *EKONOMIAZ. Revista vasca de Economía*, *78*(3), 24–47.

Restrepo, F.B., and Márquez, I.D. (2013). *The Orange Economy – An Infinite Opportunity*. Online: Inter-American Development Bank. https://publications.iadb.org/en/orange-economy-infitnite-opportunity.

Romer, C. (2018). Doctors supported to prescribe arts through new £4.5m scheme. https://www.artsprofessional.co.uk/news/doctors-supported-prescribe-arts-through-new-ps45m-scheme.

Scott, J. (2017). *Social Network Analysis* (4th edn). SAGE Publications Ltd. https://dx.doi.org/10.4135/9781529716597.

Senekal, B.A., and Stemmet, J.-A. (2014). The gods must be connected: an investigation of Jamie Uys' connections in the Afrikaans film industry using social network analysis. *Communicatio*, *40*(1), 1–19. doi:10.1080/02500167.2014.888361.

Siepel, J., Camerani, R., Masucci, M., Valez Ospina, J., Casadei, P., and Bloom, M. (2020). *Creative Industries Radar: Mapping the UK's Creative Clusters and Microclusters*. London: PEC.

Sucar, L.E. (2015). *Probabilistic Graphical Models: Principles and Applications*. London: Springer.

Swords, J. (forthcoming). *Social Network Analysis of the Creative Industries in Yorkshire and the Humber*. York, UK: University of York.

Swords, J., and Liu, X. (2015). *Visualizing Urban and Regional Worlds: Power, Politics, and Practices*. London: SAGE Publications.

Taylor, M. (2019). Who run the arts? (Men): social network analysis of directors and trustees in English arts organisations. Paper presented at the CAMEo Conference – Re-Futuring Creative Economies, Leicester, UK.

Wu, D. (2017). Rethinking creative industries research: synthesizing the creative class thesis, clustering, and global production network approaches. *Geography Compass*, *11*(12), 1–11. doi:10.1111/gec3.12348.

Zweig, K.A. (2016). Graph theory, social network analysis, and network science. In K.A. Zweig (ed.), *Network Analysis Literacy: A Practical Approach to the Analysis of Networks*. Vienna: Springer Vienna, pp. 23–55.

5. Measuring creative and cultural industries: the statistics job from taxonomies to composite indices

Alessandro Crociata and Chiara Burlina

5.1 INTRODUCTION

The current hype on the role of culture and creativity in fostering national as well as local economies calls for a comprehensive policy scheme to support the so-called creative economy. A key starting point is the unresolved issue for those seeking to fix conceptually and empirically robust definitions, characterisations and measurements. With regard to creative economy there is an unresolved issue challenging the plurality of models to size the boundaries of the well-known creative and cultural industries (CCIs) system.

So, the central challenge is to achieve more conceptually and empirically robust statistical descriptions of such complex systems to capture the broader dynamics of CCIs in boosting economic and social value in contemporary society. Scholars and policymakers over the past 20 years have fuelled a significant definitional debate, but there is currently no official and universally agreed-upon statistical definition of the creative economy in general, or of CCIs systems. As the creative economy today faces the challenges of sustainability and inclusiveness, it becomes increasingly important to achieve adequate standards of measurement. Since many closely related terms have been employed, we present here a review of the debate and a reasoned measuring toolkit to highlight the state of the art of mapping and measuring the creative economy. This chapter is structured as follows: section 5.2 reviews the literature background of the debate. Section 5.3 provides the main quantitative approaches in measuring CCIs. Section 5.4 discusses and concludes, giving suggestions on the empirical metrics as a function for setting up planning tools.

5.2   TAXONOMIES BACKGROUND

At the European level, many approaches are used to study the economics of the CCIs and to taxonomise economic activities in this system. The development of a European statistical framework for culture and creativity dates back to 1995, when the Council of the European Union decided to set up a European statistical framework for culture and creativity with the then Minister of Culture, and adopted a first resolution on the relevance of European cultural and economic statistics. Consequently, the European Commission provided for the formation of the Leadership Group on Cultural Statistics (LEG-Culture). From 1997 to 2000, LEG-Culture was involved in a programme aimed at studying and producing a statistical system that would allow homogeneous international comparisons and studies. This first statistical information system introduced a delimitation of the cultural field, categorised into eight cultural and artistic domains, with different sets of activities, practices or cultural products. The final report, *Cultural Statistics in the EU* (Eurostat, 2000), provides a harmonised approach to carry out comparative analyses on the cultural sectors of the countries of the European Commission. The framework is based on eight domains: (1) artistic and monumental heritage; (2) archives; (3) libraries; (4) books and press; (5) visual arts; (6) architecture; (7) performing arts; and (8) audio and audio-visual media/multimedia; and six functions to define the economic activities of the cultural sector: (1) preservation; (2) creation; (3) production; (4) dissemination; (5) trade/sales; and (6) education.

Apart from the need for empirical and comparative analysis, the definition of CCIs boundaries also has policy implications, as it defines the legal and budgetary scope of action for policymakers. One of most frequently quoted definitions, provided as a tool for setting policy, is from the United Kingdom, with the publication of the *Creative Industries Mapping Document* by the Department for Culture, Media and Sport (DCMS). This framework identifies the creative industries as: 'those industries which have their origin in individual creativity, skill and talent and which have a potential for wealth and job creation through the generation and exploitation of intellectual property' (DCMS, 1998: 3).

It establishes the legitimacy of the sector to be the subject of public policies, placing the cultural and creative sector at the heart of national and regional economic strategies. Notwithstanding the spread of this framework, some criticism has been raised that it arbitrarily links creative industries to the knowledge economy (O'Connor, 2008). In particular, the profound differences that exist between knowledge engaged in classical research and development (R&D) activities, that produced by business-to-business relations, and that present in the creative industries, has been raised (Garnham, 2005; Pratt, 2004).

Among the institutional contributions to the issue, studies published by the Organisation for Economic Co-operation and Development (OECD, 2006) and the European Commission (2006) fuelled the institutional debate at policy level. In 2006, the OECD introduced a new approach to map the CCIs, using the three most important types of industrial classifications: the Nomenclature of Economic Activities (NACE), the United Nations' International Standard Industrial Classification (ISIC) and the North American Industry Classification System (NAICS). This framework takes the categories used by the DCMS to which it adds computer games, software and electronic publishing. In 2006 the KEA European Affairs Report delineated the boundaries of CCIs to point out their contribution to growth and cohesion in Europe, by establishing a correspondence between the sector and its activities. The KEA framework splits the cultural sector into three. First, a non-industrial sector where non-reproducible goods and services are produced and consumed in the same moment. This category includes the field of arts such as: crafts, painting, sculpture, photography, theatre, dance, circus, festivals, museums, libraries, archaeological sites and archives. Second, an industrial sector, where reproducible goods are produced for mass consumption and distribution. This category represents cultural industries such as: film industry, radio, video games, live music and publishing. In addition to the cultural sector, as defined above, the framework also takes into account a third, creative industries sector, including activities whose outputs are functional, but which incorporates elements from the two previous layers into the production process (design, architecture, advertising).

In a review of the most widely used approaches, Throsby (2008a) presents six taxonomic models, according to the principles on which each classification system is based:

1. The DCMS model (DCMS, 1998): based on activities requiring creativity, skill and talent, with potential for wealth and job creation through exploitation of their intellectual property.
2. The symbolic texts model (Hesmondhalgh, 2002): based on industries concerned with industrial production and dissemination of symbolic texts.
3. The concentric circles model (Throsby, 2008b): based on the origin and diffusion of creative ideas in sound, text and image from core creative arts.
4. The World Intellectual Property Organization (WIPO) copyright model (WIPO, 2003): based on industries involved directly or indirectly in the creation, manufacture, production, broadcast and distribution of copyrighted works.
5. The UNESCO Institute for Statistics (UIS) trade-related model (UNESCO-UIS, 2005): based on cultural goods and services entering international trade.

6. The Americans for the Arts model (Americans for the Arts, 2005): based
    on businesses involved with the production or distribution of the arts
    ('arts-centric businesses').

A further contribution is the proposal launched by Eurostat in 2009 to renew
the European framework for cultural statistics. The European Statistical
System Network on Culture, also known as ESSnet-Culture, develops the
work of LEG-Culture by moving from the same approach to cultural domains.
In the ESSnet-Culture framework, each cultural domain is composed of several
sub-domains; so that, for example, the audio-visual sector consists of radio,
film, video, multimedia and audio recordings. For each of these sub-domains,
based on the listed functions, the related economic activities are explained.
Taking as an example the audio-visual domain, the creation function is characterised by the activities of the creation of audio-visual assets, followed,
more externally, by the processes of production and post-production, as well
as editing and publishing with regard to video, multimedia products and audio
recordings. To stick to the concept of comparability, ESSnet-Culture differs
from the previous approaches because it considers the management function
of culture, and with respect to LEG-Culture, adds the domains of advertising,
crafts and intangible heritage. Finally, in terms of the sector's boundaries, it
does not consider the natural heritage and all the activities related to software
and telecommunications, sport and tourism.

5.3   MEASURING CCIs

According to the empirical CCIs literature, there are very different aspects
to consider when measuring these industries (Ortega-Villa and Ley-Garcia,
2018). The first issue concerns the direction of analysis: from one side it
could be demand-driven, when the focus is the impact of cultural industries on
economic growth; on the other side it is product-driven, when considering the
geographical, institutional and social factors that affect the CCIs' development
(Potts, 2011; Towse, 2011; UNESCO, 2009).

Regarding the output side, among the most common variables are employment growth rate and value added or gross domestic product (GDP). Cerisola
(2018) and Piergiovanni et al. (2012) have studied the effects of different creative components on employment and value added for Italian provinces. Both
studies show that there exists a positive relation between province growth and
the presence of CCIs. Crociata et al. (2018) investigate the spatial evolution of
the creative workforce and the economic growth associated to CCIs for several
regions in Europe before the economic crisis of 2008. Their findings support
the idea that some regions attract and maintain higher percentages of creative
employees, following a clear spatial pattern across Europe. The empirical

analysis reveals that the surrounding environment plays an important role in the development and growth of CCIs.

So, do creative industries drive economic growth, or is the relationship the other way around? The study by Marco-Serrano et al. (2014) tried to solve this question by analysing regional European data for ten years between 1999 and 2008. In their study, they proxy economic growth through regional income generation, and the contribution of CCIs is represented by the number of employees in those industries. Their findings reveal that the relationship exists in both directions, insofar as CCIs attract a skilled workforce and qualified human capital, which in turn positively affect the economic growth of the European regions (Marco-Serrano et al., 2014).

Besides human capital (Marrocu and Paci, 2012) and market structures (Comunian et al., 2010), it is interesting to investigate which other factors might play a role in the creation of CCIs. Taking the local and regional perspective as the unit of analysis, Chapain and Comunian (2010) highlight four categories that affect the development of CCIs in two cities/regions in the United Kingdom (UK): the personal dimension, the operational sphere, networking aspects and regional infrastructures. The assets of these two areas, in particular their size and infrastructures, play a fundamental part in attracting creative firms. The role of networks has also been stressed by Drda-Kühn and Wiegand (2010), concerning small towns in rural areas in Germany. In contrast to Chapain and Comunian's (2010) study, where the unit of analysis was influenced by the power of the large metropolitan city of London, the case of Altenkirchen shows an environment where CCIs are still at their preliminary stages. Here, the enabling factors are represented by the strong presence of networks which connect public administration, tourism industry, business communities and local cultural community. The importance of network and cluster initiatives is supported by the study conducted in Italy and Spain by Lazzeretti et al. (2012). The authors find similar patterns as in the UK for Spain, where cultural industries are located close to big cities, while in Italy they are dispersed across the territory. These results are explained through the importance of urbanisation economies (Lorenzen and Frederiksen, 2008), which are denser in Spain than in Italy.

Another aspect that deserves attention is the economic sustainability and tolerance related to the CCIs framework (KEA and PPMI, 2019). Boschma and Fritsch (2009) study the regional distribution of the creative employees for seven European countries, with respect to tolerance and openness behaviours. Their findings support the relation between these two concepts, in particular for areas characterised by a high-skilled workforce, which contributes to higher regional growth rates and higher degrees of tolerance. In the same vein, Bagwell (2008) develops a case study on six jewellery clusters in the City Fringe Opportunity Area of London to better understand local economic development and social inclusion aspects. In this area, the prevalence of ethnic minority groups is a driver for inclusivity purposes of creative industries, along with the development of qualified human capital and public support.

As reported in previous studies, there is no clear consensus on what is the most appropriate way to measure CCIs and what is a representative unit of analysis (Markusen, 2013). The next section reports some of the variables, at different levels of analysis, that mainly describe CCIs from a quantitative viewpoint.

Available Data Sources

Studies have used different data sources according to the level of analysis to collect information on CCIs (KEA, 2018). However, due to the lack of a comprehensive and exhaustive database, the aim of this chapter is to provide robust evidence about CCIs' definitions and measurement by using available statistical information in relation to the literature presented in the previous section. We distinguish different levels of analysis: country (NUTS1), region (NUTS2), province (NUTS3) and finally, city. For the CCI sectors, we select the NACE Rev. 2 industry codes (Eurostat, 2008), following the *Guide to Eurostat Culture Statistics* (Eurostat, 2018), as reported in Table 5.1.

At country level, we include the World Bank, the United Nations Educational, Scientific and Cultural Organization (UNESCO), the United Nations Development Programme (UNPD), the European Commission and European Statistical Office (Eurostat), the United Nations Conference on Trade and Development (UNCTAD), the OECD, the Quality of Government Institute (University of Gothenburg), the International Council of Museums (ICOM) and the World Economic Forum, which were the main data sources. Some of them, such as the OECD and Eurostat, present data at regional (NUTS2) and province (NUTS3) level, that can be combined with information from the national statistic offices to allow finer-grained observations. Moreover, national statistics offices are an interesting source for city-level data. Some of these big cities (such as Berlin, Paris, Florence, Barcelona and Budapest) are the focus of a recent report by the European Commission (2019), where variables on creative and cultural cities are accompanied by other indicators of inclusivity and tolerance at city level.

Table 5.1   Nace Rev. 2 codes for CCIs

Code	Description	Code	Description
18.11	Printing of newspapers	71.11	Architectural activities
18.12	Other printing	71.12	Engineering activities and related consultancy
18.13	Pre-press and pre-media services	72.11	Research and experimental development on biotechnology
18.14	Binding and related services	72.19	Other research and exp. development on natural sciences and engineering
18.2	Reproduction of recorded media	72.2	Research and exp. development on social sciences and humanities
58.11	Book publishing	73.11	Advertising agencies
58.13	Publishing of newspapers	73.12	Media representation
58.14	Publishing of journals and periodicals	74.1	Specialised design activities
58.21	Publishing of computer games	74.2	Photographic activities
58.29	Other software publishing	90.01	Performing arts
59.11	Motion picture, video and television programme production activities	90.03	Artistic creation
59.2	Sound recording and music publishing	91.01	Library and archives activities
60.1	Radio broadcasting	91.02	Museums activities
60.2	Television programming and broadcasting	91.03	Operation of historical sites and buildings and similar visitor attractions
62.01	Computer programming activities	91.04	Botanical and zoological gardens and nature reserves activities
62.09	Other information technology and computer service activities	93.21	Activities of amusement parks and theme parks
63.91	News agency activities	93.29	Other amusement and recreation activities

Indices to Measure CCIs

A recently released report by UNESCO (2019) presents seven possible thematic indicators that might quantitively describe the CCIs:

1. Expenditure on heritage: this expresses the ratio between the sum of public and private expenditure over population; it proxies for the total expenditure on all cultural and natural heritage.
2. Culture in GDP: it represents the total amount of GDP expenditure in CCIs over the national GDP, to give an overview of the overall contribution of the culture sector to the economy in a given territory.

3. Cultural employment: this is the ratio between population employed in the creative sector over the total employed people, to understand how helpful CCIs are in increasing the overall employment.
4. Cultural business: this indicator highlights the conditions to develop cultural business; it is a trend indicator insofar as it reports a time series of the number of cultural establishments at time t with respect to time t-1.
5. Household expenditure: this indicator measures the share of household expenditure for cultural activities, and it represents how much people are willing to spend on cultural activities and related goods and services.
6. Multilingual education: this shows the number of instructional hours dedicated to official/national languages with respect to regional or local languages.
7. Culture for social cohesion: this is a composite indicator that includes tolerance, trust and gender data, and a proxy for the degree of intercultural understanding and personal acceptance.

While the first five indicators are strictly related to the creative and cultural aspects, the last two are devoted to measuring inclusivity and social sustainability. In particular, 'multilingual education' gives some feedback about the level of multilingualism promotion during the schooling years and of intercultural dialogue; the 'culture for social cohesion' indicator provides a measure of possible opportunity gaps in sexual, gender or racial disparities (UNESCO, 2019). These thematic indicators give a general overview of the main variables related to the CCIs.

Among the most important composite indexes presented in the literature, we find the Global Creativity Index (GCI) (Florida et al., 2015), based on the '3Ts' paradigm of economic development (Florida, 2002). The GCI is a broad-based measure of advanced economic growth and sustainable prosperity, and the three Ts represent: (1) technology, a standard measure of R&D effort, proxied by the share of GDP devoted to R&D, and the standard measure of innovation, based on patents; (2) talent (or human capital), which comprehends educational and occupational measures of talent; and (3) tolerance, which accounts for the openness to ethnic and religious minorities and to gay and lesbian people. Despite the very interesting framework and usefulness of this indicator, the final output is a composite index at country level, which has some pitfalls when it is statistically tested against urban income and job growth (Crociata et al., 2018; Hoyman and Faricy, 2009).

Apart from these indicators, there are other several composite indexes at country level, such as the Czech Creative Index (CZCI) (Kloudová and Stehlíková, 2010), the Composite Index of the Creative Economy (CICE) (Bowen et al., 2008), and the European Creativity Index (ECI) (KEA, 2009). An extensive review of other indicators is reported by Correia and da Silva

Table 5.2   *List of indicators*

Index	Source	Level of analysis
The Arts Index Netherlands provides facts and figures on arts and culture in the Netherlands, ranging from the number of cinema tickets sold, to the income of public libraries, to the percentage of people practising amateur arts.	Lahaut et al. (2015) Boekman Foundation	National (country)
Focused on the measurement and ranking of creative global cities, the CCI Creative City Index (CCI-CCI) covers eight dimensions, ranging from the size of creative industries, to the scale of cultural amenities, to user-created content.	Hartley et al. (2012) ARC Centre of Excellence for Creative Industries and Innovation (CCI)	City
Creative Grid highlights 10 infrastructural conditions for creative industries growth and competitiveness that go from the presence of high-profile cultural infrastructure, to support services for the creative industries, to connectedness.	Fleming, T. (2010) Creative Consultancy	No geographical level: sector-based
The Creative Space Index (CSI) comprises both quantitative and qualitative indicators grouped into five dimensions: talent, openness, cultural environment and tourism, technology, and innovation and industry.	Correia and da Silva Costa (2012) FED, Faculdade de Economia – Universidade do Porto	National (country)
The Design, Creativity and Innovation Scoreboard comprises seven dimensions: three measure the so-called creative climate (e.g. creative education, openness), and four capture creativity and design (e.g. share of creative occupations and designers).	Hollanders and van Cruysen (2009) Economic and Social Research and Training Centre on Innovation and Technology, Maastricht University	National (country)
The European Creativity Index (ECI) is aimed at assessing national competitiveness in the Creative Age by measuring talent, technology and tolerance (see also Creativity Index).	Florida and Tinagli (2004) Carnegie Mellon Software Industry Centre	National (country)
The European Creativity Index (ECI) aims to measure the interplay of various factors that contribute to the growth of creativity in the EU, by combining dimensions concerning creativity, innovation and economic performance as well as arts and culture.	KEA European Affairs (2009)	National (country)

Index	Source	Level of analysis
The Cultural Life Index aims to measure the performance of nations or provinces in terms of availability of cultural resources (e.g. number of museums, TV sets), cultural participation (e.g. admissions to cinemas) and production (e.g. number of films produced, of web hosts, etc.).	Picard et al. (2003) Prepared for the Finnish Ministry of Education and Culture	National (country) and some domestic provinces
The Creativity Index is Richard Florida's overall measure of a territory's economic potential. It combines measures of talent, technology and tolerance, such as: foreign-born and gay/lesbian population share for tolerance; patents per capita for technology; and creative class occupational share for talent.	Florida, R. (various applications)	National (country)
The Global Creativity Index (GCI) is a measure for advanced economic growth and prosperity based on the so-called '3Ts': talent, technology and tolerance.	Florida et al. (2015) Martin Prosperity Institute	National (country)
The Intercultural Cities Index is a benchmarking tool combining data on: demographics (primarily quantitative); inputs: policies, structures (primarily qualitative); and impacts: attitudes and behaviours (primarily qualitative).	Wagner (2015)	City
The Creative City Index uses three elements – an internal assessment, an external assessment and a web-based survey – to measure cities' performance across ten domains, ranging from political frameworks, to diversity and vitality, to entrepreneurship and innovation, to liveability and well-being.	Landry and Hyams (2012) Comedia with Basque Country region of Biscay and its core city Bilbao	City
The Sharpie's Creativity Index lists the UK's 20 most creative towns and cities as determined by data provided by 60 national and local organisations. It includes measures of creative sub-cultures and local environments, particularly of creative consumption.	Sharpie and The Future Laboratory (2007)	Towns and cities
The Composite Index of the Creative Economy (CICE) is a summary measure of an entity's creative capacity or capability in three key dimensions: innovation, entrepreneurship and openness.	Bowen et al. (2008) KU Leuven, Faculty of Economics and Business	Regions

Source: Adapted from Montalto et al. (2019).

Costa (2014), proposing strengths, weaknesses and major characteristics of several cultural and creative indexes. Some of these indicators are listed in Table 5.2.

The so lively debate among scholars and practitioners on CCIs and their effects on the economic and social aspects shows how the empirical metrics are articulated and focused on pointing out the capacity of culture and creativity to generate jobs and innovation, enabling the conditions for creative processes to thrive. These approaches, diversely distributed across Europe, offer a toolkit for policymakers: an opportunity to design context-specific development strategies and evidence-based policy.

5.4   CONCLUSION

The role of CCIs is gaining more relevance to foster not only the developments of the creative economy, but the overall economic scenario. The contemporary challenge is to develop a comprehensive understanding of CCIs and their performance and contribution to the economy and society, through improved indicators and characterisations at national and at EU level. The taxonomy of CCIs must confront complex, multidimensional concepts that have important implications from social, symbolic and economic perspectives. Moreover, in the modern creative economy, if CCIs are a key to fostering economic growth via innovation, it is worth considering how CCIs are conducive to achieving inclusive development, to strengthening social cohesion and sustainability. As promoted by the European Commission in the New European Agenda for Culture 2018, a CCIs-based development approach should be based not only on a flourishing creative economy, but most notably on a socially and culturally inclusive environment. There is therefore potential to develop a more comprehensive and systematic understanding of the metrics framework of CCIs. The lack of proper monitoring tools is linked to the lack of suitable and comparable data. To enrich and, to a certain extent, refine the current issue, composite indicators development techniques should be enhanced using a varied mix of data, coming both from official statistics and experimental web sources. The selection of pertinent metrics to capture culture and creativity is, however, far from being a trivial exercise.

REFERENCES

Americans for the Arts (2005). *Creative Industries 2005: The Congressional Report* [online]. Americans for the Arts. Avaliable from: https://www.americanforthearts .org/sites/default/files/pdf/about_us/2005AmericansForTheArtsAnnualReport.pdf.

Bagwell, S. (2008). Creative clusters and city growth. *Creative Industries Journal*, *1*(1), 31–46. https://doi.org/10.1386/cij.1.1.31_1.

Boschma, R.A., and Fritsch, M. (2009). Creative class and regional growth: empirical evidence from seven European countries. *Economic Geography*, *85*(4), 391–423. https://doi.org/10.1111/j.1944-8287.2009.01048.x.

Bowen, H., Moesen, W., and Sleuwaegen, L. (2008). A composite index of the creative economy with application to regional best practices. *Review of Business and Economics*, 4, 375–397.

Cerisola, S. (2018). Creativity and local economic development: the role of synergy among different talents. *Papers in Regional Science*, *97*(2), 199–215. https://doi.org/ 10.1111/pirs.12254.

Chapain, C., and Comunian, R. (2010). Enabling and inhibiting the creative economy: the role of the local and regional dimensions in England. *Regional Studies*, *44*(6), 717–734. https://doi.org/10.1080/00343400903107728.

Comunian, R., Chapain, C., and Clifton, N. (2010). Location, location, location: exploring the complex relationship between creative industries and place. *Creative Industries Journal*, *3*(1), 5–10. https://doi.org/10.1386/cij.3.1.5_2.

Correia, C.M., and da Silva Costa, J. (2014). Measuring creativity in the EU member states. *Investigaciones Regionales: Journal of Regional Research*, 30, 7–26.

Crociata, A., Agovino, M., Russo, A., and Quaglieri Domínguez, A. (2018). Creative workforce and economic development in precrisis Europe: main trends and causality relationships. *International Regional Science Review*, *41*(4), 448–479. https://doi.org/10.1177/0160017615607054.

Department for Culture, Media and Sport (DCMS) (1998). *Creative Industries Mapping Document*.

Drda-Kühn, K., and Wiegand, D. (2010). From culture to cultural economic power: rural regional development in small German communities. *Creative Industries Journal*, *3*(1), 89–96. https://doi.org/10.1386/cij.3.1.89_7.

European Commission (2006). *The Economy of Culture in Europe*.

European Commission (2019). *The Cultural and Creative Cities Monitor*. Luxembourg. https://doi.org/10.2760/257371.

Eurostat (2000). *Cultural Statistics in the EU. Final Report of the LEG*. Eurostat Working Papers. Luxembourg.

Eurostat (2008). *NACE Rev. 2*. Luxembourg. https://ec.europa.eu.eurostat/documents/3859598/5902521/KS-RA-07-015-EN.pdf.

Eurostat (2018). *Guide to Eurostat Culture Statistics*. Luxembourg. https://doi.org/10.2785/45136.

Florida, R. (2002). *The Rise of the Creative Class* (Vol. 9). New York: Basic Books.

Florida, R., Mellander, C., and King, K. (2015). *The Global Creativity Index 2015*. Tornoto: Martin Prosperity Institute, p. 64.

Florida, R., and Tinagli, I. (2004). *Europe in the Creative Age*, Carnegie Mellon Software Industry Publishing.

Florida, R., Mellander,C., and King, K.M. (2015). *The Global Creativity Index 2015*. Martin Prosperity Institute, Toronto.

Garnham, N. (2005). From cultural to creative industries: an analysis of the implications of the 'creative industries' approach to arts and media policy making in the United Kingdom. *International Journal of Cultural Policy*, *11*(1), 15–29. https://doi.org/10.1080/10286630500067606.

Hartley, J., Potts, J., MacDonald, T., Erkunt, C., and Kufleitner, C. (2012). The CCI Creative City Index. *Cultural Science Journal*, *5*(1), 1–138.

Hesmondhalgh, D. (2002). *The Cultural Industries*. London: SAGE Publications.

Hollanders, H., and Cruysen, A.V. (2009). Design, creativity and innovation: a scoreboard approach. PRO INNO Europe INNO METRICS, UNU-MERIT, Maastricht Economic and Social Research and Training Centre on Innovation and Technology, Maastricht Univeristy, Maastricht.

Hoyman, M., and Faricy, C. (2009). It takes a village: a test of the creative class, social capital, and human capital theories. *Urban Affairs Review*, *44*(3), 311–333. https://doi.org/10.1177/1078087408321496.

KEA European Affairs (2006). *The Economy of Culture in Europe*, Bruxelles, Belgium: KEA for the European Commission.

KEA (2009). *The Impact of Culture on Creativity.* Brussels. https://keanet.eu/wp-content/uploads/2019/09/impactculturecreativityfull.pdf.

KEA (2018). *Reserach for the CULT Commitee – Creative Europe: Towards the Next Programme Generation.* Brussels. https://doi.org/10.2861/079399.

KEA and PPMI (2019). *Research for CULT Committee – Culture and Creative Sectors in the European Union – Key Future Developments, Challenges and Opportunities.* Brussels. https://www.europarl.europa.eu/RegData/etudes/STUD/2019/629203/IPOL_STU(2019)629203_EN.pdf.

Kloudová, J., and Stehlíková, B. (2010). Creativity index for the Czech Republic in terms of regional similaries and geographic location. *Economics and Management, 15,* 100–109. https://www.semanticscholar.org/paper/CREATIVITY-INDEX-FOR-THE-CZECH-REPUBLIC-IN-TERMS-OF-Kloudová-Stehlíková/08dbd43098ec89572l0c9dbee1e9f4118cca5ea4.

Lazzeretti, L., Capone, F., and Boix, R. (2012). Reasons for clustering of creative industries in Italy and Spain. *European Planning Studies, 20*(8), 1243–1262. https://doi.org/10.1080/09654313.2012.680585.

Lorenzen, M., and Frederiksen, L. (2008). Why do cultural industries cluster? Localisation, urbanisation, products and projects. In P. Cooke and L. Lazzeretti (eds), *Creative Cities, Cultural Clusters and Local Economic Development* (pp. 155–179). Cheltenham, UK and Northampton, MA, USA: Edward Elgar Publishing.

Marco-Serrano, F., Rausell-Koster, P., and Abeledo-Sanchis, R. (2014). Economic development and the creative industries: a tale of causality. *Creative Industries Journal, 7*(2), 81–91. https://doi.org/10.1080/17510694.2014.958383.

Markusen, A. (2013). Fuzzy concepts, proxy data: why indicators would not track creative placemaking success. *International Journal of Urban Sciences, 17*(3), 291–303. https://doi.org/10.1080/12265934.2013.836291.

Marrocu, E., and Paci, R. (2012). Education or creativity: what matters most for economic performance? *Economic Geography, 88*(4), 369–401. https://doi.org/10.1111/j.1944-8287.2012.01161.x.

Montalto, V., Tacao Moura, C.J., Langedijk, S., and Saisana, M. (2019). Culture counts: an empirical approach to measure the cultural and creative vitality of European cities. *Cities, 89,* 167–185. https://doi.org/10.1016/J.CITIES.2019.01.014.

O'Connor, J. (2008). *The Cultural and Creative Industries: A Review of the Literature.* A Report for Creative Partnerships. London: Arts Council of England.

OECD (2006). *International Measurement of the Economic and Social Importance of Culture.* OECD Statistics Working Papers, No. 2007/03. Paris: OECD Publishing. https://doi.org/10.1787/5k92znx7sc30-en.

Ortega-Villa, L.M., and Ley-Garcia, J. (2018). Analysis of cultural indicators: a comparison of their conceptual basis and dimensions. *Social Indicators Research, 137*(2), 413–439. https://doi.org/10.1007/s11205-017-1588-2.

Picard, R.G., Grönlund, M., and Toivonen, T. (2003). *Means for Overall Asessment of Cultural Life and Measuring the Involvement of the Cultural Sector in the Information Society.* The report prepared for The Finnish Ministry of Education and Culture. Publications of The Ministry of Education. Helsinki, Finland.

Piergiovanni, R., Carree, M.A., and Santarelli, E. (2012). Creative industries, new business formation, and regional economic growth. *Small Business Economics, 39*(3), 539–560. https://doi.org/10.1007/s11187-011-9329-4.

Potts, J. (2011). *Creative Industries and Economic Evolution.* Cheltenham, UK and Northampton, MA, USA: Edward Elgar Publishing.

Pratt, A.C. (2004). The cultural economy. *International Journal of Cultural Studies*, *7*(1), 117–128. https://doi.org/10.1177/1367877904040609.

Throsby, D. (2008a). Modelling the cultural industries. *International Journal of Cultural Policy*, *14*(3), 217–232. https://doi.org/10.1080/10286630802281772.

Throsby, D. (2008b). The concentric circles model of the cultural industries. *Cultural Trends*, *17*(3), 147–164. https://doi.org/10.1080/09548960802361951.

Towse, R. (2011). *A Handbook of Cultural Economics*. Cheltenham, UK and Northampton, MA, USA: Edward Elgar Publishing.

UNESCO (2009). *Framework for Cultural Statistics*. Montreal: UNESCO Institute for Statistics.

UNESCO (2019). *Culture | 2030 Indicators*. Paris: United Nations Educational, Scientific and Cultural Organization.

UNESCO-UIS (2005). *International Flows of Selected Cultural Goods and Services, 1994–2003*. Montreal: UNESCO Institute for Statistics.

Wagner, A. (2015). Measuring Intercultural Policies: The Example of the Intercultural Cities Index. In R. Zapata-Barrero (ed.), *Interculturalism in Cities: Concept, Policy and Implementation* (pp. 115–135). Cheltenham, UK and Northampton, MA, USA: Edward Elgar Publishing.

World Intellectual Property Organization (2003). *WIPO Guide to the Intellectual Property Worldwide*. Geneva, Switzerland: WIPO.

PART II

Creative economies and entrepreneurship:
re-thinking inclusivity and business models

6. Experiences of belonging to the creative economy: narratives from northern micro-entrepreneurs

Lenita Nieminen and Arja Lemmetyinen

6.1 INTRODUCTION

This chapter contributes to place branding theory (Dudek-Mańkowska and Grochowski, 2019; Maheshwari et al., 2011; Pasquinelli, 2010) and to entrepreneurship research on the social embeddedness of an entrepreneurial process (McKeever et al., 2015; Jack et al. 2008, 2010; Jack and Anderson 2002), combining place branding with micro-entrepreneurs' narratives on the extent to which they feel a sense of belonging to the local creative ecosystem. Prior studies have explored the interface between branding theory and marketing/ entrepreneurship to investigate how the corporate branding process influences emerging entrepreneurial opportunities (Gaddefors, 2005). A recent study focuses on the relationships between the creative economy and place branding, thus combining the phenomenon of the creative economy with a specific location and creating a city as a brand (Dudek-Mańkowska and Grochowski, 2019). This study does not perceive the local creative ecosystem of the micro-entrepreneurs as a brand, and instead argues that the ecosystem could be regarded as a precursor that may evolve into a brand of an ecosystem, place, area or city. The prerequisite for an ecosystem to evolve into a brand is that the actors within it feel an affinity for the place brand (Lemmetyinen and Go, 2010).

Creative and cultural industries (CCIs) have recently been researched in connection to entrepreneurship (Artico and Tamma, 2018; Konrad, 2018; Borin et al., 2018; Schulte-Holthaus, 2018) alongside their value in promoting change and development (Goldberg-Miller and Kooyman, 2018), including regional and destination development (Mikic, 2018; Eisenbeis, 2018). However, there has not been any extensive research on cooperative networks and ecosystems in the context of CCIs. Typically, ecosystems cross industry boundaries and connect various types of business and innovation networks in an exchange that is embedded in an institutional and socio-technical environment (Aarikka-Stenroos and Ritala, 2017). The ecosystem approach, as an extension of the concept of network management, views the issue as a question of the broader societal system environment in which the business networks are embedded (Möller and Halinen, 2017). How to create suitable conditions and an ecosystem favourable for start-ups and entrepreneurs, especially focusing on how to best prepare a region for a future within the creative economy, and how to become less dependent on the automotive and machinery sectors, have been topical issues in regions such as Stuttgart (Eisenbeis, 2018). A start-up ecosystem in any region has every chance of success if it is based on the principles of smart selection, smart connection, smart capital and smart culture (Eisenbeis, 2018). The city branding process, focusing on stakeholder engagement in the post-industrial cities of Sheffield in the United Kingdom and Essen in Germany, has been a topic of research (Henninger et al., 2016). In the context of country branding, stakeholders' engagement with a place brand identity has been explored (Helmi et al., 2019).

The purpose of the present chapter is to discuss and illustrate how micro-entrepreneurs in CCIs engage with the creative economy. Our research question is: What characterises a micro-entrepreneur's sense of belonging in relation to the creative economy? The concept of the local creative ecosystem in the context of the creative economy enables connections not only between people but also between their ideas and practices as part of the connected communities (Comunian, 2011). The current research applies the concept of the local creative ecosystem (Comunian, 2011) to examine micro-entrepreneurs in CCIs and the local creative ecosystems they are supposed to be part of. In the analysis, we utilise Wenger's community of practice approach as a lens to illustrate how micro-entrepreneurs in CCIs are engaged with the creative economy. Recent context research emphasises the more subjective features of contexts and suggests that entrepreneurs actively enact or create contexts (Welter et al., 2019; Welter, 2011). For example, a longitudinal ethnographic study (Gaddefors and Anderson, 2017) shows how context determines what becomes entrepreneurial.

The chapter is structured as follows. First, we introduce the reader to the concepts of creative industries and the creative economy, and present research on the creative economy from the perspectives of entrepreneurship and ecosystems. The relationship between the creative economy and a place brand and entrepreneurial networks and embeddedness is in focus. In the methodology section, the context of the research and the data analysis are described. Finally, the narratives of the micro-entrepreneurs are presented, and the chapter ends with a discussion, implications, limitations and avenues for future research.

6.2   FROM AN UNHAPPY CITY TO A CREATIVE PLACE BRAND?

Cultural entrepreneurs operate in the complex landscape of the creative industries[1] in which their integrated development, including place branding, contributes to the efficacious utilisation of their physical, economic and social assets. Accordingly, the shift of power from large media enterprises to networks of adaptive local entrepreneurs who create value propositions in collaboration with their audiences signals a change (Go et al., 2015) that could bring a new kind of entrepreneurship to the field of creative industries, called 'everyday' or 'mundane' entrepreneurship (Dodd et al., 2021; Welter et al., 2017).

Focusing on the relationship between the creative economy and place branding combines the phenomenon of the creative economy with a specific location, and therefore creates a city as a brand (Dudek-Mańkowska and Grochowski, 2019). This follows the stream of research that investigates the influence of the creative sector on the development of cities (Boccella and Salerno, 2016; Cooke and Lazzeretti, 2008); studies focused on place branding and its importance for local development (Pasquinelli, 2010; Maheshwari et al., 2011); and studies concentrated on the process of place branding with the use of the presence of creative industries (Evans, 2015; Mengi et al., 2017). The authors of these studies see the creative city as an entity with a well-developed creative sector (economy), a dynamic creative community (society) and well-designed strategies to support creativity (policy).

Following the reasoning above (Dudek-Mańkowska and Grochowski 2019), a creative place brand acts as a kind of umbrella brand. A local creative ecosystem, introduced originally by Comunian (2011), in turn, may be seen as a pre-stage of a creative place brand, to which the micro-entrepreneurs in creative industries attach themselves. In other words, the entrepreneurs feel an affinity for the creative economy, but not necessarily for a specific place (brand) or umbrella brand. Local creative ecosystems play a role in ensuring that creative industries flourish. We suggest that there is a relationship between the creative economy and a creative place brand, and the role of the micro-entrepreneurs' engagement with a creative economy as a prerequisite of the creative place brand cannot be neglected.

In our interpretation of the literature of place brands and creative ecosystems, the 'creative place brand' (Dudek-Mańkowska and Grochowski, 2019) is the most developed form of the creative economy and is preceded by the 'local creative ecosystem' (Comunian, 2011). Interestingly, Magala (2011) considers places that are distinctive but do not yet have a unique selling point, or that are unique enough to differentiate them from other 'unhappy cities'. Further, Magala (2011: 16) explains city branding as the cultivation of imagined identities; with an emphasis on the creative input of artists, thinkers, researchers and designers playing a role in the place brand reputation game: 'Without a film festival most people would never have heard of Cannes; without pilgrims, of Rome, Mecca or Jerusalem'. According to Magala (2011), cities have a distinct brand, hence Czestochowa in Poland with its Black Madonna is different from Cannes with its beaches and film festival.

How the local creative ecosystems and creative place brand are related is illustrated in Figure 6.1, which combines the concepts of the creative place brand introduced by Dudek-Mańkowska and Grochowski (2019), the concept of the local creative ecosystem by Comunian (2011) and the idea of unhappy cities presented by Magala (2011).

Figure 6.1   *From unhappy cities to the creative place brand*

6.3   ENTREPRENEURIAL NETWORKS AND EMBEDDEDNESS

Our research question investigates what characterises a micro-entrepreneur's engagement with the creative economy and its local creative ecosystem. This kind of approach, focusing on social structures and entrepreneurial networks, has not been as extensive in the context of culture and creative business as in other entrepreneurial contexts. Earlier research emphasises that the content and nature of networks and the nature of interactions between network actors (for example, what goes on in and between ties) should be considered more extensively (Jack, 2010; Jack et al., 2010). Jack et al. (2010) claim that networking is not just about resource acquisition, but is also about softer, socialised issues, such as social learning and confidence-building through interdependence and the sharing of experience.

The often-cited study on the effects of embeddedness on the entrepreneurial process by Jack and Anderson (2002) confirms that being socially embedded not only enables knowledge, contacts, advice, information and support, but also creates opportunities, thus shaping and sustaining business. They showed that the opportunities existing in a local milieu were not available to those not embedded. It seems that place becomes something of value for entrepreneurs, offering something very special, valuable and rare that is hard to imitate and substitute; and that is a source of sustainable competitive advantage (McKeever et al., 2015).

It is evident that embeddedness is a reciprocal process of becoming accepted in the local context, and learning about and accepting the local rules (Jack and Anderson, 2002; McKeever et al., 2015). Similarly, Jack et al. (2008) perceive entrepreneurs as a product of their social environment and opportunities as influenced by social interaction. McKeever et al. (2015) talk about 'local belonging' and 'community belonging' that enable community members to understand the nature and habits of their place and how to 'play the same game'. This can only be achieved by knowing the local context and the rules of engagement.

This chapter explores the ways in which micro-entrepreneurs describe their sense of belonging to the creative economy. In the language of Wenger (1998), engagement with the locality means that individuals accept or reject opportunities to belong to a community of practice, depending on how well those opportunities fit with their sense of self and how they interpret what they do. The newcomer participates in practices valued by a community by mimicking others and picking up the jargon, behaviour and norms of a social group (Lave and Wenger, 1991; Wenger, 1998), thus attaining expertise in doing, knowing and being in a community of practice. A lack of identification with a community or a lack of access to participation may also lead to marginalisation, conflict or exclusion from a social group.

Figure 6.2 illustrates the framework of the study, presenting how belonging to a social community integrates micro-entrepreneurs' experiences (the micro level) to the local creative place and its place brand (the meso level).

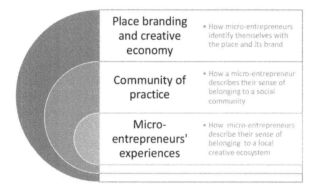

Figure 6.2   The theoretical framework of the study

In the following section we present the context of our study and findings of the narrative analysis of how the micro-entrepreneurs describe their sense of belonging to a local creative ecosystem, viewing it as a social community in which the entrepreneurs participate.

6.4   METHODOLOGY

A qualitative approach is ideal when a holistic view of the phenomenon is required (Yin, 2009). To study the nature of networks and network dynamics, more qualitative, longitudinal and multi-method work is encouraged. Jack (2010) and Jack et al. (2010), among others, claim that ethnography, participant observation, interviews and surveys provide a mechanism to study networks in context and appreciate how networks operate and how they are formed, created, maintained and utilised, and also to recognise the impact of network emergence, change and evolution. There is also a need for qualitative studies to develop ideas about entrepreneurship and the market–entrepreneurship interface, where qualitative studies allow the researcher to take account of specific characteristics such as the complex, interactive and personal nature of entrepreneurship (Gaddefors, 2005).

Context of the Research

Over the period 2009–19, we followed the 'emancipation' of the creative economy in a rural province in southwest Finland. During this period, cooperation projects with local cultural and creative actors included workshops and seminars with international expert speakers; developmental projects, and student projects within the field; and practitioners contributing to classroom teaching and seminars. The initiative offered the authors access to longitudinal and intense interactions with creative and cultural entrepreneurs who were self-employed, freelancers, artists or other cultural workers and non-governmental organisations representing a wide range of CCIs. The situation also allowed us to follow Chalmers and Shaw's (2017: 20) proposal 'to adopt methodological resources that will facilitate development of a more dynamic and context-including programme of research', and to reduce the gap between research findings and the lived world. For this study, we conducted phenomenological interviews (Cope, 2005) with four entrepreneurs in CCIs representing heritage, art, design and creative services. Formal and informal conversations, several encounters at various events with entrepreneurs and also our observations, have inevitably influenced the narratives.

We perform a narrative analysis, in which 'the researcher organises and interprets empirical data that describe some more or less consistent events, happenings and actions in a way that they construct one or more narratives that will be interpreted and discussed' (Eriksson and Kovalainen, 2016: 221). This kind of analysis is based on a dichotomy that distinguishes between the analysis of narratives and narrative analysis (Polkinhorne, 1995). The analysis of narratives involves researchers collecting stories told by people and then analysing them using various techniques. In the case of narrative analysis, the focus, as in this study, is on the narrative itself as a mode of analysis (Eriksson and Kovalainen, 2016: 221).

Analysis of the Study

In our narrative analysis, we apply Wenger's (1998) framework on belonging to a community of practice. The community of practice approach is the understanding that we identify with some communities strongly and not at all with others, and define ourselves by what we are not as well as by what we are: by the communities we do not belong to as well as those we do. These relationships change, and we also move from one community to another, and in doing so we carry a fragment of each with us. We can also be a member of many communities at the same time (Wenger, 1998; Lave and Wenger, 1991).

Wenger (1998) presents three forms of belonging – engagement, imagination and alignment – and suggests that they work best in combination. 'Engagement' requires authentic access to and interaction with other participants; that is, doing things together, talking and producing artefacts. 'Alignment' means becoming part of something big by connecting local efforts to broader discourses. The work of alignment often entails convincing and inspiring others. 'Imagination' refers to viewing oneself through the eyes of an outsider, being 'in someone else's shoes' (Wenger, 1998).

6.5   NARRATIVES OF MICRO-ENTREPRENEURS

In this section, we present the narratives and our interpretation of the ways in which Wenger's forms of belonging manifest in the micro-entrepreneurs' narratives.

Pamela: Visual Artist

Pamela is a visual and performance artist who operates an art gallery and a perfume shop. She has created cultural service packages for tourists around her artistic activities. Pamela identifies herself as an artist, and she says that 'art is my number one [interest] and doing art and showing it to people is my first priority and then comes my shop and tourism'. It is apparent that art is her true passion and an outlet for sharing her feelings with her audience. She lives and works in her family home, and it is quite evident that, for Pamela, family history is the basis for her creative work.

Pamela says that her mother's cosmetics shop (established in 1936) was the first of its kind in rural Finland. The local perfume shop back then sold the same lipsticks used by actors Marlene Dietrich and Greta Garbo. Twenty-five years ago, when her mother died, Pamela inherited the shop and was unsure what to do with it. For her mother, the shop was 'quite an ordinary shop', but for Pamela, it developed into something different. Now, clients book an appointment at her perfume salon, and they are served sparkling wine while Pamela conducts a 'tasting' to identify an appropriate perfume in the unique milieu of her grandparents' old house, decorated with her colourful paintings. For Pamela, perfume tasting is not a sales tactic, but more of an art performance.

In addition, Pamela and her husband arrange an annual open light art event in November at the darkest time of the year in the garden of the art gallery. The two-week art event has a grand opening in which Pamela exhibits a dance performance that attracts a great number of visitors, as well as a lot of media attention. Pamela states that she has learned from the local art council that every time a new exhibition opens, it is of the utmost importance to send a press release and arrange a press conference. She says, 'I'm a gallerist so I've collected a list of about 100 people who I bomb with invitations to my exhibition'.

Pamela reports belonging to a couple of cultural networks. One is an association for artists in a nearby town. She has also been a member of a local network that consists of about five to ten entrepreneurs in arts and handicrafts with whom she has had some sporadic business connections. The local cultural office has also helped to coordinate a network between local artists. Pamela's product packages are also available in a tourist office in the nearby town, and on the internet.

Pamela definitely sees parallels between her own entrepreneurship and her family's traditions. In our interpretation, imagination appears in the narrative in her honouring of her family's history. For example, she has decorated a room for a small perfume museum in the art gallery where she displays the cosmetics from the period when her mother ran the shop. Both the museum and the perfume shop are decorated with furniture made by her grandfather. Pamela identifies herself as a performance artist and considers the four pillars – an atelier, a perfume shop, a gallery and a residence – as her 'complete artwork'. In our interpretation, the perfume museum is a kind of an artefact that connects Pamela's efforts to a broader discourse, thus indicating alignment. She has also created service packages for tourists around her artistic activities. Every time she opens a new exhibition, she sends a press release and arranges a press conference. She has managed to get a few contacts among the journalists who visit her four or five times a year. Pamela is seemingly quite independent, and her engagement with her entrepreneur colleagues in the local ecosystem hardly exists.

Ellen: Owner of a Design Sauna

Ellen set up her business in 2010 in what could be termed a designer sauna. The building was designed by the world-famous Finnish architect Alvar Aalto in the 1940s. At the time, it functioned as both a sauna and a laundry for the workers in the neighbouring factories. Today, the property houses an elegant cafeteria decorated with Aalto furniture, a sauna, a design shop and an art gallery. In 2005, Ellen's father noticed that the sauna was for sale, so Ellen and her brother decided to buy it. Ellen says, 'It feels like this building is meant for us'. The building has a lot of sentimental value to her. Ellen's family was born in the Ironworks Village,[2] and her mother, father and grandfather all worked at the factory. They lived in a house that was also designed by Aalto, and Ellen describes how she grew up in this architectural environment, even though her family belonged to the working class. Ellen says that she has her roots in the Ironworks Village and the sauna, so it is rather easy for her to tell people about its history.

Ellen has a wholehearted commitment to the Ironworks Village. She has been devoted to the area since childhood, and her affinity for the village has become even stronger since she began her business in the area. So far, the process of becoming an entrepreneur has taken so much of Ellen's time that she has been too busy to develop her products. Ellen describes her working days as a circus, and says, 'I still have to learn how it works ... I have dreams for this'. Before owning the sauna, Ellen worked as a caretaker at an institution for people with disabilities, and it is her dream to combine her background as an art therapist with the design sauna. It is noteworthy that, like the other interviewees, she does not use the word 'business' when she talks about her entrepreneurial endeavours.

Ellen explains that she belongs to a network of local artists and artisans, and was a bit surprised but happy that she was asked to join these networks. She also notes that some of the handicraft artisans have closed their businesses, and some have moved away from the area. Ellen mentions several times how pleased she would be to collaborate with others, but it is not so easy for her to leave the 'house'. She also spoke of a local cultural festival that was arranged a couple of times, but the cooperation was not 'very rosy', and she and her brother had to do a lot of work on their own.

For Ellen, engagement appears in the way she speaks of belonging to a group of local artisans, artists and micro-entrepreneurs in the tourism business. She is proud of having been invited to participate in the community of CCIs. She would welcome greater collaboration with other local entrepreneurs, but her involvement with her own business based around her house constrains her. Ellen has a wholehearted commitment to the brand identity of the place. She has been devoted to this area since childhood, and this feeling of affinity has become even stronger since she began her business in the area. However, many practical routines have taken so much of Ellen's time that she has been too busy to develop her products. Ellen's endeavour to preserve and promote the cultural heritage of the place can be categorised under 'imagination'. Her dream is to combine her background as an art therapist with her work at the design sauna, so she seeks to connect her competence and activities to a broader context, indicating alignment.

Kate: Owner of an Art House

After inheriting an old family estate in 2005, Kate had the idea to start a cultural centre to display her artwork and paintings, and also to generate some income to cover the costs of the house. For Kate, the house itself is important, and it represents the heritage she values most, that is, that embodied by authenticity. In all her activities, she tries to find ways that could bring income for the maintenance of the house. Kate organises cooking, reading, music, poetry and art, for example. She says:

> When I inherited this house, it was obvious that I would do everything that I could afford to keep the house and myself alive, so I thought I could create a cultural centre where the doors would be open and I could provide people with different services, experiences and, most importantly, my art, which is the most essential way to make ends meet.

Kate categorises herself as a handicraft artist. She sees a resemblance between the Ironworks Village and the area of Fiskars village, which is a popular and fast-growing community of local handicraft artists and micro-entrepreneurs in southern Finland. Kate says that activities in Fiskars are concentrated in a small geographical area, which makes it easier to develop the area. Kate's art house is not located at the heart of the Ironworks Village, so she feels somewhat excluded. She is critical of the tendency of the municipality to concentrate on the development of the Ironworks Village, which excludes the handicraft artists and entrepreneurs on the outskirts of the village: 'I have a feeling that the Ironworks Village takes all the potential visitors'. Kate therefore plans to offer a cultural package of her own, encompassing two minor tourist attractions located nearby. She says that for her, Facebook has been a good way to market her cultural products and services.

In summer, Kate's products are available in the café in the Ironworks Village. She has also distributed brochures and business cards. She often attends exhibitions around the region, but she finds it rather time-consuming and requiring too much effort; however, she recognises that it is an important route to selling her art: 'One should try all the time to get to the places which give you and your products more visibility'. Kate seems somewhat disappointed that the locals do not show that much interest in her art. She considers handicraft artisans, including herself, to be very talented and believes that although they differ from one another, they are all creating their art from their hearts.

When asked about the networks she might belong to, Kate says that, professionally, she does not have any. She does not belong to the local artists' association, and now does not take part in local development projects, feeling that they have not helped her. She feels strongly that she alone will have to be responsible for her business:

> I do not want to take part in those events any more, since I am doing this work alone and everything that happens here is because of me. I plan and make my products, I market them, and try to communicate about them, I clean my house and do everything by myself.

However, Kate evidently sees the benefits of more intense forms of local cooperation.

For Kate, the house itself is important, and in all her activities she tries to find ways that could bring in income to support the maintenance of the house. She does not mention the local community of artists and handicraft entrepreneurs. When Kate speaks of Fiskars village, which is a famous community of artists, artisans and cultural entrepreneurs in Finland, she imagines it as a creative place brand. She does not see engagement in a local creative ecosystem as relevant for her. Neither does she belong to the local artists' association. She feels very strongly that in the end she alone has to take responsibility for her business. Kate promotes her products through traditional media and Facebook, but it seems that her efforts to convince and inspire her audience remain insufficient.

Maria: Former Owner of a Small Spa and Resort

Maria is an entrepreneur and the former owner of a small spa and resort that was located in a historic villa area outside of a larger industrial town. Maria is interested in the cultural heritage of this historic area of summer homes that dates back to the 1850s and is among one of the best-preserved villa areas in Finland. She bought an old villa and renovated it to create both a spa and a private home. Maria's vision was to offer customers the experience of country living as it used to be, albeit modified in a modern style. In her blog, Maria introduces herself as a conceptual designer for the lifestyle and service business. She writes about her inexhaustible enthusiasm for the lifestyle world, service concepts and the creation of unique experiences for customers, and says that this makes her approach to business unique. In 2020, she introduced herself as a creative leader and brand ambassador.

In formal and informal conversations with Maria and at local cultural business events, she always speaks with great determination and conviction of her vision of an umbrella brand which she refers to as 'Nordic Country Living'. She believes in the attractiveness of the Nordic lifestyle, which is of interest to tourists from around the world; in the same way, the Danish concept of *hygge* (cosiness) exemplifies how cold has become 'cool' and how cosiness, comfort and social connectivity create a good quality of life marked by simple pleasures. She envisages her spa business as part of such a joint brand.

Maria is not afraid to speak out about how the local authorities have shown no interest in revitalising the villa area, and how the regional destination management organisation sees no value in rebranding it as a cultural tourism destination. She says that she has been left alone by her 'own people': 'But I cannot do this alone. What is needed is cooperation between education, research, and the regional development agency, and also the city [administration] needs to be for the idea'.

A year ago, Maria was forced to give up her spa business. However, she still believes in the concept of Nordic Country Living and eco-luxury cultural services. She says that only recently had she been able to gather a 'tribe' of people 'with the appropriate mindset and story' that believes in her. Maria is proud of listing the expertise she has managed to gain, for example, in 'digitalisation and systems thinking, concept design, business, interior design, investment, tourism, strategic management, brand storytelling and preservation of cultural heritage'. Currently, Maria runs a start-up project with the aim of developing a platform for companies offering 'luxury services in unique cultural destinations for niche travellers'.

Maria envisioned how a brand ecosystem could be constructed through a virtual network of relationships with business partners. She has taken an initiator role in co-creating an ecosystem in cultural tourism. Apparently, Maria's engagement in a virtual creative ecosystem is strong, while her engagement in a place is weak. She is extremely good at developing interactions with people whose competence matches with the ecosystem, and she is constantly searching for such people. Moreover, she is convincing and inspiring when visualising a virtual platform combining service providers, investors, consultants and experts, and professionals from a range of fields. Speaking of ecosystems and branding is characteristic of her.

In the following section, we discuss the implications and conclusions of our narrative analysis of how micro-entrepreneurs feel an affinity with the local creative economy and place brand.

6.6   DISCUSSION, IMPLICATIONS AND LIMITATIONS

This study contributes to both entrepreneurship and place branding research and complements earlier studies on branding and entrepreneurship focused on embeddedness and networks (Gaddefors, 2005; Möller and Halinen, 2017; McKeever et al., 2015; Jack et al., 2008; Jack and Anderson, 2002). We combined the meso-level concepts of a creative place brand and a local creative ecosystem (Dudek-Mańkowska and Grochowski, 2019; Comunian, 2011) with the micro-level experiences of the creative and cultural small business entrepreneurs to illustrate how they identify with the local creative ecosystem and the place and its brand. Indeed, some perhaps perceive the place and its brand as not sufficiently unique to differentiate itself from other places (Magala, 2011).

For the micro-entrepreneurs in CCIs, the local creative ecosystem may be important in the sense of how the intangible heritage of the place becomes a core of their service offering. However, the commitment to a place brand is rather limited if the reason for running a business is to generate income; for example, for the maintenance of an old family house. The commitment to a place brand is strong when a brand ecosystem is constructed through a virtual network of business partners who are mainly not from the local area. Interestingly, the creative place brand then acts as a kind of an umbrella brand linked more closely to the vision of network cooperation than to a specific place.

When analysing how the entrepreneurs perceived their sense of belonging to the creative economy, it became obvious that entrepreneurship as such was not the primary feature defining their identity. The micro-entrepreneurs did not refer to themselves as entrepreneurs, but characterised themselves as artists or passionate art lovers. They did not use the word 'business' when they spoke of their entrepreneurial endeavours. For some of the micro-entrepreneurs, their individual family history and passion for art are the most dominant characteristics of their sense of belonging to the local creative ecosystem. For some micro-entrepreneurs, the preservation of the family estate and the architectural infrastructure provides the reason for their entrepreneurship.

The micro-entrepreneurs contributing to our study represent a typical mundane or everyday form of entrepreneurship (often referred to as necessity entrepreneurship), with little potential for innovation and economic growth (Welter et al., 2019) other than maintaining a family property. In focusing on entrepreneurship as an everyday activity propelled by a variety of motivations other than the economic (Dodd et al., 2021) – for example, honouring an ancestor's life's work or the architectural heritage of a place – this study offers a more multifaceted view of both conducting and training for entrepreneurship.

As a long-term qualitative study utilising various data-gathering methods, the study is not easily replicated. In using narrative analysis as a data analysis method, the researchers' interpretation of what is relevant plays a major role in how the narratives are constructed. The purpose of narrative research is not to produce one definite truth about something that is out there, but to offer one version of it (Eriksson and Kovalainen, 2016: 226), and 'it is always possible to narrate the same events in a different way'. Riessman's (1993) criteria to evaluate narrative studies ask whether the interpretation is reasonable and convincing, and let the readers evaluate that. The correspondence between the researchers and the participants has allowed the participants to check the interpretations. We have followed the micro-entrepreneurs in their natural environment for a decade, to show that the resulting interpretation is more than an ad hoc judgement. The study will be useful as a basis for future research, suggesting that a similar kind of research setting may be used in other cities or places.

NOTES

1. The United Nations Conference on Trade and Development (UNCTAD) classification depicts four broad groups of creative industries: heritage, including cultural sites and traditional cultural expressions; arts, including performing and visual arts; media, including publishing and audio-visuals; and functional creations, including new media, design and creative services (UNCTAD, 2008).
2. Having emerged around iron and paper industries, the Ironworks Village is considered a culturally relevant destination. In the heart of the industrial area is an old ironworks that was set up in the late fifteenth century. A large corporation owns most of the historic buildings in the area that formerly housed company officials and employees. The corporation also operates a line of service businesses targeted at business-to-business clients. A well-known Finnish architect, Alvar Aalto, left his footprint in the area during the 1940s by designing buildings, most of which are owned by the corporation. Quite recently, the corporation announced that it would sell most of those buildings. During the last ten years, the municipality has coordinated development projects that attempted to attract tourists and new residents to the area by strengthening a brand based on the cultural heritage of the Ironworks Village.

REFERENCES

Aarikka-Stenroos, L. and Ritala, P. (2017). Network management in the era of eco-systems: systematic review and management framework. *Industrial Marketing Management*, 67, 23–36.

Artico, C.I. and Tamma, M. (2018). Culture-based products: integrating cultural and commercial strategies. In: Innerhofer, E., Pechlaner, H. and Borin, E. (eds), *Entrepreneurship in Culture and Creative Industries*. Cham: Springer, 11–24.

Boccella, N. and Salerno, I. (2016). Creative economy, cultural industries and local development. *Procedia – Social and Behavioral Sciences*, 223, 291–296.

Borin, E., Donato, F. and Sinapi, C. (2018). Financial sustainability of small- and medium-sized enterprises in the cultural and creative sector: the role of funding. In: Innerhofer, E., Pechlaner, H. and Borin, E. (eds), *Entrepreneurship in Culture and Creative Industries*. Cham: Springer, 45–62.

Chalmers, Dominic M. and Shaw, Eleanor (2017). The endogenous construction of entrepreneurial contexts: a practice-based perspective. *International Small Business Journal*, 35 (1), 19–39.

Comunian, R. (2011) Rethinking the creative city. *Urban Studies*, 48, 1157–1179.

Cooke, P. and Lazzeretti, L. (2008). Creative cities: an introduction. In: Cooke, P. and Lazzeretti, L. (eds), *Creative Cities, Cultural Clusters and Local Economic Development*. Cheltenham: Edward Elgar Publishing, 1–24.

Cope, J. (2005). Researching entrepreneurship through phenomenological inquiry: philosophical and methodological issues. *International Small Business Journal*, 23 (2), 163–189.

Dodd, S., Anderson, A. and Jack, S. (2021). 'Let them not make me a stone' – repositioning entrepreneurship. *Journal of Small Business Management*. https://doi.org/10.1080/00472778.2020.1867734.

Dudek-Mańkowska, S. and Grochowski, M. (2019). From creative industries to the creative place brand: some reflections on city branding in Poland. *Place Branding and Public Diplomacy*, 15, 274–287.

Eisenbeis, U. (2018). Relevant locational factors for creative industries startups. In: Innerhofer, E., Pechlaner, H. and Borin, E. (eds), *Entrepreneurship in Culture and Creative Industries*. Cham: Springer, 281–296.

Eriksson, P. and Kovalainen, A. (2016). *Qualitative Methods in Business Research*. London: SAGE.

Evans, G. (2015). Rethinking place branding and place making through creative and cultural quarters. In: Kavaratzis, M., Warnaby, G. and Ashworth, G. (eds), *Rethinking Place Branding*. Cham: Springer.

Gaddefors, J. (2005). Creating context – entrepreneurial opportunities in a consumer market setting. *Journal of Enterprising Culture*, 13 (3), 199–224.

Gaddefors, J. and Anderson, A.R. (2017). Entrepreneurship and context: when entrepreneurship is greater than entrepreneurs. *International Journal of Entrepreneurial Behavior and Research*, 23 (2), 267–278.

Go, F., Lemmetyinen, A. and Hakala, U. (2015). Introduction. In: Go, F., Lemmetyinen, A. and Hakala, U. (eds), *Harnessing Place Branding through Cultural Entrepreneurship*. Basingstoke: Palgrave Macmillan, 1–28.

Goldberg-Miller, S.B.D. and Kooyman, R. (2018). In: Innerhofer, E., Pechlaner, H. and Borin, E. (eds), *Entrepreneurship in Culture and Creative Industries*. Cham: Springer, 183–196.

Helmi, J., Bridson, K. and Casidy, R. (2020). A typology of organizational stakeholder engagement with place brand identity. *Journal of Strategic Marketing*, 28 (7), 620–638.

Henninger, C.E., Foster, C., Alevizou, P. and Frohlich, C. (2016). Stakeholder engagement in the city branding process. *Place Branding and Public Diplomacy*, 12 (4), 285–298.

Jack, S.L. (2010). Approaches to studying networks: implications and outcomes. *Journal of Business Venturing*, 25 (1), 120–137.

Jack, Sarah L. and Anderson, Alistair (2002). The effects of embeddedness on the entrepreneurial process. *Journal of Business Venturing*, 17 (5), 467–487.

Jack, Sarah L., Dodd, Sarah D. and Anderson, Alistair R. (2008). Change and the development of entrepreneurial networks over time: a processual perspective. *Entrepreneurship and Regional Development*, 20 (2), 125–159.

Jack, S.L., Moult, S., Anderson, A.R. and Dodd, S.D. (2010). An entrepreneurial network evolving: patterns of change. *International Small Business Journal*, 28 (4), 315–337.

Konrad, E.D. (2018). Entrepreneurial behavior and financing structures in the German creative industries. In: Innerhofer, E., Pechlaner, H. and Borin, E. (eds), *Entrepreneurship in Culture and Creative Industries*. Cham: Springer, 25–44.

Lave, J. and Wenger, E. (1991). *Situated Learning: Legitimate Peripheral Participation*. Cambridge: Cambridge University Press.

Lemmetyinen, A. and Go, F. (2010). Building a brand identity in a network of Cruise Baltic's destinations – a multi-authoring approach. *Journal of Brand Management*, 17, 519–531.

McKeever, Edward, Jack, Sarah and Anderson, Alistair (2015). Embedded entrepreneurship in the creative re-construction of place. *Journal of Business Venturing*, 30 (1), 50–65.

Magala, S. (2011). Imagined identities of existing cities. In: Govers, R. and Go, F. (eds), *International Place Branding Yearbook 2012: Managing Reputational Risk*. New York: Palgrave Macmillan, 12–24.

Maheshwari, V., Vandewalle, I. and Bamber, D. (2011). Place branding's role in sustainable development. *Journal of Place Management and Development*, 4 (2), 198–213.

Mengi, O., Durmaz Drinkwater, S.B., Öner, A.C. and Velibeyoglu, K. (2017). Place management of a creative city: The case of Izmir. *International Journal of Knowledge-Based Development*, 8 (3), 271–291.

Mikic, H. (2018). Cultural entrepreneurship and rural development: case study of Pirot, Serbia. In: Innerhofer, E., Pechlaner, H. and Borin, E. (eds), *Entrepreneurship in Culture and Creative Industries*. Cham: Springer, 245–264.

Möller, K. and Halinen, A. (2017). Managing business and innovation networks – from strategic nets to business fields and ecosystems. *Industrial Marketing Management*, 67, 5–22.

Pasquinelli, C. (2010). The limits of place branding for local development: the case of Tuscany and the Arnovalley brand. *Local Economy: The Journal of the Local Economy Policy Unit*.

Polkinghorne, D. (1995). Narrative configuration in qualitative analysis. *Qualitative Studies in Education*, 8 (1), 5–23.

Riessman, C. (1993). *Narrative Analysis*. Qualitative Research Methods Series, No. 30. Newbury Park, CA: SAGE.

Schulte-Holthaus, S. (2018). Entrepreneurship in the creative industries. In: Innerhofer, E., Pechlaner, H. and Borin, E. (eds), *Entrepreneurship in Culture and Creative Industries*. Cham: Springer, 99–154.

UNCTAD (2008). *Creative Economy Report 2008. The Challenge of Assessing the Creative Economy: Towards Informed Policy-Making*. UNCTAD.

Welter, F. (2011). Contextualising entrepreneurship: conceptual challenges and ways forward. *Entrepreneurship Theory and Practice*, 35 (1), 165–184.

Welter, F., Baker, T., Audretsch, D.B. and Gartner, W.B. (2017). Everyday entrepreneurship – a call for entrepreneurship research to embrace entrepreneurial diversity. *Entrepreneurship Theory and Practice*, 41 (3), 311–321.

Welter, F., Baker, T. and Wirsching, K. (2019). Three waves and counting: the rising tide of contextualisation in entrepreneurship research. *Small Business Economics*, 52, 319–330.

Wenger, E. (1998). *Communities of Practice: Learning, Meaning and Identity*. Cambridge: Cambridge University Press.

Yin, R.K. (2009). *Case Study Research: Design and Methods*. Thousand Oaks, CA: SAGE Publications.

7. Cultural entrepreneurship: ethnicity and migrant communities

Annette Naudin

7.1 INTRODUCTION

This chapter considers the impact of public policies aimed at cultural entrepreneurs from diverse ethnic and migrant communities, as a means of understanding their potential barriers. The British policy context is noteworthy, because in contrast with other European countries, the United Kingdom (UK) identifies ethnicity in public policies, creating an opportunity to focus attention on individuals from diverse ethnic and migrant communities. The outcome of this research suggests that targeting policy interventions at different ethnic groups can result in further discrimination, but there are opportunities for a better understanding of cultural entrepreneurship as experienced by individuals from diverse ethnic and migrant communities.

For the purposes of this chapter, my working definition of 'cultural entrepreneur' is individuals working in the cultural and creative industries (CCIs) as freelancers, owners of micro-enterprises and self-employed cultural workers (see also: Leadbeater and Oakley, 1999; Naudin, 2018; Oakley, 2014). This definition includes those who balance a portfolio career, people engaged in a range of activities comprising of some unpaid work and possibly operating between amateur and professional practices. It should be noted that it is rare for cultural entrepreneurs to self-identify as 'cultural entrepreneurs'. Most individuals in the sector tend to focus on cultural, media or creative sub-sectors to describe their practice. For example, they might present themselves as a performer, dancer, web designer, film director or television producer, or increasingly there is evidence to suggest that a person's practice can be so varied that pinning it down to a professional identity is difficult. As work shifts from fundraising, to project and events management, alongside cultural, media or creative practice, there is a tendency to develop a hybrid identity. However, this chapter is concerned with self-employment in the CCIs and links to policies which seek to develop entrepreneurial modes of work. While scholars from entrepreneurship studies might challenge the degree to which the entrepreneurs in this study can be described as 'real' entrepreneurs, given the extent to which entrepreneurship has become associated with the sector (Oakley, 2014; McRobbie, 2011) the term 'cultural entrepreneur' seems appropriate.

The chapter outlines the public policy context before describing the approach to the case study, which is based on a local policy intervention in Birmingham, UK. This is followed by findings and observations which contribute to our understanding of cultural entrepreneurship amongst diverse ethnic and migrant communities in relation to place and local policies.

7.2   CULTURAL POLICY CONTEXT

Over the last 20 years, many British cities have engaged in projecting a 'creative city' agenda through policies which have sought to exploit the contribution of the CCIs. Encouraged to emphasise their cultural distinctiveness, city councils have supported local CCIs, as a means of differentiating themselves from other European cities, through a myriad of interventions including the development of cultural quarters and support for cultural entrepreneurship (Landry, 2008). In the UK, the New Labour government's (1997–2010) desire to represent a multicultural Britain placed an emphasis on 'diversity' in UK cultural policy, particularly through Arts Council England (ACE) schemes which aimed to encourage audience and workforce development (Mirza, 2009). For ethnic and immigrant communities, diversity policies enabled funding to be available through programmes such as Decibel (Hammonds and Bhandal, 2010). As Mirza (2009: 56) argues, the lived experience of diversity policies is not without its problems for those on the receiving end, 'relying as it does on a particular emphasis on ethnic identity which is bound to specific communities'. Furthermore, diversity policies did little to address workers outside of cultural institutions, such as freelancers and micro-entrepreneurs. While cultural entrepreneurs from diverse ethnic and migrant communities were not specifically left out of policies which focused on CCIs' economic contribution, they were not expressly targeted in the development of cultural quarters and city centre initiatives.

As Bell and Oakley (2015) have argued, policies which supported creative economy development and culture-led regeneration often ignored the significance of social relationships which underpin much CCI work. If ethnic and immigrant cultural workers were not engaging with key networks, contributing to economic agendas and city centre initiatives, it is likely that funding and entrepreneurial opportunities were not directed at them:

the creative economy model that has been pursued nationally, locally and internationally is not only insensitive to the time and the local knowledge needed to support localised production centres, it is actively undermining the conditions of their existence. (Oakley, 2016: 169)

Social relationships are critical to cultural work, and in cities they form the glue which enable CCIs to thrive, establishing formal and informal relationships encouraged by cultural quarters and co-working environments (Bell and Oakley, 2015; Long and Naudin, 2019), usually in city centres. The 'cultural melting pot', which has been described as an ecosystem (Warwick Commission, 2015), is deliberately deployed for cultural development and re-branding cities, integrating CCIs into all aspects of urban planning (Bell and Oakley, 2015). Yet, as we know from the work of scholars such as Rosalind Gill, the social and professional connections created through informal networks are far from 'egalitarian' (Gill, 2002); rather, they tend to bolster strong ties (Granovetter, 1973) over diverse new relationships. This becomes significant when we analyse the specificity of the local by exploring where and how CCIs tend to be based and whether, in translating national policies, local policymakers consider the distinctive characteristics of diverse communities. Beyond the core geographic heart of the city centre, we find cultural entrepreneurs positioned outside of creative economy policies, who operate through different sets of social networks, cultural values and practices. As Banks and O'Connor (2017) have argued, creative practices engaged communities well before the focus on the so-called 'creative industries', developing relationships between localised cultural activities and community groups which operate in the margins of the subsidised sectors. What is significant here is that national policies, through either the Department for Digital, Culture, Media and Sports (DCMS) or funding bodies such as ACE, have limited opportunities to consider the finer detail in more localised approaches to the cultural entrepreneurship (Oakley, 2016). Cities with a changing demographic present a complex environment for local cultural policymakers.

Fast forward to more recent times, and this study explores how, at a localised level, funded projects provide support which aims to address any discrimination and to tackle a perceived lack of support for cultural entrepreneurs from so-called 'diverse' backgrounds. In this chapter, I investigate the impact of 'diversity' and 'creative city' policies on black and ethnic minority cultural entrepreneurs. I interrogate local cultural policy by investigating how cultural entrepreneurs negotiate their position in a multicultural city and their experience of policy interventions aimed at diverse communities.

7.3   SUPER-DIVERSITY AND ENTREPRENEURSHIP

The context for this research is a multicultural city, described by some scholars as 'super-diverse'. The use of the term 'super-diverse' is not common but it has gained traction amongst academics who feel that it reflects contemporary society and demographic changes taking place in major British and European cities (Creese and Blackledge, 2018). When exploring super-diversity attention is drawn to the mix of individuals in a place: 'old' and 'new' international migrants, native established populations and resident minorities (Grzymala-Kazlowska and Phillimore, 2018). In this sense, super-diversity aligns itself with critical approaches which seek to gain a deeper understanding of the experiences of communities, acknowledging the tensions and contradictions. While the specific ethnicities of participants is not the subject of study, the idea of super-diverse communities offers a helpful context for an exploration of the lived experience of cultural entrepreneurship.

Evidence from the Global Entrepreneurship Monitor suggests that ethnic minorities and immigrants to the UK are twice as likely as white Britons to be early-stage entrepreneurs (Aston University, 2018). Discrimination and a lack of social capital are reasons for becoming self-employed, but motivation can also come from the potential financial rewards and wanting to make a difference to their community (Aston University, 2018). Despite the potential for a high number of cultural entrepreneurs from black, ethnic minority and immigrant groups, there is little data and understanding of their characteristics and of their experiences in relation to local cultural policies. In general, ethnic entrepreneurship is underresearched (Volery, 2007), and it is acknowledged that the term is problematic as it bundles together disparate groups only loosely connected by the idea of being 'other' from the dominant Western white norm. Ethnic community dynamics, characterised by culture, religion and social diversity of ethnic groups, differentiate ethnic entrepreneurs in complex ways (Kontos, 2007), but do policymakers acknowledge or understand this?

Support for entrepreneurship can be traced back to Thatcher's enterprise culture in the 1980s (Drakopoulou-Dodd and Anderson, 2001) through to Blair's New Labour policies. As Devins (2009) argues, this included a regional policy of promoting enterprise in deprived areas as a means of addressing both economic decline and social inclusion. For individuals from black, ethnic and migrant communities, cultural entrepreneurship might present the only or easiest way to engage in professional cultural production, specifically for those who appear to be 'hidden' from policymakers (Long and Warren, 2019). To interrogate cultural policies and gain insights into the experiences of black, ethnic and immigrant cultural entrepreneurs, this chapter focuses on a British city with a diverse multicultural population.

7.4   APPROACH

The data for this chapter is drawn from evaluations of projects supported by Birmingham City Council (BCC) which took place between 2016 and 2019, and which sought to address inequalities by targeting policy interventions at 'diverse' cultural workers. The findings are based on several evaluations, including the following funded programmes: ASTONish, RE:Present and the BAME[1] Arts Development Programme. I led a small team of researchers to produce the evaluations, which involved interviews, observations during training programmes, attending events, tracking social media discussions, online surveys and cultural policy documents such as Birmingham's *Cultural Strategy 2015–2019* and ACE's *The Creative Case for Diversity*. Other than RE:Present, all the programmes were focused on communities living and/or working in north Birmingham, defined by BCC boundary maps as the Aston, Newtown and Lozells areas. Some projects received additional funding from ACE and support through local universities in the form of venues, speakers and mentors.

For the BAME Arts Development Programme, our brief was to explore the impact of the projects and the degree to which the funding made a difference in terms of developing talent in cultural leadership and entrepreneurship, addressing barriers for cultural workers, and gaining an understanding of the relation between focusing on cultural support in specific geographical areas and cultural shifts within those areas. The team at BCC invited a robust and critical evaluation report, with the aim of obtaining real insights to inform future policies. This chapter combines the data from evaluating these local cultural policy interventions, to explore critical questions about the relationship between policy, locality and cultural entrepreneurs from diverse ethnic and migrant communities. The data analysis is framed by two theoretical debates: firstly, literature which highlights inequalities in the CCIs (Ahmed, 2012; Khan, 1976; Mirza, 2009); and secondly, the significance of place and the relationship between cultural work and location (Banks, 2006; Long and Warren, 2019; Naudin, 2018).

7.5   BIRMINGHAM'S SUPER-DIVERSITY

According to the Office for National Statistics, Birmingham's resident population was 1 137 100 in 2017, and based on the 2011 Census, international migration has increased the city's population (238 313 residents were born overseas from a wide range of countries including Poland, Pakistan, India, Romania and Somalia). While some parts of the city remain predominantly white, Aston and Newtown have a higher percentage of people born overseas.

In Aston, 43.7 per cent of the population were non-white, of which the largest ethnic group was Asian or Asian British ethnicity which made up 69.1 per cent of the local population, the second-largest being black or black British ethnicity which was 16.4 per cent (2011). Newtown had a population of 12 485, with black and black British being the highest ethnic group making up just over 39 per cent of the local population, followed by 29 per cent of Asian and Asian British ethnicity (2011). As a possible indication of wealth or status, Aston has over 50 per cent of households described as 'owner occupied', which compares to only 20 per cent of Newtown's households, where over 50 per cent are rented from the local authority. The 2011 Census demonstrates that 42 per cent of the population classified themselves as from an ethnic background other than white, and current trends suggest that Birmingham is soon to become a majority minority city (Birmingham City Council, 2018). In this case study, geographical areas within the city were important because the programmes we evaluated focused predominantly on Aston and Newtown, which as the data shows, have high numbers of people who describe themselves as being of either black and black British or Asian and Asian British ethnicity, as well as being areas with high levels of deprivation. It is within this super-diverse demographic context that policymakers are setting out cultural, social and economic priorities in contemporary European cities. And although statistical data demonstrates the super-diversity of Birmingham in terms of ethnic differences, it says little about the environment in which individuals live, work, experience and navigate the city as cultural entrepreneurs.

7.6   BIRMINGHAM'S CULTURAL POLICIES AND DIVERSITY

For a number of years, BCC set out the 'A Creative City' strategy, including policy interventions to reach wider markets, identifying skills gaps, providing a city-wide programme of business start-ups and campaigns to share best practice in the use of finance and availability of grants (Birmingham City Council, 2017). This took the form of cultural quarters, as evidence of how dedicated parts of the city can be identified as hubs or clusters of CCI activities: Digbeth/ Eastside and the Jewellery Quarter are good examples of this (Chapain and Comunian, 2010). Furthermore, a significant aspect of Birmingham's cultural distinction has been expressed through a celebration of its diversity in bids to be European Capital of Culture 2008 (BBC, 2003), and in the 2018 bid for Channel 4 to relocate its headquarters. But evidence from a local cultural entrepreneur suggests that there is a perception that funding in Birmingham tends to favour established arts organisations, with a lack of diversity in terms of their programmes, their leadership and the workforce (see blog posts by Hemmings, 2016 and Talwar, 2016). Although the BCC's website describes a vision for a successful local economy and engagement in the arts through activities co-designed with local residents, the city council also acknowledges that inequalities persist, particularly in Birmingham's most deprived neighbourhoods (Brookes et al., 2016).

In terms of Aston and Newtown, The Drum (opened in 1998) provided an intercultural arts centre and was perceived as a major cultural asset, serving north Birmingham communities. Built on the site of Aston Hippodrome, the venue reflected the already highly diverse communities in the area through a varied programme including drama, music, exhibitions, comedy and dance. It should be noted that the creation of The Drum was building on a rich history of black cultural talent based in north Birmingham, including bands such as Steel Pulse, the poet Benjamin Zephaniah, and organisations such as the Handsworth Cultural Centre, described in detail by Kieran Connell in his book *Black Handsworth* (Connell, 2019). The centre was originally established as the UK's national centre for black British and British Asian arts, but played a major role in serving local communities until its closure in 2016. Funding for BCC's BAME Arts Development Programme focused specifically on the gap created by the closure of The Drum (Laws, 2016), creating a policy intervention to target diverse cultural leaders, entrepreneurs and artists which might have benefited from the venue. In our interviews, cultural entrepreneurs discussed the significance of The Drum as a venue for the local black and ethnic minority community: for local audiences, cultural performers, artists and producers. As I have outlined, on the one hand BCC encouraged cultural entrepreneurship as part of its creative city agenda; on the other hand, a key venue and focal point for black and ethnic minority arts and culture was shut down, leaving a vacuum for local cultural activities.

7.7 THE HYPERLOCAL CONTEXT

Situated on the edges of Aston, The Drum separated Aston and Newtown from Birmingham city centre and all its cultural organisations, creating a kind of border or acting as a kind of gatekeeper. As one interviewee explained:

> I think there's still a lot of work to be done in Aston and Newtown and I think sometimes in our communities we're hung up on a building [The Drum], we're hung up on a provision specifically for us and I think sometimes that cuts you out of a whole other exciting network of stuff that's going on. (Interviewee 5)

This reveals the tensions and ambiguities which the closure of The Drum exposes for local audiences and cultural entrepreneurs alike. The Drum was celebrated as a showcase for local CCI work, but simultaneously restricted local cultural entrepreneurs, isolating them from the city centre and other prestigious venues or business opportunities. The closure of The Drum instigated the policy intervention made by BCC in collaboration with the ACE, realising the need to provide support and build capacity, particularly with black and ethnic minority cultural entrepreneurs and producers. The interviews which informed this study presented an opportunity to explore this intervention with participating cultural entrepreneurs. Locality begins to have meaning beyond geographical boundaries, and the concept of 'hyperlocal' can help us to challenge assumptions based on presumed notions of how culture is produced, consumed and valued. Although the term 'hyperlocal' tends to be used in relation to community journalism (Barnett and Townend, 2014), I am using it here to emphasise the close relationship between place-based cultural entrepreneurs, their relationship to their immediate locality (in contrast to the city centre initiatives) and local historical context. In the projects we evaluated, cultural entrepreneurs who live and/or work in Aston and Newtown felt a strong sense of commitment to their local community, describing city centre venues as 'mainstream' and making a distinction between spaces which they understand as not inclusive of their community:

> I've always been of the thinking that we need mainstream organisations to value what we offer as a cultural offer and to programme it within their walls, so that people in Birmingham, whether north, west, east, south, feel that they can go to mainstream venues and see work of quality and of value to their lives. I don't think you have to have a specific building in the north of Birmingham. I really think that's a ghettoisation of arts, I really do. (Interviewee 5)

Historically, the existence of The Drum created a focus for the local community, keeping other spaces and venues in a kind of hinterland, rendering them invisible, remote and beyond the reach of cultural entrepreneurs based in Aston and Newtown. Participants in our study appear to be disenfranchised from both cultural institutions and the cultural quarters which make up what the Warwick Commission report described as the 'UK's Cultural and Creative Industries Ecosystem derived from a richly diverse and multicultural society' (Warwick Commission, 2015: 18). Aston and Newtown are home to a rich mix of cultural enterprises (singers, poets, performers, visual artists, festival organisers, and so on), cultural traditions, histories and diverse values, but the co-dependency between practitioners tends to be limited to the area, to the hyperlocal:

> in Aston and Newtown, well I do challenge this idea that art is dead in that part of the city or is simmering. It is very much alive … There are so many musicians in Aston and Newtown, so many, who just don't crossover into the other spaces of the city. (Interviewee 7)

Whether borders and the lack of access to resources are imagined positions or not, cultural entrepreneurs from diverse ethnic and migrant communities experience their practice through the hyperlocal context, rather than as part of a wider 'creative city' agenda. They do not benefit or contribute to city centre economic development initiatives, part of creative city regeneration projects. Instead, their cultural work is undertaken in and around local communities, in venues for their community such as The Drum, but also in churches, schools, community centres and local parks. There is no sense that the participants in this study are not proud of their local cultural contribution, but they do demonstrate an awareness that they are left out of significant city centre activities: they 'don't crossover'.

7.8 HAND-HOLDING ACROSS IMAGINED BORDERS

In the context of this study, our evaluation described how individual projects were delivered by facilitators who could be described as cultural intermediaries: interpreting local policy initiatives as part of the training they offered, and acting as a bridge between structures and cultural entrepreneurs (Durrer and O'Brien, 2014). The role of cultural intermediaries appeared to be significant in two ways: through their access to networks, and in their ability to interpret local cultural policies for black and ethnic minority cultural entrepreneurs. Cultural intermediaries can be in powerful positions by shaping social interactions locally and deploying certain contacts to make introductions across networks or 'imagined borders'. For instance, between mainstream cultural institutions and cultural entrepreneurs from diverse ethnic and migrant communities, whose networks and contacts have been limited to Aston and Newtown. As interpreters of cultural policy initiatives, their role as intermediaries can influence models of work and create particular kinds of opportunities, often shaped by their own positions and dispositions. In a large city, cultural intermediaries arrive at the position by using symbolic strategies to secure their role as gatekeepers, opening doors for cultural entrepreneurs but also, potentially, restricting opportunities. A key aspect of the brokering role is a kind of 'cultural translation' of the language of cultural policy or cultural milieus, to support a cultural entrepreneur crossing over into a new spaces and networks. What was significant in this study was that cultural intermediaries had to acknowledge the 'imagined border' and demonstrate an 'authentic' acknowledgement of the kinds of barriers and challenges described by cultural entrepreneurs from ethnic and migrant communities:

> So, for me, knowing who the [the organiser] was, knowing the profile of some of the facilitators [cultural intermediaries], I thought, why not just challenge myself, to put myself in a different network, to see what I can learn, what I could gain. (Interviewee 9)

For cultural entrepreneurs disconnected from core structures, an introduction from a trusted individual is critical to mustering the courage to engage with unfamiliar organisations, ways of working and different cultural values (Belfiore, 2018). Having established a level of trust, there was evidence of cultural intermediaries becoming unofficial spokespeople for anything related to ethnic or migrant cultural workers, or as the 'go to' person for making connections. The outcome can be a sense that cultural entrepreneurs from diverse ethnic and migrant communities have been consulted when the 'go to' cultural intermediary is involved in discussions targeting any ethnic minorities, and an overreliance on very few individuals. Individual cultural intermediaries, however well intentioned, cannot represent a multiplicity of perspectives, knowledge, experience and understanding in a super-diverse environment. This resonates with Ahmed's discussion on 'institutionalising diversity', in which she explains that by being appointed into a position, people of colour feel that simply being there is enough, and that it represents the organisation's compliance with diversity policies, rather than being evidence of a real attempt to address inequalities in the workforce (Ahmed, 2012: 23). The following section investigates this issue from the perspective of UK cultural entrepreneurs, targeted by policymakers as ethnically diverse.

7.9   LIVING IN A TICK BOX AREA

As stated at the start of the chapter, the UK is relatively unusual in identifying ethnicity in most public policies and research, resulting in the use of the term 'BAME', which refers to 'black, Asian and minority ethnicity'. Many scholars have been critical of the use of terms such as 'diversity' and 'BAME' in cultural policy (Ahmed, 2007, 2012; Saha, 2017), but until recently, through campaigns such as BAMEOver, it was the preferred term used by policymakers. At a local level, some participants from Aston and Newtown were offended by these terms, and acknowledged that when public funding is directed at their area, there was a level of cynicism about the policy intervention:

> I feel like Aston and Newtown get a lot of organisations or people using them as a tick box area and so there's a lot of mistrust around whether the people coming in

are actually coming to try and actually make a difference or whether it's just because they've got funding to do so. (Interviewee 8)

Ahmed (2007) argues that although 'diversity' can unify, too often it tends to refer to poor individuals and suggests a state of being that is fixed, rather than pointing to underlying structural disadvantages, allowing racism and inequalities to be overlooked. We found BAME cultural entrepreneurs to be only too aware of being part of a 'tick box' exercise and, as a result, some interviewees engaged in the process of self-diversity making or diversifying themselves:

> We are diverse. Well, we're not diverse in one sense because we're all black women from the Caribbean, born here, you know, but we are in that box, aren't we, of diversity. (Interviewee 9)

When investigated in a local context, diversity policies seem to encourage an acceptance of social sorting, so that instead of addressing inequalities, the result is alienating and segregates communities. Amongst the black community, difference is also felt between cultural entrepreneurs from Africa, and black British Caribbean who are often second or third generation and whose cultural practice appears to be less 'exotic':

> What I get is if you are a Black artist from either the Caribbean or mainland Africa coming come here to do stuff you are more likely to get attention than if you are British born. I don't think anyone is particularly interested in the Black British voice because we are not exotic enough, we are not different enough, we don't have a separate language. (Interviewee 10)

The experience does not emerge overnight, but rather it is born out of years of being treated as 'other', as one interviewee explained: '[I] got sick 20 years ago of being the brown artist for Birmingham' (Interviewee 16, 2018). An understanding of this position is described by another interviewee, who recalls being suspicious of the programme we evaluated, based on his experience of previous policy interventions in the local area:

> So, I went really to the first meeting out of curiosity and just to ensure that it wasn't basically … keeping it honest, it wasn't just white, upper class organisation, that had come in, parachuted into the inner-city area to just take the money because, obviously, the Hippodrome got a large chunk of the money and we're not blind to that. So, I was quite concerned that quite a well-established, well-resourced organisation came in to almost just take the little scraps that the local community had. So, I kind of came with a frustration, agenda, if I be honest. (Interviewee 9)

We also found that having felt alienated from mainstream institutions and cultural policies, participants explained the problems they have in finding the right language to talk about their practice, in a way that is confident but not arrogant. This was discussed within the context of not always appreciating one's self-worth, and how that translates in financial terms when costing a cultural service or product. As the recipients of funding aimed at 'BAME' or 'diverse' individuals, it is easy to see that cultural entrepreneurs might feel targeted as a means of box ticking rather than for their potential talent or cultural contribution, resulting in this lack of confidence. It seems particularly shocking when, as discussed earlier in this chapter, black and ethnic minority communities in north Birmingham have been engaging in internationally renowned cultural production since the 1970s and 1980s. But as Connell (2019) points out, the relationship to state funding might explain the vulnerability of local infrastructure, while perpetuating a sense of being part of a box ticking exercise.

7.10   CONCLUSION

It is over 40 years since Naseem Khan's (1976) influential report, *The Arts Britain Ignores*, charted the range of arts practices amongst ethnic minority communities that were invisible and unsupported by national institutions. How much has changed since then? This chapter explores locality as central to understanding how cultural policies can address or exacerbate inequalities in the cultural workforce, specifically for entrepreneurial modes of work. The cultural entrepreneurs from ethnic and migrant communities in this study benefited from the policy intervention that we evaluated, but the research uncovered entrenched problems, beyond an assessment of the programme. We found that the programme of activities had a positive impact, but through our evaluation, participants revealed a more complex picture rooted in location. The experiences of those we interviewed appeared to be linked to a historical relationship between publicly funded cultural policy interventions in north Birmingham and local communities. We uncovered an underlying lack of appreciation for the barriers and challenges faced by diverse urban communities, in contrast with other CCI workers engaged in city centre initiatives. It could be argued that cultural entrepreneurs from ethnic and migrant communities were not perceived to be part of the city's economic development plan. Simultaneously, there is a need for a more nuanced understanding of the experiences of individuals in super-diverse cities, a need to respect how barriers constrain and the degree to which this is felt by a community, in a well-defined part of the city. While local policymakers should aim to reach a broad range of talent, this should be supported with a more astute understanding of diverse communities, including consideration of networks, values, barriers and histories. For cities across Europe, the impact of demographic changes in the population is difficult, and a lack of resources will exacerbate the challenge.

A starting point could be recognising the barriers and complexities, as demonstrated by the role of the cultural intermediary, and an openness to re-evaluate underlying values in public policies (Belfiore, 2018; Saha, 2017). However, cultural intermediation cannot be left to a few individuals; rather, the process should recognise the full breadth of super-diversity in the community, including the hyperlocal context, and engage in multiple-level 'translation' and relationship building for the city's CCIs. Cultural entrepreneurs do not operate in a vacuum, and local policymakers need to appreciate the connections between super-diverse communities, locality, structure and the values which underpin these relationships.

NOTE

1. The use of the term 'BAME' in this chapter refers specifically to the title of the Birmingham City Council programme. The author wishes to acknowledge the BAMEOver campaign and the unhelpful way in which the acronym blends ethnicity, geography and nationality, and in doing so reduces people to 'other'.

BIBLIOGRAPHY

Ahmed, S. (2007), 'You end up doing the document rather than doing the doing: diversity, race equality and the politics of documentation', *Ethnic and Racial Studies*, 30 (4), 590–609.

Ahmed, Sara (2012), *On Being Included: Racism and Diversity in Institutional Life.* Durham, NC: Duke University Press.

Aston University (2018), 'Immigrants "twice as entrepreneurial as white Britons"', https://www2.aston.ac.uk/news/releases/2018/july/immigrants-twice-as-entrepren eurial-as-white-britons (accessed 15 July 2018).

Banks, Mark (2006), 'Moral economy and cultural work', *Sociology*, 40 (3), 455–472.

Banks, M. and J. O'Connor (2017), 'Inside the whale (and how to get out of there): moving on from two decades of creative industries research', *European Journal of Cultural Studies*, 20 (6), 637–654.

Barnett, S. and J. Townend (2014), 'Plurality, policy and the local', *Journalism Practice*, 9 (3), 332–349. Doi.org/10.1080/17512786.2014.943930.

BBC (2003), 'Birmingham's highlights', http://www.bbc.co.uk/birmingham/capital_of _culture/highlights.shtml (accessed 15 July 2018).

Belfiore, E. (2018), 'Whose cultural value? Representation, power and creative industries', *International Journal of Cultural Policy*, 26 (3), 383–397, doi.org/10.1080/ 10286632.2018.1495713.

Bell, David and Kate Oakley (2015), *Cultural Policy.* London: Routledge.

Birmingham City Council (2017), '£500,000 awarded for Aston & Newton arts projects', https://www.birmingham.gov.uk/news/article/51/500000_awarded_for_aston _and_newton_arts_projects (accessed 15 July 2018).

Birmingham City Council (2018), 'Community Cohesion Strategy for Birmingham Green Paper: forward together to build a fair and inclusive city for everyone', https://www.birminghambeheard.org.uk/economy/community-cohesionstrategy/ supporting_documents/Birmingham%20Community%20Cohesion%20Strategy %20Green%20Paper%20%20FINAL.pdf (accessed 15 July 2018).

Blommaert, Jan, Massimiliano Spotti and Jef Van der Aa (2017), *Complexity, Mobility, Migration*. London: Routledge.

Brookes, N., J. Kendall and L. Mitton (2016), 'Birmingham, priority to economics, social innovation at the margins', in T. Brandsen, S. Cattacin, A. Evers and A. Zimmer (eds), *Social Innovations in the Urban Context* (pp. 83–96). Cham: Springer International Publishing.

Chapain, C. and R. Comunian (2010), 'Enabling and inhibiting the creative economy: the role of the local and regional dimensions in England', *Regional Studies*, 44 (6), 717–734.

Collis, C., E. Felton and P. Graham (2010), 'Beyond the inner city: real and imagined places in creative place policy and practice', *Information Society*, 26 (2), 104–112.

Connell, Kieran (2019), *Black Handsworth: Race in 1980s Britain*. Oakland, CA: University of California Press.

Creese, Angela and Adrian Blackledge (eds) (2018), *The Routledge Handbook of Language and Superdiversity*. London: Routledge.

Devins, D. (2009), 'Enterprise in deprived areas: what role for start-ups?', *International Journal of Entrepreneurship and Small Business*, 8 (4), 486–498.

Drakopoulou-Dodd, S. and A.R. Anderson (2001), 'Understanding the enterprise culture: paradigm, paradox and policy', *International Journal of Entrepreneurship and Innovation*, 2 (1), 13–26.

Durrer, Victoria and Dave O'Brien (2014), 'Arts promotion', in Jennifer Smith Maguire and Julian Matthews (eds), *The Cultural Intermediaries Reader* (pp. 100–112). London: SAGE Publishing.

Ellmeier, A. (2003), 'Cultural entrepreneurialism: on changing the relationship between the arts, culture and employment', *International Journal of Cultural Policy*, 9 (1), 3–16.

Geldorf, Dirk (2016), *Superdiversity in the Heart of Europe: How Migration Changes Our Society*. Leuven: Acco.

Gill, R. (2002), 'Cool, creative and egalitarian? Exploring gender in project-based new media work', *Information, Communication and Society*, 5 (1), 70–89.

Granovetter, M. (1973), 'The strength of weak ties', *American Journal of Sociology*, 78 (6), 1360–1380.

Grzymala-Kazlowska, A. and J. Phillimore (2018), 'Introduction: rethinking integration. New perspectives on adaptation and settlement in the era of diversity', *Journal of Ethnic and Migration Studies*, 44 (2), 179–196.

Hammonds, W. and L. Bhandal (2010), 'Where to next for diversity? An assessment of Arts Council England's race equality and cultural diversity policies and emerging trends', *Journal for Policy Research in Tourism, Leisure and Events*, 3 (2), 187–200.

Hemmings, R. (2016), 'Birmingham's big problem', *Arts Professional*, https://www.artsprofessional.co.uk/magazine/blog/birminghams-big-problem (accessed 5 August 2017.

Khan, Naseem (1976), *The Arts Britain Ignores: The Arts of Ethnic Minorities in Britain*. London: Community Relations Commission.

Kontos, Michalis (2007), 'Immigrant entrepreneurs in Germany', in Leo-Paul Dana (ed.), *Handbook of Research on Ethnic Minority Entrepreneurship: A Co-evolutionary View on Resource Management* (pp. 445–463). Cheltenham, UK and Northampton, MA, USA: Edward Elgar Publishing.

Landry, Charles (2008), *The Creative City: A Toolkit for Urban Innovators*. London: Routledge.

Laws, R. (2016), 'The Drum arts centre in Aston set to close down after funding crisis', https://www.birminghammail.co.uk/whats-on/drum-arts-centre-aston-set-11124615 (accessed 15 July 2018).

Leadbeater, Charles and Kate Oakley (1999), *The Independents*. London: Demos.

Loaker, B. (2013), 'Becoming "culturpreneur": how the "neoliberal regime of truth" affects and redefines artistic positions', *Culture and Organization*, 19 (2), 124–145.

Long, Paul and Annette Naudin (2019), 'Producing values: Impact Hub Birmingham as co-working and social innovation space', in Rosalind Gill, Andrew Pratt and Tarek Virani (eds), *Creative Hubs in Question: Dynamics of Virtual Work* (pp. 211–227). Cham: Palgrave Macmillan.

Long, Paul and Saskia Warren (2019), 'An area lacking cultural activity researching cultural lives in Urban Space', in Paul Jones, Beth Perry and Paul Long (eds), *Cultural Intermediaries Connecting Communities* (pp. 97–114). Bristol University Press.

McRobbie, Angela (2002), 'From Holloway to Hollywood: happiness at work in the new cultural economy', in Paul Du Gay and Michael Pryke (eds), *Cultural Economy* (pp. 97–115). London: SAGE.

McRobbie, A. (2011), 'Re-thinking creative economy as radical social enterprise', http://www.variant.org.uk/ (accessed 15 July 2018).

Mirza, M. (2009), 'Aims and contradictions of cultural diversity policies in the arts: a case study of the Rich Mix Centre in East London', *International Journal of Cultural Policy*, 15 (1), 53–69.

Naudin, Annette (2018), *Cultural Entrepreneurship: The Cultural Worker's Experience of Entrepreneurship*. London: Routledge.

Oakley, K. (2011), 'In its own image: New Labour and the cultural workforce', *Cultural Trends*, 20 (3–4), 281–289, DOI: 10.1080/09548963.2011.589709.

Oakley, Kate (2014), 'Good work? Rethinking cultural entrepreneurship', in Chris Bilton and Stephen Cummings (eds), *Handbook of Management and Creativity* (pp. 145–159). Cheltenham, UK and Northampton, MA, USA: Edward Elgar Publishing.

Oakley, K. (2016), 'Whose creative economy? Inequality and the need for international approaches', *Les Enjeux de l'information et de la communication*, 17 (2), 163–171.

O'Brien, D. and K. Oakley (2015), 'Cultural value and inequality: a critical literature review', https://ahrc.ukri.org/documents/project-reports-and-reviews/cultural-value-and-inequality-a-critical-literature-review/ (accessed 15 July 2018).

Pratt, A.C. (2008), 'Creative cities?', *Urban Design Journal*, 105 (Spring), 35.

Pratt, A.C. (2011), 'The cultural contradictions of the creative city', *City, Culture and Society*, 2 (3), 123–130.

Saha, Anamik (2017), *Race and the Cultural Industries*. Cambridge: Polity Press.

Shane, S. (2009), 'Why enouraging more people to become entrepreneurs is bad public policy', *Small Business Economics*, 33 (2), 141–149.

Talwar, A. (2016), 'White noise: improving diversity in the arts', *Arts Professional*, https://www.artsprofessional.co.uk/magazine/blog/white-noise (accessed 5 December 2017).

Volery, Thierry (2007), 'Ethnic entrepreneurship: a theoretical framework', in Dana Leo-Paul (ed.), *Handbook of Research on Ethnic Minority Entrepreneurship: A Co-evolutionary View on Resource Management* (pp. 30–41). Cheltenham, UK and Northampton, MA, USA: Edward Elgar Publishing.

Warwick Commission (2015), *Enriching Britain: Culture, Creativity and Growth*, Warwick: The Warwick Commission Report on the Future of Cultural Value.

8. Creative entrepreneurship in 2022 and beyond: some implications for higher education

Ruth Bridgstock

8.1 INTRODUCTION

Nearly ten years ago I wrote a conceptual journal article named 'Not a dirty word: arts entrepreneurship and higher education' for the *Journal of Arts and Humanities in Higher Education* (Bridgstock 2013). At that time, entrepreneurship was gaining a presence in higher education creative degree programmes in the United Kingdom (UK) and Australia. In part, it was finding purchase in curricula because of scrutiny around graduate outcomes and, in some institutions, creative industries discourse. However, there was still a sense that by addressing entrepreneurship in creative degrees, universities might be compromising their commitment to disciplinary depth and critical engagement for instrumental graduate outcomes and neoliberalism. Some were worried that the art school and conservatoire were being invaded by the business school, bringing with it curricula of questionable relevance to creative practice, and a profit motive at odds with deeply held creative values.

In that article my intention was to reassure creative practitioners and educators that there are ways of thinking about creative entrepreneurship that are actually highly congruent with the creative ethos. My argument was that all creative practitioners are entrepreneurs (whether pushed or pulled to it), and all can learn to hone these capabilities for their benefit. A pragmatic approach does not absolve governments of responsibility to support a strong subsidized arts sector, or regulate for fair working conditions. Nor does it condone precarious labour and exploitative working practices. In the article I also argued that it did not seem appropriate for most students of creative practice to learn entrepreneurship skills through courses that do not address the nuances of creative practice and contexts.

In this chapter I take my 2013 article as a base and explore how thinking and practice in creative entrepreneurship has changed and developed over the last decade. I consider shifts to creative entrepreneurship because of networks, the fourth industrial age and what this means for creative entrepreneurship education going forward.

8.2   CREATIVE ENTREPRENEURSHIP: ONGOING DEFINITIONAL ISSUES AND A PRAGMATIC APPROACH

Entrepreneurship has now become a fairly mature area of research in business. Entrepreneurship research relating to specific sectors and disciplines remains much less well established. For example, Hausmann and Heinze (2016) reviewed 50 articles relating to creative, cultural and arts entrepreneurship, and found little consensus around definitions of entrepreneurship. Scholars tended to agree with the broad idea that creative entrepreneurship relates to the creation of novel or innovative ideas, products or services, and then bringing them to markets or audiences in some way. However, they differ widely in terms of emphasis on different entrepreneurial processes (for example, innovation or project management of events or business start-up), locations of entrepreneurship (inside organizations or freelance) and scale (for example, individuals or organizations or cities).

Another area of contention in the creative entrepreneurship literature is concerned with whether the subject of enquiry is entrepreneurship as it relates to the cultural industries, the creative industries or the arts. The distinctions between these terms and associated practices and sectors continue to be somewhat blurry, but they point to a diversity of creative practice that can be concerned with economic, cultural or other outcomes (or indeed a combination of these), and might occur in all kinds of places inside or outside organizations in different industry sectors. Creative practice can be publicly subsidized or not, and it can produce products/artefacts, services and experiences, or indeed contribute creative value to other products, services or experiences. The diversity just described is an important and distinctive feature of creative entrepreneurship and has implications for creative entrepreneurship education, as will be discussed further below.

This chapter takes a pragmatic approach to definitional issues. It will engage with, and emphasize, aspects of creative entrepreneurship that are of relevance to creative practitioners, and educators who are tasked with fostering practitioner capabilities for creative entrepreneurship. Individual creative practitioners may well work within, across and even outside creative and/or cultural industries. Different students in the same degree cohort may end up working in vastly different contexts, with different aims and different outcomes. It makes sense to acknowledge and cater to this diversity rather than educating for a sub-set of possibilities.

In my 2013 article I outlined three senses in which creative entrepreneurship seems to be relevant to practitioners and educators: creative entrepreneurship as 'new venture creation', involving venture start-up and management; 'being enterprising', recognizing or creating an opportunity to add creative value of some kind; and career self-management and being employable. The three senses have much in common. For instance, in order to build a sustainable creative career (career self-management), a creative practitioner may establish a new business or organization (new venture creation), which meets the needs of markets or audiences and adds a certain type of aesthetic, cultural or experiential creative value (being enterprising). Each of these senses will be explored briefly in the next sections of this chapter.

8.3 CREATIVE ENTREPRENEURSHIP AS NEW VENTURE CREATION

The 'new venture creation' sense is a traditional view which corresponds the most closely to laypeople's notions of entrepreneurship. New venture creation encompasses activities documented by Hausmann and Heinze's (2016, p. 11) review which included 'creat(ing) a micro-business', 'starting a not-for-profit organisation', and the establishment of 'economically sustainable cultural enterprises'. New venture creation entrepreneurship education involves students learning skills and knowledge for starting and growing a creative enterprise, including legal issues, sales and marketing, finance and business strategy (Burns 2017). In studies of creative practitioners' reflections on their initial training, new venture creation skills are most commonly cited as needed but deficient or missing in degree programmes (Hennekam and Bennett 2017; Haukka 2011).

New venture creation capabilities seem to be important to many creative practitioners. More than one-third of all job roles in the UK creative and cultural industries are self-employed job roles rather than employee job roles (Department for Digital, Culture, Media and Sport 2019), compared with about 16 per cent across the economy. In the United States Bureau of Labor Statistics (Vilorio 2018) data suggests that 44 per cent of creative roles in that country are self-employed or freelance. Some types of creative practitioners are more likely to be self-employed than others: in Australia, for instance, the most recent iteration of Throsby and Petetskaya's (2017) survey of artists' careers, *Making Art Work*, showed that more than 80 per cent of practising professional arts practitioners in that country were self-employed in their principal artistic occupation, whereas the self-employment rate across creative occupations is closer to 30 per cent.

Many emerging creative practitioners will find foundational training in new venture creation and management skills beneficial. However, they may not need in-depth skills in all aspects of their ventures. Bridgstock et al. (2011) found that of the outstandingly successful artists and designers that they studied, the majority of participants were strategic in choosing to not engage with the 'on the ground' activities of venture creation and management. Rather, they knew enough about these topics to work effectively with specialists in these areas. They also fostered professional relationships with these specialists. From the findings of these case studies, many practitioners may require business basics only, along with skills in their creative disciplines and the ability to network professionally (Bridgstock et al. 2011). Specialist business topics such as taxation law or accrual accounting may not need to be included in creative entrepreneurship curricula.

8.4   CREATIVE ENTREPRENEURSHIP AS 'BEING ENTERPRISING'

Creative entrepreneurship education initiatives that target broader capabilities, such as opportunity recognition, knowledge creation or resilience, are prioritizing the 'being enterprising' sense of creative entrepreneurship. This 'being enterprising' sense of creative entrepreneurship is concerned with the identification of creative opportunities, and the exploitation of those opportunities in order to add creative value (Scott 2012). The value can be financial, cultural or social (Bacigalupo et al. 2016).

Creative entrepreneurship in the enterprising sense is closely related to notions of creativity and innovation in the literature. For instance, in Hausmann and Heinze's (2016) review, they found references in creative entrepreneurship literature to expressions such as 'novel ideas', 'innovations or improvements of existing offerings' and 'innovative applications'. It can occur within self-employment or while working as an employee, through the phenomenon of intrapreneurship, where entrepreneurial behaviour occurs inside existing firms, through doing new things, departing from the customary or pursuing innovative opportunities (Antoncic and Hisrich 2003).

One might wonder what differentiates the creative entrepreneur from creative practitioners in general. By definition, all practitioners are creative. My suggestion in response would be that it is opportunity identification and the creation of value that differentiates entrepreneurial creative practice from creative practice in general. Enterprising creative practitioners are outwardly engaged, at least to some extent, looking for opportunities to apply their creative disciplinary skills and to find a market or audience.

Many lists of attributes for successful entrepreneurship in the enterprise sense exist, and some of these may have applicability to creative entrepreneurship. These lists tend to emphasize either qualities (such as determination or prosociality) or broad meta-theoretical constructs involving higher-level cognitive, affective and behavioural processes. 'Five minds for the entrepreneurial future' (Duening 2010) provides a very broad theoretical framework of transferable capabilities for success in entrepreneurship in the enterprise sense that may be used to inform creative entrepreneurship education, as the constructs can be adapted to different creative practices and contexts. Duening's enterprising 'minds' are: (1) The Opportunity Recognizing Mind; (2) The Designing Mind; (3) The Risk Managing Mind; (4) The Resilient Mind; and (5) The Effectuating Mind.

First, the Opportunity Recognizing Mind identifies distinctive patterns in the practitioner's context (such as audience behaviour, collaborator availability or resources) as creating an opportunity. The Designing Mind then moves to exploit that opportunity, by creating a new creative product or service, or redesigning a product or service to meet that opportunity. The Risk Managing Mind minimizes risk in the venture, through internal (adaptation) strategies, or external (management) strategies such as diversifying investors. The Resilient Mind is responsible for emotional, financial and reputational rebounding from failure. Finally, the Effectuating Mind undertakes focused and goal-directed action, to ensure that the venture (or project, or idea) becomes reality.

8.5   CREATIVE ENTREPRENEURSHIP AS CAREER SELF-MANAGEMENT AND EMPLOYABILITY

The third sense of creative entrepreneurship relates to the practitioner's ability to repeatedly acquire or create work and build a sustainable career through career self-management. Career management is the process of managing the interaction of work, learning and other aspects of life in intentional ways throughout life (Haines et al. 2003). It occurs through an ongoing process of decision-making, evaluation and reflection, based on knowledge of industry and the world of work and awareness of one's own values, needs and skills (Bridgstock 2009). In some ways effective career self-management mirrors creative enterprise, in that it involves recognizing and making the most of opportunities in value-congruent ways, although the opportunities are about work creation or education and training. Also, like enterprise, career self-management can require adaptation to meet changes in the world of work and individual needs over the life span. It relies on specific knowledge of sector-specific nuances and protocols around gaining work.

Creative work is characterized by portfolio working, in which individuals are involved in 'multiple work and/or development activities simultaneously' (Pollard 2013, p. 54), which may include concurrent or overlapping work as an employee, self-employment and education/training activities inside or outside the practitioner's creative work. In some other occupations, people can still rely on organizational or professional structures for career development and progression. However, creative practitioners tend to have the individual responsibility for continually obtaining or creating employment, so it makes sense that possessing developed career management skills would be beneficial. In Bridgstock (2011) I provided empirical support for this. I conducted survey-based research into the capabilities and career outcomes of beginning and established creative practitioners. This research found that the propensity and ability to career self-manage was positively related to both objective (for example, earnings) and subjective (for example, career satisfaction) measures of career success.

From the above discussion it can be seen that most creative practitioners will need to be entrepreneurial, at least to some extent, in all three senses of the term. They are responsible for their own career development, which often involves an unfolding portfolio of work at least in part conducted through self-employment. Creative work will always involve creating value of some kind, through identifying and then exploiting opportunities.

It might be assumed that creative entrepreneurship looks similar for all practitioners. In fact, creative entrepreneurship is enormously diverse and heterogeneous, in terms of the sectors, places and contexts where practitioners work; the fields and types of practice they engage in; and the kinds of creative value that they add. As Rae (2005: 186) states, 'creative entrepreneurs are diverse, from self-employed artists to owners of global businesses'. Diversity in entrepreneurial practice is found in other sectors and industries, but it is a defining feature of creative entrepreneurship and it has important implications for education, which needs to cater to this diversity. Creative entrepreneurship is distinctive because of value chains, labour processes, demand for creative outputs, the regulatory environment and the diversity of products/ services (Caves 2000). The next section of this chapter explores the distinctive and diverse features of creative entrepreneurship, including the contextual and industry sectoral features of creative work, the processes of creative work, the kinds of value that creative work can add, and the motivations and identities of the practitioner.

8.6   DISTINCTIVE FEATURES OF CREATIVE ENTREPRENEURSHIP

Creative Motivations and Identities

The first distinctive feature of creative entrepreneurship relates to the motivations and identities of practitioners. In contrast to the stereotype of the business entrepreneur, who aspires to venture success and profit as an outcome, it has been argued that creative practitioners have 'protean careers' (Waters et al. 2015) and tend to aspire to the achievement of personally determined goals such as career sustainability and outcomes of practice, rather than profit. It must also be acknowledged that entrepreneurs in all sectors and industries bring a variety of motivations and aspirations to their work; but the personal identities of creative practitioners are often distinctively tied closely with their creative practices. The protean career involves: (1) strong intrinsic motivations for, and personal identification with, career (Hall 2004); and (2) personal construction of career and recurrent acquisition or creation of work (which is likely to occur on a freelance or self-employment basis). A highly distinctive feature of creative careers is a blurring of the boundaries between life and work (Leadbeater and Oakley 1999).

The creative protean career has been documented as being underpinned by intrinsic motivations including doing what the practitioner loves, meeting complex challenges and developing their skills. However, creative practition- ers also report extrinsic motivations such as contributing to their discipline or to the community, and seeking peer or audience recognition (Bartleet et al. 2020). Of course, there are also some creative artists who are strongly moti- vated by profit. For instance, Warhol famously stated: 'making money is art and working is art and good business is the best art'.

Entrepreneurs are often thought of as 'pulled' to entrepreneurship, driven by challenge or innovation. By contrast, creative practitioners are suggested to be 'pushed' to entrepreneurship through necessity in the context of 'precarious- ness and constraint' (Oakley 2013), and may have minimal 'natural' inclina- tion towards business ownership or commercial endeavours. This has led some scholars to argue that creative practitioners who have never shown interest in being self-employed, but are instead adapting their work to their contexts, are not entrepreneurs (Leadbeater and Oakley 1999).

The possession of an adaptive and adaptable entrepreneurial identity is central to developing the mindsets and practices of creative entrepreneurship (Werthes et al. 2017; Bridgstock 2013). Werthes et al. (2017) suggested that it is possible for creative practitioners to develop meta-identities that reconcile the creative and entrepreneurial. In Gotsi et al.'s (2010) terms, they become 'practical artists' (or perhaps pragmatic artists), who exercise creativity with some autonomy, but within constraints and parameters of context. Rather than being resistant to this, they seem to be reasonably happy to accommodate and reconcile their experiences. Crucial for creative entrepreneurship educators to note is that this process of identity development occurs through entrepreneurial experience, interaction with other creative entrepreneurs and reflection.

Creative Practice, Social Networks, Bricolage and Co-creation

Related to the notion of the practical or pragmatic creative identity which prac- tices within constraints is the entrepreneurial behaviour of bricolage, argued to be an important element of both opportunity identification and effectuation (bringing creative ideas to fruition) (de Klerk 2015). Bricolage is about making the most of whichever resources are at hand to meet opportunities or solve problems. Entrepreneurial bricolage often relies upon social capital (Valliere and Gegenhuber 2014) in the context of resource constraints. De Klerk points out that in creative practice, bricolage is often collaborative and transcends short-term project goals to meet longer-term visions via mentoring and supporting one another, and sharing resources. Bricolage is one way that practitioners tackle the challenge of precarious work: they share with, and nurture, one another towards future goals, even in the face of significant competition for creative work.

It can be seen that social networks and interaction with other practitioners are beneficial to entrepreneurship in terms of identity development and resource acquisition. Social networks are central to creative practice in terms of direct creative collaboration as well. It is the combination and recombination of people, perspectives and creative contributions in project teams through networks that has long been recognized as a distinctive feature of creative practice, and a key driver of innovation. The phenomenon can extend to co-creation and co-evolution with audiences and consumers, a phenomenon that has been extensively documented in digital media practice (Malmelin and Villi 2017) and the performing arts (Heim 2016).

Multiple Bottom Lines and Hybrid Enterprises

Related to the previously discussed creative protean career, with its emphasis on individual motivations for career, is the next distinctive feature of creative entrepreneurship: multiple bottom lines. Creative practitioners often balance multiple aims and purposes in their work, and there can be tensions between these goals and outcomes that the practitioner negotiates in an ongoing way (Neck et al. 2009). Juggling and blending multiple entrepreneurial bottom lines is central to creative entrepreneurship and the successful creative career (Caves 2000). The ability to practice in a value-congruent way that meets one's personal needs, and also makes the most of opportunities to add creative value in different ways, is a challenging balancing act that is central to creative practice, yet it is often not explicit and it is rarely addressed in creative entrepreneurship education programmes.

The idea of multiple bottom lines in creative practice has some congruence with triple bottom line theory in the business literature, which captures values and criteria for venture success beyond the commercial, and has been a part of the entrepreneurship literature since the late 1990s. Arising out of the corporate social responsibility movement, multiple bottom line theory suggests that enterprises can and should add economic, social and environmental value concurrently (Elkington 1998). Hawkes (2001) augmented triple bottom line theory with a fourth bottom line that can be of relevance to creative practice: that of culture (or cultural vitality). Chell (2007) points out that even quadruple bottom line theory misses important potential outcomes of creative entrepreneurship, such as belongingness, community, friendship and development of one's capabilities.

Just as creative entrepreneurs can juggle and blend multiple entrepreneurial bottom lines, their portfolio career arrangements mean that they can also practice across government subsidized creative activities and commercialized creative activities, either concurrently or on an overlapping basis. There are significant differences between ventures in a subsidized context and ventures in a commercial context. For instance, a commercially orientated practitioner may need to know about raising finance and venture capital, small business taxation and intellectual property law; whereas an artist working in a subsidized context will need to know about grantsmanship and cultural stakeholder management. This means that creative practitioners may need to be at least somewhat across both types of entrepreneurship, as well as at least some of the legal complexities of managing both at once (although, as previously pointed out, they may be able to rely on their networks for in-depth legal advice). In some respects, there are parallels to this distinction in terms of hybrid business models involving commercial and social entrepreneurship elsewhere (Chell 2007), but what is consistently different about creative practice is that in the context of creative work, engaging in subsidized and commercial creative activities at once can be very common, and provide a way to build the sustainability of the enterprise. For instance, the creative director of a performing arts production company might apply for a grant to stage an experimental theatre piece, at the same time as staging a commercial cabaret show, and offering events management services and equipment hire.

Intrapreneurship and Entrepreneurship

Census analysis of creative employment in Australia and the UK indicates that one-third of creative practitioners work as employees 'embedded' outside the creative sectors, in sectors as diverse as government, education or healthcare (Digital Media Research Centre 2018). These census analyses have strong implications for creative entrepreneurship education. Embedded creative practitioners have the same job titles as creative practitioners working in the creative sectors, but their working contexts, skill requirements, career configurations, working and social networks, and trajectories are distinctive (Hearn et al. 2014).

Embedded creative practitioners are employed to provide creative expertise, often by large firms where the core business is non-creative, whereas those in the creative sectors tend to be self-employed, or employed in a micro-business or small or medium-sized enterprise alongside other practitioners. Embedded creative practitioners are more likely to be employed on an ongoing part-time or full-time basis, and they earn more than their creative sector counterparts. For the embedded creative worker, the 'client' who provides the task brief may often be intra-firm; whereas for the specialist creative, the client is always external to the firm. Of course, creative practitioners can and often do work concurrently across embedded and specialist employment arrangements, and this can be a risk management strategy for the portfolio career, with embedded work providing some stability and security.

Creative practitioners may also work in 'non-creative' roles either within or outside creative sectors, and there can be creative intrapreneurship opportunities in this work as well. Bridgstock and Cunningham (2016) report on a longitudinal study of more than 900 creative graduates up to six years after undergraduate course completion. An unexpected finding was that more than half of those engaged in 'non-creative' work were nonetheless using the creative disciplinary skills they had acquired during creative degrees. Examples from the study included the administrative assistant who designed the company website, ran their social media marketing campaign or designed and wrote the marketing materials; or the retail worker who designed store displays.

Opportunity Creation

The final key distinctive feature of creative entrepreneurship relates to opportunity and risk, and the fact that the appeal of creative products and services is often not predictable (Caves 2000). Sarasvathy et al. (2005) conceptualize opportunity identification as falling somewhere on the scale from low-risk opportunity recognition, to medium-risk opportunity discovery, to high-risk opportunity creation. At one end of the continuum, opportunity recognition involves known supply and known demand, such as in franchising.[1] In the middle, there is opportunity discovery, with some degree of either known supply or demand. At the other end of the spectrum, there is opportunity creation, with unknown supply and demand; that is, a new product/service, perhaps also with some uncertainty around resourcing, and unknown demand. It can be argued that creative entrepreneurship more often corresponds with the high-risk opportunity creation category, with practitioners creating something new that may or may not find audience appeal.

This means that there can be significant uncertainty in creative entrepreneurship, and a high degree of personally adopted risk, particularly for creative practitioners in self-employment or small enterprise contexts. In Duening's (2010) terms, creative entrepreneurs will often need to have highly developed Risk-Managing and Resilient Minds: they will need to be adaptable and responsive to early warning signals, and recover well from failure. High risk has led to the development of personal risk management strategies such as the embedded portfolio career described above, where practitioners ensure that they have a steady income at the same time as engaging in higher-risk creative ventures on a self-employment basis. Creative entrepreneurs also risk manage through diversification of resourcing, such as through bricolage, described above, and through ensuring agility in their creative processes. In Duening's (2010) terms, the Designing Mind helps to ensure that the creation of both creative products and services and the creative enterprises themselves will be successful, by engaging in rapid creative prototyping and testing, often in partnership with audiences or consumers, with investment in each single prototype minimized, and with each successive iteration inching towards a successful outcome.

It can be seen that creative entrepreneurship is distinctive, and can require advanced skills because creative work is by its nature highly creative (and therefore risky), because resources can be scarce, because creative work is collaborative and networked, and because the practitioner's personal identity is often caught up in their practice. Leadbeater and Oakley (1999) discuss creative entrepreneurs as blurring demarcation lines between consumption and production, work and non-work, individualism and collaboration. Recently, creative entrepreneurship practice has also been affected by rapid technological change and other twenty-first-century influences, discussed briefly in the next section.

8.7   CREATIVE ENTREPRENEURSHIP IN 2021

A discussion of creative entrepreneurship written in the year 2021 would not be complete without some treatment of the impact of the fourth industrial revolution (Schwab 2016). The fourth industrial revolution literature suggests that we stand on the brink of an era in which artificial intelligence (AI), automation, robots and digital networks will transform the way we live, work and learn. Some writing in this category contains deterministic predictions of 'robots coming for our jobs', arguing that between 20 and 60 per cent of job roles will disappear over the coming decades under the influence of automation, robotics and AI. Others emphasize the creation of entirely new jobs that are based on technological advances. A third category of future-focused literature emphasizes qualitative and task-based changes to job roles.

Creativity is one category of capability that has been suggested to be uniquely human, or at least less susceptible to automation than other categories (Bakhshi et al. 2015). In turn, job roles that involve significant creativity may also be less susceptible to automation. According to some sources, and in line with contemporary arguments about the creative economy (Bakhshi et al.

2015), such job roles may add greater value in the future world of work than other kinds of roles.

This is not to suggest that creative practice will be less precarious in the future. If we take media industries as being one of the first sectors to be disrupted by technology in this way, we have actually seen an increase in self-employment and project-based work over the last few years. This is because of a combination of factors such as changing consumer behaviour, regulatory uncertainty, ubiquitous connectivity and amateur content creation, facilitated by digital networks and the internet (World Economic Forum 2020).

Precarity has been intensified by the Covid-19 pandemic, which has had an enormous impact on how creative work is undertaken, business models and revenue streams, access to audiences and, for many, ongoing viability (Comunian and England 2020). Comunian and England (2020) argue that the Covid-19 crisis has further exposed pre-existing structural and policy vulnerabilities in the creative sector, along with challenges associated with increasingly digital practice, including accessibility, acquisition of required new skills and challenges in finding and implementing effective models of monetization. Arguably, the pandemic has also led many creative entrepreneurs to innovate and find new business models, products and services, and ways to reach audiences (Bonin-Rodriguez and Vakharia 2020). There has also been renewed recognition of the value of creative work in some quarters, with creative practitioners and their work playing an important role in helping humanity through the crisis (Essig 2020).

Across all sectors, creative enterprises often exist in contexts characterized by rapid technological and social/cultural change. They are subject to greater fluctuations in demand than other kinds of enterprises, as their products and services are often discretionary rather than essential. Competition between enterprises can be significant.

Thus, in 2021 the Opportunity Recognizing Mind of Duening (2010) is challenged to move beyond recognizing patterns in current resources, collaborators and markets, and must also scan the horizon for developments in technology, disciplinary practice, consumer and audience behaviour, the social and community context and the regulatory environment. They then need to translate this foresight into behaviour, through a process of agentic adaptability (Bandura 2001); an overall process which I describe as 'adaptive foresight'. In the early twenty-first century, it seems that networks have become central to foresight and horizon-scanning. In Bridgstock (2016) I described the professional learning strategies of professionals and fast-moving digital media fields, and discovered that they often relied on distributed networks to obtain on-demand, 'just in time' quick-turnaround information and skills via social networking sites, obtaining information quickly and then passing it along.

Practitioners engaged actively in a process of sense-making of this information to anticipate trends and big moves in their fields.

Networks are important to other elements of twenty-first-century creative entrepreneurship apart from foresight and learning, bricolage and user co-creation for innovation functions discussed earlier. Networks are ideal mechanisms of information allocation and flow, and also the formation and maintenance of weak social ties (Bridgstock 2019b). As such they are useful to creative entrepreneurs for career development and self-promotion, as well as promotion of creative products and services. Over the last decade, individual branding, digital networking, online portfolios and showreels have become expected ways to enhance careers (Nikitkov and Sainty 2014). Digital networks are also important sources of career information, and have become focal venues for some of the processes involved in professional networking (Bridgstock 2016).

Thus, networked promotion of creative work has become a highly sophisticated and strategic endeavour for some creative practitioners. Micro-celebrity and self-branding via social media (Marwick 2015) involve not only promotion of creative work, but also promotion of the creator of that work, their process, lifestyle and/or life. The creative practitioner fosters ties with audience members through self-presentation and signalling authenticity, accessibility, presence and connectedness (Cunningham and Craig 2017). Critical studies argue that this type of self-promotion mythologizes creative work, that it underplays the persistent emotional labour involved and, further, that it can actually perpetuate precarity (Duffy and Wissinger 2017).

Another trend in twenty-first-century creative entrepreneurship is diversification of creative practice:

> You're a musician and a photographer and a poet; a storyteller and a dancer and a designer – a multiplatform artist, is the term one sometimes sees. Which means that you haven't got time for your 10 000 hours in any of your chosen media … the point is versatility. Like any good business, you try to diversify. (Deresiewicz 2015)

Some disciplinary diversification among creative entrepreneurs can be to do with the necessity of working through digital platforms in the twenty-first century; in these contexts it is advantageous for everyone to have basic skills in photography, video, visual design, promotional writing and social media. But the point Deresiewicz (2015) makes is that diversification of creative practice is another risk management strategy for creative entrepreneurs. It increases the likelihood that the practitioner will be able to add creative value of some kind in a multiplicity of scenarios, or at least the perception of this (Koppman 2016). Diversification can also afford the practitioner an entrepreneurial niche, because of the unique combination of capabilities that they possess, which may flow through to the creation of unique creative products and services. Successful innovation is fostered by exposure to new people and new ideas, particularly through transdisciplinary social input (Granovetter 2005), or by individual expertise in multiple disciplinary areas that affords a unique perspective on a problem or opportunity (Bridgstock 2013). However, as Deresiewicz (2015) points out, too much diversification may mean that the creative practitioner is not in a position to put their '10 000 hours' towards expertise and depth in their primary creative discipline. The learning of primary and other disciplinary creative skills becomes another balancing act, based on the practitioner's interests, values and motivations, along with their perceptions of what might be needed or valued in their work.

8.8   LEARNING CREATIVE ENTREPRENEURSHIP IN HIGHER EDUCATION

This chapter has presented a case that entrepreneurship, in three senses (enterprise, new venture creation and career self-management) is a central part of creative practice. It has covered several ways that creative entrepreneurship is distinctive, including creative motivations, co-creation and bricolage, multiple bottom lines and hybrid enterprises, concurrent intrepreneurship and entrepreneurship, and opportunity creation. It has also engaged with some ways that creative entrepreneurship is changing in the early part of the twenty-first century, including rapid change and the need for foresight and agentic adaptability, the centrality of digital networks to many aspects of practice, and diversification of creative work. Successful creative entrepreneurship is nuanced and individualized, and develops and changes over time through experience.

So, what are the implications of these findings for university educators of creative students? Entrepreneurship education is now found in a wide variety of disciplines in higher education, aside from its traditional home in the business school (Winkel 2013). There is also a reasonably mature body of literature that addresses pedagogic approaches for entrepreneurship education, ranging from 'supply'-oriented, often classroom-based models that provide lectures, readings, case studies and so on, that raise awareness and understanding; through to 'demand'-oriented, hands-on, experiential methods including simulations and authentic learning in the world of work, often accompanied by student reflection; and interactive models that emphasize communication, discussion and interaction, such as through industry mentoring, debates or networking. Analysis suggests that all three kinds of approaches can be beneficial, particularly if interwoven meaningfully (Nabi et al. 2017; Fayolle and Gailly 2015). Put another way, entrepreneurship education programmes in general have been agreed to optimally include a taught element, hands-on practice, interactions and university support (Hartshorn and Hannon 2005). These elements seem to be universally popular no matter what the disciplinary context, but their design, application and content must be highly discipline-specific to be relevant. For instance, in terms of content, Damásio and Bicacro (2017) discuss entrepreneurship education in film schools, and the importance that students be able to identify and make the most of the opportunities afforded by the digital revolution's impact on the media value chain (from capture to post-production, distribution and exhibition). Familiarity with these phenomena and associated opportunities might come about through exploration of case studies and theory in the classroom, mentoring and discussion with practitioners or hands-on, lived experience, or all three providing complementary perspectives and an overall more nuanced picture.

I suggest that undergraduate creative higher education degree programmes should not attempt to provide exhaustive canvassing of how to be a successful creative entrepreneur in addition to developing in-depth disciplinary skills and knowledge (an exception might be if the learners are undertaking two entire degree programmes; for example, the University of Technology Sydney Bachelor of Creative Intelligence and Innovation offered as a double degree with a creative disciplinary degree). However, they should also avoid tokenism and relegating it to capstone subjects, electives or even the co-curricular space, as seems to still be common practice (Bridgstock 2019a). Rather, the foundational development of adaptive entrepreneurial identity should be woven into the fabric of disciplinary degree programmes, with an explicit understanding that learning will continue outside and beyond the degree. The degree programme could even set up mechanisms for this ongoing development to occur, such as through the establishment of alumni entrepreneurship communities of practice or industry mentoring relationships.

An adaptive entrepreneurial identity underpins and directs learning, and drives career and entrepreneurship behaviour. It is developed through a cyclical learning process between learning activities, where the student 'tries on for size' different identity possibilities, along with learning through social interaction with peers and industry/community (Bridgstock 2013). Educators play a key role in scaffolding processes of reflective and emergent meaning-making throughout. Students build critical capabilities and learn to self-manage their learning through this process, as well as actively construct adaptive entrepreneurial identities. Learners should therefore be given the opportunity to interact with professionals to forge and 'test' their emerging career identities, such as through informational interviewing processes or career mentoring. Through the curriculum, the student then reflects on their successive experiences and interactions, in the light of an increasing understanding of their own values and interests.

The process of adaptive entrepreneurial identity construction aligns beautifully with the 'deliberate practice' process for learning entrepreneurship skills proposed by Read and Sarasvathy (2005). Engaging in both, through the same learning cycle, develops both identity and capabilities. Deliberate practice involves systematic and purposeful doing based on small, realistic goals, requiring focused attention and acting on feedback. For instance, a learner might practice developing and pitching a creative entrepreneurial idea for venture capital, and in the process affirm through discussions with their teacher that their creative practices and motivations align better with social enterprise. The learning around ideation and pitching is not lost when the learner then decides to write a grant application: it can be honed for the social enterprise and grant writing context.

Thus, if possible, creative entrepreneurship education should involve multiple possible learning experiences which learners can progressively customize to their needs. As Kariv et al. (2019) suggest, delivering only one type of entrepreneurial learning experience does not produce high-level learning outcomes or effectively support identity development. The experiences might involve placements within or outside creative industry sectors, service learning, start-up entrepreneurial opportunities, hackathons, international mobility learning and multidisciplinary consultancies.

I could have made the previous recommendations about learning creative entrepreneurship in my 2013 article. The points remain relevant today. But what are the implications of the twenty-first-century influences on creative entrepreneurship education, canvassed earlier in this chapter, that require foresight and agentic adaptability, judicious diversification of creative practice and constant reinvention? A key challenge for creative entrepreneurship educators in the twenty-first century is currency and relevance. While the creative entrepreneurial landscape is constantly morphing because of digital, social, economic and other innovation disruptions, creative entrepreneurship education offered in a static curriculum can easily start to lag behind (Kariv et al. 2019). The key to staying up to date once again seems, in part, to be offering authentic, experiential learning opportunities (Kolb and Kolb 2009) in which students are exposed to, and operate within, real-world and current practice. Authentic learning in real-world contexts updates itself. However, students must also be exposed to authentic learning experiences that require them to look forward, seek to make the most of upcoming and potential opportunities as well as existing ones, and develop learning networks that will encourage them to constantly 'scan the horizon' and create opportunities. Explicit mentoring and community of practice-based learning may support students to normalize and become comfortable with self-reinvention and practice reinvention, while maintaining a sense of congruent creative identity. Arguably, adaptive foresight learning is among the least well-developed aspects of contemporary entrepreneurship education, and it is particularly important for creative fields that are in flux because of fast-moving digital technology developments.

Finally, while much important creative entrepreneurship learning is practice-based, it should not be done unthinkingly. At university level it is also worthwhile to expose learners to critical perspectives on issues such as precarious labour, controversies surrounding self-presentation via social media and diversification of disciplinary practice. As well as developing capable practitioners and entrepreneurs, we should also aim to foster creative entrepreneurship literacy, and thus support learners to make informed and value-congruent choices about their creative careers.

NOTE

1.   Although franchising as a risk management strategy (Koh et al. 2018) may not always work in the case of shifting consumer or audience demand; for example, McDonald's customer preferences shifting towards healthier and more sustainable options through the 2000s, necessitating innovation in its fast food product line.

REFERENCES

Antoncic, B. and R.D. Hisrich (2003), 'Clarifying the intrapreneurship concept', *Journal of Small Business and Enterprise Development*, **10** (1), 7–24.

Bacigalupo, M., P. Kampylis, Y. Punie and G. Van den Brande (2016), *EntreComp: The Entrepreneurship Competence Framework*, Luxembourg: Publication Office of the European Union.

Bakhshi, H., F. Frey and F. Osborne (2015), *Creativity vs. Robots: The Creative Economy and the Future of Employment*, London: Nesta.

Bandura, A. (2001), 'Social cognitive theory: an agentic perspective', *Annual Review of Psychology*, **52** (1), 1–26.

Bartleet, B.L., Bennett, D., Bridgstock, R., Harrison, S., Draper, P., Tomlinson, V., and Ballico, C. (2020), *Making Music Work: Sustainable Portfolio Careers for Australian Musicians*. Australia Research Council Linkage Report. Brisbane: Queensland Conservatorium Research Centre, Griffith University.

Bonin-Rodriguez, P. and N. Vakharia (2020), 'Arts entrepreneurship internationally and in the age of COVID-19', *Artivate*, **9** (1), 3–7.

Bridgstock, R. (2009), 'The graduate attributes we've overlooked: enhancing graduate employability through career management skills', *Higher Education Research and Development*, **28** (1), 27–39.

Bridgstock, R. (2011), 'Skills for Creative Industries graduate success', *Education and Training*, **53** (1), 9–26.

Bridgstock, R. (2013), 'Not a dirty word: arts entrepreneurship and higher education', *Arts and Humanities in Higher Education*, **12** (2–3), 122–137.

Bridgstock, R. (2016), 'Educating for digital futures: what the learning strategies of digital media professionals can teach higher education', *Innovations in Education and Teaching International*, **53** (3), 306–315.

Bridgstock, R. (2019a), 'Creative industries and higher education: what curriculum, what evidence, what impact?', in S. Cunningham and T. Flew (eds), *A Research Agenda for the Creative Industries*, Cheltenham, UK and Northampton, MA, USA: Edward Elgar Publishing, pp. 112–130.

Bridgstock, R. (2019b), 'Employability and career development learning through social media: exploring the potential of LinkedIn', in J. Higgs, D. Horsfall, S. Cork and A. Jones (eds), *Challenging Future Practice Possibilities*, Rotterdam: Sense-Brill Publishers, pp. 143–153.

Bridgstock, R. and S. Cunningham (2016), 'Creative labour and graduate outcomes: implications for higher education and cultural policy', *International Journal of Cultural Policy*, **22** (1), 10–26.

Bridgstock, R., S. Dawson and G. Hearn (2011), 'Cultivating innovation through social relationships: a qualitative study of outstanding Australian innovators in science, technology, and the creative industries', in A. Mesquita (ed.), *Technology for Creativity and Innovation: Tools, Techniques and Applications*, Hershey, PA: IGI-Global, pp. 104–120.

Burns, P. (2017), *New Venture Creation: A Framework for Entrepreneurial Start-Ups*, Basingstoke: Palgrave Macmillan

Caves, R.E. (2000), *Creative Industries: Contracts Between Art and Commerce*, Cambridge, MA: Harvard University Press.

Chell, E. (2007), 'Social enterprise and entrepreneurship: towards a convergent theory of the entrepreneurial process', *International Small Business Journal*, **25** (1), 5–26.

Comunian, E. and L. England (2020), 'Creative and cultural work without filters: Covid-19 and exposed precarity in the creative economy', *Cultural Trends*, **29** (2), 112–128.

Cunningham, S. and D. Craig (2017), 'Being "really real" on YouTube: authenticity, community and brand culture in social media entertainment', *Media International Australia*, **164** (1), 71–81.

Damásio, M.J. and J. Bicacro (2017), 'Entrepreneurship education for film and media arts: how can we teach entrepreneurship to students in the creative disciplines?', *Industry and Higher Education*, **31** (4), 253–266.

de Klerk, S. (2015), 'The creative industries: an entrepreneurial bricolage perspective', *Management Decision*, **53** (4), 828–842.

Department for Digital, Culture, Media and Sport (DCMS) (2019), 'DCMS Sectors Economic Estimates 2018: Employment', *National Statistics*, 26 June, accessed 1 January 2021 at https://www.gov.uk/government/statistics/dcms-sectors-economic-estimates-2018-employment.

Deresiewicz, W. (2015), 'The death of the artist – and the birth of the creative entrepreneur', *The Atlantic*, **315** (1), 92. https://www.theatlantic.com/magazine/archive/2015/01/the-death-of-the-artist-and-the-birth-of-the-creative-entrepreneur/383497/.

Digital Media Research Centre (2018), *The Creative Economy in Australia*, accessed 1 January 2021 at https://research.qut.edu.au/dmrc/wp-content/uploads/sites/5/2018/03/Factsheet-1-Creative-Employment-overview-V5.pdf.

Duening, T.N. (2010), 'Five minds for the entrepreneurial future: cognitive skills as the intellectual foundation for next generation entrepreneurship curricula', *Journal of Entrepreneurship*, **19** (1), 1–22.

Duffy, B.E. and E. Wissinger (2017), 'Mythologies of creative work in the social media age: fun, free, and "just being me"', *International Journal of Communication*, **11** (20), 4652–4671.

Elkington, J. (1998), 'Partnerships from cannibals with forks: the triple bottom line of 21st century business', *Environmental Quality Management*, **8** (1), 37–51.

Essig, L. (2020), 'A Covid prompt from Artivate', *Creative Infrastructure*, 4 April, accessed 1 January 2021 at https://creativeinfrastructure.org/2020/04/04/a-covid-19 -prompt-from-artivate/.

Fayolle, A. and B. Gailly (2015), 'The impact of entrepreneurship education on entrepreneurial attitudes and intention: hysteresis and persistence', *Journal of Small Business Management*, **53** (1), 75–93.

Gotsi, M., C. Andriopoulos, M.W. Lewis and A.E. Ingram (2010), 'Managing creatives: paradoxical approaches to identity regulation', *Human Relations*, **63** (6), 781–805.

Granovetter, M. (2005), 'The impact of social structure on economic outcomes', *Journal of Economic Perspectives*, **19** (1), 33–50.

Haines, K., Scott, K., and Lincoln, R. (2003), *Australian Blueprint for Career Development*, accessed 15 January 2006 at http://www.dest.gov.au/directory/ publications/australian_blueprint.pdf [no longer available].

Hall, D. (2004), 'The protean career: a quarter-century journey', *Journal of Vocational Behaviour*, **65** (1), 1–13.

Hartshorn, C. and P. Hannon (2005), 'Paradoxes in entrepreneurship education: chalk and talk or chalk and cheese? A case approach', *Education + Training*, **47** (8–9), 616–627.

Haukka, S. (2011), 'Education-to-work transitions of aspiring creatives', *Cultural Trends*, **20** (1), 41–64.

Hausmann, A. and A. Heinze (2016), 'Entrepreneurship in the cultural and creative industries: insights from an emergent field', *Artivate: A Journal of Entrepreneurship in the Arts*, **5** (2), 7–22.

Hawkes, J. (2001), *The Fourth Pillar of Sustainability: Culture's Essential Role in Public Planning*, Melbourne: Common Ground.

Hearn, G., R. Bridgstock, B. Goldsmith and J. Rodgers (2014), 'Creative work beyond the creative industries: an introduction', in G. Hearn, R. Bridgstock, B. Goldsmith and J. Rodgers (eds), *Creative Work Beyond the Creative Industries: Innovation, Employment and Education*, Cheltenham, UK and Northampton, MA, USA: Edward Elgar Publishing, pp. 1–22.

Heim, C. (2016), *Audience as Performer: The Changing Role of Theatre Audiences in the Twenty-First Century*, London: Routledge.

Hennekam, S. and D. Bennett (2017), 'Creative industries work across multiple contexts: common themes and challenges', *Personnel Review*, **46** (1), 68–85.

Kariv, D., H. Matlay and A. Fayolle (2019), 'Introduction: entrepreneurial trends meet entrepreneurial education', in A. Fayolle, D. Kariv and H. Matlay (eds), *The Role and Impact of Entrepreneurship Education*, Cheltenham, UK and Northampton, MA, USA: Edward Elgar Publishing, pp. 1–11.

Koh, Y., Y. Rhou, S. Lee and M. Singal (2018), 'Does franchising alleviate restaurants' vulnerability to economic conditions?', *Journal of Hospitality and Tourism Research*, **42** (4), 627–648.

Kolb, A.Y. and D.A. Kolb (2009), 'Experiential learning theory: a dynamic, holistic approach to management learning, education and development', in S.J. Armstrong and C. Fukami (eds), *The SAGE Handbook of Management Learning, Education and Development*, London: SAGE Publications, pp. 42–68.

Koppman, S. (2016), 'Different like me: why cultural omnivores get creative jobs', *Administrative Science Quarterly*, **61** (2), 291–331.

Leadbeater, C. and K. Oakley (1999), *The Independents: Britain's New Cultural Entrepreneurs*, London: Demos.

Malmelin, N. and M. Villi (2017), 'Co-creation of what? Modes of audience community collaboration in media work', *Convergence*, **23** (2), 182–196.

Marwick, A.E. (2015), 'Instafame: Luxury selfies in the attention economy', *Public Culture*, **27** (75), 137–160.

Nabi, G., F. Liñán, A. Fayolle, N. Krueger and A. Walmsley (2017), 'The impact of entrepreneurship education in higher education: a systematic review and research agenda', *Academy of Management Learning and Education*, **16** (2), 277–299.

Neck, H., C. Brush and E. Allen (2009), 'The landscape of social entrepreneurship', *Business Horizons*, **52** (1), 13–19.

Nikitkov, A. and B. Sainty (2014), 'The role of social media in influencing career success', *International Journal of Accounting and Information Management*, **22** (4), 273–294.

Oakley, K. (2013), 'Good work? Rethinking cultural entrepreneurship', in C. Bilton and S. Cummings (eds), *Handbook of Management and Creativity*, Cheltenham, UK and Northampton, MA, USA: Edward Elgar Publishing, pp. 145–159.

Pollard, E. (2013), 'Making your way. Empirical evidence from a survey of 3,500 graduates', in D. Ashton and C. Noonan (eds), *Cultural Work and Higher Education*, Basingstoke: Palgrave Macmillan, pp. 45–66.

Rae, D. (2005), 'Cultural diffusion: a formative process in creative entrepreneurship?', *International Journal of Entrepreneurship and Innovation*, **6** (3), 185–192.

Read, S. and S.D. Sarasvathy (2005), 'Knowing what to do and doing what you know: effectuation as a form of entrepreneurial expertise', *Journal of Private Equity*, **9** (1), 45–62.

Sarasvathy, S.D., N. Dew, S.R. Velamuri and S. Venkataraman (2005), 'Three views of entrepreneurial opportunity', in Z.J. Acs and D.B. Audretsch (eds), *Handbook of Entrepreneurship Research*, New York: Springer-Verlag, pp. 141–160.

Schwab, K. (2016). *The Fourth Industrial Revolution*, Geneva: World Economic Forum.

Scott, M. (2012), 'Cultural entrepreneurs, cultural entrepreneurship: music producers mobilising and converting Bourdieu's alternative capitals', *Poetics*, **40** (3), 237–255.

Throsby, D. and K. Petetskaya (2017), *Making Art Work*, Melbourne: Australia Council for the Arts.

Valliere, D. and T. Gegenhuber (2014), 'Entrepreneurial remixing: bricolage and postmodern resources', *International Journal of Entrepreneurship and Innovation*, **15** (1), 5–15.

Vilorio, V. (2018). *Careers for People Who Are Creative*, accessed 1 January 2021 at https://www.bls.gov/careeroutlook/2018/article/creative-careers-update.htm.

Waters, L., D.T. Hall, L. Wang and J.P. Briscoe (2015), 'Protean career orientation: a review of existing and emerging research', in R.J. Burke, K.M. Page and C.L. Cooper (eds), *Flourishing in Life, Work and Careers*, Cheltenham, UK and Northampton, MA, USA: Edward Elgar Publishing, pp. 235–260.

Werthes, D., R. Mauer and M. Brettel (2017), 'Cultural and creative entrepreneurs: understanding the role of entrepreneurial identity', *International Journal of Entrepreneurial Behavior and Research*, **24** (1), 290–314.

Winkel, D. (2013), 'The changing face of entrepreneurship education', *Journal of Small Business Management*, **51** (3), 313–314.

World Economic Forum (2020), 'Four digital trends in the media industry', *Digital Transformation*, accessed 1 January 2021 at http://reports.weforum.org/digital -transformation/digital-trends-in-the-media-industry/.

PART III

Creative economies: focus on networks, place and mobilities

9. This must be the place: creative workers' evaluations of cities as enabling contexts for work

Lorenzo Mizzau, Fabrizio Montanari, Damiano Razzoli and Stefano Rodighiero

9.1 INTRODUCTION[1]

Cities are important spatial contexts that affect different realms of individual and collective life, and provide individuals and organisations with crucial resources and capabilities for their social, economic and cultural activities (e.g., Glaeser, 2013; Hall, 2014; Nash, 2020). Cities represent nowadays the social aggregation that hosts more than half of the population worldwide (World Bank, 2015), thus representing the privileged spatial nexus where individuals perform their work, attend educational activities, engage in social interactions and settle down. Accordingly, there has been widespread attention into how policymakers, planners and administrators can manage cities in ways that tackle pressing socio-economic issues such as liveability and safety, socio-economic development, and sustainability. Within this context, a great deal of attention has been put on policies and actions aimed at sustaining creativity, which is considered a key resource for local development (European Commission, 2019).

As highlighted by the organisational and sociological literatures, creative labour is highly complex and uncertain, and creative workers usually face several hurdles in pursuing their careers (e.g., Lingo and Tepper, 2013; Rowlands and Handy, 2012). Indeed, creative labour markets are characterised by precariousness, lack of formal labour regulations and a skewed distribution of incomes (Alacovska, 2018; Eikhof and Haunschild, 2007; Menger, 1999). For these reasons, it is important to understand what city-related features are more relevant in facilitating the work of creatives. Cities in fact provide important contextual conditions that could favour (or hinder) collaboration, learning and the seizing of job opportunities, particularly for creative workers (e.g., Comunian et al., 2010; Scott, 2010).

The relationship between cities and creative workers has been mainly addressed in terms of the factors that affect creatives' locational choices (e.g., Lawton et al., 2013; Wojan et al., 2007). In so doing, scholars have often adopted a 'macro' approach by modelling locational choices as a function of the presence of given amenities and 'production systems' in given sectors (e.g., Florida, 2005; Storper and Scott, 2009). This has been done mostly by 'objective' measures related to city features, or via surveys aimed at understanding what kind of factors were the most relevant in determining choices to live in a city (e.g., Asheim and Hansen, 2009; Musterd and Gritsai, 2013). Another stream of research has delved more into the perceived subjective experience, providing a more nuanced picture of why people move and remain in certain cities (e.g., Brown, 2015; Markusen, 2013). In so doing, scholars have investigated both immaterial elements (signs, traditions, aesthetic stimuli and so on) and material elements (informal spaces, cultural institutions and so on) that sustain the work of creatives, stimulating creative process, sustaining professional development and forming positive expectations related to possible career paths (e.g., Drake, 2003; Merkel, 2019; Montanari et al., 2018).

In this chapter, we aim at delving into this subjective element in order to provide a fine-grained understanding of how creative workers perceive a city as an enabling (or inhibiting) context for their work. In other words, we want to highlight what features of the urban context are perceived by creative workers as enabling factors for their work, and how they play out in practice. To address our purpose, we present a qualitative study of creative workers living in a medium-sized city in northern Italy, Reggio Emilia.

9.2   URBAN CONTEXT AND CREATIVE WORKERS: A COMPLEX RELATIONSHIP

Within the economic geography and urban studies literature, a stream of research has studied the city-related characteristics that are more suitable to sustain the work of creative workers in terms of factors contributing to creative workers' attraction into places (e.g., Lawton et al., 2013; Musterd and Gritsai, 2013). Accordingly, proponents of the 'people follow jobs' thesis argued that creatives are attracted to a place primarily by employment opportunities available within local production systems or clusters (e.g., Rantisi and Leslie, 2010; Storper and Scott, 2009). In other terms, creative workers decide to move to cities where the presence of thick labour markets offer relevant (actual or potential) employment opportunities. Conversely, proponents of the 'jobs follow people' thesis claimed that individuals are attracted to a place by attributes such as a vibrant cultural offer, a climate of tolerance for and openness to the new, or the availability of 'third places' such as cafes and bookstores for people to meet (Clark et al., 2002; Wojan et al., 2007).

More nuance to the debate has been added by studies addressing the matter of what features of the urban context shape creative workers' choices to remain in cities. For example, Brown (2015) studied international creative migrants working in Birmingham, highlighting how locational choices are driven by personal quests and desires (for example, education, travelling, exploring another culture), and sometimes by chance (for example, an unsearched job offer) or pure experimentation, rather than being linear and rational (that is, oriented to maximise potential career outcomes). Further, this study pointed out that the networking opportunities provided upon arrival in a place were 'vital for enabling migrants to become quickly networked into the local creative "scene"' (Brown, 2015: 9). This is consistent with the model of knowledge-based talent attraction that emerged from the analysis of several Canadian cities (Grant, 2014), which pointed to universities as primary factors in providing access not only to job opportunities, but also to personal networks such as friends and family.

Echoing these results, several studies highlighted how people remain in the places where they were born, raised or have studied, because of the dense personal and professional networks that they have developed over time (e.g., Chapain and Comunian, 2010; Musterd and Gritsai, 2013). Others pointed to a variety of factors such as liveability and sustainability (e.g., Hracs et al., 2011; Lewis and Donald, 2010), proximity to metropolitan areas (Denis-Jacob, 2012; Waitt and Gibson, 2009) and the availability of informal spaces and organisations that sustain creative workers in connecting to relevant creative communities (e.g., Markusen, 2013; Montanari et al., 2018).

Another stream of research has investigated how the work of creatives is sustained by immaterial factors such as the traditions, signs and symbols of a place. For example, Scott (2000) proposed that places develop as stratifications of cultural and social raw materials (prominently, signs and symbols) that become embedded into the economic and cultural fabric of the city, creating competitive advantages for local clusters and 'gravitation effects' for creative workers. Drake (2003) gave an account of how craft artists rely on multisensorial stimuli in their environments to get inspiration for their work. Florida (2005) raised the issue of how creative workers could be attached to a city when they perceive it as unique in terms of factors such as history, built environment and opportunities to interact with other creatives. Finally, Chapain and Comunian (2010: 725) highlighted how a strong regional identity – that is, 'the inspirational role of place in terms of its people, its cultural assets, and its industrial past' – was considered an enabling factor by creative workers in the Newcastle–Gateshead area.

Taking the above-reviewed ideas further, we aim at providing more nuance to the understanding of the relationship between city and creative workers. In particular, we extend the scope of the city-related features that can impact on how creative workers feel sustained (or hindered) in performing their work. In other words, we elucidate the urban features contributing to creative workers' evaluation of cities as enabling (or hindering) contexts for their work. In doing so, we aim to contribute to the extant literature by delving into the process through which individuals interpret urban contexts as providing opportunities to carry out their work.

9.3   SETTING AND METHODOLOGY

This qualitative study was conducted on creative workers living in Reggio Emilia, a medium-sized city in the north of Italy. The city represents an interesting setting as it is home to the third-largest artistic cluster in the administrative region of Emilia-Romagna, although it is not usually associated to the typical features of the 'creative city' (Florida, 2005; Landry and Bianchini, 1995). Indeed, the city is still mostly associated with its industrial footprint in the manufacturing and agri-food sectors, which have contributed to positioning it as one of the most resilient industrial areas in Italy (Unioncamere Emilia-Romagna, 2017).[2] Moreover, with 170 000 inhabitants in the municipality, Reggio Emilia shows the typical features of small to medium-sized cities that, although chosen by a large number of creative workers, have been traditionally overlooked by studies of creative places (Lingo and Tepper, 2013; Markusen, 2006).

The study[3] consists of 210 in-depth semi-structured interviews that we conducted between October 2016 and December 2018, lasting 30–50 minutes each. In order to identify the creative workers to interview, we started by collecting existing databases from different sources (mainly a built-in database by the municipality of Reggio Emilia, and one developed by the Italian Association of Artists). We eliminated duplications and validated the databases with the help of three informants embedded into the local context (one journalist of the local newspaper, the city councillor of creative and educational activities and one manager working in the Department of Culture of the municipality). Then, we proceeded to contact people, and resorted to the snowballing technique (that is, asking each contacted person to nominate five other creative workers in the city), so as to cover a wide range of potentially relevant informants (Biernacki and Waldorf, 1981).

Our final sample consists of 193 creative workers (124 males and 69 females), 62 per cent of whom are originally from the municipality, while 38 per cent were born somewhere else and then moved to Reggio Emilia. Interviewees are aged between 18 and 64 (mean age of 31); 60 per cent of them are in the early to middle stage of their career, the remaining 40 per cent in the middle to established stage. These workers operate in different creative sectors: music (29 per cent), photography and visual arts (21 per cent), communication and advertising (11 per cent), graphic design (10 per cent), handicrafts (8 per cent), theatre and dance (8 per cent), writing (8 per cent), architecture (3 per cent) and fashion (2 per cent).

During the interviews, we asked creative workers questions related to four areas of interest: (1) personal, educational and professional background; (2) present work condition (for example, employment status, most relevant projects and collaborations, other jobs held); (3) professional needs, career expectations and evaluation of outcomes achieved; and (4) most- and least-liked features of the city, particularly in relation to facilitating (or hindering) creative work. Interviews were digitally recorded and transcribed. All the interviewees were guaranteed anonymity, hence in the results section we will report job title and ID instead of the interviewee name.

While we were still collecting data, we progressed with our analytical process in order to grasp the most salient themes (Miles and Huberman, 1994). In more detail, each author independently read the transcripts of the interviews in order to develop personal impressions. Then, as we proceeded to collect new data, we shared and discussed impressions and interpretations until we reached a common understanding and agreement on the emerging themes. In doing so, we focused on the main features of the urban context depicted as most relevant in sustaining (or hindering) creative work. As a result of the analysis of the transcripts, which were manually coded, we were able to distil nine city features. Then, we aggregated them into three higher-level dimensions affecting how creative workers perceive a city as an enabling (or inhibiting) context for creative work: life quality, network and city identity.

9.4   RESULTS

As mentioned above, we identified nine city features, each grouped under one of three dimensions that can affect how creative workers perceive a city as an enabling working context: quality of life, network and city identity. In the following, we describe these dimensions, providing evidence of how creative workers make sense of each of the city features.

Quality of Life

The first dimension relates to three main features: amenities, geographical position and public services. Amenities include all those elements such as natural sites, leisure activities and cultural offer, which contribute to making the city more liveable and vibrant (Clark et al., 2002; Florida, 2005). While geographical position refers to the physical location of the city and the related climatic characteristics, public services encompass all the services provided by public institutions in the transportation, educational, health and welfare domains.

Our analysis shows that creative workers evaluate these three city features based on the standards provided in terms of quality of life. For example, regarding amenities, all interviewees appreciate Reggio Emilia because of its affordability, and a general work attitude that is industrious but not over-whelming. Indeed, the reduced cost of living (for example, house and office rents) 'gives you the chance to live the city in a much more relaxed way, as you can save money for other aspects of life and not consume all of your time for work related issues' (#139, architect, 48 years). Similarly, individuals appreciate the compact scale of the city (contrasted with the urban sprawl typical of metropolitan areas), its pedestrian-friendly zones – 'Reggio is the city which you can walk through with no problems' (#91, graphic designer, 48 years) – and the easily reachable 'green areas that abound in the city' (#136, fashion designer, 40 years). While some interviewees criticise the high levels of traffic and pollution, they mostly agree that Reggio Emilia is a pleasant city 'with a beautiful city centre that really astonishes you every time you walk through it' (#23, photographer, 27 years). Furthermore, they appreciate its convenient geographical position 'that allows you to be in larger cities [for example, Bologna and Milan], but also seaside and skiing in less than two hours' (#98, musician, 50 years).

In addition, creative workers appreciate the possibility of benefiting from high-quality services, especially in the welfare and education domains, where the innovative approach adopted in the municipal kindergartens is internationally renowned (Thornton and Brunton, 2014). The opportunity to receive an outstanding education for children (at the average cost of standard public nurseries in Italy) affected the choice of some creatives to relocate to Reggio Emilia from larger metropolitan areas. For example, one video maker states: 'I moved from Milan to Reggio primarily for family reasons. I looked at the city from the point of view of a father: Reggio has excellent kindergartens, and the primary schools offer a great service too' (#103, 32 years).

All in all, creative workers appreciate the liveability of the city. Indeed, they perceive that it provides a context which is functional to their work, at the same time enabling the cultivation of personal and societal goals (for example, work–life balance, engagement in social activities). On a different note, some interviewees (particularly the younger ones) complain about the limited number of cultural activities and their excessive conservative features, as in the following example: 'Yes, Reggio Emilia is close to more vibrant cities, but it is not exactly the same thing of living there; here it is too quiet' (#26, communication manager, 36 years). However, most of them are generally satisfied with what goes on in the city. In particular, interviewees appreciate the quality standards and accessibility of the local cultural offer, which is 'different from the more extensive offer that could be thrilling but difficult to enjoy in large cities' (#123, communication specialist, 33 years). Besides the presence of leisure venues such as restaurants, bars and cafes, interviewees highlight the presence of 'important and internationally renowned cultural institutions and events such as Aterballetto and Collezione Maramotti' (#106, graphic designer, 28 years),[4] which give the opportunity to attend high-quality cultural events 'that otherwise you can only see in the theatres of European capitals' (#65, dancer, 21 years).

Network

As for the second dimension, interviewees highlight the important role played by three features of the city: places and events; key organisations; and personal ties. 'Places and events' refer to all formal and informal gatherings, that range from professional workshops and cultural events, to artist studios and co-working spaces. 'Key organisations' refer to all those local actors (for example, municipality, university, prominent cultural institutions) that play an important role in sustaining connections among creative workers. 'Personal ties' refer to all relationships that a creative worker develops with other creative workers as well as members of the local community.

Creative workers' consideration of these elements as enabling factors is based on the extent to which they provide a sense of being in an inclusive urban context; that is, where it is easy to meet and interact with other people, particularly other professionals. Most interviewees evaluate Reggio Emilia positively, as it offers various places and events favouring spontaneous encounters with other professionals, which in turn are key conduits for the dissemination of information and ideas, as well as for informal job-search networks. To illustrate, a disc jockey (DJ) noted: 'I met most of my work contacts during events such as Eleva [a local electronic music festival]' (#121, DJ, 27 years). Similarly, a dancer said that 'the ballet shows hosted in the local theatre and the rehearsals of Aterballetto are always a great opportunity to meet other choreographers and dancers, and exchange ideas with them' (#66, 38 years).

The majority of interviewees appreciate the relational dynamics characterising the city more generally, which contribute to increasing their enmeshment in the local community. In this regard, interviewees appreciate the possibility to easily develop friendship ties with neighbours and colleagues, and parents of their children's friends. Such a diffused sociality also translates into socio-emotional support, as interviewees state that they could tap into it to receive 'help with childcare in times of family emergencies, which really makes your life easier and work better' (#128, video maker, 41 years). Moreover, the perceived presence of dense, cohesive networks sustains the feeling of being in a supportive environment, which in turn could be conducive to pursue new professional projects. To illustrate, one DJ told us: 'Reggio is my comfort zone; that's why I started here. When you start a career as freelance you already experience a lot of uncertainty. I needed something certain' (#67, 23 years).

It is interesting to note that several interviewees highlight the important role played by private houses, as it is very common for creative workers in the city to invite colleagues and other creatives to their households in order to discuss work issues, new projects or simply facilitate acquaintance between people. To illustrate, a musician highlighted:

> I worked with a musician from Tangeri, Morocco, who used to live here; I once went to his place and there were two other impressive musicians – I think they were Iranian. This was happening in a house in the city centre of Reggio Emilia. There are many things that I am not aware of: I went to that musician's home and I happened to listen to something so unexpected. This proves me that this city often hides several interesting things behind its corners. (#107, 55 years)

However, as an inhibiting factor, some interviewees warn that it is not always easy to get access to local networks, since the relevance of private places for social networking favours the development of secluded cliques 'rather than sustaining the feeling of a common creative scene' (#104, illustrator, 35 years). On a similar note, other creative workers are critical toward the relational patterns characterising the city's creative scene, since 'knowing almost everyone and having your family and best friends here can feel a little too much' (#23, photographer, 27 years). That is, they fear that being immersed in an environment with a limited renewal of people could be detrimental to their work. In this sense, they claim the importance of attracting creatives from other geographical areas, who could bring new perspectives and ideas as well as open up new professional opportunities. To this end, they would like to have more landmark events, as 'Fotografia Europea [the major international event in the city, a photography festival] is alright, but Reggio needs something else: I don't know, something like a Linux Day could help attract professionals from other cities' (#118, co-founder of media company, 40 years).

City Identity

The third dimension emcompasses all the city features that contribute to construct the city identity, which refers to a specific form of 'collective identity based on perceived uniqueness and meanings of place' (Jones and Svejenova, 2017: 203). More specifically, city identity comprises three elements: distinctive traits, material features and narratives. 'Distinctive traits' includes all those traits and outlooks that creative workers perceive as central, distinctive and persistent, thus making the city unique and recognisable (Bell and de-Shalit, 2011; Hall, 2014). 'Material features' relate to those elements such as historical buildings, squares and monuments that characterise the urban fabric visually and aesthetically, thus contributing to shaping its identity (Jones and Svejenova, 2017; Molotch, 2002). 'Narratives' include all the stories to which creative workers refer when asked to explain their idea of the city (Kalandides, 2011).

Analysis shows that creative workers evaluate these features based on the extent to which they contribute to developing an affective attachment to the city. Accordingly, creative workers consider the city as an enabling context when they feel a strong alignment with its traits. For example, interviewees agree that Reggio Emilia is characterised by 'a great social openness and deep-rooted solidarity, which have been built over the years thanks to the cooperative movement, the Resistance movement in the WWII [World War II] period, and [subsequently] to the movements for the workers' rights' (#93, video maker, 37 years). Interviewees further substantiate that such a collectivist spirit is evident in the strong presence of unions in the local economy, and in the diffusion of the cooperative organisational model, but plays also out in more 'vernacular' terms in the everyday life of neighbourhoods. To illustrate, one interviewee notes: 'Reggio Emilia is the city of people and you notice that every day. I don't know [what it is], but even when you go to the supermarket you feel that people do actually listen to you and pay attention to your needs' (#142, communication manager, 47 years). Interviewees acknowledge the 'attitude to productivity' as another trait characterising the city, and contributing to a feeling that 'you can start up your creative work here' (#119, co-founder of a communication company, 52 years). Interviewees acknowledge 'openness' as a further trait characterising the city, namely by referring to 'the mentality of being open and hospitable toward newcomers and foreigners' (#113, video maker, 37 years) and 'the strong impetus to continuously innovate in all the societal fields' (#51, social media manager, 28 years). Interviewees appreciate this trait as it contributes to the feeling of being 'in an innovation-friendly environment' (#131, communication manager, 44 years).

Most interviewees exhibit high appreciation for the material features of the city that showcase the city's distinctive history, culture and image. To illustrate, one architect notes: 'I think that Piazza Fontanesi has really inspired my creative activity: it is the most beautiful square in Reggio Emilia and it is nice to photograph people there walking on the street during the market' (#19, 37 years). As far as narratives are concerned, interviewees mention particularly the historical events, periods and imprints (of cultural, political and/or social significance) in which Reggio Emilia had a prominent role, and to which they attach particular emotional and symbolic meanings. For example, they frequently cite the role that the city played for the Italian political scenario in the aftermath of World War II up until the 1970s, when several strikes took place in one of the landmark industrial sites of the city: 'My grandfather worked at Officine Reggiane [a major industrial plant just outside the actual city centre, now reconverted], he was one of the occupants at the times of the "great strikes" and his stories are still vivid memories for me' (#100, visual artist, 42 years). Moreover, interviewees mention the cultural scene that took place in the city in the 1980s and 1990s, when 'people came to Reggio from all over Italy' (#135, DJ, 55 years) thanks to the presence of some famous music clubs and of several indie and techno bands from the city and the surrounding areas.

Overall, creative workers appreciate the city identity, as it contributes to deriving a strong sense of attachment to the place: 'I live in the house where [Massimo] Zamboni [one of the most important musicians of the local indie scene] used to live; living and working here means a lot to me' (#140, copywriter, 38 years). Such an affective bond developed with the city sustains creative workers' engagement in the work domain to the point that sometimes they perceive that their artefacts are imbued by the identity features of the locality: 'When I work in other cities, people always tell me that my style and vision are strongly informed by the city where I come from; indeed, I think it is my DNA' (#100, visual artist, 42 years).

However, there are also more critical comments, pointing to different interpretations of the city traits, material features and narratives. Some interviewees complain about the lack of a multivocal identity, criticising the city's 'overwhelming collectivistic spirit that generates excessive homogenising effects' (#84, restorer, 49 years). In some cases, interviewees display a neutral approach to the material features of the city: 'you know, Reggio Emilia is nice, but after all it does not change so much my work as I collaborate with people and clients from other cities' (#117, graphic designer, 41 years). In other cases, they highlight that common narratives about the city are outdated: 'Reggio Emilia used to be innovative, [it was] the capital of "indie" culture in Italy. There were incredible places such as Maffia [a now-closed music club]. Now times have changed, but people still think to live in the yesteryear' (#98, musician, 48 years). An interviewee even pointed to a mismatch between the local culture and the possibility of being appreciated as a creative worker: 'people here don't understand what I do for a living: for them it's much easier to understand what's like producing bolts' (#82, co-founder of a co-working space, 36 years). In all these cases, creative workers do not feel a positive attachment to the city, and its particular city identity may become more a hindrance than an enabling factor.

9.5   DIMENSIONS OF URBAN CONTEXT AFFECTING CREATIVE WORKERS: A MODEL

This study shows what features of the urban context are important for creative workers, and how such features play out from creative workers' real voice. Our analysis highlights three dimensions of the urban context that creative workers consider relevant in terms of enabling or inhibiting their creative work: quality of life, network and city identity. The perceptions of the three dimensions provide a cognitive framework that helps individuals to make sense of how they can perform their work in a given environment.

More precisely, evaluation of the three dimensions is situation-specific, as it depends on the key features that an individual might look for in a given stage of their life and career in terms, for example, of liveability versus search for cultural vibrancy, nurturing long-lasting relationships versus being open to new encounters, or settling down versus being prone to mobility (see also Hracs and Stolarick, 2014). Figure 9.1 summarises our theoretical model.

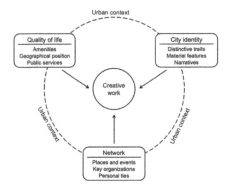

Figure 9.1   The dimensions of urban context affecting creative work

Our first dimension – quality of life – consists of all the city amenities, geographical position and public services that individuals experience in their daily lives. Individuals consider this dimension by evaluating the extent to which they are, in each moment, prone to a quiet, tranquil way of living, possibly sacrificing a higher level of the place's amenities (for example, cultural vibrancy). Accordingly, those individuals who describe an urban context that is quiet and offers high standards in terms of quality of life, consider it to be enabling since they can derive extra resources (for example, temporal and cognitive resources) for cultivating personal, professional and societal goals, which in turn can make them more inspired at work. In other words, individuals might trade quiet, less vibrant urban contexts for a better quality of life, which eventually could help them to focus on their work or even be more satisfied with the work–life balance achieved. On the other hand, individuals seeking cultural vibrancy and 'buzz' may not appreciate such a context, leading them to consider the urban context as inhibiting for their work.

Our second dimension – network – includes all the ties that creative workers form with other people with whom they interact in the city. As boundaries between work and free time are blurred for creative workers (Wittel, 2001), formal and informal social encounters take place within a situated context of places, organisations and events in the city. Individuals evaluate this urban dimension according to the extent to which they like being part of close and tightly knit networks. Here, individuals may appreciate a certain degree of network closure. Indeed, cohesive networks can sustain creative work, leading individuals to perceive that they can share ideas with a reduced risk of opportunistic behaviour and/or criticism (see also Perry-Smith and Mannucci, 2017). As a result, creative workers who appreciate the social fabric of the city tend to evaluate the urban context as enabling for their work. On the contrary, when individuals perceive that local networks are too closed and self-referential, they suffer from limited opportunities for new encounters. In these cases, creative workers may consider the urban context as inhibiting for their work, as it limits the potential for creative exploration, cross-fertilisation and new collaborations.

Our third dimension – city identity – includes all the perceived distinctive traits and material features that make up the character of an urban context (Molotch et al., 2000). Moreover, city identity is the result of images from the past and current interpretations that individuals share through narratives (see also Jones and Svejenova, 2017). Creative workers consider this dimension by evaluating the extent to which they feel identified with and attached to a place. When individuals feel 'in tune' with a city's identity, they may derive extra motivational and emotional resources, thus perceiving the context as an enabling one. On the contrary, if a creative worker is 'out of tune' with the city's identity, the context may become an impediment and inhibit their work.

This study contributes to a deeper understanding of how creative workers perceive their urban context as sustaining (or hindering) their work. In so doing, we complement the extant literature with a micro, subjective perspective that illuminates the urban dimensions perceived as more relevant by creative workers, and how they are evaluated by individuals. Our results also shed light on the micro-foundation of cities' attraction of creative talent. In particular, this study lends support to approaches that question the rationale behind simplistic place-based policies aimed at attracting creative workers (e.g., Markusen, 2006; Storper and Scott, 2009). Although policymakers may choose to re-brand and package a city as a creative hub, our results support a more nuanced picture of the elements that concur to subjective evaluations of a city as an enabling context for creative work. Thus, policymakers and city administrators should invest in actions that take more into account the emotional, affective and cognitive processes through which creatives perceive quality of life, networks and city identity in relation to their creative work.

An initiative recently launched by the territorial development agency of Milan could provide an interesting example of actions that policymakers could deploy to affect creative workers' perception of their city as an enabling context for their work. The agency launched a 'Neighbourhood Campaign' to raise awareness about – and encourage people to discuss – the character-istics of the city's neighbourhoods. Local associations, citizens and other components of the social fabric of the city gathered together to express their vision of the future of their neighbourhoods, or to make practical requests to the municipality. In the debate, many of the issues which emerged are among those highlighted in our model, such as quality of life (for example, pointing to excellence in terms of services or position), connections (for example, refer-ring to key spots or places of gathering) and identity and image (for example, how citizens of other areas perceive their neighbourhood, and how locals feel about it). While such initiatives pertain more to the realm of narratives or storytelling about the city, other policies could apply to the creation of 'third places' or shared infrastructures that can help creative workers gather together. This could be particularly relevant for creatives in the early stages of their career, for whom the need to perceive social support is typically higher. This is all the more relevant at the present time, where during the Covid-19 pandemic the geographies of (creative) work are changing, and a proportion of the workers may flow away from large metropolitan areas, to more peripheral places (see Mariotti et al., 2021). Seen from this point of view, in these places it is also important to provide a cultural offer which is appreciated by creative workers, so as to attract and retain them in the medium term. A final set of policies aims at residential initiatives (such as controlled rents and co-housing initiatives) that could sustain creative workers, particularly in those cities where the cost of living is high; this can help to combat the 'centrifugal forces' that are arising in particular from large metro areas, while also contributing to the perceived quality of life standards provided by a city.

Our study also points to avenues for future research. For example, it would be interesting to include in the analysis creative workers who have left a city for another place. Taking into consideration those who disliked a city or could not find a job that realised their aspirations could help to draw a more complete picture of the city identity, and how it impacts on creative work. Research would also benefit from developing 'matched pair' case studies, where to those living in a certain kind of city (for example, small, quite liveable, economically vibrant, 'not very creative', as in our case) one could add a study of another, different city (for example, a large regional centre, more culturally vibrant, more characterised in terms of creative industries), to extend the scope of the results. Finally, it would be interesting to adopt a quantitative approach to measure creative workers' identification with a city and its effects on creativity or career outcomes.

NOTES

1. The research was conducted before the Covid-19 outbreak. In the final section, we discuss how our findings may be interpreted in light of the contemporary situation, still characterised by the pandemic, also informing the development of public policies aimed at sustaining creative work.
2. For example, Reggio Emilia shows a 68.4 per cent employment rate (nine points higher than the Italian average) and ninth-highest gross domestic product per capita among all Italian cities (Camera di Commercio di Reggio Emilia, 2018). Within this economic context, creative workers account approximately for 5.5 per cent of the labour force of the urban economy, and creative firms for 10 per cent of overall firms; data in line with the national trends (Emilia-Romagna Valorizzazione Economica Territorio, 2018).
3. The data analysed for this study were collected as part of a wider research project aimed at investigating the creative dynamics of the city, from which three other papers originated: Razzoli et al. (2020), Montanari et al. (2021a) and Montanari et al. (2021b).
4. Established in 1977, Aterballetto is Italy's foremost contemporary ballet company. Collezione Maramotti is a private art institution established in 2007 by a local prominent fashion company (the Max Mara Group).

REFERENCES

Alacovska, A. (2018). Informal creative labour practices: A relational work perspective. *Human Relations*, *71*(12), 1563–1589.

Asheim, B., and Hansen, H.K. (2009). Knowledge bases, talents, and contexts: On the usefulness of the creative class approach in Sweden. *Economic Geography*, *85*(4), 425–442.

Bell, D.A., and de-Shalit, A. (2011). *The Spirit of Cities. Why the Identity of a City Matters in a Global Age.* Princeton, NJ: Princeton University Press.

Biernacki, P., and Waldorf, D. (1981). Snowball sampling: Problems and techniques of chain referral sampling. *Sociological Methods and Research*, *10*(2), 141–163.

Brown, J. (2015). Home from home? Locational choices of international 'creative class' workers. *European Planning Studies*, *23*(12), 2336–2355.

Camera di Commercio di Reggio Emilia (2018). *7° Rapporto sulla Coesione Sociale in Provincia di Reggio Emilia.* Available at: www.re.camcom.gov.it/allegati/Abstract %20Rapporto%20coesione%20sociale%202018_181211044622.pdf.

Chapain, C., and Comunian, R. (2010). Enabling and inhibiting the creative economy: The role of the local and regional dimensions in England. *Regional Studies*, *44*(6), 717–734.

Clark, T.N., Lloyd, R., Wong, K.K., and Jain, P. (2002). Amenities drive urban growth. *Journal of Urban Affairs*, *24*(5), 493–515.

Comunian, R., Chapain, C., and Clifton, N. (2010). Location, location, location: Exploring the complex relationship between creative industries and place. *Creative Industries Journal, 3*(1), 5–10.

Denis-Jacob, J. (2012). Cultural industries in small-sized Canadian cities: Dream or reality? *Urban Studies, 49*(1), 97–114.

Drake, G. (2003). 'This place gives me space': Place and creativity in the creative industries. *Geoforum, 34*(4), 511–524.

Eikhof, D.R., and Haunschild, A. (2007). For art's sake! Artistic and economic logics in creative production. *Journal of Organizational Behavior, 28*(5): 523–538.

Emilia-Romagna Valorizzazione Economica Territorio (2018). *Economia Arancione in Emilia-Romagna – Cultura, Creatività, Industria.* Available at: www.ervet .it/wp-content/uploads/downloads/2018/06/1_Economia_Arancione-in-Emilia -Romagna_Parte-I-Mappe-Vol-I.pdf.

European Commission (2019). *The Cultural and Creative Cities Monitor, 2019 Edition.* Available at: composite-indicators.jrc.ec.europa.eu/cultural-creative-cities -monitor/docs-and-data.

Florida, R.L. (2005). *Cities and the Creative Class.* New York: Routledge.

Glaeser, E.L. (2013). Triumph of the city: How our greatest invention makes us richer, smarter, greener, healthier, and happier. *Journal of Economic Sociology, 14*(4), 75–94.

Grant, J.L. (2014). *Seeking Talent for Creative Cities: The Social Dynamics of Innovation.* Toronto: University of Toronto Press.

Hall, P. (2014). *Cities of Tomorrow: An Intellectual History of Urban Planning and Design Since 1880.* New York: Wiley.

Hracs, B.J., Grant, J.L., Haggett, J., and Morton, J. (2011). A tale of two scenes: Civic capital and retaining musical talent in Toronto and Halifax. *Canadian Geographer / Le Géographe canadien, 55*(3), 365–382.

Hracs, B.J., and Stolarick, K. (2014). Satisfaction guaranteed? Individual preferences, experiences and mobility. In J. Grant (ed.), *Seeking Talent for Creative Cities: The Social Dynamics of Innovation* (pp. 99–118). Toronto: University of Toronto Press.

Jones, C., and Svejenova, S. (2017). The architecture of city identities: A multimodal study of Barcelona and Boston. In M.A. Höllerer, T. Daudigeos and D. Jancsary (eds), *Multimodality, Meaning, and Institutions* (pp. 203–234). Bingley: Emerald Publishing.

Kalandides, A. (2011). The problem with spatial identity: Revisiting the 'sense of place'. *Journal of Place Management and Development, 4*(1), 28–39.

Landry, C., and Bianchini, F. (1995). *The Creative City.* London: Demos.

Lawton, P., Murphy, E., and Redmond, D. (2013). Residential preferences of the 'creative class'? *Cities 31*, 47–56.

Lewis, N.M., and Donald, B. (2010). A new rubric for 'creative city' potential in Canada's smaller cities. *Urban Studies, 47*(1), 29–54.

Lingo, E.L., and Tepper, S.J. (2013). Looking back, looking forward: Arts-based careers and creative work. *Work and Occupations, 40*(4), 337–363.

Mariotti, I., Manfredini, F., and Giavarini, V. (2021). *La geografia degli spazi di coworking a Milano. Una analisi territoriale.* Milano Collabora. Comune di Milano. Available at: https://www.comune.milano.it/-/lavoro.-milano-sperimenta-nuovi -spazi-e-modi-di-lavorare-per-una-citta-a-15-minuti.

Markusen, A. (2006). Urban development and the politics of a creative class: Evidence from a study of artists. *Environment and Planning A: Economy and Space, 38*(10), 1921–1940.

Markusen, A. (2013). Artists work everywhere. *Work and Occupations*, *40*(4), 481–495.

Menger, P.M. (1999). Artistic labor markets and careers. *Annual Review of Sociology*, *25*(1), 541–574.

Merkel, J. (2019). 'Freelance isn't free'. Co-working as a critical urban practice to cope with informality in creative labour markets. *Urban Studies*, *56*(3), 526–547.

Miles, M.B., and Huberman, A.M. (1994). *Qualitative Data Analysis: An Expanded Sourcebook*. London: SAGE.

Molotch, H. (2002). Place in product. *International Journal of Urban and Regional Research*, *26*(4), 665–668.

Molotch, H., Freudenburg, W., and Paulsen, K.E. (2000). History repeats itself, but how? City character, urban tradition, and the accomplishment of place. *American Sociological Review*, *65*(6), 791–823.

Montanari, F., Mizzau, L., and Razzoli, D. (2021a). 'Start me up': The challenge of sustainable cultural entrepreneurship for young cultural workers. In: L. Biondi, P. Demartini, L. Marchegiani, M. Marchiori, and M. Piber (eds), *Cultural Initiatives for Sustainable Development: Management, Participation and Entrepreneurship in the Cultural and Creative Sector* (pp. 143–160). Cham: Springer.

Montanari, F., Mizzau, L., Razzoli, D., and Rodighiero, S. (2021b). City context and subjective career success: How does creative workers' need for recognition filter city identity? *Human Relations*, *74*(5), 729–750.

Montanari, F., Scapolan, A., and Mizzau, L. (2018). Embeddedness and locational choices: A study of creative workers in a dance organization. *Urban Studies*, *55*(5), 1121–1138.

Musterd, S., and Gritsai, O. (2013). The creative knowledge city in Europe: Structural conditions and urban policy strategies for competitive cities. *European Urban and Regional Studies*, *20*(3), 343–359.

Nash, L. (2020). Performing place: A rhythmanalysis of the city of London. *Organization Studies*, *41*(3), 301–321.

Perry-Smith, J.E., and Mannucci, P.V. (2017). From creativity to innovation: The social network drivers of the four phases of the idea journey. *Academy of Management Review*, *42*(1), 53–79.

Rantisi, N.M., and Leslie, D. (2010). Materiality and creative production: The case of the Mile End neighborhood in Montréal. *Environment and Planning A: Economy and Space*, *42*(12), 2824–2841.

Razzoli, D., Rodighiero, S., Mizzau, L., and Montanari, F. (2020). Need for space. How artists rely on space to face precarious work conditions. *Sociologia del lavoro*, *157*, 164–185.

Rowlands, L., and Handy, J. (2012). An addictive environment: New Zealand film production workers' subjective experiences of project-based labour. *Human Relations*, *65*(5), 657–680.

Scott, A.J. (2000). *The Cultural Economy of Cities*. Thousand Oaks, CA: SAGE.

Scott, A.J. (2010). Cultural economy and the creative field of the city. *Geografiska Annaler: Series B, Human Geography*, *92*(2), 115–130.

Storper, M., and Scott, A.J. (2009). Rethinking human capital, creativity and urban growth. *Journal of Economic Geography*, *9*(2), 147–167.

Thornton, L., and Brunton, P. (2014). *Bringing the Reggio Approach to your Early Years Practice*. New York: Routledge.

Unioncamere Emilia-Romagna (2017). *Rapporto 2017 sull'Economia Regionale.* Available at: imprese.regione.emilia-romagna.it/notizie-primo-piano/2017/rapporto -2017-sulla-economia-della-emilia-romagna-prima-regione-per-crescita.

Waitt, G., and Gibson, C. (2009). Creative small cities: Rethinking the creative economy in place. *Urban Studies, 46*(5–6), 1223–1246.

Wittel, A. (2001). Toward a network sociality. *Theory, Culture and Society, 18*(6), 51–76.

Wojan, T.R., Lambert, D.M., and McGranahan, D.A. (2007). Emoting with their feet: Bohemian attraction to creative milieu. *Journal of Economic Geography, 7*(6), 711–736.

World Bank (2015). *World Development Indicators: Urbanization.* Available at: wdi .worldbank.org/table/3.12.

10. Crafting professionals: exploring the spatial and social mediation of professional networks in craft higher education

Lauren England

10.1 INTRODUCTION

Concerns over creative graduate outcomes have recently become more audible as the costs of higher education (HE) have risen, and critique of precarious employment has grown (McRobbie, 2016; Hjelde, 2015). This has brought the debate over entrepreneurial and career management skills development in creative education to the forefront (Ball et al., 2010; Bridgstock, 2011), including the role of networks (Hearn and Bridgstock, 2010). This chapter seeks to contribute to this growing body of literature and to respond to the call for 'greater recognition of the societal networks and advantage and disadvantage within which our Art Schools are located' (Orr and Shreeve, 2017: 51).

The chapter draws from a qualitative study of craft HE and professional development in the United Kingdom (UK) conducted between 2016 and 2018. While there are numerous definitions of craft (Adamson, 2010), the focus of this chapter is on the production of three-dimensional (3D) contemporary craft objects/artefacts in core craft materials: ceramics, furniture, glass, jewellery, metal crafts, silversmithing and textiles (Crafts Council, 2016). Findings are presented from a thematic analysis (Braun and Clarke, 2006) of semi-structured interviews on the provision and experience of professional development education with 15 craft educators and 26 final-year undergraduate students from four HE providers in England: Plymouth College of Art (PCA), Staffordshire University, London Metropolitan (London Met) and the University of Sunderland.

While this study is geographically limited to England for consistency in HE policy, which differs across the devolved nations of the UK,[1] the inclusion of four regional case studies enabled the exploration of how spatial dynamics can influence HE experience and professional development in association with significant variations in creative industries distribution, policies and investment favouring the capital (Mateos-Garcia and Bakhshi, 2016; Watson, 2020; Stark et al., 2013), but also broader regional socio-economic inequalities (McCann, 2016). It is presented that this influences creative students' professional processes, their perceptions of and opportunities for work (Faggian et al., 2013; Noonan, 2015). This research includes case studies from three cities that have experienced significant post-industrial decline and high levels of deprivation (Ministry of Housing, Communities and Local Government, 2019): Sunderland (North East), Stoke-on-Trent (West Midlands) and Plymouth (South West), alongside a London case.[2] It is suggested that this approach has relevance for the wider UK in considering interregional inequality in the creative economy (Watson, 2020; Stark et al., 2013), and wider European contexts with regional disparities and industrial decline (Iammarino et al., 2019). Internationally, there are also potential parallels with Australia, where comparative work on creative graduate outcomes has been undertaken (Brook et al., 2022), reflecting similarities in UK and Australian cultural and creative industries (CCIs) policies and HE systems.

This chapter begins by discussing the literature on the role of networks in creative career development, with reflection on the limited understanding of how professional networks – primarily contacts with creative professionals and CCIs organisations, but also manufacturing companies – are developed in creative education and craft, specifically beyond work experience/internships and live briefs (Allen et al., 2013; Orr and Shreeve, 2017). This includes discussion on links between HE and the creative economy (Comunian et al., 2015), and the role of place in educational contexts (Noonan, 2015).

Two key and connected mediators of networks within HE – place and educators – are then presented, with discussion on the opportunities and challenges for professional network development when mediated by these spatial and social factors. First, the methods of network development in HE are identified. It is then discussed how place plays a role in the practices and pathways that students are exposed to through the use of local networks and resources. The potential advantage of one location over another is considered here, highlighting regional differences in the local/regional economy, as well as CCIs markets and industry structures (Mateos-Garcia and Bakhshi, 2016) and associated socio-economic implications for creative career development (Brook et al., 2020; Oakley et al., 2017). The role of educators as creative network brokers and mediators (Foster and Ocejo, 2015) is also discussed here, as educators are seen to play a key role in determining students' engagement with other – local and non-local – artists, professionals and organisations throughout the degree. It is presented that this, in combination with geographical exposure, influences students' identification of potential career pathways. The chapter concludes with reflection on the role of networks in early-career craft career development and the implications of their spatial and social mediation, including the potential for inequalities in accessing craft careers to be reinforced.

10.2   CRAFT, HIGHER EDUCATION AND NETWORKS IN CREATIVE CAREERS

It is acknowledged that networks 'play a vital role in the creative community' (Harvey et al., 2012: 534), particularly when entering precarious creative labour markets (Lee, 2011) and in accessing resources and opportunities (Granovetter, 1977; Lin et al., 1981; Bourdieu, 2010). Craft networks have been explored in relation to skills sharing and communities of practice (Amin and Roberts, 2008), and clusters (Thomas et al., 2013), with some investigation of the role they play in craft career development (Hunt et al., 2010; England and Comunian, 2016). Hunt et al. (2010) suggest that craft students engage with multiple networks including formal professional networks, informal (family and friends), industry (work placement) and university (tutors, visiting artists) networks. However, the role these networks play in early career development and the influence of networks developed during the HE period on students' professional practice remains underexplored. England and Comunian (2016), however, highlight the influence of universities on professional network development and maintenance in craft careers for educators and local artists, indicating the importance of considering the role of HE providers in network development during the educational period. This is supported by the wider literature which acknowledges connections between higher education institutions (HEIs), industries and localities (Goddard and Vallance, 2013), including in the creative economy, where HEIs have been identified as contributing through cultural production and preservation, and the generation of creative human capital (Comunian and Gilmore, 2016), the provision of soft and hard infrastructure, governance and markets (England and Comunian, 2016).

In the wider literature on creative industries, professional networks and support systems are noted as critical both prior to and following graduation (Caves, 2000; Comunian et al., 2011; Ball et al., 2010; Mills, 2011). The transition from education to creative work is acknowledged as being reliant on 'who you know' (Bridgstock, 2011) and word-of-mouth recruitment is prominent (Allen et al., 2013). Here, networking is positioned as 'mandatory' (Lee, 2011), favouring those who are already socially 'networked' (Banks and Oakley, 2016), which exacerbates structural class, race and gender barriers to creative careers (Caves, 2000). Unequal access to network building opportunities during educational training, such as internships and work experience, have also been noted in relation to arts students' extant networks and social capital (Orr and Shreeve, 2017; Allen et al., 2013), which may render them more reliant on the university or their tutors to create networks on their behalf.

The concept and function of network brokerage – 'a complex process involving search, selection, co-production, and tastemaking functions that are accomplished by brokers in multiple formal roles (gatekeeper, coordinator, representative, etc.)' (Foster and Ocejo, 2015: 416) – has been explored extensively in creative industries literature. This chapter aims to reflect on the role of educators as brokers in craft HE – connecting those from outside an organisation (artists and industry partners) to those inside it (students), and connecting students to artists and industry – but also considers how their relationships with external, spatial factors influence network development.

The advantage of brokerage positions is acknowledged in studies on creative networks (Foster and Ocejo, 2015), but limits to network advantage have also been identified, including acknowledgement that 'tastemaking' can form exclusionary validations of particular forms of creative expression and expertise (Orr and Shreeve, 2017; Patel, 2020b). Gaps in employability skills development from creative HE have been associated with a lack of connections between HE and industry, and subsequently limited opportunities for developing industry awareness or experience (Bennett, 2016). The delivery of professional development training within a university context (workshop, studio or classroom) may therefore contribute to some of the challenges faced by craft (and other creative) graduates upon establishing their own practice outside of the security of the university studio. There have been calls to embed enterprise education in the curriculum through projects or work experience rather than deliver it as an 'add on' (Carey and Naudin, 2006), and to provide authentic, hands-on professional experience (Billett, 2009) and learning environments (Ashton, 2016) in which 'vocational practices, social capital and entrepreneurial expertise [can] be developed in situ' (Guile, 2010: 480). In this chapter the use of networks is considered in core curricula and extracurricular activities, and engagement inside and outside of the university.

It can be argued that inequalities in creative work (Brook et al., 2020) and craft specifically (Patel, 2020a) could be reproduced within the HE system through a lack of engagement with or challenge to the barriers experienced (in the UK, but also internationally) based on gender, race, class and disability. Another recognised limitation of networks is lock-in – 'a lack of openness and flexibility' (Boschma, 2005: 62) – which can be caused by 'geographical cognitive, organisational, social or institutional proximity' (*ibid*: 61). Considering geographic limitations, Karlsson asserts that 'local networks can be too closed, too exclusive and too rigid' (2011: 100–101). Within craft or creative careers this could be caused by closely clustered industries reliant on personal connections (Lee, 2011), regional isolation (Swords and Wray, 2010) or highly specialised practice such as a craft discipline – ceramics, glassmaking, etc. (England and Comunian, 2016).

Allen and Hollingworth (2013) and Noonan (2013, 2015) have also indicated that place influences the career planning and identities of creative students. Noonan (2013: 142) in particular states that 'place is part of the learning process', and notes 'clear triangulation between their institution, the creative economy and the geographical place both occupy'. Place also plays a significant role in the development of craft markets (Brown, 2014), influenced by factors such as local infrastructure, governance, soft infrastructure and local markets (Chapain and Comunian, 2010). Drake's (2003) study of micro and small creative businesses, including craft makers, also identifies connections between place and creative processes. This suggests that, in addition to the university learning environment, local resources, networks and infrastructure influence professional pathways. Studies on UK cultural labour markets and graduate trajectories have also highlighted the dominance of London and the South East (Faggian et al., 2013), and the potential for this spatial inequality to reinforce social inequality (Oakley et al., 2017). Place is therefore considered in this chapter to understand how regional/local networks and resources may be of significance in professional development (England and Comunian, 2016; Comunian and Gilmore, 2016), and the potential spatial advantages and disadvantages experienced by craft students across England.

This chapter seeks to bring together this diverse literature on creative HE, networks and creative careers to investigate the gaps in relation to craft education and career development. In connecting previous research on place and network brokerage in craft HE, it seeks to address limitations in our understanding of how professional networks are used, developed and mediated in this context, and how this creates geographical advantages and disadvantages in professional development which intersect with regional socio-economic inequalities, with implications for improving diversity in craft.

10.3   NETWORK DEVELOPMENT IN CRAFT HIGHER EDUCATION

In supporting students' awareness of professional pathways and their choice of career path, craft educators emphasised the identification of role models (other artists, designers and makers producing work in the style that students aspired to), and their professional trajectories and activities. From this, students would then identify their own goals and action plan. Exposure to professionals and different practices was therefore positioned as a key method of professional preparation, both in setting aspirations for students' own practice and in developing their understanding of available pathways.

Table 10.1   *Professional network development practices in craft higher education brokered by educators*

Professional network development in craft HE	
Outside HE	Inside HE
Core curricula provision	
Studio/industry/exhibition visits (local, UK)	Live briefs (set by industry partners)
Off-site creative projects	Visiting speakers
Sales events/pop-up stalls	Developing educator and peer-based network
Exhibition experience	
International fieldtrips	
Extracurricular provision	
Competitions/briefs	Competitions/briefs
Off-campus engagement with alumni	On-campus engagement with alumni
Summer schools (limited scholarships available)	Artists-in-residence programmes
Work experience/internships	Assisting on projects (internal work experience/internship)

Such exposure via guest speakers, site visits and live projects was identified by students as key to their understanding of creative careers and the identification of their own professional pathway, supporting the inclusion of these practices in the programme and their role in professional development. The professional experiences and networks of tutors and technicians with their own practices were also of value to the students, particularly those who were part-time educators with current industry experience.

To capture how networks were identified as being developed in the craft HE context (by students and educators), a framework is presented, including both on- and off-campus educational practices and core curricula and extracurricular activities (Table 10.1).

While many of the activities identified were common across the four regional case studies, what emerged was the significant differences in who they were engaging with in relation to the geographical locations of their university, and the availability of local resources and creative networks and markets in the region that could support their professional development. The regional differences between the four locations are important to highlight as they each present unique opportunities and challenges. The challenges presented by locality also appeared to encourage the promotion of engagement with non-local networks and opportunities that drew heavily on the personal networks and experiences of educators.

10.4   PLACE, PATHWAYS AND PERSONAL NETWORKS

Each location represented in this study (London, Plymouth, Stoke-on-Trent and Sunderland) presented unique opportunities and challenges for students in developing professional networks and gaining exposure to different forms of professional practice. In the cases of Staffordshire (Stoke-on-Trent) and Sunderland universities, this included connecting with their industrial craft heritage as well as new contemporary production taking place locally (Comunian and England, 2019), while PCA and London Met drew more on the prominence of creative business (of different scales) in the region.

Educators from Staffordshire emphasised the region's reputation (historical and contemporary) for ceramics production and the university's connections with local ceramics manufacturers as a means through which students were introduced to industrial processes and able to identify potential industry career opportunities:

> obviously we can benefit from uh the ceramic industry … So that might be having exhibitions there, working on live projects, having um, tours, talks, uh studio design, studio visits which I think is really, really key to see where the students can go … we've also got students that have progressed onto working in those companies as well, so we do try and link as much as possible. (Staffordshire Educator 1)

This suggests that the location of the course and presence of regional industry had some influence on opportunities for professional engagement through live briefs and other practices identified in Table 10.1. However, as reflected in the quotation below, the importance of exposing students to non-regional practices and organisations in order to expand their view of professional practice, and raise their ambitions to engage with the national and global craft and design sector, was also recognised. This nevertheless creates a reliance on educators leveraging their own professional connections to provide such opportunities, the implications of which are discussed in the next section:

> I send them off to studios in London and contacts I have in London so it's not all very, we don't, you know we don't want them to be provincial, parochial, we try and enlighten them in a way that's much, you know more ambitious I suppose in where they might go. (Staffordshire Educator 2)

In Sunderland the connection between the university and the National Glass Centre (NGC) was utilised to engage students with the exhibition programme, retail opportunities and work experience, including working in the NGC hot shop, gallery or on facilitation projects with visiting artists. Involvement in local or regional creative projects and commissions which could be embedded into professional development and creative modules was also identified:

> in the second year we have a module which is designing for making for space, site-specific contexts. So that would include working in a park in Gateshead ... they'll exhibit alongside professional artists, it's called Enchanted Parks. (Sunderland Educator 4)

Engagement with local industry via the course was limited by supply (Comunian and England, 2019), with the exception of a collaboration with a car manufacturer. Engagement with creative networks in the North East and regional artist projects and facilitation/fabrication opportunities were, however, promoted on-campus and off-site. In order to develop non-local networks, students were encouraged to engage with national and international opportunities, particularly Northlands Creative in Scotland and the summer programme at Pilchuck Glass School in the United States, again associated with educators' own connections. It was noted that a small number of scholarships were available to support students in accessing these opportunities.

At PCA, links were made with the high proportion of independent makers in the South West and associated professional associations and events such as the Devon Guild of Craftsmen and Bovey Tracey Contemporary Craft Fair. These were used to provide exhibition and work experience opportunities for students and to deliver a guest speaker programme. Connections were also made with creative organisations and venues, including local studio spaces and the Plymouth School of Creative Arts, for live projects and pop-up shops. As reflected in the quotation below, educators at Plymouth noted the lack of industry in the region and therefore the lack of opportunities for students to engage with industrial processes, in comparison to places such as Stoke-on-Trent where there is still an active manufacturing base:

> I mean it's all very uh being self-employed down here, because there is no industry ... if people want to do work placements in the South West they're working with usually very small [enterprises] you know artists on their own or SMEs [small and medium-sized enterprises]. (PCA Educator 4)

Projects, competitions and opportunities with local businesses such as Plymouth Gin and Princess Yachts were, however, offered through extra-curricular projects run across the college. There was also an emphasis on non-regional and international engagement with creative organisations, and trips to key sector events and exhibitions such as the London Design Festival and the British Ceramics Biennial: 'I think it's really important that they get out and see things in London and abroad and have a greater understanding' (PCA Educator 1). However, educators also noted financial barriers to students travelling independently for such opportunities, which could create or exacerbate socio-economic differences in students' HE experiences (Allen et al., 2013) and subsequent access to creative careers (Brook et al., 2020).

At London Met the co-location with the design industry and the wealth of cultural resources in London was used to create a network and exhibition opportunities for students, tapping into high-profile design events such as Clerkenwell Design Week and London Design Festival. Here an educator reflects on the university's location:

> We're right in the centre of a very creative hub, Brick Lane … you just turn around a corner and there's another furniture show room or a product, and it's all really up and coming designers and work that's not on the high-street. (London Met Educator 5)

Being based in London was also positioned as facilitating visits from and to professionals, including alumni. As articulated by an educator below, students based in London were also seen as having a key advantage in accessing work experience opportunities at short notice; drawing on educators' own local networks, but also by having lower travel expenses than those based outside of London, which could increase their likelihood of being selected for opportunities. While excluding non-local students may be undertaken to reduce the cost implications of taking part in (unpaid or low-paid) work experience, this nevertheless exacerbates regional inequalities in access to formative opportunities, that may be more likely to take place in London due to the concentration of cultural labour markets in the city (Oakley et al., 2017), as well as economic inequalities in only offering opportunities to those students able to afford to live and study in the capital. On the other hand, the cost of living in London was identified as negatively impacting upon students' capacity to take on extracurricular activities due to other work commitments:

> lots of our students go on to work with people that we know … it just wouldn't happen if they were outside of London … if I need a hand I don't ask for people who don't live locally, because I can't expect them to like travel on the train … So, if they're in London they can go and help someone at the weekend. (London Met Educator 1)

There were limits to localised partnerships, such as network lock-in and the mediation of professional opportunities by large organisations (England and Comunian, 2016) that emerged across the regions. As such, the types of practices students were exposed to locally could close off other pathways and practices if reliant on local resources. The inclusion of national and international field trips facilitated an expanded view of craft practice and potential pathways, although again there are financial implications, making these inaccessible for some students. A lack of exposure to industry, based on geographical location, could also impact upon students' awareness of large-scale production processes and the potential application of craft processes in this area. In the next section the implications of a reliance on educators using their personal networks to expand students' engagement with non-local professionals both on- and off-campus is discussed.

As identified earlier, educators often supported students' network development through the use of their own contacts, including alumni and in connection with local resources/networks but also non-local (UK and international) opportunities. This facilitated guest presentations on creative and professional practice, industry partnerships for live briefs, competitions and exhibitions, work experience opportunities, and opportunities for students to work with educators and other professionals on-campus. Across the four case studies, the brokerage role (Foster and Ocejo, 2015) of educators was highlighted (by the educators themselves and by students) in facilitating student involvement in such experiences, and their influence on pathway identification. Below, an educator reflects on the connections with artists that they opened up to students through (extracurricular) assisting roles on an artist residency programme:

> I think part of the service that I've been offering or been open to probably over the last ten, 13 years here is the artist access schemes … [students] come and work with me if I'm making work for a visiting artist … I think that is a very informalised way of actually getting right into the nitty gritty of working as a professional. (Sunderland Educator 2)

This highlights the role of HE in creative clusters and ecosystems in how the educators act as network facilitators both within and outside their walls (Comunian et al., 2011; Comunian and Faggian, 2014; Comunian et al., 2015; Comunian and Gilmore, 2016). Although references (by educators and students) to being in a 'creative bubble' at university and institutional networks that were heavily reliant on educators' personal networks also highlights the potential for network lock-in (Boschma, 2005).

From the student perspective, connections between the university, educators and the wider art scene at local, national and international levels were seen as contributing to the types of practices and opportunities they were exposed to. There was also an awareness that the status, size and specialism of a local art scene could also facilitate or hinder relevant professional network development, through both the university and independent activity. For example, Staffordshire students often referred to the location's ceramics heritage and the opportunities that afforded in terms of both reputation and the opportunities available. Similar remarks were made by Sunderland students in relation to glassmaking. It was noted, however, that other disciplines were not equally represented in the area:

> Stoke's obviously known for ceramics but I wouldn't say it has much for met-alsmiths, sort of if you went to London maybe there would be more opportunities out there for that sort of thing. (Staffordshire Student 2)

Students in Sunderland, Staffordshire and Plymouth suggested that their counterparts based in London had an advantage due to their proximity to industry, other creatives and cultural organisations, but also due to the relative wealth of the local population and subsequent market opportunities. This advantage was also acknowledged by all of the students based in the city; one student who had moved to London following a foundation diploma in Cornwall (South West) reflected on the comparative advantage of London in relation to network building during university, also noting the implications for students 'starting from fresh' if relocating (to London) after university:

> It's very easy visiting people in London I think, as opposed to being in Falmouth, that was a problem. Obviously it was only a foundation so it doesn't matter but a lot of my friends who stayed down there you then relocate to London or they come home and then suddenly you're kind of starting from fresh whereas a lot of stuff I think I've built up this year. (London Met Student 4)

In contrast, a student commented that the relative lack of opportunities in Plymouth had taught them a valuable lesson regarding the distribution of the UK's creative economy, and that this helped them in understanding how to position themselves and their professional practice:

> it's given me a realistic view in that not all places are the same, so certain areas are more creative, certain places are growing, it teaches you how to direct yourself and to mould yourself depending on the area in which you're in. (PCA Student 4)

Students' awareness of spatial disadvantages (and associated economic implications) may increase as they engage more with local and national CCIs through their degree, but may not inform their university choice, while others may experience limited opportunities for geographical mobility (Donnelly and Sol, 2018); while some students cited advantageous local infrastructure (i.e. the ceramics industry in Stoke) as a factor in their degree choice, material engagement opportunities and equipment (i.e. glassblowing) and proximity to home (regional or closer) were dominant considerations.

Such location-based choices reflect wider trends in reduced student mobility associated with the rising costs of HE, a phenomenon which disproportionately affects students from disadvantaged groups and exacerbates existing inequalities (Donnelly and Sol, 2018). This also has potential implications for graduate mobility and employment opportunities. This suggests that spatial and social advantages and disadvantages, prior to, during and post-HE, can be accumulative and should therefore be considered as connected to both student and graduate experiences and outcomes.

Overall, these findings indicate that the practices that inform creative career preparation through exposure to practitioners and pathways vary depending on their geographical context. This was particularly visible in references by educators and students, from all locations, to London as a creative hub with privileged access to networks, markets and opportunities; but also in references to Staffordshire having the advantage of being at the heart of the ceramics industry. While this presents potential advantages for regions with a strong craft heritage (Sunderland and Stoke-on-Trent) to capitalise on local networks and resources and potentially drive new contemporary market development (Comunian and England, 2019), the uneven distribution of CCIs markets (jobs, events, institutions and consumers and so on) (Faggian et al., 2013; Watson, 2020) can be seen to intersect with wider regional socio-economic divisions in the UK (McCann, 2016; Oakley et al., 2017).

10.5   DISCUSSION

This chapter has sought to highlight methods of professional network development in craft HE and its mediation by spatial and social factors. The role of spatial factors (availability of industry networks, opportunities for work experience or employment and the status of the local art scene) highlighted in this study supports the argument that place informs students' learning experiences (Noonan, 2015). In particular, the perceived value of different places according to their symbolic status in the creative economy, and the tangible resources and opportunities they offered to students, in both cosmopolitan cities and regional areas, emerges (Noonan, 2013; Allen and Hollingworth, 2013). It also suggests that links between HE and the creative economy (Comunian and Gilmore, 2016; Comunian et al., 2015), and the role of local networks in professional development (England and Comunian, 2016), should be carefully considered in relation to creative graduate pathways. The potential advantage of one location over another (London) links with wider debate around regional disparity in cultural investment and the distribution of the creative industries (Stark et al., 2013), and wider class-based inequalities in creative work (Brook et al., 2020). Here the local infrastructure and the professional networks of educators may facilitate or hinder professional development, depending on relative levels of access and provision.

In considering educators as network brokers and mediators (Foster and Ocejo, 2015) it is argued that their facilitation of network development in and outside of HE has the potential to reduce students' reliance on extant social networks and capital in accessing professional development opportunities (Orr and Shreeve, 2017). It is nevertheless acknowledged that students may continue to leverage their personal connections to support their career development during and post-HE. Furthermore, it is suggested that a reliance on educators' professional networks and local infrastructure could facilitate or hinder professional development, depending on relative levels of access and provision. This presents an issue of what practices are legitimised or delegitimised (Orr and Shreeve, 2017), and what narratives of creativity (Taylor and Littleton, 2012) and professional practice students are exposed to (in addition to geographic influences), thus problematising the tastemaking function of the brokerage position (Foster and Ocejo, 2015). Particular challenges highlighted here include the potential for lock-in (Boschma, 2005), given the reliance on educators' personal networks.

There is, however, potential for the recent move online associated with the Covid-19 pandemic, and development of remote teaching and learning practices, to support greater equality in online network participation and engagement that across a distributed and de-centred community, opportunity to engage beyond place. Further opportunity for a regional levelling-up across craft markets is also presented by the rise of online craft consumption (Crafts Council, 2020), and the further development of regional creative clusters and micro clusters both within and outside of big cities (Siepel, 2020).

10.6   CONCLUSION

It is argued that the spatial and social assets and limitations that impact upon professional network opportunities need to be accounted for in the development (and marketing) of degree programmes. The importance of educator networks also has implications for what knowledge can be brought into HE, and the opportunities that can be facilitated by strategic staffing choices. It is argued that students need to be exposed to a wide variety of practices and pathways, and for non-local networks to be established, in order to develop their understanding of the viability of different pathways and strategies for sustaining a professional creative practice after graduation (England, 2022). Additional institutional support may also be needed to enable students with limited financial resources to engage in such formative activities.

While it has been acknowledged that university quality, discipline, degree qualification and location make a difference to graduate outcomes both within and outside of the creative economy (McGuinness, 2003; Comunian et al., 2011; Faggian et al., 2013), further research and theoretical models are needed to understand the multi-level connections between individual characteristics, the creative educational experience (including location, staffing, curricula and more) and graduate trajectories that can be applied to both craft and other disciplines.

NOTES

1. Funding systems for HE in the UK differ across the devolved nations: annual tuition fees paid by students (often supported by a student loan) are currently £9250 in England, £9000 in Wales and £4395 in Northern Ireland, with no fees in Scotland. There are also differences in degree structures and duration: in England, Wales and Northern Ireland bachelors honours degrees are typically three years full-time; in Scotland they take four years.
2. It is acknowledged that high levels of deprivation are also found in London boroughs.

REFERENCES

Adamson, G. 2010. *The Craft Reader*, Oxford: Berg.
Allen, K. and Hollingworth, S. 2013. 'Sticky subjects' or 'cosmopolitan creatives'? Social class, place and urban young people's aspirations for work in the knowledge economy. *Urban Studies*, 50, 499–517.
Allen, K., Quinn, J., Hollingworth, S. and Rose, A. 2013. Becoming employable students and 'ideal' creative workers: exclusion and inequality in higher education work placements. *British Journal of Sociology of Education*, 34, 431–452.
Amin, A. and Roberts, J. 2008. Knowing in action: beyond communities of practice. *Research Policy*, 37, 353–369.
Ashton, D. 2016. From campus to creative quarter: constructing industry identities in creative places. *Higher Education and the Creative Economy*, London: Routledge.
Ball, L., Pollard, E. and Stanley, N. 2010. *Creative Graduates Creative Futures*, CGCF Higher Education.
Banks, M. and Oakley, K. 2016. The dance goes on forever? Art schools, class and UK higher education. *International Journal of Cultural Policy*, 22, 41–57.
Bennett, D. 2016. Developing employability in higher education music. *Arts and Humanities in Higher Education*, 15, 386–395.
Billett, S. 2009. Realising the educational worth of integrating work experiences in higher education. *Studies in Higher Education*, 34, 827–843.
Boschma, R. 2005. Proximity and innovation: a critical assessment. *Regional Studies*, 39, 61–74.
Bourdieu, P. 2010. *The Forms of Capital (1986)*, Chichester: John Wiley & Sons.
Braun, V. and Clarke, V. 2006. Using thematic analysis in psychology. *Qualitative Research in Psychology*, 3, 77–101.
Bridgstock, R. 2011. Skills for creative industries graduate success. *Education + Training*, 53, 9–26.
Brook, O., O'Brien, D. and Taylor, M. 2020. *Culture is Bad for You: Inequality in the Cultural and Creative Industries*, Manchester: Manchester University Press.
Brook, S., Comunian, R., Corcoran, J., Faggian, A., Jewell, S. and Webb, J. 2022. *Gender and Creative Careers*, London: Palgrave.
Brown, J. 2014. *Making it Local: What Does this Mean in the Context of Contemporary Craft*. London: Crafts Council.

Carey, C. and Naudin, A. 2006. Enterprise curriculum for creative industries students: an exploration of current attitudes and issues. *Education + Training*, 48, 518–531.

Caves, R.E. 2000. *Creative Industries: Contracts between Art and Commerce*, Cambridge, MA: Harvard University Press.

Chapain, C. and Comunian, R. 2010. Enabling and inhibiting the creative economy: the role of the local and regional dimensions in England. *Regional Studies*, 44, 717–734.

Comunian, R. and England, L. 2019. Creative clusters and the evolution of knowledge and skills: from industrial to creative glassmaking. *Geoforum*, 99, 238–247.

Comunian, R. and Faggian, A. 2014. Creative graduates and creative cities: exploring the geography of creative education in the UK. *International Journal of Cultural and Creative Industries*, 1, 19–34.

Comunian, R., Faggian, A. and Jewell, S. 2011. Winning and losing in the creative industries: an analysis of creative graduates' career opportunities across creative disciplines. *Cultural Trends*, 20, 291–308.

Comunian, R. and Gilmore, A. 2016. *Higher Education and the Creative Economy: Beyond the Campus*, London: Routledge.

Comunian, R., Gilmore, A. and Jacobi, S. 2015. Higher education and the creative economy: creative graduates, knowledge transfer and regional impact debates. *Geography Compass*, 9, 371–383.

Crafts Council UK. 2016. *Studying Craft 16: Trends in Craft Education and Training*, London: Crafts Council UK.

Crafts Council UK. 2020. *The Market for Craft*, London: Crafts Council UK.

Donnelly, M. and Sol, G. 2018. *Home and Away: Social, Ethnic and Spatial Inequalities in Student Mobility*, London: Sutton Trust.

Drake, G. 2003. 'This place gives me space': place and creativity in the creative industries. *Geoforum*, 34, 511–524.

England, L. 2022. Crafting professionals: entrepreneurial strategies for making a living through passionate work. *Innovation*, DOI:10.1080/14479338.2021.2019043.

England, L. and Comunian, R. 2016. Support or competition? Assessing the role of HEIs in professional networks and local creative communities: the case of glassmaking in Sunderland. In R. Comunian and A. Gilmore (eds.), *Higher Education and the Creative Economy*, London: Routledge, 177–195.

Faggian, A., Comunian, R., Jewell, S. and Kelly, U. 2013. Bohemian graduates in the UK: disciplines and location determinants of creative careers. *Regional Studies*, 47, 183–200.

Foster, P. and Ocejo, R.E. 2015. Brokerage, mediation, and social networks in the creative industries. In C. Jones, M. Lorenzen and J. Sappeed (eds.), *The Oxford Handbook of Creative Industries*. Oxford: Oxford University Press, 405–420.

Goddard, J.B. and Vallance, P. 2013. *The University and the City*, London: Routledge.

Granovetter, M.S. 1977. The strength of weak ties. *Social Networks*. Elsevier.

Guile, D.J. 2010. Learning to work in the creative and cultural sector: new spaces, pedagogies and expertise. *Journal of Education Policy*, 25, 465–484.

Harvey, D.C., Hawkins, H. and Thomas, N.J. 2012. Thinking creative clusters beyond the city: people, places and networks. *Geoforum*, 43, 529–539.

Hearn, G.N. and Bridgstock, R.S. 2010. Education for the creative economy: innovation, transdisciplinarity, and networks. In D. Araya and M.A. Peters (eds.), *Education in the Creative Economy: Knowledge and Learning in the Age of Innovation*. New York: Peter Lang Publishing Inc., 93–116.

Hjelde, K. 2015. Paradox and potential: fine art employability and enterprise perspectives. *Art, Design and Communication in Higher Education*, 14, 175–188.

Hunt, W., Ball, L. and Pollard, E. 2010. *Crafting Futures: a Study of the Early Careers of Crafts Graduates from UK Higher Education Institutions*. Institute for Employment Studies, Brighton/University of the Arts London, London/The Crafts Council, London.

Iammarino, S., Rodríguez-Pose, A. and Storper, M. 2019. Regional inequality in Europe: evidence, theory and policy implications. *Journal of Economic Geography*, 19, 273–298.

Karlsson, C. 2011. Clusters, networks and creativity. In Andersson, D.E., Anderson, Å.E. and Mellander, C. (eds.), *Handbook of Creative Cities*. Cheltenham, UK: Edward Elgar, 85–114.

Lee, D. 2011. Networks, cultural capital and creative labour in the British independent television industry. *Media, Culture and Society*, 33, 549–565.

Lin, N., Ensel, W.M. and Vaughn, J.C. 1981. Social resources and strength of ties: structural factors in occupational status attainment. *American Sociological Review*, 46, 393–405.

Mateos-Garcia, J. and Bakhshi, H. 2016. *The Geography of Creativity in the UK*, London: Nesta.

Mccann, P. 2016. *The UK Regional-National Economic Problem: Geography, Globalisation and Governance*, London: Routledge.

Mcguinness, S. 2003. University quality and labour market outcomes. *Applied Economics*, 35, 1943–1955.

McRobbie, A. 2016. *Be Creative: Making a Living in the New Culture Industries*, Cambridge: Polity Press.

Mills, C. 2011. Enterprise orientations: a framework for making sense of fashion sector start-up. *International Journal of Entrepreneurial Behavior and Research*, 17, 245–271.

Ministry of Housing, Communities and Local Government. 2019. *The English Indices of Deprivation 2019*. London: MHCLG.

Noonan, C. 2013. Smashing childlike wonder? The early journey into higher education. In D. Ashton and C. Noonan (eds.), *Cultural Work and Higher Education.* London: Palgrave Macmillan, 133–153.

Noonan, C. 2015. Professional mobilities in the creative industries: the role of 'place' for young people aspiring for a creative career. *Cultural Trends*, 24, 299–309.

Oakley, K., Laurison, D., O'Brien, D. and Friedman, S. 2017. Cultural capital: arts graduates, spatial inequality, and London's impact on cultural labor markets. *American Behavioral Scientist*, 61, 1510–1531.

Orr, S. and Shreeve, A. 2017. *Art and Design Pedagogy in Higher Education: Knowledge, Values and Ambiguity in the Creative Curriculum*, London: Routledge.

Patel, K. 2020a. Diversity initiatives and addressing inequalities in craft. In S. Taylor and S. Luckman (eds.), *Pathways into Creative Working Lives*, Cham: Palgrave Macmillan, 175–191.

Patel, K. 2020b. *The Politics of Expertise in Cultural Labour: Arts, Work and Inequalities*, Lanham, MD: Rowman & Littlefield Publishers.

Siepel, J. 2020. Small engines of growth: understanding creative microclusters. Available from: https://pec.ac.uk/blog/small-engines-of-growth-understanding -creative-microclusters (accessed 19 November 2020).

Stark, P., Gordon, C. and Powell, D. 2013. Rebalancing our cultural capital. Available from: http://www.gpsculture.co.uk/downloads/rocc/Rebalancing_FINAL_3mb.pdf.

Swords, J. and Wray, F. 2010. The connectivity of the creative industries in North East England – the problems of physical and relational distance. *Local Economy*, 25, 305–318.

Taylor, S. and Littleton, K. 2012. *Contemporary Identities of Creativity and Creative Work*, Farnham: Ashgate.

Thomas, N.J., Harvey, D.C. and Hawkins, H. 2013. Crafting the region: creative industries and practices of regional space. *Regional studies*, 47, 75–88.

Watson, A. 2020. Not all roads lead to London: insularity, disconnection and the challenge to 'regional' creative industries policy. *Regional Studies*, 54 (11), 1574–1584.

11. Emerging spatial relations of artists and art scenes through the lens of art schools in Manchester and Leipzig

Silvie Jacobi

11.1 INTRODUCTION

This chapter provides an overview of empirical research on the location choice, place engagements and mobility dynamics of art school students and graduates in Manchester and Leipzig. It highlights, firstly, the importance of place within creative industries research as interconnected and relational phenomena, and questions the reliance on talent attraction and sector clusters to make a successful creative city. Secondly, the chapter outlines a focus on practice in understanding the formation of sense of place and spatial relations in the art world. Key literature is introduced to allow for a better positioning of the research question and subject area of contemporary art and the art world within the field of creative cities and regions, after which place concepts and theories are introduced to detail from what theoretical perspective empirical findings were analysed. After outlining case study contexts, the empirical section discusses findings between the cases of Manchester and Leipzig and their respective art schools, with the aim to summarise key findings and analyse them in terms of their significance for understanding geographical dynamics of the art world as an example of mobilities in creative work and networks.

11.2 LITERATURE REVIEW

Creative Cities and Talent Migration

Existing research and critique on the creative city and creative regions (Andersson et al., 2011), including dynamics of clustering in the creative industries, have often emerged through a single-sited view in urban studies issues or on economic impact in a city or region (e.g. Bagwell, 2008; Waitt and Gibson, 2009; Harris and Moreno, 2010; Gilmore et al., 2016) and less so from connectivity with other places, despite Florida's (2005) creative class being considered a highly mobile class. From a single-sited context, solutions were often derived for creative industry policy to, for example, support narratives of regional growth (Bagwell, 2008), retention of talent (Comunian and Faggian, 2014; Gilmore et al., 2016) and the establishment of top-down creative hubs, clusters or quarters (Mould and Comunian, 2015). A better understanding is needed of geographical dynamics of creative professionals through an empirical account of mobility, rather than focusing on policy mobility (Prince, 2012) as abstract forms of empirical reality, which does not necessarily reveal underlying cultural and artistic practices that make cities creative. In much of the creative city literature we see a repeated instrumentalisation of artistic production in making a city more attractive, and as a guaranteed mechanism to attract talent (Burdack et al., 2009; Comunian and Faggian, 2014). The value of this chapter lies in questioning the place attraction narrative and favouring a view of interconnectedness and dynamism between places determined by practice, despite the focus on art schools as place-bound institutions.

Furthermore, the focus on a single site is limited in a context of geographical debate in which a global sense of place (Massey, 1991) has put the identity of a specific place into the context of its relations with multiple others. Creative industry professionals, for example, navigate multiple places through their work and may even live in two or more places at the same time. The most extreme of this case might be that of digital nomads (Müller, 2016) who do not have a permanent place to live. Existing perspectives on mobility in this context include bohemian graduates navigating the creative industries on a much larger scale than the place of their study (Comunian and Faggian, 2014), investigations of rural creative clusters and their relationship with the urban (Harvey et al., 2012), and the mobility of modern artists from art historical research (Hellmanzik, 2009).

Contemporary Art, the Art World and Fine Art Education

This chapter specifically focuses on the case of the art world and how emerging contemporary artists navigate it today as they go through and beyond art school. The research investigates fine art education as a discipline taught within art schools, which is predominantly concerned with the production of contemporary art and, to some extent, participating in the art market and/or being engaged in artist-led activity. This is important, as fine art is the discipline from which art schools originally emerged, and which is least connected with a monetised economic value chain which could be referred to as an 'industry'. Rather than looking into creative higher education generally, along the lines of what have been defined as bohemian graduates (Faggian et al., 2013), the aim for this chapter is to look specially into education environments at art schools (Madoff, 2009), raising their profile as important infrastructure of the city and its art scene, and allowing a geographical angle of investigation of artistic production.

In the art world, artists and educators are less involved with the art market, which is primarily navigated by gallerists, auction houses and collectors, and could be understood as an industry in itself. Curators and critics are perhaps the only link with the production environment (Birnbaum and Graw, 2008). This discipline-specific outlook helps creative industry researchers and policymakers to understand that place-specific dynamics are defined by practices unique to each sector or sub-discipline. Therefore this chapter not only contributes to an understanding of an expanded sense of place in which creative talent mobility and place attachment are connected processes beyond one place (Massey, 1991, 2012), but it also retires overstretched policy concepts relating to the creative industries as homogenous in policy aspirations and support mechanisms. For example, there is some contention from within the contemporary art sector as to whether artists can even be considered as part of the creative industries, as their work and practices are considered not strictly economical due to a social and symbolic value regime (Abbing, 2008; Beech, 2015).

Place and Spatial Relations

The definitions of place (Cresswell, 2015) and spatial relations play an important part to appreciate the global sense of place concept (Massey, 1991; Harvey, 2012). The literature outlines how place is space that has been shaped by human processes (Casey, 1997; Vickery, 2011; Cresswell, 2015), which points to the importance of social and cultural practices in understanding place, and in the case of this chapter this extends also to artistic practices. A 'global' understanding expands notions of place and rootedness beyond a singular identity, emphasising that mobility and multiple places are as important in how we construct place as internal place characteristics.

In contrast to place, spatial relations refer to structural conditions such as a city's size, density or distances between places, which determine the conditions within which social, cultural or artistic practices evolve. Art scenes and the art world, however, themselves have spatial relations, more broadly referred to as geographies, which as shown in the findings are determined through practice more so than mere spatial configuration. The focus on practice is why the communities of practice concept (Wenger, 1998) has been applied to understand how learning in practice-based environments has a socially and spatially organised form, which also allows for a spatial understanding of art scenes as landscapes of practice (Wenger-Trayner and Wenger-Trayner, 2014). Although the latter concept of landscapes of practice is not primarily a geographical phenomenon, it can explain how art scenes are spatially con-figured through practice rather than through a singular place as a boundary.

11.3   CASE STUDY CONTEXT AND METHODOLOGY

As this research was carried out within the framework of a joint PhD between King's College London and Humboldt University Berlin, empirical research took place between Germany and the United Kingdom (UK). The compara-tive angle not only allows for geographical analysis, but also looks into how a state-funded education in Germany can result in different geographical formations compared to a privatised system in the UK. The Leipzig case was chosen because of previous research that I conducted there which revealed the importance of the art school in the emergence of the New Leipzig School, a movement that made Leipzig known internationally for its representational painting; whereas I selected Manchester School of Art on the basis of its open-ness to participate in the research, as well as choosing Manchester as a place that had comparable spatial relations.

Both art schools have a long-standing history within the art scenes and economy of their city, with Manchester School of Art founded in the early nineteenth century to feed design talent into the needs of industrialisation, and the Leipzig Academy of Fine Arts founded in the mid-eighteenth century to initially focus on drawing, and a century later to support the growing publish-ing industry.

The Manchester school is now attached to Manchester Metropolitan University and is one of the most popular schools in terms of volume of appli-cations from within the UK, benefiting from being a culturally vibrant city and having a diversity of high-quality art and design courses. Art schools in the UK are in most cases part of universities, but have their roots in independent art schools, which later on became polytechnics and subsequently universities (Chatterton, 2000; Banks and Oakley, 2016).

Leipzig Academy is renowned for the New Leipzig School (Gerlach, 2008; Rehberg and Schmidt, 2009) movement of painters during the 1990s, which attracted many students from across Germany interested in skill-based train-ing which was still nurtured at the school despite changes after the German Democratic Republic (GDR) opening up to other art media training there. Leipzig presents a case of a city that is experiencing unprecedented growth after a sustained period of shrinkage during the 1990s and 2000s follow-ing German Reunification (Bontje, 2005). The city is known for a strong sub-cultural and artist-led scene (Raabe and Waltz, 2014), which emerged in empty factories and houses.

Compared to the density of arts organisation for the size of the city in Leipzig, Manchester is considered to have a small visual arts scene.

Manchester and Leipzig are both post-industrial cities (Mace et al., 2004) and feature former cotton mills, some of which are now used as workspaces for creatives. The cities are attractive places as university and regional cultural hubs, with Manchester being a driver behind the Northern Powerhouse and decentralisation of the UK's economy.

11.4   EMPIRICAL EVIDENCE AND ANALYSIS

The first step into understanding the emerging sense of place and spatial relations of artists was to examine why they decided to attend a specific art school and what motivated them to go there. For some respondents this choice was due to the place of the school, especially in the Manchester case, where students repeatedly compared its affordability yet good size and cultural diversity with London, which was associated with artistic learning being 'stifled' due to lack of space and time to focus on studying. In the Leipzig case, however, many students were attracted to the school because of its unique repertoire of teaching framed in the traditional master–student system, with the New Leipzig School signalling its excellence for representational painting (Gerlach, 2008). Since the 1960s, with the shift towards conceptual art and an expansion of what practice and artistic medium mean (Krauss, 1979; Buchloh, 1990), painting and in particular its representational modes alongside life drawing were not compulsory and/or completely vanished from the curriculum. Leipzig kept this specialism alive as its professors practised in representational style during the GDR era, and after its collapse continued to engage with this legacy in new ways.

In comparison, many UK art schools including the Manchester school have less of a specialist profile due to the hybridity of fine art degrees and regularly changing teaching staff. This may offer more opportunities for exchange and innovation, as boundaries between communities of practice are more often crossed; however, it also can mean less permanence for artists in establishing their artistic positions. In the Manchester case students entering art school were generally aged between 18 and 21, with only a few mature students and career changers; whereas Leipzig Academy students ranged between 18 and 40 years of age, with some already having a solidified understanding of their artistic interests and positions are when they enrolled. Along with a longer time frame in which students undertake their studies (five years to complete a diploma), this increased the students' understanding of association or disassociation with place.

The arrival at art school in both institutions was perceived as a step into learning not only the language of art, but also that of place. This evolves informally at the beginning of the course with students navigating their new city, as well as becoming engaged in the student art scene through attending or setting up exhibitions within and externally to the schools. Part of the curriculum in both institutions is an optional engagement in modules that sit at the intersection between art and geography (Hawkins, 2013), in which students explore expanded practices and learn to become 'streetwise' and use place as an extended learning environment. This context highlights the importance of place in art school education, as art is exhibited and produced in, and influenced by the world around it:

> Through the school's activities space is involved. Because at the school you can work and make things, you have to show this somewhere. And we visit these shows together and familiarise ourselves with them. Despite this happening geographically outside of the school, it somehow remains part of the academic activity ... For exhibitions there is no book where you can read how to develop them. It is not a theoretical undertaking but a practical form of learning. That's why the involvement in a location and with an exhibition space is always part of a learning process, because each exhibition has its own unique challenges. There is always something you don't know yet, and that is the learning process. That's why the connection between the city and the school is clear. (Media Art Graduate and Lecturer from Leipzig Academy, lives and works in Leipzig and Berlin)

This engagement has resulted in analytical and material engagement with space and place through artist-led activities, and for some students this shapes their practice for many years to come:

> I remember the early activities, assignments that we were given were very much like Psycho-geography and kind of exploring the city. I remember the first day we were split into groups and there was a map of Manchester. We were given a square of Manchester that we had to just go out to find, to walk around it. I think we just had to make rubbings and bring stuff from that area. Then we all came back and made a map out of everyone's different things ... I always still walk past the square where we did that. (Sculpture Graduate from Manchester School of Art)

These are examples of practices that are discussed as 'expanded' (Krauss, 1979), which relate to place and space in manifold ways, as Hawkins (2013) itemises. While at Manchester these practices would fall under the loosely structured sculpture pathway within the fine art department, in Leipzig this falls under the category of 'media art', taught in the old-fashioned master–student system in which students are allocated a professor whose practice becomes a role model.

To illustrate some of the place engagements that these kind of practices produce, I will give several short examples. Students in Manchester were particularly engaged in the city's history around socialism, Marx and protest movements, following some introduction through their lecturers in tutorials, or site visits in which they engaged in psychogeographical methods. They used conventional qualitative research methods and archival research as a means to establish context and subject matter for their work, which resulted in performance works re-enacting historical realities in the context of the city today, turning place into temporary art and political event spaces for their mainly student audiences. Other colleagues were more invested in creating affordable production conditions for their work, and with it opportunities to create exhibition spaces, as the city has little opportunity otherwise to show in an institutional context. These spaces required a re-thinking of conventions of what a gallery is and how exhibiting can also be an intervention in urban space; for example through a group of students led by a visiting lecturer who hired a hotel room to stage a show. These engagements forge relationships with the material aspects of the city, that is, the built environment, and through practices enacted in these, space becomes place (Cresswell, 2015).

In Leipzig, where a lively artist-led scene and empty spaces provided a playground for artistic experimentation, students in media art established studios in spaces outside of the school as they do not have permanent space there during their studies. Some of the students as a result became involved in the refurbishment of properties, communal living and setting up residency projects to work with international artists, as well as running their own exhibition spaces. Some of the lecturers, however, considered these activities as too time-consuming or politically engaged, which they considered a form of instrumentalisation of artistic practice rather than a form of autonomy. Some of the students argue in response to this that it is essential to conduct such activities in order to develop artistic opportunity beyond the institutional and art market context, as a way to secure a livelihood often based on an alternative economy. This was possible until very recently, as Leipzig maintained relatively high vacancy levels in the built environment as an effect of long-term shrinkage, and rent levels being among the lowest in Germany. For artist-led spaces this meant that artists used spaces for free in exchange for their upkeep. Although Manchester has affordable rents compared to other UK cities, artist-led projects emerged on a fluctuating basis as space came with a price-tag, and currently studio projects are being pushed to the fringes of the city.

For painters in Leipzig, the studio and industrial urban environment of the city elicited a specific feeling, in which interviewed artists reported being particularly productive. However, those engaging in media art practice in both Leipzig and Manchester felt that place could be exhausted, and they needed to apply their methods (that is, socially engaged practices, installation art, new exhibition formats) in other cities, to encounter new perspectives and be more connected with people who are also engaged in similar forms of practice:

> You learn to paint in that specific place. You have created yourself an environment there in which you learned how to paint. I think it is hard to dispute the importance of how one is integrated in that place ... How does the atelier fit in with the sur-

rounding urban environment? You need life in a city. Change that makes a change in your work. The ability to be part of this change by doing things yourself. (Painting Graduate of Leipzig Academy, lives and works in Leipzig)

While painters did not directly engage with place as subject matter, their place attachment in Leipzig was very strong, which was evidenced through the city as the environment of inspiration, locus of a permanent studio and practice-specific support networks. The relationship that painters built with Leipzig is also linked to the prevailing repertoire in which they become embedded when they start studying. Yet students who directly engaged with place through media art practices felt the need to be mobile and to relocate in pursuit of new opportunities, as the repertoire and with it associated exclusivities, alienated them. This is also likely because painterly practices require a certain permanence in a studio setting (Buren and Repensek, 1979), which expanded practices move away from, for example through working in communities, public space or temporary sites. Likewise Manchester graduates, whose practices were less specialised than those of Leipzig graduates, noted how the city had its limitations once they had explored artist-led spaces and exhibited, as one artists expressed it, 'everywhere'.

It could be expected that expanded art practices (for example, socially engaged practices, media art, installation, film and so on) require active engagement with place that creates more intense connections with it, but this research has shown how this does not necessarily result in greater place attachment, as artists look for newness and therefore need new places to navigate. This poignantly underlines the necessity of analysing intricate practices within a sector of the creative industries to understand geographical form and processes. It also points to the need to look at connectivity between places as a source for understanding innovation in a sector.

While I have highlighted how sense of place is closely connected with artistic practices and certain ways of teaching within a specific repertoire, students develop spatial relations over their time in education. These are relations with place, and places beyond, on the basis of size, density, proximity to other places and what this means for the purpose of pursuing an artistic livelihood. Relations with the place in which young artists study are often expressed through analysis of places beyond, and in both cases to the capital cities of London and Berlin, which are in relative proximity. Here, especially London was evaluated critically in terms of its size, density and standing in the national and international hierarchy of cities, resulting in issues with unaffordable student housing, lack of studio space and lack of time resulting from employment needed to support student studies. In the German case this scenario played out less on an economic scale, as Berlin is still considered affordable. However, culturally, Berlin's size was considered too large for a coherent sense of belonging in art scenes to be experienced, as they were perceived as too fragmented and constantly changing. It can be assumed that regional cities, in the cases of Leipzig and Manchester, were considered productive for the duration of artistic study, because some of their cultural limitations created a focus and a stable environment that global cities could not provide.

Spatial relations are furthermore developed at the moment when art students graduate and need to make a decision as to whether they should stay in or leave their place of study. This ranges between place attachment and mobility, which I am illustrating here as an interconnected process, as both are recurrently negotiated by artists. There are some respondents in both cases who underlined how students should make use of the local networks and infrastructure already established in their city of study; however, this is perhaps too linear as an assumption. Communities of practice can disperse geographically, depending on where artists find a productive platform for their artistic position and livelihood; for example, for media art students of the Leipzig Academy the relationship with Berlin was essential to develop their identities as artists and their professional networks. This means although their practice emerged from the Leipzig Academy and has a shared repertoire amongst people who trained there, this network expands geographically as members of the community move to Berlin to find better conditions for their work. This can be transferred to how we understand art scenes as geographically dispersed or as geographically imagined. A lecturer detailed how some of his current students and alumni from Leipzig often meet in the same study group constellation in Berlin:

> In my experience people look towards Berlin. For painting the connection with being here [Leipzig] is still tight. All the students of Neo Rauch are rooted here and work here, at Spinnerei [artist studio hub in Leipzig] mostly. They made it, but others move away. Leipzig does remain a point of reference amongst them in Berlin, however. They meet in a similar constellation. (Media Art Student at Leipzig Academy)

Although the community, which can be understood as the art scene, is affiliated with Leipzig, its physical location has become affiliated with Berlin. This is a case in which art scenes can be understood as landscapes of practice, as they are not strictly determined by its physical geography and boundaries, but by geographical imaginaries determined by practice and spatialised practice boundaries. As the teaching at Manchester School of Art in fine art is much more hybrid and less defined by a specific repertoire, art students tend to disperse geographically as they graduate, and there is less of a capacity to trace their communities according to their practice profile, but more so around further education or economic opportunities.

Spatial relations are also determined by the function that places hold within the art world; for example, while Manchester is considered a favourable place for artistic study, it has fared less well in terms of providing access to an art market. Here young artists are still required to have connections with London or to travel frequently in order to advance their careers, meet gallerists and collectors. However, this poses barriers for those with less financial backing and creates inequality in a power geometry of time-space (Massey, 2012). There is also a notion that as soon as an artist has made a name for themselves, they are less dependent on location and they have the benefit of financial resources to travel:

> Based in London someone can call me up to come to the studio. Those things aren't impossible for Manchester but you need to be at a certain point in your career where someone is going to take a 2-hour train journey. (Painting Graduate from Manchester School of Art, lives and works in London)

> I have exhibited a lot cross regional in the last few years. This is something that annoys me. I liked to do it for a few years but I am tired of it now. But it is part of it if you don't just want to show in Leipzig ... Having to continuously travel, reacting to new spaces, situations, people, conditions that I encounter there. Despite often not receiving any money, they expect you to do it, still. With all these decisions you think about your portfolio. Where you exhibited is always good to read. International is even better, to be part of something to give you status. (Media Art Graduate from Leipzig Academy, lives and works in Leipzig)

While this media art graduate travels to overcome the limitations of her site-specific work in Leipzig, other locally based artists, especially those engaged in painting, benefit from the local market around the New Leipzig School repertoire and hype, which has allowed a considerable number of graduates to thrive locally and build a strong although exclusive scene.

The notion of the local artists in Leipzig seems to allow for enhanced reputation in the art world because of the recollection of the schools' repertoire alongside the New Leipzig School movement on the international scale. With Manchester not having a distinct local school of art, the status of the local artist has even been considered as a patronising concept, as it does not take into account the interconnectivity of Manchester-based or emerged artists with other places. Some feel that it is limiting for an artist to produce and show locally, and to be labelled as a local artist, while the reality of the art world is geographically networked.

11.5 RELEVANCE FOR GEOGRAPHICAL RESEARCH IN ART AND ON THE CREATIVE INDUSTRIES

These findings highlight how artists' location decisions are determined by modes of artistic practice and productive processes in the art world, rather than originating from specific spatial conditions and relations themselves. This is important for how the geography of each sector should be understood through mapping practices, and for understanding how they influence the spatial decisions of creative workers. Practice is also the source through which scenes (Bennett and Peterson, 2004; Straw, 2004, 2006) – in this case, art scenes – can be understood as a geographical phenomenon through the landscapes of practice concept (Wenger-Trayner and Wenger-Trayner, 2014). This is relevant for understanding not only the clustering of creatives in one fixed place, but also how communities of practice can be imagined geographies in which practice bonds them rather than location.

Within this frame of reference, I outlined how identity of place has become relational, and that place attachment cannot be discussed without perspectives on the mobility of creative workers. Therefore narratives around clustering need to be complemented with perspectives on mobility, which has in theoretical terms been explained through the buzz and pipeline model (Bathelt et al., 2004), or the maintaining of weak and strong ties (Granovetter, 1973). Less so have these concepts been applied to a cultural geography context, as they are primarily used to explain processes in economic geography where in-depth practices can often be overlooked in favour of quantification and systematisation of processes and roles. Hence the communities and landscapes of practice theory allows for a clearer focus on practice and its importance for determining spatial relations in the art world. Through these concepts we can not only understand the importance of learning in the emergence of practice, but also transfer this to mapping art scenes.

A multiplicity of dimensions can unfold through the practice focus; for example, that of creative workers being part of multiple communities (or scenes) and navigating spatially dispersed landscapes of practice, while at the same time engaging with local-level activities. A one-dimensional narrative of economic success through retention of creative talent and clustering (Comunian and Faggian, 2014; Gilmore et al., 2016) is therefore limited and cannot sufficiently explain the complex and qualitatively rich contexts I have set out with the practice focus. For example, based on my findings, I argue that the quality and value of creative, cultural and artistic practice should be accounted for as a source of understanding the cultural and creative industries, and with this, inform policies such as creative cities and clusters.

REFERENCES

Abbing, H. (2008) *Why are Artists Poor? The Exceptional Economy of the Arts.* Amsterdam: Amsterdam University Press.

Andersson, D.E., Andersson, E. and Mellander, C. (2011) *Handbook of Creative Cities.* Cheltenham, UK and Northampton, MA, USA: Edward Elgar Publishing.

Bagwell, S. (2008) 'Creative clusters and city growth', *Creative Industries Journal*, 1(1), pp. 31–46.

Banks, M. and Oakley, K. (2016) 'The dance goes on forever? Art schools, class and UK higher education', *International Journal of Cultural Policy*, 22(1), pp. 41–57.

Bathelt, H., Malmberg, A. and Maskell, P. (2004) 'Clusters and knowledge: local buzz, global pipelines and the process of knowledge creation', *Progress in Human Geography*, 28(1), pp. 31–56.

Beech, D. (2015) *Art and Value: Art's Economic Exceptionalism in Classical, Neoclassical and Marxist Economics.* Leiden: Brill.

Bennett, A. and Peterson, R.A. (2004) *Music Scenes: Local, Translocal and Virtual.* Nashville, TN: Vanderbilt University Press.

Birnbaum, D. and Graw, I. (2008) *Canvases and Careers Today: Criticism and Its Markets.* Berlin: Sternberg.

Bontje, M. (2005) 'Facing the challenge of shrinking cities in East Germany: the case of Leipzig', *GeoJournal*, 61(1), pp. 13–21.

Buchloh, B.H.D. (1990) 'Conceptual art 1962–1969: from the aesthetic of administration to the critique of institutions', October, 55, pp. 105–143.

Burdack, J., Lange, B. and Ehrlich, K. (2009) *Creative Leipzig? The Views of High-Skilled Employees, Managers and Transnational Migrants.* AMIDSt, University of Amsterdam.

Buren, D. and Repensek, T. (1979) 'The function of the studio', *October*, 10, pp. 51–58.

Casey, E. (1997) *The Fate of Place.* Berkeley, CA: University of California Press.

Chatterton, P. (2000) 'The cultural role of universities in the community: revisiting the university-community debate', *Environment and Planning A*, 32(1), pp. 165–182.

Comunian, R. and Faggian, A. (2014) 'Creative graduates and creative cities: exploring the geography of creative education in the UK', *International Journal of Cultural and Creative Industries*, 1(2), pp. 19–34.

Cresswell, T. (2015) *Place: An Introduction*, 2nd edn. Oxford: John Wiley & Sons.

Faggian, A. et al. (2013) 'Bohemian graduates in the UK: disciplines and location determinants of creative careers', *Regional Studies*, 47(2), pp. 183–200.

Florida, R. (2005) *Cities and the Creative Class.* New York: Routledge.

Gerlach, S. (2008) 'From famed to shame – the transition of a former East German arts academy to the talent hotbed of a contemporary painters' school. The Hochschule für Grafik und Buchkunst, Leipzig', in Jordan, M. and Miles, M. (eds), *Art and Theory after Socialism*, Bristol: Intellect, pp. 9–20.

Gilmore, A., Gledhill, D. and Rajkovic, I. (2016) 'Staying and making it in regional creative cities – visual arts graduates and infrastructures for professional development', in Gilmore, A. and Comunian, R. (eds), *Higher Education and the Creative Economy*, London: Routledge, pp. 164–183.

Granovetter, M.S. (1973) 'The strength of weak ties', *American Journal of Sociology*, 78(6), pp. 1360–1380.

Harris, A. and Moreno, L. (2010) *Creative City Limits: Urban Cultural Economy in a New Era of Austerity.* London: UCL Urban Lab & AHRC.

Harvey, D. (2012) 'From space to place and back again: Reflections on the condition of postmodernity', in Bird, J. et al. (eds), *Mapping the Futures: Local Cultures, Global Change*, London: Routledge, pp. 3–29.

Harvey, D., Hawkins, H. and Thomas, N. (2012) 'Thinking creative clusters beyond the city: people, places and networks', *Geoforum*, 43(3), pp. 529–539.

Hawkins, H. (2013) 'Geography and art. An expanding field: site, the body and practice', *Progress in Human Geography*, 37(1), pp. 52–71.

Hellmanzik, C. (2009) *Artistic Clusters and Modern Artists' Mobility – An Empirical Study*. Dublin: The Institute for International Intergration Studies Disscussion Paper Series.

Krauss, R. (1979) 'Sculpture in the expanded field', *October*, 8, pp. 31–44.

Mace, A., Porsch, L., Braun, R. and Pfeiffer, U. (2004) 'Shrinking to grow? The urban regeneration challenge in Leipzig and Manchester', *Town Planning Review*, 77(5), pp. 625–634.

Madoff, S.H. (2009) *Art School (propositions for the 21st Century)*. Cambridge, MA: MIT Press.

Massey, D. (1991) 'A global sense of place', *Marxism Today*, 38, pp. 24–29.

Massey, D. (2012) 'Power-geometry and a progressive sense of place', in Bird, J., Curtis, B., Putnam, T. and Tickner, L. (eds), *Mapping the Futures: Local Cultures, Global Change*, New York and Abingdon: Routledge.

Mould, O. and Comunian, R. (2015) 'Hung, drawn and cultural quartered: rethinking cultural quarter development policy in the UK', *European Planning Studies*, 23(12), pp. 2356–2369.

Müller, A. (2016) 'The digital nomad: buzzword or research category?', *Transnational Social Review*, 6(3), pp. 344–348.

Prince, R. (2012) 'Metaphors of policy mobility: fluid spaces of "creativity" policy', *Geografiska Annaler: Series B, Human Geography*, 94(4), pp. 317–331.

Raabe, M. and Waltz, M. (2014) 'Swinging Leipzig: Subkulturelles Image und Marketing'. Deutschlandfunk, 07/02/2014 Radio broadcast.

Rehberg, K. and Schmidt, H. (2009) *60/40/20 Kunst in Leipzig seit 1949*. Leipzig: Seemann.

Straw, W. (2004) 'Cultural scenes', *Loisir et société/Society and Leisure*, 27(2), pp. 411–422.

Straw, W. (2006) 'Scenes and sensibilities', in *E-Compós*, Vol. 6.

Vickery, J. (2011) *Beyond the Creative City – Cultural Policy in an Age of Scarcity*. Birmingham: MADE Centre for Placemaking.

Waitt, G. and Gibson, C. (2009) 'Creative small cities: rethinking the creative economy in place', *Urban Studies*, 46(5–6), pp. 1223–1246.

Wenger, E. (1998) *Communities of Practice: Learning, Meaning, and Identity*. Cambridge: Cambridge University Press.

Wenger-Trayner, E. and Wenger-Trayner, B. (2014) 'Learning in a landscape of practice: A framework', in Wenger-Trayner, E. and Wenger-Trayner, B. (eds), *Learning in Landscapes of Practice*, London: Routledge, pp. 27–44.

12. Exploring contemporary visual arts careers in Italy: education, mobility and project work

Jessica Tanghetti

12.1 INTRODUCTION

The chapter explores career patterns of contemporary visual artists in Italy. In general, careers in the creative sector have been widely investigated for their peculiarities and unstable structures (Lam, 2018; Allen and Hollingworth, 2013; Comunian and Jewell, 2018). However, within this broader literature, the work of contemporary visual artists – especially at the start of their careers – has not received much attention. Careers in contemporary visual arts (CVA) depend on a multitude of social, personal and professional factors, including country of origin, education, networks and mobility. Scholars agree that the career pathway for CVA is governed by a complex and dynamic network of players, which are part of an art ecosystem (McIntyre, 2004). In this ecosystem multiple actors, such as art schools, art professionals, galleries, public spaces, private collections and museums, play a crucial role in allowing artists to gain recognition and legitimation. The role of creative intermediaries (Heinich, 2012; Comunian et al., 2022; Lee and Lee, 2016) is also critical in the development of creative careers.

Based on the existing literature and previous work done in the field, the study builds on a longitudinal analysis of the career pathways of emerging contemporary visual artists in Italy. More specifically, the study analyses the relation between the curricula vitae (CVs) of artists and career progress, considering together education, professional experiences, networks and mobility. In doing so, attention will be paid to gender disparity and geographical and mobility aspects.

In particular, firstly, I explore the creatives' career patterns in the literature, focusing on key aspects such as the role of networks, education, mobility and gender. Secondly, I contextualise the CVA sector in Italy, highlighting its features and geographical patterns. I then introduce the study, focusing on the methodology and sample development, and reveal the findings of the analysis, deepening issues related to networks, mobility, gender and artists' work legitimation. In conclusion, I highlight the main implications of this study, underlining final remarks and future research directions.

12.2 NETWORK, MOBILITY AND GENDER ISSUES IN CREATIVE CAREERS

There is extensive literature on the challenges faced by creatives to establish a sustainable career (Ross, 2007; Bridgstock, 2011; Zelenko and Bridgstock, 2014; Daniel, 2016; Brook and Comunian, 2018), often defined as 'protean' (Hall, 2004), 'boundaryless' (Arthur and Rousseau, 1996) and typified by do-it-yourself career management (Bridgstock 2005). Generally, the creative and cultural sector is characterised by high rates of underemployment (for example, intermittent work, voluntary work and part-time work) and by an oversupply of artists and creative workforce capacity (Ashton, 2014; Bridgstock and Carr, 2013; Jeffri, 2004; Menger, 1999). Also, it has been proven that often visual and performing arts graduates a few months after graduation earn far less than graduates in other sectors who have comparable human capital characteristics (Bridgstock, 2005; Comunian et al., 2010). CVA careers feed into contemporary debates about the nature of cultural labour (Ross, 2003), particularly the degree to which cultural labour forms part of a new global precariat subject to increased pressures and shocks (Tanghetti et al., 2022/forthcoming).

The literature acknowledges some specific dynamics in the labour market of visual arts (Menger, 1999). Many authors have underlined the relational structure of the contemporary art market (Becker, 1988; Jyrämä, 2002; Rouget et al., 1991). The social network theory proposed by many as explaining access to jobs and job markets (Lin, 1982) can be interesting in examining the interaction of actors in the art market and its effect on the integration of young artists. This social network-based approach is akin to sociological analyses of art worlds, where the value of art results from the interaction between many actors, including producers and distributors (Martin, 2007). Although studies of how artists use their social and professional networks to further their careers are not numerous, there is some empirical evidence that artists' social capital has a strong impact on whether they continue to be employed in the arts, and how successful they are in the fields of visual art (Giuffre, 1999; Greffe, 2002). Art is in fact considered as a 'total social fact' (Chateau, 1998), requiring intense identification and evaluation efforts by various actors (Scott, 1987), known as 'legitimating bodies' (Rouget et al., 1991). More specifically, careers in the arts can be interpreted as a collective construction where the qualification of artists and their work are part of a social process composed by, as argued by Martin (2007), artistic tests, set up by various actors in the market such as cultural institutions, gallery owners, collectors and critics which, interconnected and taken together, constitute the career path of a young artist entering the visual arts market.

As acknowledged by scholars, like most sectors in the creative and cultural industries (CCIs), the visual arts reflect a broader trend whereby specific moments and patterns play a significant role in career success. Therefore, the career patterns of artists increasingly resemble a patchwork CV characterised by a series of work and learning experiences (Bridgstock, 2005). The first fundamental role in an artist's career development is played by art schools: the artist enters the market when they graduate (Galenson, 2005; Martin, 2007). In the international context, enrolments in arts programmes in higher education are increasing (Siddins et al., 2016), and the relationship between graduates and career outcomes has been investigated by scholars. Comunian and Faggian (2014) looked statistically at the career outcomes (such as salary and job security) of creative graduates and concluded that arts graduates tend to struggle to secure jobs and stable salaries, and that in the sector there is a consistent gender pay gap. England and Comunian (2016) explore how higher education in itself can facilitate or hinder opportunities for local graduates. Similarly, Ashton and Comunian (2019) explore the role of higher education as a hub for the development of creative graduates and local economies. Finally, art schools play a role in excluding certain social classes from artistic careers (Banks and Oakley, 2016).

Alongside the role of the art ecosystem (McIntyre, 2004), other social, economic and personal factors impact on artists' careers, including spatial factors such as mobility and migration. Geography, including the country of origin, the city and institution of education, have important consequences on career advancement. Research on the role of mobility in creative workers' careers (Comunian and Faggian, 2014) has been carried out. A study of classical musicians (Bennett, 2010) found that migration plays a role in their career and professional development. Focusing on the visual arts, O'Hagan and Kelly (2005) examined prominent artists' birth and work locations, and their consequential patterns of labour movement during several long periods; while O'Hagan and Hellmanzik (2008) analysed established artists' migration for four periods.

Within these broader dynamics, questions of gender equality, and inclusivity and diversity in general, have also been raised (Boeltzig et al., 2009; Miller, 2016; Eikhof and Warhurst, 2013; Baia Curioni at al., 2015). Gender inequality in the visual arts has been investigated in the United Kingdom (McMillan, 2018), identifying how gender changes the career pathways for artists. A similar study in Italy (Iaquinta and Simoncelli, 2018) has explored the presence of female artists in different CVA contexts, such as commercial galleries, public institutions and the Venice Biennale, highlighting a significant underrepresentation of women artists. Barriers to success for women in the arts have been identified by scholars in recurring unemployment, career interruption and instability (McCaughey, 1985; Noble, 1987); low pay and intangible rewards (Sang, 1989); and the difficulty in balancing competing personal and family roles and obligations (Kavaler-Adler, 1993; Stohs, 1992).

However, beyond the acknowledgement of the complexity of these factors and the range of actors involved, there is still very little known about the role that each plays in CVA careers development. Also, building on previous literature, it might be of interest to explore the connection between the actors involved and factors such as mobility, spatial dimensions and gender.

12.3 THE CONTEMPORARY VISUAL ART SECTOR IN ITALY

The Italian market share for post-war and CVA is estimated to account for less than 1 per cent of the global value of the sector in 2020 (McAndrew, 2021), and 9 per cent of the volume. On a national level, in 2020 the whole CCIs generated €85 billion (-8 per cent on 2019), employing approximately 1.4 billion workers (-3.5 per cent on 2019) (Symbola, 2021). The most significant regions in terms of value generated and employment are represented by Lombardy (€22.7 billion of added value and approximately 340 000 workers) and Lazio (€13 billion of added value and approximately 190 000 workers). An important role is also played by the region of Piemonte, with €7.5 billion of added value and approximately 122 000 workers. Milan represents the Italian city with the highest incidence of the cultural and creative sector on the local economy: the added value generated by CCIs in the city counted for 9.7 per cent of the economy in 2020, while the total number of workers in the sector was 9.8 per cent of the total employment in the city (Symbola, 2021). In terms of the incidence of CCIs in the local economy, Milan is followed by Rome (8.7 per cent added value and 8 per cent of employment) and Turin (8 per cent added value and 8 per cent of employment).

Focusing on performing and visual arts, the sector in 2020 employed approximately 95 000 workers in Italy, generating an added value of roughly €4 million (Symbola, 2021). The industry reflects the same trends identified for the CCIs as a whole, highlighting the primary role played by the hubs of Milan, Rome and Turin. Among the CCIs, the performing and visual arts sector has been the most impacted upon by the Covid-19 pandemic, recording a decrease of 26 per cent in added value and 12 per cent in employment in 2020.

From a qualitative point of view, the Italian contemporary art ecosystem (McIntyre, 2004) is based on a supply chain that originates from educational institutions, arriving at museums and collectors in a system including non-profit spaces, fairs and galleries (Symbola, 2019). Therefore, the Italian artists' validation process is characterised by the relevance of personal networks, leading the artists, especially at the earliest stages of their careers, to invest heavily in the accumulation of relational capital (Zorloni, 2005).

Focusing on education, in Italy there are 49 art schools distributed throughout the country. In 2019–20 there were approximately 39 000 students enrolled in the academies of fine arts in Italy (Miur, 2021), considering both private and public institutions, of which 67 per cent were females and 22 per cent were foreigners. In terms of the number of students enrolled, the most popular in 2019–20 were Accademia di Brera (Milan, 4497 students) and NABA Nuova Accademia di Belle Arti (Milan, 4390 students), followed by Accademia di Belle Arti di Napoli (Naples, 3332 students) and Accademia di Belle Arti di Roma (Rome, 3020 students). With a total of approximately 9000 students, it is possible to define Milan as the leading Italian art educational hub.

A fundamental role in the artists' career development is also played by artist-in-residence programmes, whose presence and prestige have been increasing throughout the last decade. According to Art in Residence (AIR, 2020), in Italy there are 92 residencies: the majority of them, 43, are in the North (47 per cent), 27 (29 per cent) are in the Centre, while 22 (24 per cent) are in the South. In addition to having the highest number of art residencies, the Northern area of Italy also hosts the most recognised ones, as Dolomiti Contemporanee (Pordenone), Fondazione Antonio Ratti (Como), VIR Via Farini (Milan) and Fondazione Bevilacqua La Masa (Venice), enforcing the role of the area as a formative hub for the education and training of young artists.

Focusing instead on the institutional sphere, the Centre of Italy has the highest number of public contemporary art museums and institutions (49 per cent), thanks to the key role played by Rome; while 20 per cent of the total are in the South and 31 per cent in the Northern regions (Associazione Civita, 2020). The Italian predominance is in the city of Rome, which hosts contemporary art institutions such as Galleria Nazionale d'Arte Moderna e Contemporanea and MAXXI Museums, which registered approximately 215 000 and 204 000 visitors in 2018, respectively; this is followed by Turin, with Galleria d'Arte Moderna e Contemporanea and Castello di Rivoli visited by 185 000 and 125 000 people, respectively, in 2018.[1] Therefore, the main institutional contemporary art hubs are represented by Rome and Turin. Despite the presence of significant institutions such as PAC and Museo del 900, an institutional contemporary art museum is still missing from Milan.[2]

Alongside museums, a prominent role in the sector is played by contemporary art foundations, non-profit organisations open to the public, usually founded by private or corporate collectors, showcasing their own collections and temporary exhibitions, thereby having a substantial impact on the territory they are based in. The highest number of foundations, 22 (57 per cent), is in the

North of Italy (Associazione Civita, 2020), where the prominent Fondazione Prada (Milan) and Fondazione Sandretto Re Rebaudengo (Turin)[3] are also based. There are then eight art foundations in the Centre of Italy (20 per cent), and nine (23 per cent) in the South (Associazione Civita, 2020).

Focusing on the commercial side of the sector, with an estimation of 950 galleries, Italy reached fifth position in the global ranking related to art galleries' presence (Resch, 2016). In this context the predominance of Milan is clear: with 190 galleries (20 per cent of the national total), it is in the international top ten of the art galleries cities.

The analysis of the Italian scenario highlights the primary role of the North of Italy as a formative hub (academies, residencies), and its central position from a commercial point of view (galleries, fairs). The Centre of Italy is instead the primary institutional contemporary art institutional hub, while the role played by the South of Italy in the sector is almost irrelevant.

An increasingly important role in the sector is played by contemporary art fairs, which are not only trading contexts, but also curated shows with articulated programmes and side events. With 55 000 visitors in 2019 and 208 exhibitors (of which 62 per cent were from abroad), Artissima, taking place in November in Turin, is confirmed to be the most important Italian art fair in Italy. In terms of prominence, the second Italian art fair is instead miart, taking place in Milan in April,[4] which attracted 185 exhibitors (of which 38 per cent were from abroad) for its 2019 edition. Following the international experiences, art fairs became the foundation for the development of art weeks, with a dense programme of events, talks, openings and exhibitions, involving local art institutions and galleries, taking place for the whole fair week, as happens during the Turin and Milan art weeks.[5]

As mentioned above, networks are at the basis of the Italian contemporary art system. In this respect, it is possible to note that the connection between players happens not only on a vertical level, but also from a horizontal perspective: the sector in fact highlights a high level of collaboration between players belonging to the same category, with the purpose of achieving common objectives. An example is represented by the Associazione dei Musei d'Arte Contemporanea Italiani (AMACI), a not-for-profit association of the most important contemporary art museums in Italy, established in 2003 to develop a 'network of museums active in the field of contemporary art, based on the profitable exchange of information, ideas and experiences ... and the sharing of models for the growth and improvement of the standards of quality of our institutions' (AMACI, 2020). A similar perspective is also present at a commercial level, as in the case of the Associazione Nazionale delle Gallerie d'Arte Moderna e Contemporanea (ANGAMC), an association of Italian art galleries which aims to support and strengthen the category from a practical and legal point of view, also developing proposals in order to improve the conditions of the sector. In addition, private art foundations joined together in the Comitato Fondazioni d'Arte Contemporanea, an association founded in 2014 aiming to provide models of collaboration between the public and private sectors, sharing methodologies and best practice.[6]

12.4　METHODOLOGY AND DATA

Since 2018, in Italy, the think tank and art magazine ExibArt has published '222 Artists worth investing in' (Biasini Selvaggi, 2019), a guide to the most promising emerging artists based in Italy, selected by prominent curators, gallerists and critics. Our sample has been based on data from the 2019 publication. More specifically, I based the analysis on artists featured in the publication born between 1985 and 1990 in Italy, identifying the names of 76 artists in these cohorts (Table 12.1). Unfortunately, the initial sample was quite unbalanced gender-wise, especially in the years 1986–88, where out of a total of 48 artists I found only 11 female artists.

Table 12.1　Artists research sample by year of birth and gender

Year of birth	Male	Female
1985	4	4
1986	18	4
1987	8	7
1988	11	0
1989	6	5
1990	5	4
Total	52	24

Focusing on the region of origin (Table 12.2), the analysis highlights that the large majority of artists, 44 (58 per cent), come from the North of Italy, especially from the Lombardy and Veneto regions, where the most recognised art schools (Academy of Brera, Milan and IUAV University, Venice) are based. Artists from the North of Italy highlight a more balanced distribution gender-wise, with 26 male and 18 female artists. There are then 18 artists (24 per cent) from the Centre of Italy, where Tuscany, with seven artists, is the most represented region. With only four female artists, the gender gap in the area is quite high.

Fourteen artists come from the South of Italy, where the regions of Puglia and Campania show the highest population (four artists each). Female representation is almost irrelevant, with only two women artists in the whole area.

Table 12.2   *Artists sample by gender and geography*

Region	Male	Female
North of Italy	26	18
Lombardy	7	6
Veneto	5	5
Piemonte	4	2
Friuli Venezia Giulia	4	1
Liguria	3	0
Emilia Romagna	3	4
Centre of Italy	14	4
Lazio	3	1
Marche	2	1
Abruzzo	2	1
Toscana	6	1
Umbria	1	0
South of Italy and Islands	12	2
Puglia	3	1
Calabria	2	1
Campania	4	0
Sicilia	2	0
Sardegna	1	0

The analysis then focused on artists' education, exploring the city, institution and year of degree for each artist belonging to the preliminary sample. Data were extrapolated from artists' CVs, found on artists' personal websites or on those of their representative galleries (as indicated in the ExibArt publication). The analysis highlights a predominance of artists who graduated from the Academy of Brera in Milan and IUAV in Venice, with ten artists each. To conduct meaningful comparisons, I decided to restrict the analysis to the artists in these cohorts. Therefore, the final sample (Table 12.3) is composed of 20 artists, with a slight predominance of male artists (12 male and 8 female artists).

The large majority of artists belonging to the sample come from the North of Italy, especially from Lombardy and Veneto (seven artists from each region), where the Academy of Brera and IUAV are based. However, the rest of the North of Italy regions are also represented. With eight female and ten male artists, the North of Italy shows a substantial balance between genders. There are then two male artists from the rest of Italy: one from the Centre of Italy

Table 12.3   *Final sample: artists graduated from the Academy of Brera (Milan) and IUAV (Venice)*

Year of birth	Male	Female
1986	6	3
1987	2	3
1988	0	0
1989	2	1
1990	2	1
Total	12	8

Table 12.4   *Final sample: geographical provenance*

Region	Male	Female
North of Italy	10	8
Lombardy	4	3
Veneto	2	5
Piemonte	1	0
Friuli Venezia Giulia	1	0
Liguria	1	0
Emilia Romagna	1	0
Centre of Italy	1	0
Marche	1	0
South of Italy	1	0
Puglia	1	0
Total	12	8

(from Marche) and one from the South (from Puglia); while no female artists come from those areas (Table 12.4).

Based on the artists' CVs, I extrapolated data on their education and career paths, focusing on education, residencies, awards and solo exhibitions. In doing so, attention was paid to spatial, temporal and gender factors. The results from the analysis are shown in section 12.5.

12.5   CONTEMPORARY VISUAL ARTS CAREERS IN ITALY: GEOGRAPHY, HUBS AND MOBILITY

Mobility to Study: Education and Geography

From the analysis of the CVs, I explored the whole educational path undertaken by artists, focusing also on a geographical perspective. As mentioned above, the final sample is composed of artists who studied and achieved a degree at the Academy of Brera in Milan or IUAV in Venice, including also those studying at these institutions for their second degree.

Most artists in the sample obtained their BA at the targeted institutions, except four artists, who first graduated from other Italian universities (Politecnico, Turin; Academy of Carrara; University of Alghero; University of Verona). It is interesting to note that there are no graduates from universities based abroad. Almost all the artists in the sample continued their studies after the first degree, except for four artists (three male artists from Brera and one female artist from IUAV). Almost half of the sample (nine) achieved their MA at the same university at which they obtained their BA (five from Brera and four from IUAV); while, as mentioned above, four artists studied at Brera and IUAV (two at Brera and two at IUAV) after having obtained a degree from another university. The rest of the sample (three), after the BA at IUAV (two) and Brera (one), continued their studies at other institutions in Italy (IUAV after the BA at Brera, and Ca' Foscari Venice after IUAV). In only one case was the MA obtained at a university based abroad (ZHDK, Photography, Zurich). Even if the role played by education abroad is almost irrelevant in this sample, it is interesting to note that seven artists undertook an Erasmus exchange programme in Europe (UDK Berlin, Germany; KASK Belgium; Luca School of Arts, Belgium; LMA Riga, Latvia; Academy of Fine Arts Warsaw, Poland; Bilgi University of Istanbul, Turkey; Hochschule fur Bildende Kunste, Dresden, Germany). Only two artists undertook a PhD (one in Italy, at the University of Alghero, and the other in the United States, at Harvard University); while three artists attended a specialisation course at an institution abroad after the completion of their MA (at Sandberg Institute, Amsterdam; SoundImageCulture, Brussels; Ecole Nationale Supérieure des Beaux-Arts, Paris).

From Training to Work: The Artist-in-Residence Programmes

A fundamental role in the education, training and professional development of artists is played by the artist-in-residence programmes, which provide artists with the opportunity to live and work outside of their usual environments, reflecting, researching and producing work (Neuendorf, 2016). These programmes are key steps in an artist's career development, allowing them to build their network, elevate their art and strengthen their CV. The artist-in-residence programmes are quite competitive and coveted by artists, who can access them through invitation or open call, depending on the kind of programme. Thus, especially at the beginning of their careers, artists mainly focus on finding residency opportunities, both nationally and internationally.

I investigated the level of mobility linked to artist-in-residence programmes experienced by the artists in the sample from the beginning of their careers until 2020. The majority of artists in the sample had at least one artist-in-residence experience, except two (both male artists graduated from Brera). The average number of residencies undertaken by artists is four, with a peak of 11 residencies for a female artist who studied at IUAV, and a minimum of one programme for four artists (two male artists and two females, graduated from Brera). It is interesting to note that seven artists (35 per cent) had an artist-in-residence programme experience in the same city they graduated from, namely Fondazione Bevilacqua La Masa for five artists graduated from IUAV, and VIR ViaFarini-in-Residence for two artists from Brera.

Considering the total amount of residencies undertaken by the artists in the sample, there is a slight predominance of programmes undertaken in Italy (56 per cent), even if the number of international ones is significant overall (43 per cent). While there are some Italian residencies that are quite popular in the sample, the international ones have instead been attended by the targeted artists just once. The most popular artist-in-residence programme in Italy is that offered by Fondazione Bevilacqua La Masa in Venice, which has been attended by five artists from IUAV. There are three programmes attended by three artists each, namely VIR Via Farini and Careof in Milan, Fondazione Spinola Banna in Turin, and BoCS Art Cosenza in Cosenza; while Dolomiti Contemporanee in Pordenone has been attended twice. The majority of artists who attended at least two residencies included both national and international experiences. In only two cases did they attend exclusively international programmes.

Focusing on the international residences, there is a high degree of fragmentation: the programmes attended by the targeted artists are quite diverse and spread across and beyond Europe. The most popular residence destination in Europe is France, even if with only three artists experience residencies there, followed by Denmark, Finland, Belgium, the United Kingdom and Serbia (two artists each). The rest of the residences, attended by only one artist from the sample each, are disseminated across Europe, in Germany, Portugal, the Czech Republic, Holland, Malta and Poland, and beyond Europe in Argentina, the United States, India, China, Libya, Iceland, South Korea, Israel and Morocco.

Mobility to Work: The Artists' Solo Exhibitions

Solo exhibitions are undoubtedly milestones in an artist's career. They can be organised independently by the artists themselves in their studios or in artist-run spaces, or in collaboration with commercial galleries or institutions such as museums or foundations.

In reviewing the CVs of the artists belonging to the sample, I focused on the solo exhibitions they had in the period 2010–19, paying attention to the kind of space hosting the shows and city/country in which they were located. I decided to exclude 2020 from the analysis as, due to the Covid-19 restrictions, many exhibitions were cancelled and the artists' mobility was severely limited. During the considered period of time, the artists had a total of 127 exhibitions, quite balanced gender-wise (54 per cent by male artists and 46 per cent by female artists). Nevertheless, two female artists did not have any solo shows in the entire period.

It is interesting to note that the first solo exhibitions of these artists took place in the same city they were studying in. In 2010–11, in fact, two artists from IUAV had their first solo show in Venice, one in a gallery and the other in an independent space; while three artists from Brera had their first solo exhibition in Milan, two of them in a gallery and the other one in an independent space. It is mainly after the BA (2011–12) that the territorial presence of these artists overcomes their city of education's boundaries, with solo exhibitions in some of the main Italian cities, such as Turin and Rome, alongside Milan and Venice; while their international presence has still been minimal, with just two of them having solo exhibitions abroad, one in an independent space in Berlin, the other in a gallery in Brussels. During the MA or at its completion (2013–14), the majority of the artists (65 per cent) belonging to the sample had at least one solo show, mainly in commercial galleries and independent spaces, but in a few cases also in minor museums, sometimes linked to the educational hub they were based in (for example, Ca' Rezzonico Museum in Venice). Their solo exhibitions abroad were at that time always connected to an international educational experience or the attendance of a artist-in-residence programme: in two cases the artists managed to have a solo show in a gallery based in the city of their Erasmus exchange programme (Brussels and Warsaw), while another two cases were in a gallery in the same city of their residence programme (Helsinki and Ceska Briza). In the period of the completion of the MA (or just after it) (2015–16), the percentage of artists achieving a solo show grew significantly (75 per cent), with four artists having more than one solo show a year. This stage represented a kind of turning point in the artists' career development, because they started to exhibit their work in cities and places not connected to their educational path or their residency experiences. It is possible to assume that these shows were the result of a network development activity undertaken by artists, based on personal and professional relationships, an essential part of an artist's path. The exhibitions took place in galleries and independent spaces mainly located in the Italian main cities, such as Rome, Venice, Milan and Bologna, with a slight predominance of those based in Milan (28 per cent of the total of the solo shows by these artists in 2015–16). It is also interesting to underline that during this period five artists (25 per cent of the sample) had more than one solo exhibition a year (two shows for three artists, and three shows for two artists), combining in three cases a national and international presence. In only one case we had instead the recognition of an artist's work at a major Italian museum, such as Villa Croce in Genova.

During their career progress, the large majority of artists (80 per cent) had at least one solo show a few years after their degree (2017–18), with almost half of them (40 per cent) having more than one solo exhibition a year. It is interesting to note that there is a high diversification of organisations hosting the shows in this period, with the introduction of foundations and corporate spaces, and the greater presence of museums. In 2017–18 the artists had a total number of 43 exhibitions, 44 per cent of them taking place in Milan, which is clearly the most important exhibition hub for emerging artists in Italy. Except for one case, for the artists exhibiting their work more than once a year in that period, their shows never took place in the same city, highlighting the high level of mobility required for artists to progress in their careers. However, the international mobility of artists is still limited, with only 25 per cent of the sample having exhibitions abroad, half of them (12.5 per cent) connected to their previous artist-in-residence places (Warsaw and London) or educational experience (Harvard). The rest of the international exhibitions took place instead in Ibiza, Krakow and San Paolo. Focusing on the exhibitions in Italy, there is a high concentration of those taking place in the North (84 per cent), where as well as Milan the cities hosting shows were Bologna, Piacenza, Turin, Venice, Vicenza, Livorno, Verona, Brescia and Varese. The Centre of Italy played a marginal role (11 per cent), mainly thanks to the role of Rome, where half of these shows took place, while the rest were in commercial galleries in Siena and Civitanova Marche. The role of the South is almost irrelevant, with only two exhibitions (5 per cent) taking place in Palermo.

The last full year I considered for the analysis is 2019, as in 2020 many shows were been cancelled or postponed due to Covid-19. During that year, 60 per cent of the artists had at least one solo show, with 42 per cent of them having multiple solo exhibitions. The analysis highlighted that no artists in the sample exhibited their work in a space in which they had already done so in the past, underlining a high fragmentation of their careers. The international presence is higher in 2019, with 35 per cent of shows taking place abroad and one of the artists exhibiting only internationally. During this year, the exhibitions' cities/countries were entirely connected to places where artists undertook a residence programme (New York, USA; Panjib and Mumbai, India; Beijing, China; Belgrade, Serbia; Valletta, Malta). It is important therefore to note that, even after years of exhibitions, no artists have been represented by an international commercial gallery, and that the international experiences are balanced between male and female artists.

Looking at the Italian scenario, the landscape is quite fragmented, with 62 per cent of the exhibitions taking place in the North of Italy (Milan, Modena, Bergamo, Turin), 31 per cent in the Centre (Siena, Prato, Rome) and 8 per cent in the South (Lecce). Milan is again the city where artists mainly exhibited their work (31 per cent). These artists' solo shows have been hosted by different kinds of organisations, ranging from museums, private collections, foundations, independent spaces and commercial galleries, to corporate spaces and cultural institutions.

The Artists' Work Recognition: The Awards

Awards represent fundamental achievements for artists, especially at the early stage of their careers, as they allow them to gain recognition in the system, making them and their work known and, often, obtaining monetary support for their career development. From the CVs of the artists belonging to the sample, I analysed the awards they received or were shortlisted for, from 2013 to 2020.

Seventy-five per cent of the targeted artists mentioned at least one award in their CVs (achieved or shortlisted for), and the average number of awards for artists was three. The greatest number of awards was 12 and was achieved by a male artist who graduated from IUAV; while two male artists and two female artists had not obtained (or been shortlisted for) even one award. In total, the artists in the sample had achieved or been nominated for 64 awards, precisely divided between males and females (32 each). Only four awards (6 per cent) were international, and referred to international grant programmes (Step Travel Grant, European Cultural Foundation), national public grants (Handle with care for public art project in Galerija Museum of Contemporary Art Metelkova (MG/MSUM), Ljubljana, Slovenia), educational institutions (Harvard University, Department of Visual and Environmental Studies, Graduate School of Arts and Sciences Fellowship and Summer Research Award) and emerging international artists dedicated prizes (Ecole des regards-young talents, Aix-en-Provence – Marseille). The international awards were mainly achieved by male artists (three males and one female).

Focusing on the national prizes, the most popular ones were the Combat Prize and Francesco Fabbri Prize, both mentioned six times in the CVs of the artists belonging to the sample.

The Combat Prize is an award promoted by the Museum G. Fattori in Livorno, 'aimed at promoting and enhancing Contemporary Art'. The competition entails the selection of 80 artworks from five different categories, such as painting, drawing, photography, video arts – performance, sculpture and installation. It culminates in the exhibition of the finalists' works, the publication of a catalogue and the awarding of prize money (€6000 to the winner of the painting, sculpture and installation categories;[7] €4000 to the winner of the photography category; and €3000 to the winner of the drawing and video arts – performance categories). The competition is open to all contemporary artists worldwide and there are no age restrictions or thematic constraints. Within the sample, one female and one male artist won the first prize in the sculpture and installation category, and a female artist in the photography category; one artist obtained a special mention, while another has been shortlisted for the award twice.

The Francesco Fabbri Prize is an award promoted by the Francesco Fabbri foundation focused on 'Emerging Art' (artists under 35 working in any kind of media) and contemporary photography. The winners receive €5000 and their artwork becomes part of the prestigious Francesco Fabbri foundation collection, enhancing their careers. One male artist of the sample won the first prize for Emerging Art, while five others (three males and two females) were shortlisted for the award.

Other nationally recognised awards mentioned in the artists' CVs twice include the Cairo Prize, focused on emerging artists; the Termoli Prize, focused on public interventions; Premio Ora, dedicated to creating collaborations between emerging artists and galleries; and Movin'Up, promoted by the Italian Ministry of Culture with the purpose of promoting Italian artists' work abroad.

12.6   DISCUSSION

This study analyses the career patterns of a selection of emerging artists in Italy, focusing on their education, mobility, training and working experiences, also considering gender aspects (McMillan, 2018; Iaquinta and Simoncelli, 2018). Central to the analysis is also the role of the contemporary art market's networks (Becker, 1988; Jyrämä, 2002; Rouget et al., 1991).

As already mentioned (section 12.4), the sample is quite gender-balanced, being composed of 12 males and eight females, while their geographical provenance is completely unbalanced (O'Hagan and Kelly, 2005), as 90 per cent of the artists come originally from the North of Italy. I was in fact interested in investigating potential common career patterns for artists having a similar background, and the fact of having studied in the same art school (either Academy of Brera or IUAV in Venice) is an interesting starting point. Education is in fact the preliminary step for entering the market (Martin, 2007), and our data show that it is considered essential by the artists in the sample: all of them achieved a BA in art and only four did not continue their studies after it.

The analysis highlighted the limited mobility of artists (Comunian and Faggian, 2014) during their educational path: 40 per cent continued their studies in the same institution, while only 35 per cent of them undertook a period of study abroad (Erasmus exchange programmes, mainly in Belgium, Germany and Eastern Europe). There are, then, just a few cases of artists studying abroad for specialisation courses, and one for a PhD. According to our data, international experiences seem not to be seen as essential from an educational point of view, while it seems that staying local, especially in key cities in the Italian art scene such as Milan and Venice, benefits artists for networking (Lin, 1982), training and working opportunities. This emerges clearly when looking at the preliminary experiences that artists in the sample undertook: a consistent number of artists had an artist-in-residence programme and/or their first solo show in the same cities they were studying in. This can be interpreted from two angles: on the one hand, the educational hub becomes an emerging art local cluster, where artists may have the opportunity to experience some of the essential steps of their careers (England and Comunian, 2016; Ashton and Comunian, 2019); on the other hand, this may be seen as a disincentive for art students to undertake experiences abroad, also underlining the limited international opportunities offered to artists at the early stages of their careers.

Although limited, the Erasmus experiences of the targeted artists have clearly been rewarding, as they often resulted in a solo exhibition in the city where the programme took place, and in the development of an international network for the artist. It is in fact possible to see that those having these experiences in many cases have had more international exposure in the progress of their careers. The most consistent international experiences I found in the artists' CVs are represented by the artist-in-residence programmes (43 per cent of the residencies experienced by artists). It is interesting to note that artists having more than one residence experience combined national and international programmes. While in Italy the programmes attended by artists are quite recurrent, at an international level it is not possible to trace clear mobility trajection patterns, as programmes undertaken by artists are fragmented across and beyond Europe. Data highlight the key role of international artists-in-residence programmes in furthering artists' careers, as all of the international solo shows that the artists in the sample had in the early stages of their careers took place in the cities of these programmes, alongside those connected to Erasmus experiences.

Focusing on the artists' working achievements, such as solo shows and awards, the sample is gender-balanced: 54 per cent of the total number of solo shows were dedicated to the male artists of the sample, with 46 per cent to females; and 50 per cent of the awards resulting from the CVs were connected to male artists, with 50 per cent to female. In relation to the solo exhibitions, our data confirm the role of Milan as the main commercial hub, as the greater number of shows took place in this city.

The development of the artists' careers shows a consistent increase year by year of the number of solo shows, and a related geographical diversification, mainly in Italy and in main hubs such as Milan, Rome and Turin. It is also possible to note a progressive crescendo in the diversification of the categories of spaces hosting the exhibitions, which range from galleries, artist-run spaces and independent spaces mainly in the early career stage, to foundations, museums and corporate spaces some years after graduation (Martin, 2007; McIntyre, 2004). The artists' career paths are in general discontinuous (Bridgstock 2005): our data highlight the lack of stable collaboration relationships between artists and galleries, and the need of artists to move from city to city (mainly in Italy) in order to exhibit their work.

12.7   CONCLUSIONS AND FUTURE RESEARCH

This study aims to investigate the role of hubs, mobility, working and training opportunities for emerging artists in Italy, also considering gender aspects. It exposes the role of the city of education as an emerging art cluster, providing growth opportunities to artists in terms of training and work; questioning whether this, although positive for career advancement, could potentially obstruct a national and international mobility of artists, also reducing the possibility to access to the opportunities offered by the cluster to artists based outside it. Although data show a limited international mobility of artists, it is clear that these experiences have been rewarding for career advancement and network development.

This study embraces the social network theory (Lin, 1982), showing the multitude of actors that, at a different level, an artist should engage with in order to further their practice; and it puts the gender issue in a positive light, demonstrating a generalised balance in the access to training and working opportunities, and in relation to work recognition.

Being aware of the fact that the sample I used is quite restricted, I believe that this study can represent the starting point for future research, potentially adopting an international comparative approach.

NOTES

1.   Data released by the institutions themselves.
2.   The project of a contemporary art museum in Milan (MAC), which was supposed to be inaugurated in 2011, was approved by the public administration of Milan and architect Daniel Libeskind was commissioned. After a couple of years of delay, in 2013 the new administration decided to allocate the budget on other projects, blocking the realisation of the museum.
3.   They were founded by collectors Miuccia Prada and Patrizio Bertelli, and Patrizia Sandretto Re Rebaudengo, respectively.

4. Due to Covid-19, the 2020 edition of the fair was cancelled and replaced by an online-only edition which took place in September.
5. They take place during the Artissima and miart fairs.
6. The association was founded in 2014, after the Minister of Cultural Heritage and Tourism, Dario Franceschini, requested Patrizia Sandretto Re Rebaudengo to develop proposals for a fruitful collaboration between the private and public sectors.
7. One prize for each category.

REFERENCES

AIR (2020). The network of residences. Available: https://www.artinresidence.it (accessed 30 September 2020).

Allen, K., and Hollingworth, S. (2013). 'Sticky subjects' or 'cosmopolitan creatives'? Social class, place and urban young people's aspirations for work in the knowledge economy. *Urban Studies*, 50(3), 499–517.

AMACI (2020). Associazione dei Musei d'Arte Contemporanea Italiani. Available: https://www.amaci.org/en/about-us (accessed 30 September 2020).

Arthur, M.B., and Rousseau, D.M. (1996). *The Boundaryless Career: A New Employment Principle for a New Organisational Era*. New York: Oxford University Press.

Ashton, D. (2014) Creative contexts: work placement subjectivities for the creative industries. *British Journal of Sociology of Education*. Available: https://doi.org/10.1080/01425692.2014.916602.

Ashton, D., and Comunian, R. (2019). Universities as creative hubs: modes and practices in the UK context. In Gill, R., Pratt, A.C., and Virani, T. (eds), *Creative Hubs in Question: Place, Space and Work in the Creative Economy*. Cham: Palgrave Macmillan, pp. 359–379.

Associazione Civita (2020). Le organizzazioni private dell'arte contemporanea in Italia. Report Civita.

Baia Curioni, S., Forti, L., and Leone, L. (2015). Making visible. In Velthius, O., and Baia Curioni, S. (eds), *Cosmopolitan Canvases: The Globalisation of Markets for Contemporary Art*. Oxford: Oxford University Press.

Banks, M., and Oakley, K. (2016). The dance goes on forever? Art schools, class and UK higher education. *International Journal of Cultural Policy*, 22(1), 41–57

Becker, H.S. (1988). *Les Mondes de l'art* (translation of *Art World*, 1982). Paris: Flammar.

Bennett, D. (2010). Creative migration: a Western Australian case study of creative artists. *Australian Geographer*, 41(1), 117–128.

Biasini Selvaggi, C. (2019). 222 Artists worth investing in, *ExibArt*. Rome.

Boeltzig, H., Sullivan Sulewski, J., and Hasnain, R. (2009). Career development among young disabled artists. *Disability and Society*, 24(6), 753–769. DOI: 10.1080/09687590903160258.

Bridgstock, R.S. (2005). Australian artists, starving and wellnourished: what can we learn from the prototypical protean career? *Australian Journal of Career Development*, 14(3), 40–48.

Bridgstock, R. (2011). Skills for creative industries graduate success. *Education and Training*, 53, 9–26.

Bridgstock, R., and Carr, L. (2013). Creative entrepreneurship education for graduate employability in the creative arts. In J. Holmes (ed.), *The CALTN Papers: The Refereed Proceedings of the Creative Arts Learning and Teaching Network Symposium 2013*. Hobart, Australia: Tasmanian College of the Arts, University of Tasmania and the Creative Arts Learning and Teaching Network, pp. 8–35.

Brook, S., and Comunian, R. (2018). 'Dropping out and working': the vocational narratives of creative graduates. In *The Palgrave Handbook of Creativity at Work*. Cham: Palgrave Macmillan, pp. 125–141.

Chateau, D. (1998). *Lan comme fait social*. Paris: L'Harmattan.

Comunian, R., and Faggian, A. (2014). Higher education and the creative city. *International Journal of Cultural and Creative Industries (IJCCI)*, 1, 18–34.

Comunian, R., Faggian, A., and Li, Q.C. (2010). Unrewarded careers in the creative class: the strange case of bohemian graduates. *Papers in Regional Science*, 89(2), 389–410.

Comunian, R., and Jewell, S. (2018). 'Young, talented and highly mobile': exploring creative human capital and graduates mobility in the UK. In Biagi, B., Faggian, A., Rajbhandari, I., and Venhorst, V.A. (eds), *New Frontiers in Interregional Migration Research*. Cham: Springer, pp. 205–230.

Comunian, R., England, L., and Hracs, B.J. (2022). Cultural intermediaries revisited: lessons from Cape Town, Lagos and Nairobi. In B.J. Hracs, T. Brydges and T. Haisch (eds), *Culture, Creativity and Economy: Collaborative Practices, Value Creation and Spaces of Creativity*. London: Routledge, pp. 109–123.

Daniel, R. (2016). Creative artists, career patterns and career theory: insights from the Australian context. *Australian Journal of Career Development*, 25(3), 91–98.

Eikhof, D.R., and Warhurst, C. (2013). The promised land? Why social inequalities are systemic in the creative industries. *Employee Relations*, 35(4), 495–508.

England, L., and Comunian, R. (2016). Support or competition? Assessing the role of HEIs in professional networks and local creative communities: the case of glass-making in Sunderland. In Comunian, R., and Gilmore, A. (eds), *Higher Education and the Creative Economy*. London: Routledge, pp. 177–195.

Galenson, D.W. (2005). Anticipating artistic success (or how to beat the art market): lessons from history. Working Paper 11152. Cambridge: National Bureau of Economic Research.

Giuffre, K. (1999). Sandpiles of opportunity: success in the art world. *Social Forces*, 77(3), 815–832.

Greffe, X. (2002). *Arts and Artists from an Economic Perspective*. London: Economica.

Hall, D.T. (2004). The protean career: a quarter-century journey. *Journal of Vocational Behaviour*, 65(1), 1–13.

Heinich, N. (2012). Mapping intermediaries in contemporary art according to pragmatic sociology. *European Journal of Cultural Studies*, 15(6), 695–702.

Iaquinta, C., and Simoncelli, S. (2018). Donne Artiste in Italia: presenza e rappresentazione. NABA Report.

Jeffri, J. (2004). Research on the individual artist: seeking the solitary singer. *Journal of Arts Management, Law and Society*, 34, 9–23.

Jyrämä, A. (2002). Contemporary art markets – structure and actors: a study of art galleries in Finland, Sweden, France and Great Britain. *International Journal of Arts Management*, 4(2), 50–65.

Kavaler-Adler, S. (1993). *The Compulsion to Create: A Psychoanalytic Study of Women Artists*. New York: Routledge.

Lam, A. (2018). Boundary-crossing careers and the 'third space of hybridity': career actors as knowledge brokers between creative arts and academia. *Environment and Planning A: Economy and Space*, 50(8), 1716–1741.

Lee, S.H., and Lee, J.W. (2016). Art fairs as a medium for branding young and emerging artists: the case of frieze London. *Journal of Arts Management, Law, and Society*, 46(3), 95–106.

Lin, N. (1982). Social resources and instrumental action. In P.V. Marsden and N. Lin (eds), *Social Structure and Network Analysis*. Beverly Hills, CA: SAGE, pp. 131–145.

Martin, B. (2007). How visual artists enter the contemporary art market in France: a dynamic approach based on a network of tests. *International Journal of Arts Management*, 9(3), 16–33.

McAndrew, C. (2021). The art market 2021. Art Basel and UBS report. Available: https://www.artbasel.com/about/initiatives/theartmarket2021pdf (accessed 30 October 2021).

McCaughey, C. (1985). Feminine dominance of the arts: woman as producer and consumer. In *The Arts-Women and Politics: Arts Research Seminar No. 2*. Ottawa: Canada Council, Working Document 600-133, pp. 22–26.

McIntyre, M.H. (2004). *Taste Buds: How to Cultivate the Art Market: Executive Summary*. Arts Council England.

McMillan, K. (2018). Representation of female artists in Britain. Freeland Foundation Report.

Menger, P.M. (1999). Artistic labor markets and careers. *Annual Review of Sociology*, 25, 541–574.

Miller, D.L. (2016). Gender and the artist archetype: understanding gender inequality in artistic careers. *Sociology Compass*, 10(2), 119–131.

Miur (2021). Iscritti istituti AFAM 2021 Available: http://ustat.miur.it/dati/didattica/italia/afam-istituzioni-autorizzate-afam (accessed 30 October 2021).

Neuendorf, H. (2016). Art Demystified: How Do Artist Residencies Work? *Artnet Online*. Available at: https://news.artnet.com/art-world-art-demystified-artist-residencies-649592 (accessed 30 September 2021).

Noble, K.D. (1987). The dilemma of the gifted woman. *Psychology of Woman Quarterly*, 11, 367–378.

O'Hagan, J., and Hellmanzik, C. (2008). Clustering and migration of important visual artists: broad historical evidence. *Historical Methods: A Journal of Quantitative and Interdisciplinary History*, 41(3), 121–136. DOI: 10.3200/HMTS.41.3.121-136.

O'Hagan, J., and Kelly, E. (2005). Identifying the most important artists in a historical context: methods used and initial results. *Historical Methods*, 38, 118–125.

Resch, M. (2016). *The Global Art Gallery Report*. Phaidon. Available: https://www.magnusresch.com/wp-content/uploads/2020/12/GlobalArtGalleryReport2016byMagnusResch.pdf (accessed 30 September 2021).

Ross, A. (2003). *No-Collar, the Humane Workplace and its Hidden Costs*. New York: Basic Books.

Ross, A. (2007). Nice work if you can get it: the mercurial career of creative industries policy. *Work Organisation, Labour and Globalisation*, 1(1), 13–30.

Rouget, B., Sagot-Duvauroux, D., and Plieger, S. (1991). *Le marché de l'art contemporain en France: prix et stratégies*. Paris: La Documentation Française.

Sang, B.E. (1989). Psychotherapy with women artists. *The Arts in Psychotherapy*, 16, 301–307.

Scott, W.R. (1987). The adolescence of institutional theory. *Administrative Science Quarterly*, 32, 493–511.

Siddins, E., Daniel, R., and Johnstone, R. (2016). Building visual artists' resilience capabilities: current educator strategies and methods. *Journal of Arts and Humanities*, 5(7).

Stohs, J.H. (1992). Career patterns and family status of women and men artists. *Career Development Quarterly*, 40, 223–233.

Symbola (2019). Io Sono Cultura 2019. Available: https://www.symbola.net/ricerca/io -sono-cultura-2019/ (accessed 30 September 2020).

Symbola (2021). Io sono cultura 2021 Available: https://www.symbola.net/ricerca/io -sono-cultura-2021/ (accessed 30 October 2021).

Tanghetti, J., Comunian, R., and Dent, T. (2022/forthcoming). Covid-19 opened the Pandora Box of the creative city: creative and cultural workers against precarity in Milan, *Cambridge Journal of Regions, Economy and Society*.

Zelenko, O., and Bridgstock, R. (2014). Developing agency in the creative career: a design-based framework for work integrated learning. In G. Hearn, R. Bridgstock, B. Goldsmith and J. Rodgers (eds), *Creative Work beyond the Creative Industries: Innovation, Employment and Education*. Cheltenham, UK and Northampton, MA, USA: Edward Elgar Publishing, pp. 211–225.

Zorloni, A. (2005). Structure of the Contemporary Art Market and the Profile of Italian Artists. *International Journal of Arts Management*, 8(1), 61–71.

PART IV

Creative economies re-imagined

13. Re-futuring creative economies: beyond bad dreams and the banal imagination

Mark Banks

At a time when it is becoming more urgently necessary to question the capitalist foundations of economic life, supporting 'growth', free markets and unfettered accumulation remain the foundational premises of 'creative economy'[1] policy. In the United Kingdom (UK), for example, the dominant claim is that investment in culture and creativity boosts economic activity and national output, outlined in publications such as *Culture is Digital* (DCMS, 2018), the *UK Digital Strategy* (DCMS, 2017), *The Culture White Paper* (DCMS, 2016), the *UK Industrial Strategy* (HM Government, 2017, 2018), the *Independent Review of the Creative Industries* (Bazalgette, 2017) and in the complementary work of industry-facing agencies such as the Creative Industries Federation (2016). Such claims are echoed in the policy framings of other economically powerful European nations such as France (France Créative, 2013) and Germany (BMWi, 2017), and have been consolidated at European Union (EU) level through growth-oriented initiatives such as Creative Europe 2014–2020. Current EU plans for funding culture and creativity beyond 2020 seem set to further reinforce the growth-led agenda (European Commission, 2018, 2021). The creative economy policies of Australia (Government of Australia, 2013) and Canada (Canada Heritage, 2017) are similarly fixed on economic expansion as the primary objective. At a wider level, while the United Nations Educational, Scientific and Cultural Organization (UNESCO) through its *Convention on the Diversity of Cultural Expressions* (UNESCO, 2005), *Creative Cities Network* (UNESCO, 2017) and publications such as the *Creative Economy Report Special Edition* (UNESCO/UNCP, 2013), might more strongly advocate for more socially just and locally sensitive economic progress, they tend to do so from within the confines of a conventional (gross domestic product-focused, capital-led) 'sustainable development' approach (see Isar, 2015; Throsby, 2017). There is very little in this policy discourse that seeks to question capitalistic growth as the primary socio-economic objective, or that considers the more damaging and deleterious consequences of a commitment to ceaseless economic expansion. Indeed, this policy and advocacy work tends to more generally lack any explicitly environmental or (wider) ecological[2] priorities or perspectives.

In an era of unfolding and urgent crises,[3] and growing concerns for climate justice, such a lack seems – to say the least – both inadequate and inappropriate. For those of us who accept that the current economic crisis is not a passing phase but enduring and systemic, and very much integrated with social inequalities and a growing abundance of environmental crises (Banks, 2018), it seems there is no better time for exponents of the creative economy to be thinking about more genuinely different and sustainable models of organising and producing. This means ways of making arts, media and culture that do not rest on assumptions of unchecked growth, and expansive exploitation of physical and human resources, but seek instead to divert from (or challenge) these conventional understandings, norms and practices. In this respect, of course, there are now a whole range of established and incipient 'socially just', 'inclusive', 'ecological', 'transitional', 'post-growth', 'decolonised' and 'co-operative' forms of cultural industries production that appear to offer different ways of producing the creative economy (see e.g., de Peuter and Cohen, 2015; Fletcher, 2016; Imagine 2020 (2018); McHattie et al., 2019; O'Dair, 2015; Sandoval, 2018; Serafini, 2020). These are vital, valuable and worthy of our support, yet they also remain quite marginal, undervalued and outside of the orthodox imaginary of the creative economy. I see the task of any kind of critical creative economy studies as to bring these counter-initiatives further to the fore, while continuing to challenge established and hegemonic practices, and the range of imaginaries, metaphors and myths that sustain them.

I stress this latter point since here I wish to draw particular attention to how orthodox narratives of creative economy have come to fix a set of what I would term 'banal utopian imaginaries' in government, in organisations, in universities, in commercial life: positive stories and images of tomorrow that might initially appear complex and plural, but are actually quite restricted in the range of creative futures they desire and present. These tend to be most avidly fashioned by those driving the upsurge in creative economy policy and advocacy, particularly now that this activity has come to be so strongly tied to technology, state industrial strategies, and faith in machines to deliver progressive and equitable social futures. To my mind, however, this positivity begins with its own negation: a denial of the existence of many of the problems with how the creative economy currently operates, and a refusal to acknowledge that delivering pacific social futures might be as much undermined by the creative economy as enhanced by it. What is more, as I will argue, these banal imaginaries not only serve to secure existing arrangements of power and inequality, and offer much less than they promise, but they also work to close down the possibilities of other, potentially progressive and non-capitalistic, forms of creative economy developing or coming into being.

CREATIVITY ECONOMY AND ECOLOGICAL CRISIS

First, though, it is worth thinking briefly about how we might have got to this point of neglect. In the last 20 years, the creative economy has become an important policy focus internationally. Governments – especially in the richest nations – have turned to the creative economy to help drive post-industrial (and now, post-financial crisis) economic growth, employment and social cohesion, partly based on assumptions that the creative sectors are greener, more socially inclusive and more sustainable than traditional industries (ACE, 2017; British Council, 2010; European Commission, 2018). However, the evidence base supporting these assumptions is remarkably thin, and their opposite more likely true. A growing body of research in the arts, humanities and social sciences has argued that the creative economy is highly resource- and energy-intensive, socially exclusive and, ultimately, at current levels of activity, ecologically unsustainable (Banks, 2018; Caraway, 2017; Maxwell and Miller, 2012, 2017; Murdock, 2018; Oakley et al., 2018).

Yet when it comes to ecological matters, governments and exponents of the creative economy have tended generally towards quietism or indifference. Compared to manufacturing industries or primary extraction, creative industries tend to be (erroneously) presented as 'greener' (and therefore 'good') by nature (Maxwell and Miller, 2017). We also know that while the creative economy still tends to be favoured as a 'positive' solution to problems of social and economic restructuring, a large body of research has revealed the persistent spread of clearances, gentrifications, displacements and exclusive (and usually resource-hungry) developments that have occurred in the name of cultural regeneration or reanimation of 'dead' urban space (see Grodach et al., 2017; Oakley, 2015; Pratt, 2011). And even within the cultural quarters and districts that house the apparently equitable professional enclaves of cultural, media and creative industries, we know that deep-rooted workforce inequalities are not only persisting, but often also expanding (Banks, 2017; Saha, 2018).

Researchers and campaigners in the Global South have alerted us to the plight of workers involved in the global extraction and supply chain of raw materials, or in processes of sweatshop manufacture producing creative economy goods for consumption in rich countries, as well as those involved in the global trade and circulation of waste, e-waste and detritus of the creative economy which creates problems of disposal, disassembly, toxic hazard, ill-health and death (see e.g., Chan et al., 2016; Cubitt, 2015; Grossman, 2016; Murdock, 2018; Taffel, 2016).

Many producers and policymakers tend to stick to the optimistic claim that technological innovations and efficiency savings in production will eventually overcome these ingrained problems and negative externalities, sufficient to ensure that economic growth can continue without fatally damaging ecological capacity. But the assumption that capitalistic growth can be absolutely (rather than simply relatively) decoupled from ecological impacts looks increasingly like delusion (Jackson, 2017). In creative tech, the rapidly expanding demand for electronic communications, entertainment and content is tending to generate environmental and energy costs that outstrip any savings made by efficiency improvements in the manufacture and design of individual technologies themselves (Caraway, 2017), the so-called Jevons Paradox. The fashion industry might be pioneering new ways of making clothes more 'renewably' and 'responsibly' but the vast resources thrown at pricking the demand for new product and the staggering levels of waste and disposal this generates seems likely to offset any efficiency gains made (Thomas, 2019). The music industry – seemingly relocated to the dematerialised ether – creates and drives traffic through the expanding network of servers, generators, cables, devices and accessory hardware. As research is now revealing, the emissions and waste profile is displaced and made indirect, but not necessarily reduced (Devine, 2019). There are, of course, many other examples that we could cite.

While most supporters of the creative economy have tended to gloss over these inconveniences, it is of course the case that some mainstream ecological approaches (such as 'sustainable development', 'inclusive growth', 'green growth', 'urban prosperity', and so on) have now been mooted for some greater coupling to the creative economy; I am thinking here of the work of the Organisation for Economic Co-operation and Development (OECD), World Bank, UNESCO, and others.[4] Yet these tend to take for granted continued growth within an established economic framework, one where you can have more of the same if you make some well-meaning but minor concessions; but the direction of travel overall remains unchanged (see e.g., Florida, 2017). But even if the economy improves, the idea of economic development premised on continually expanding gross domestic product (GDP) and 'sustainably developing' (that is, using up) existing resources will eventually hit some unavoidable biospherical limits (Hickel and Kallis, 2019). In parallel, since none of these approaches foreground labour issues or politics, societies must somehow address the absolute and relative poverty inequality and insecurity being accelerated by current economic and ecological transformations, which will, for many, increasingly challenge the sustainable bases of social cohesion, community and life itself; and it is no longer acceptable to pretend that cultural, creative and media industries are not implicated in this, because they are.

CREATIVE ECONOMIES OF TOMORROW?

This, then, offers some prelude or context, but I especially want to address how the creative economy's own banal and orthodox futurology – its stories, imaginaries and visions of tomorrow – has remained markedly indifferent to, or unaffected by, the need for system change. Indeed, while we might be suffering the expanding effects of sustained economic and eco-crises, you would not necessarily know this by looking at any kind of orthodox discourse on the creative sectors. Just in the UK alone, the current Industrial Strategy – including the Creative Industries Sector Deal and Arts and Humanities Research Council (AHRC) Creative Clusters research programme – the Creative Industries Federation, most university innovation centres and business schools, and the British Council abroad, have maintained faith in the dominant imaginary. This is the one that identifies the creative economy as a wealth-creating machine driven by enterprising individuals transacting in free markets, with upbeat growth projections, unfettered production of commodities, and unlimited technological expansion, consumption and national accumulation; the only real future considered palatable or imaginable:

> The UK's future will be built at the nexus of our artistic and cultural creativity and our technical brilliance. The Centre for Economics and Business Research 2018 World Economic League Tables identify this particular blend of creativity and technology skills as the driving force behind the UK's strong economic prospects over the long term; a powerful combination of talents to project to the world as we prepare to leave the EU. (Matt Hancock, *Culture is Digital*, 2018)

> Looking forward fifteen or twenty years to what our future economy could be like, in every scenario the Creative Industries are of central importance to the UK's productivity and global success. We have two great assets: the English language and our national capacity for creativity. But the skills and business models of this sector and of the wider creative economy are those which many experts judge to be of increasing importance: blended technical and creative skills; collaborative interdisciplinary working; entrepreneurialism and enterprise ... The cultural and creative sectors are the engine of the UK's international image and soft power. (Bazalgette, 2017)

True, tokenistic nods to social inclusion, 'sustainability' and economic transition might garner some mentions; but mainly to prove that the powerful are not ogres. History shows that those in government and the organisation with a real commitment to progressive change tend to find themselves blocked or stymied. Ultimately, then, it seems the powerful will continue to trust the market to make any necessary social adjustments as it expands once again into infinite space. But this is a future that is built on past assumptions and expectations that can no longer hold.

The narrow optimism of this economic projection is mirrored in the thinness of the social world such speculation now anticipates and imagines. What is at stake here is not simply a forecast about likely economic performance, but a whole set of assumptions about the organisation and relations of tomorrow's common life. Orthodox creative economy imaginaries have become so tightly harnessed to a script that states simply 'culture is digital', 'culture is immersive' or that culture is simply benign and 'good for growth', and need only be properly harnessed and arraigned in order to bring goods for all. Yet this masks a dubious disavowal of politics and the deeply commercial and disaggregating logic that underpins the strategy – one where social and political problems (such as questions of material inequality, cultural inclusion, participation and justice) – can too easily be reduced to problems of inadequate connectivity or failures of individual engagement or enterprise. The true beneficiaries are, of course, those emboldened and enabled corporations investing in monopoly-building across platforms, software commodities, artificial intelligence (AI) systems, algorithmic computing and machine learning. The social worlds they imagine seem to mirror their own corporate fantasies of digitally afforded, frictionless and aseptic human encounter. The dominant stock-imaged sociality of the creative economy is one which seems perversely obsessed with well-dressed, VR-helmeted male monads groping blindly into the future, bedazzled by the profundity of their own interiorised experience. Such imagery also reinforces the assumption that the primary use and mode of the engagement of creative economy tech is personal: geared around fulfilling the satisfactions of the capable and empowered consumer-individual interfacing with the co-present experience, entertainment or augmented reality in hand.

We should note also that creative economy advance never really appears as initially operative in any kind of real geographical context other than this characteristic landscape of corporate interiors: sanitised modular offices, labs, co-working spaces and work-pods, or other similarly indistinguishable non-places largely unmarked by difference or social complexity. Such environments bear no traces of crisis or its potential, but tend only to reproduce the idea that no kind of restriction or limitation on the expansionist tendencies of creative class professionals will ever be truly necessary.

It is not just big tech, here, of course. Translated and taken into the art space, or gallery or museum, we are told that creative economy approaches are justified because they are driven by the increased expectations of established audiences and consumers for new kinds of 'immersive experience': the desire for new stories and sensations told and sold through interactive technology. Some of this stuff is highly admirable, good and impressive; dazzling, even. Some of it, less so. But whether immersion entails anything other than absorption in personalised consumer experience (even if those experiences are shared) is not yet clear, and how it supersedes or extends the more traditional 'immersions' able to be provided by arts and culture remains to be seen. The policy nexus is in thrall to the privatised, commercial application of technology, much more than the cultivation of cultural democracy, or the production of convivial social tools in the broadest interests of the community. This raises questions about the democratic and inclusive potential currently enabled by the creative economy monies now being directed at the arts. This is certainly not to deny the many good things that arts organisations and their partners are doing in terms of using funding and resources to make arts and culture more socially accessible and engaging to non-established users. But what seems less prominent in any kind of orthodox discourse on creative economy is recognition that the capacities for immersion and imaginative futurity are socially endowed as much as technologically driven. They rely on 'immersive' investment in democratic education, engagement and access programmes across the whole social field, and not just the existing coterie of socially advantaged audience-users. They also require well-trained and fairly paid staff working in a diversity of sustainable and valued organisations, certainly as much as on any kind of disassociated 'roll-out' of 'content' amidst digitally optimised 'solutions'. Additionally, immersion in a real future of the arts and culture – as opposed to a romanticised or individualised digital utopia – demands a much closer engagement with the likely consequences of a world increasingly shorn of the securities provided by carbon- and resource-rich economies underpinned by a relatively stable social democratic polity.

Why is it, then, that the creative economy seems blind to those emergent crises that will fundamentally transform its own conditions of possibility? Partly the usual reasons: vested power and interests. But it is also a wider societal problem of disbelief: as the political philosophers have argued (e.g., Forrester, 2017), it has always been easier to abdicate responsibility for the future in order to focus on the immediate needs of the present, partly because it has been seen as more justified to extend a moral obligation to the living rather than to non-existent future persons. But such an orientation is only justified in a world where further material progress can be assumed and ecological limits need barely be considered. Where the future was once a remote and misted abstraction which societies gradually evolved towards from the greater clarity of the present, now the future seems to be rudely reversing into the present, and it is the escalating arrival of the far away in the here-and-now that seems most urgently to matter. So we might say that while the orthodox creative economy – as it most commonly appears – might wish to be seen as exciting and futuristic, it now appears paradoxically anachronistic: increasingly and wilfully stuck in a rapidly receding past, a world of possibility now seriously on the wane. But we should not of course discount the seated power of its projections: orthodox creative economy futures are not simply sets of stories and images to be dismissed, but constitutive elements of the desired futures of the powerful in the present, and must be addressed critically insofar as they remain capable of shaping decision-making and orienting human action.

We need to challenge the limitations of these projections because, to my mind, and to borrow from the design philosopher Tony Fry (2015; and see Escobar, 2017), they are at risk of de-futuring the future. The most orthodox imaginaries of the creative economy appear to be instrumentally and artificially narrowing (rather than expanding) the range of possible ways of thinking about culture, economy and technology, and ways of doing and being human; an approach which, while being cloaked in the rhetoric of openness, may actually be closing us down at the worst imaginable time. And such imaginaries fail to acknowledge how they are actually sustaining the unsustainable in the limited range of their own economic, social and environmental assumptions and practices. In this respect we might say that the creative economy is now culpably 'de-worlding' us: literally, in its accelerated contributions to ecological crisis; and figuratively, and conceptually, in its pre-emptive closing down of the cultural imagination and all the diverse possibilities and promises that we know culture and arts can offer.

TOWARDS RE-FUTURING?

So where now? Though there has never been any ideal state of grace, it is important to keep hold of and extend those progressive elements of the social, and of politics, that have long proved sustaining and energising to cultural academics, producers and activists (see Banks, 2017; de Peuter and Cohen, 2015). We must also keep up the critique of actually existing conditions. But I would also say, in the face of de-futuring, that we might also look to re-future. To re-future is to reject the authority of the already prescribed future-present in order to re-think the fundamental categories we live by – in our case, 'economy', 'creation', 'growth', 'inclusion' and 'choice', for example – and to work in pursuit of more socially situated media, technologies and forms of art and cultural production that are not 'decontextualised and value neutral, but embodied, place based, convivial and conducive to care' (Escobar, 2017: 35). The creative economies of tomorrow might serve us better if they drew more on heterodox, feminist and ecological social and economic thought, where production is not imagined as a limitless and empty abstraction, but more concretely understood in the context of different human (and non-human) needs, and connected to the ongoing obligations, contradictions and challenges of our shared social and ecological reproduction. Such a holistic perspective might help to inform the creation of worlds of cultural production, circulation and exchange that focus less on GDP and 'sustainable development' and more on sustainable prosperity: worlds where human (and non-human) well-being can finally be disassociated from crude, economistic formulas (Jackson, 2017;

Oakley et al., 2018; Weeks, 2011). In re-futuring we might also find licence to engage in the kind of genuine 'open thinking' (and I mean more in the sense of a Theodor Adorno or a Donna Haraway, rather than a Google or Facebook) that allows us to move outside of the accepted and banal discourse on creative economy and posit for alternative or transitional creative economies, ways of being and provisioning in the cultural sphere, that take seriously the need for progressive and egalitarian change, in all social domains.

There is real possibility here, because what art, culture and aesthetic production will look like, sound like, feel like or aspire to be under crisis or transition is not yet anywhere near being on the policy agenda. But it should be, and we can help to put it there. We already have innumerable social utopias (both good and bad) fomenting in public discourse, many new 'post-work', 'post-growth' and other ecological imaginaries emerging across the humanities and social sciences, and actually existing alternative economic futures being constructed and lived in practice. Now would be a good time to see some new 'creative economy imaginaries' emerging, because while our critical inventories of existing harm and inequality are valuable, they are also perhaps insufficient. The social facts of the present could be used to better inform our own more ambitious attempts at re-worlding; that is, for us to say collectively what kinds of alternative futures we might wish to see. These might be conceived in the form of 'real utopias', as the late Erik Olin Wright (2010) suggested: practical and existing ways of living together better; or explored in the idea of 'utopia as method' proposed by Ruth Levitas (2017), where the future is cast as a constant and unending experiment in better ways to prosper and thrive, rather than a riddle to be solved or fixed with the correct solution or masterplan.

In taking these steps academics and practitioners can avoid falling into the trap of thinking that our critical work is not important; that the culture, arts and media industries are somehow going to be mere distractions to the more ominous challenges to come. But whatever future transpires, it will undoubtedly be cast in the imagination, created, aestheticised and sensed; it will be pervasively mediated, screened and projected, and (of course) intensively laboured over, by many of the same individuals, communities and organisations that have always laboured. I want to propose, then, that the job of critical creative economy scholars and activists is not simply to make those futures apparent, but also to contribute positively to their progressive imagining and building.

NOTES

1.   The creative economy has no single definition. For UNCTAD (2018, n.p.), 'It is an evolving concept which builds on the interplay between human creativity and ideas and intellectual property, knowledge and technology. Essentially it is the

knowledge-based economic activities upon which the "creative industries" are based'. For Nesta (2013: 34), it is 'those economic activities which involve the use of creative talent for commercial purposes'. I use the term as a shorthand to capture the full range of the designated 'cultural and creative sectors' (European Commission, 2018): the arts, media, and cultural and creative industries.

2. I use the term 'ecological' to refer generally to the symbiotic and integral relations between people, animals, processes and environment; and more specifically the relations between the social and cultural, the economic and the environmental.

3. As I write, in early 2020, Australian bushfires, flooding in Indonesia and the emerging COVID-19 virus pandemic loom largest.

4. See, for example, OECD (2020), UNESCO (2017) and World Bank (2012).

REFERENCES

ACE (2017) *Sustaining Great Art.* London: Arts Council England.

Banks, M. (2017) *Creative Justice: Cultural Industries, Work and Inequality.* London: Rowman & Littlefield International.

Banks, M. (2018) Creative Economies of Tomorrow: Limits to Growth and the Uncertain Future. *Cultural Trends* 27 (5), 367–380.

Bazalgette, P. (2017) *The Independent Review of the Creative Industries.* London: DCMS. https://www.gov.uk/government/publications/independent-review-of-the-creative-industries.

BMWi (2017) *Cultural and Creative Industries Monitoring Report.* Berlin: Federal Ministry for Economic Affairs and Energy.

British Council (2010) *The Creative Economy: An Introductory Guide.* London: British Council.

Canada Heritage (2017) *Creative Canada Policy Framework.* Government of Canada. https://www.canada.ca/en/canadian-heritage/campaigns/creative-canada/framework.html.

Caraway, B. (2017) Literal Media Ecology: Crisis in the Conditions of Production. *Television and New Media* 9 (5), 486–503.

Chan, J., Pun, N. and Selden, M. (2016) Chinese Labor Protest and Trade Unions. In Maxwell, R. (ed.) *The Routledge Companion to Labor and Media.* New York: Routledge, pp. 290–302.

Creative Industries Federation (2016) *The C- Report.* https://www.creativeindustries federation.com/publications/c-report-2015-2016,

Cubitt, S. (2015) Integral Waste. *Theory, Culture and Society* 32 (4), 133–145.

DCMS (2016) *The Culture White Paper.* London: DCMS.

DCMS (2017) *UK Digital Strategy.* London: DCMS.

DCMS (2018) *Culture is Digital.* London: DCMS.

de Peuter, G. and Cohen. N. (2015) Emerging Labor Politics in Creative Industries. In Oakley, K. and O'Connor, J. (eds) *The Routledge Companion to the Cultural Industries.* London: Routledge, pp. 305–318.

Devine, K. (2019) *Decomposed: The Political Ecology of Music. Popular Music.* Cambridge, MA: MIT Press.

Escobar, A. (2017) *Designs for the Pluriverse.* Durham, NC, USA and London, UK: Duke University Press.

European Commission (2018) *A New European Agenda for Culture: Background Information.* https://ec.europa.eu/culture/news/new-european-agenda-culture_en.

European Commission (2021) *Horizon Europe.* https://ec.europa.eu/info/horizon -europe_en (accessed April 2021).

Fletcher, K. (2016) *Craft of Use: Post-Growth Fashion.* Abingdon: Routledge.

Florida, R. (2017) *The New Urban Crisis.* London: Oneworld.

Forrester, K. (2017) The Problem of the Future in Postwar Anglo-American Political Philosophy. *Climatic Change* 151 (1), 55–66.

France Créative (2013) *Création sous tension 2e Panorama de l'économie de la culture et de la creation en France.* http://francecreative.org/.

Fry, T. (2015) *City Futures in the Age of A Changing Climate.* London: Routledge.

Government of Australia (2013) *Creative Australia: National Cultural Policy.* http://apo.org.au/node/33126.

Grodach, C., O'Connor, J. and Gibson, C. (2017) Manufacturing and Cultural Production: Towards a Progressive Policy Agenda for the Cultural Economy. *City, Culture and Society* 10, 17–25.

Grossman, E. (2016) The Body Burden: Toxics, Stresses and Biophysical Health. In Maxwell, R. (ed.) *The Routledge Companion to Labor and Media.* New York: Routledge, pp. 65–77.

Hancock, M. (2018) Foreword, in *Culture is Digital,* London, DCMS.

Hickel, J. and Kallis, G. (2019) Is Green Growth Possible? *New Political Economy* (published online first September) https://www.tandfonline.com/doi/full/10.1080/13563467.2019.1598964.

HM Government (2017) *Building our Industrial Strategy.* London: HMRC. https://www.gov.uk/government/uploads/system/uploads/attachment_data/file/664563/industrial-strategy-white-paper-web-ready-version.pdf.

HM Government (2018) *Creative Industries Sector Deal.* London: HMRC. https://www.gov.uk/government/publications/creative-industries-sector-deal.

Imagine 2020 (2018) *Art and Climate Change.* http://www.imagine2020.eu/about/.

Isar, R. (2015) Widening Local Development Pathways: Transformative Visions of Cultural Economy. In Oakley, K. and O'Connor, J. (eds) *The Routledge Companion to the Cultural Industries.* London: Routledge, pp. 477–488.

Jackson, T. (2017) *Prosperity without Growth: Economics for a Finite Planet.* London: Earthscan.

Levitas, R. (2017) Where There is No Vision, the People Perish: A Utopian Ethic for a Transformed Future. CUSP Essay No 5. http://www.cusp.ac.uk/wp-content/uploads/05-Ruth-Levitas-Essay-online.pdf.

Maxwell, R. and Miller, T. (2012) *Greening the Media.* Oxford: Oxford University Press.

Maxwell, R. and Miller, T. (2017) Greening Cultural Policy. *International Journal of Cultural Policy* 23 (2), 174–185.

McHattie, L.M., Champion, K. and Johnson, M. (2019) Crafting the Local: The Lived Experience of Craft Production in the Northern Isles of Scotland. *Cultural Trends* 28 (4), 305–316.

Murdock, G. (2018) Media Materialities: For a Moral Economy of Machines. *Journal of Communication* 68 (2), 359–368.

Nesta (2013) *A Manifesto for the Creative Economy.* London: Nesta.

Oakley, K. (2015) *Creating Space: A Re-evaluation of the Role of Culture in Regeneration.* AHRC Cultural Value Project. http://eprints.whiterose.ac.uk/88559/.

Oakley, K., Ball, M. and Cunningham, M. (2018) Everyday Culture and the Good Life. CUSP Working Paper No 9. https://www.cusp.ac.uk/themes/a/wp9/.

O'Dair, M. (2015) Collaborative, Co-operative and Collective Business Models in the 'New' Music Industries: A Literature Review. http://ualresearchonline.arts.ac.uk/14653/.

OECD (2020) *Inclusive Growth.* https//www.oecd.org/inclusivegrowth/~introduction (accessed April 2021).

Pratt, A. (2011) The Cultural Contradictions of the Creative City. *City, Culture and Society* 2 (3), 123–130.

Saha, A. (2018). *Race and the Cultural Industries.* Cambridge: Polity.

Sandoval, M. (2018) From Passionate Labour to Compassionate Work: Cultural Co-ops, Do What You Love and Social Change. *European Journal of Cultural Studies* 21 (2), 113–129.

Serafini, P. (2020) Cultural Production beyond Extraction? A First Approximation to Extractivism and the Cultural and Creative Industries in Argentina. In Oakley, K. and Banks, M. (eds) *Cultural Industries and Environmental Crisis.* New York: Springer, pp. 51–64.

Taffel, S. (2016) Towards an Ethical Electronics? Ecologies of Congolese Conflict Minerals. *Westminster Papers in Communication and Culture.* https://www.westminsterpapers.org/article/10.16997/wpcc.210/.

Thomas, D. (2019) The Real Cost of Your Blue Jeans. *Newsweek* 9 March. https://www.newsweek.com/2019/09/20/real-cost-blue-jeans-labor-environment-fashionopolis-book-extract-1457027.html.

Throsby, D. (2017) Culturally Sustainable Development: Theoretical Concept or Practical Policy Instrument? *International Journal of Cultural Policy* 23 (2), 133–147.

UNCTAD (2018) *Creative Economy Programme.* http://unctad.org/en/Pages/DITC/CreativeEconomy/Creative-Economy-Programme.aspx.

UNESCO (2005) *Convention on the Diversity of Cultural Expressions.* https://en.unesco.org/creativity/convention/texts (accessed February 2020).

UNESCO (2017) *Creative Cities Network: Mission Statement.* https://en.unesco.org/creative-cities/content/management-documents.

UNESCO/UNDP (2013) *Creative Economy Report Special Edition: Widening Development Pathways.* New York: United Nations.

Weeks, K. (2011) *The Problem With Work: Feminism, Marxism, Antiwork Politics, and Postwork Imaginaries.* Durham, NC, USA and London, UK: Duke University Press.

World Bank (2012) *Inclusive Green Growth: The Pathway to Sustainable Development.* Washington, DC.

Wright, E.O. (2010) *Envisioning Real Utopias.* London and New York: Verso.

14. Growth of what? New narratives for the creative economy, beyond GDP

Jonathan Gross

14.1 INTRODUCTION

How do we know when creative economies are doing well? What does success look like? When the United Kingdom (UK) government defined the 'creative industries' in its influential and contentious 1998 *Creative Industries Mapping Document* (DCMS 1998), it prioritised two measures: the number of people employed in these areas of activity, and contribution to gross domestic product (GDP).[1] In the years since, the creative industries – and now the 'creative economy' – have achieved policy prominence in part due to the efficacy of such pithy statistics regarding their contribution to national economies. But there is a groundswell of critique of GDP. These critiques have come from a variety of directions. GDP is a limited indicator of prosperity, doing a very partial job of letting us know whether, overall, people are doing well. In respect of the creative economy specifically, critiques of using GDP as the primary measure of success range from its disregard for the environmental destructiveness of these supposedly low-carbon activities, to the limits it places on 'cultural imagination' (Banks 2018).

Building upon these critiques, what needs to be paid attention to is the startling success of GDP. We need to historicize this indicator, appreciating how it was born, what it was intended to do, and the unexpectedness of the hegemonic role it has come to play. In this chapter I argue that GDP's power derives in part from its capacity to establish a simple narrative framework: coordinates against which to tell a story of collective progress. GDP is the rising tide that lifts all ships. The bellwether of prosperity. Within this worldview, the immense complexity of economies can be neatly aggregated to a single figure, and if that number increases we know that we are headed in the right direction. In challenging the dominance of GDP, therefore, it is necessary to understand the power of its capacity to set the terms for storytelling, and to consider what might be alternative grounds for narrating the 'success' of economies, and of creative economies in particular.

Within policy studies, narrative has been employed as an analytical lens for some years, particularly since the publication of Emery Roe's (1994) *Narrative Policy Analysis*. Within that field, debates have at times centred on whether narrative analysis of public policy is inherently committed to constructivist and post-structuralist epistemologies and ontologies, or whether it can be used in alignment with positivist methodologies (Jones and McBeth 2010). Within economic research, narrative analysis has yet to take off, but Robert J. Schiller has recently made the case for economists to develop such an approach within their field. The case he makes for the significance of narrative is quite specific. What Schiller is particularly interested in is how economic stories go viral and cause economic events. In his view this has been overlooked for too long, and economists need to develop new methods through which to understand the economic stories that circulate and the effects they have on people's economic behaviour (Schiller 2019). But economic narratives play more fundamental, structuring roles, beyond exerting a causal influence on specific economic events. In this chapter I address perhaps the most important of these roles at the present time: the way in which GDP, as the prevailing measure of economic success, has come to constitute a dominant narrative framework for public policy.

Within cultural policy studies there have been just a handful of substantial analyses in terms of narrative. These include Meyrick, Phiddian and Barnett's exploration of the relationship between narrative and quantification within processes of cultural evaluation (Meyrick et al. 2018), and Bilton and Soltero's Gramscian examination of cultural policies in the UK and Mexico as 'mythical narratives', leading to their proposal of a research agenda for narrative analysis within cultural policy scholarship. Such research, they suggest, could aim 'not only to understand implicit values and ideology in cultural policy but to challenge them', identifying and gathering 'the "other stories" and other voices behind or within the dominant narrative into an alternative, counter-hegemonic narrative' (Bilton and Soltero 2020: 694). In my own work, I have explored the potential for cultural policies to deliberately support conditions conducive to new individual and collective stories being told at micro, meso and macro scales (Gross 2019).[2] Cultural policies may thereby expand 'space for political imagination' (Gross 2021: 451), in some cases by being aligned with broader political narratives, such as the Green New Deal (Gross and Wilson 2020), that extend well beyond the conventional concerns of culture ministries and arts funding agencies. But there is much more work to be done to understand the ways in which cultural policy processes operate via – and make possible – practices of storytelling. In this chapter I make one contribution to that broader task, by examining recent discourses of 'creative industries' and the 'creative economy' in respect of the narrative frameworks within which their economic success has been storied.

14.2   DEFINING AND MEASURING THE CREATIVE ECONOMY

The history of the creative economy is the history of its contested definition and measurement. A key moment within this history was the definition and mapping of the creative industries by the UK government in the first months of Tony Blair's New Labour government (DCMS 1998). There is a long pre-history to the idea of the creative industries, which in a literature review Justin O'Connor traces back through related terms such as the cultural industries – associated particularly with the progressive politics of the Greater London Council in the 1980s – and the culture industry, Adorno and Horkheimer's famously critical take on what they saw to be the corrupting industrialization of aesthetic production (O'Connor 2010). From soon after its publication, the 1998 DMCS definition[3] and measurement of the creative industries was a matter of much debate, and there have been innumerable challenges made to their validity (see, e.g., Galloway and Dunlop 2007). Twenty years after its publication, I undertook an oral history of the process through which the *Mapping Document* was created, examining why, how and with what consequences it was developed (Gross 2020b). Here I want to draw out just one insight from that research. Namely, the function that the definition and measurement of the creative industries was intended to serve for the purposes of political storytelling.

A central figure in this history is the film producer and Labour member of the House of Lords, David Puttnam. During the mid-1990s, whilst Labour was still in opposition, he was 'basically funding an informal … creative industries thinktank' (Puttnam, quoted in Gross 2020b: 6), developing ideas for how to better support the UK film industry and the wider creative sector. When Labour came to power in 1997, he was one of the original members of the Creative Industries Task Force that produced the *Mapping Document*. I asked him why the document was developed, and he explained as follows:

> No one really knew what the scale of the creative economy was. We were talking about something that no one, frankly, fully understood. And that's where … the idea of a mapping document emerged from. It emerged from the fact that we found ourselves desperately ignorant … We had two problems. How to define the creative economy, and then trying to put a number on actually what it was worth … We needed a starting point. We needed to know what we were talking about. I also remember … we agreed at the time that we do a second one in five years … We needed a direction of travel, we needed to know where we were in order to be sure where we were going, and whether we were heading in the right direction … Once you defined a sector, once you've mapped out what its growth is, then that allows you to start prioritising different areas of policy development. (Puttnam, quoted in Gross 2020b: 8)

The ability to tell a story of growth was central to this whole project of defining and mapping the creative industries. The intention was that by establishing what we might call a protagonist – this newly identified sector of the economy – and telling the story of its progress, policymakers would take notice and do much more to support this sector to grow. As O'Connor puts it, "'7.9% of GDP", "4x faster than the rest of the economy" – such figures represent its indisputable right to attention' (O'Connor 2020: 2).

How efficacious has this project of storytelling been? For my research participants, all of whom were involved in the development of the *Mapping Document*, in some ways the intervention was extremely successful, with the idea of the creative industries being adopted by governments around the world to an extent they had never anticipated. On the other hand, most were disappointed that the UK government did not develop more sustained, concrete policies in support of the sector. I discuss these findings in greater detail else-where (Gross 2020b). Here I am using this pivotal moment in the history of the definition and measurement of the creative 'sector' for the specific purpose of introducing my central point in this chapter. Namely, that how the relationship between creativity and economy is conceptualized and measured needs to be understood in terms of political storytelling; and that for those for whom existing definitions and measurements of the creative industries – and now the creative economy – remain conceptually and/or politically problematic, it is important to consider the broader (economic) narrative framework within which the story of the creative economy is told.

What do I mean by 'narrative framework' here? There is a huge literature addressing the nature of narrative. In this chapter I follow Bilton and Soltero in understanding it to be 'the representation of events in time'. As they indicate, whilst usages of the term are 'ever evolving and disputed', this definition of narrative 'has garnered consensus as a starting point' (Bilton and Soltero 2020: 684). But shared narratives – collective representations of events in time – are dependent upon a range of contextual understandings that enable the central characters and action to come into focus and be understood, and for causal relationships between different events to be inferred. For example, when Virginia Woolf includes a World War I veteran, Septimus Warren Smith, amongst her characters in *Mrs Dalloway* (Woolf 2000 [1925]), she does not need to provide readers with a history of the Great War. The veteran's experiences and actions in the novel can be fluently taken in by the reader in relation to their assumed existing knowledge of the war, and their sense of what active service might have been like. Narratives that successfully communicate – representing the relationship between events in time in ways that can be grasped – do so by drawing upon backgrounds of shared knowledge and meaning, and this applies across a range of scales. Narrative frameworks – these shared background understandings of settings, events and the scope of possible action

– are involved in storytelling everywhere, from getting home in the evening and narrating an experience at the office to a loved one, to the stories of societal progress with which politicians make a claim for re-election, and the grand narratives that structure national identities over the course of generations. In each case, background knowledge makes the foreground story possible.

It is perhaps something of this sense of narrative framework that O'Connor has in mind when he writes that '[t]he field of "creative industries", closely bound to the Big Bang of a specific policy moment, must stand with the validity of that moment or risk falling with it' (O'Connor 2020: 1). What he is alluding to here is specific components of late twentieth century economic thinking in the context of which New Labour's politics developed. As has been much discussed (e.g., Garnham 2005), the idea of the creative industries established traction within policy discourse in the context of wider conversations about the overall transformation of industrialized economies at the turn of the millennium, with much commentary on the purported emergence of 'post-industrial economies', 'knowledge economies', and/or 'the information society'. Within this broader narrative framework of economic change, the conceptualization and measurement of the relationship between creativity and economy has of course continued to develop since 1998. In particular, and as the title of this book exemplifies, the idea of the creative economy has emerged, and now operates alongside its slightly older sibling. The main impetus for this shift in discourse has been the need to recognize the ways in which creativity operates in economies outside of the creative industries themselves.

This new terminology, creative economy, has been accompanied by ongoing efforts to develop effective measurements. Hasan Bakhshi, head of the creative economy programme at Nesta,[4] provides a brief history of these efforts, in which Nesta played a significant role (Bakhshi 2020). He highlights some of the conceptual and technical limitations of the 1998 DCMS mapping, and describes how subsequent work has sought to provide a more 'dynamic' account of creative occupations and industries across the economy as a whole. This includes the development of the 'creative trident' model (Higgs et al. 2008), in which sub-sectors of the economy are classified as creative according to their 'creative intensity', measured in terms of the proportion of workers within that sub-sector identified as working in 'creative occupations'. The creative economy, in this approach, is therefore constituted by three types of occupation (hence the trident image): creative occupations inside the creative industries, creative occupations outside the creative industries, and 'non-creative' roles within the creative industries. Bakhshi indicates that one of the advantages of this approach is that it makes possible internationally comparable statistics, as it draws on the widely recognized Standard Industrial Codes (SIC) and Standard Occupational Codes (SOC). A further advantage of the trident model is that it is sensitive to the fact that the creative intensity of sub-sectors can change over time, rather than simply fulfilling a binary position of creative or not-creative. But Bakhshi also highlights the limitations of this dynamic mapping, including the shortcomings of official government statistics, with the SIC and SOC classifications 'too aggregated to accurately identify creative activity from other activity', and that 'the sample frames of official surveys and the nature of administrative data sources mean that they do not always pick up creative businesses' (Bakhshi 2020: 11). He highlights that experiments are taking place in data scraping company websites to collect more fine-grained information about which businesses are doing creative work, and suggests the value of further developing approaches such as this, which may enable measurement independently of the use of SIC codes.

Notwithstanding developments such as these – or rather, as indicated by their ongoing limitations – it is clear that the challenges of defining and measuring the creative economy remain considerable. Part of the difficulty of reaching a solution to these conceptual and empirical challenges is that they are ultimately inseparable from political questions. As Christiaan De Beukelaer and Kim-Marie Spence (2019: 14) put it, how this sector of the economy is named and classified is 'a political act'. Describing creative economy as having been established as a 'global orthodoxy', Philip Schlesinger criticizes the way in which this discourse has denied space for alternative understandings of the relation between creativity and economy, and – as others have also addressed at length (Oakley and O'Connor 2015) – Schlesinger highlights the importance of the reintroduction of the word 'culture' into these discussions. He suggests that recent interest in reviving the language of 'cultural economy' is 'part of an international counter-discourse to that of the creative economy' (Schlesinger 2017: 81). Indeed, conceptualizations and measurements of the creative sector continue to be critiqued from a variety of perspectives, with a range of voices calling for the 'politicization' (Da Costa 2016) or re-politicization of creative economy discourse.

De Beukelaer and Spence, for example, who favour use of the term 'cultural economy', call for re-politicization in the context of their work to de-centre 'western' models and classifications (De Beukelaer and Spence 2019). Hye-Kyung Lee also calls for re-politicization, doing so via her analyses of how discourses of creative economy have developed within the specific institutional, political, social and economic contexts of South Korea (Lee 2016, 2020). Responding to Stuart Cunningham's (2009) article, 'Trojan horse or Rorschach blot?' – which considers whether the creative industries discourse has been a means of neoliberalizing economies around the world, or whether governments have instead made use of the discourse for their own purposes – Lee argues that the South Korean case demonstrates that the answer can be 'both', and that alertness is required to the political dynamics of these discourses as they circulate internationally, and as they develop within specific political contexts. Eleonora Belfiore, meanwhile, though a case study of contrasting representations of the British Roma community in a local museum and in the Channel 4 television series *My Big Fat Gypsy Wedding*, argues that counter to straightforward celebration of the growth of the creative industries, incommensurable forms of value can be at stake within this growth: competing priorities that cannot always be reconciled (Belfiore 2020). Choices will have to be made. And these choices – in this case, between the dignified self-representation of the British Roma community, and their highly profitable but exploitative portrayal on Channel 4 – are deeply political choices. They involve contestations of value and resources.

In contributing to these ongoing discussions of the need to re-politicize and 're-future' (Banks 2018) creative economy discourse – beyond the uncritical celebration of achieved and potential growth – in this chapter I am suggesting that interventions can usefully be made 'upstream', examining the narrative frameworks within which policy stories of the creative economy are told. In particular, I want to address the background assumptions of economic success that have predominated only since World War II, but which have been naturalized. This means asking: when we talk about growth, *growth of what?*

14.3   GDP AND POLITICAL STORYTELLING

Much of the time politicians and journalists refer to growth without even naming GDP. 'Growth' or 'economic growth' is now synonymous with GDP growth. But '[f]or thousands of years no one had heard of growth' (Pilling 2018: 9), and GDP actually has a fairly brief history. In attending to that history not only do we de-naturalize this very particular measurement of economic activity, but we can also appreciate that it was not intended to fulfil the purpose to which it is so often put today: serving as an indicator of overall economic health. In *GDP: A Brief But Affectionate History*, Diane Coyle shows how this measurement was originally developed for quite particular purposes; namely, to support responses to the Great Depression and preparation for World War II (Coyle 2014). Governments needed to know what their productive capacities were, what effects their policy interventions were having, and to be able to make the case for borrowing and investment. In helping them to develop that knowledge, GDP's design was very much entwined with the economic conditions and concerns of a specific point in capitalist history, the manufacturing age, and in this context GDP was specifically intended as a measurement of industrial production. What activities count as economically productive – the question of 'the production boundary' – has been a matter of contestation since at least the eighteenth century (Mazzucato 2018). For much of that time, economists treated the state as outside of productive economic activity. As Coyle puts it, '[f]or two centuries, "the economy" was the private sector' (Coyle

2014: 16). But in the early twentieth century significant changes took place in the relationship between economic measurement and government's ability (and willingness) to intervene in economics. During the nineteenth century the potential scope of public policy expanded hugely, as in response to the profound socio-economic changes that came with industrialization – particularly in sprawling urban centres – governments had to think in new ways about how to meet their populations' needs. It was partly this, the necessity of responding to the 'social question', that paved the way for GDP.

In his pre-history of the British welfare state, Chris Renwick shows how developments in social science, including efforts to measure poverty and unemployment, went hand-in-hand with the expansion of the scope and ambition of public policy. In the years before emerging as the principal architect of the welfare state, in 1909 William Beveridge published *Unemployment: A Problem of Industry*, in which he argued that if governments had adequate data they could understand and alleviate unemployment as a structural phenomenon, rather than treat it as a consequence of individual moral failings. Making such links between socio-economic measurement and effective public policy was a growing trend, and '[d]uring the interwar years, the idea that it was possible to use quantitative methods to identify where governments might intervene and then evaluate their impact on social welfare spread across the social sciences' (Renwick 2018: 185). It was in this context of the developing relationship between social science and public policy that GDP was developed; and, as Coyle indicates, it was the creation of this aggregate measure of economic activity that made modern macroeconomics possible, thereby also enabling Keynesian public policy interventions (Coyle 2014).

The first published calculations of GDP were presented by the governments of the UK and the United States in the 1930s. But around the same time, governments in Holland, Germany and the Soviet Union were also developing the concept and measurement of GDP (Coyle 2014). Contrary to the air of scientific neutrality with which GDP is so often presented, these calculations involved value judgements. Strikingly, the economist most centrally responsible for the initial development of GDP calculations, Simon Kuznets, argued against treating a national income estimate – the total monetary value of all goods and services produced within a country in a year – useful in itself, as a general indicator of national welfare. Instead, for the purposes of assessing welfare, he proposed to exclude activities such as arms sales and advertising, removing from the monetary total those activities which 'from the standpoint of a more enlightened social philosophy than that of an acquisitive society represent dis-service rather than service' (Kuznets, quoted in Coyle 2014: 13). At GDP's foundational moment, economists were arguing over whether production or welfare should be prioritized, and which of these the new measure was actually measuring. It was the former that won out, but it has subsequently come to stand in for the latter. In this sense, recent critiques of GDP are the re-opening of an 'old debate' (Coyle 2014: 121) that took place at the point of its inception.

Despite outlining many of its shortcomings, Coyle argues for the ongoing value of this measure. She notes the importance 'not to confuse GDP with social welfare', and yet argues that GDP is still one of the most valuable available tools we have for promoting social welfare. Unlike commentators who simply describe GDP as a measure of production, she argues that GDP defines what production is, which (technically complex) statistics then indicate. In this context, she argues, it is important to recognize that 'the economy' is not a given or natural phenomenon, but is subject to ongoing processeses of (re) definition. The statistical tools required will, in turn, continue to develop. For Coyle, this potentially means making use of the Human Development Index (discussed further below), or a dashboard of indicators including time use surveys. But she argues that GDP will continue to be a valuable part of our toolkit. Of course GDP is flawed, she writes, and yet it:

> does a good job of measuring how fast (or not) the output of 'the economy' is growing, and GDP growth is closely linked to social welfare. GDP struggles with measuring innovation, quality, and intangibles, but it does a better job than any currently available alternative. There are some alternatives for measuring welfare rather than output, but these two concepts are distinct and should not be muddled ... At present, we are in a statistical fog, without the information needed about either the negative aspects of growth when it is unsustainable and depletes the natural and other assets available for the future, or the positive aspects, when it delivers innovations and creativity. GDP, for all its flaws, is still a bright light shining through the mist. (Coyle 2014: 136, 140)

In *The Growth Delusion: The Wealth and Well-Being of Nations*, David Pilling also adopts a position recognizing the value of GDP and the social welfare benefits that GDP growth can represent. Whilst discussing at length the many technical and political limitations of GDP, he is keen not to throw the baby out with the bathwater. 'It is important to state something unequivocally. Growth – and by that I mean even raw growth as measured imperfectly by GDP – has the power to transform people's lives' (Pilling 2018: 150). However, in contrast to Pilling's more fully elaborated criticisms of GDP's shortcomings, in my view Coyle's discussion is too sanguine about the limitations of GDP. It does not give sufficient weight to environmental concerns, and nor does it engage sufficiently with how GDP growth has been mobilized to serve specific political ends. Having emerged hand-in-hand with Keynesian economic policy and the welfare state, GDP has now become a key tool of neoliberal statecraft. Governments around the world have employed rhetorics of GDP growth in the service of 'modernization' processes that typically involve privatization.

In doing so, they frequently invoke another important feature of the neoliberal discursive formation: the figure of the 'sovereign consumer' (Aldred 2009). Within this neoliberal paradigm of political economy – centred on GDP and the sovereign consumer – markets provide the most effective mechanism for distributing resources, and the state should step back and allow consumers to make their choices 'freely'.

Due to the hegemonic position that these ideas have occupied for the past few decades, there is a danger that economics and neoliberal economics become conflated. For example, Bill Jordan frames 'social value' as a challenge to 'economic' approaches to public policy (Jordan 2008). Whilst my argument in this chapter is aligned with Jordan's emphasis on pluralizing what the aims of public policy could and should be, I think it is a conceptual and strategic error to cede the ground of economics to a particular capture of economic thought and policy, neoliberalism, that took place during the second half of the twentieth century. Ha-Joon Chang argues for the importance of recognizing the diversity of approaches to economics, and appreciating its historical development as an academic discipline and professional field. He suggests that this affords citizens greater ability to challenge economists who present their views as unquestionable scientific facts, and thereby constitutes 'a contribution to our collective effort to make the subject better serve humanity'. Developing economic knowledge of these kinds has significant political potential, enabling people to challenge policymakers who tell them that 'there is no alternative' (Chang 2014: 163–164). Economic thought was previously connected much more visibly to political thought. Indeed, up until the end of the nineteenth century what we now refer to as 'economics' was known as 'political economy'. It was only in the early twentieth century that some economists sought to separate economic and political analysis, seeking to establish their discipline on epistemological terms equivalent to those of the natural sciences. As Chang argues, it is a matter of considerable importance that economic and political analysis be reconnected. For example, we need to recognize that competing economic positions contain competing formulations of 'freedom' (Chang 2014: 175). Notions of individual liberty and consumer choice have been central to neoliberal discourse, and we need to directly address questions of freedom within discussions of economic progress. I do this below in relation to Amartya Sen's capability approach to human development, a sustained challenge to GDP in which the idea of people having 'substantive freedoms' (capabilities) to live a good life is central.

Much, then, has now been written about the problems of GDP and its position within prevailing neoliberal economic discourse. These problems are technical, environmental, conceptual and political in nature. They are technical because the measurement of GDP is very complicated and many countries lack data of sufficient quality to make their GDP figures reliable, and because GDP measurement remains better equipped to count manufactured goods than it does to count more immaterial goods and services (Pilling 2018; Coyle 2014). They are environmental because the focus on GDP growth – and its equation not only with economic success but also with public policy success – is ultimately incompatible with a global ecosystem conducive to sustained human habitation (Jackson 2017). They are conceptual because GDP only measures monetary exchanges, and as feminists have argued for decades, this excludes care work and unpaid labour that holds up at least half the sky (Tronto 2013). They are political for all the preceding reasons, but also because GDP has come to occupy a hegemonic function. GDP has established a narrative framework within which the dominant political stories of the past several decades have been told. How to offer an alternative to that narrative framework is a pressing political question.

14.4 RECLAIMING ECONOMICS FROM NEOLIBERALISM: DEVELOPMENT AS FREEDOM

One answer to that question – at least in terms of alternative economy concepts, if not necessarily in terms of political strategy – is offered by Kate Raworth's *Doughnut Economics: Seven Ways to Think Like a 21st-Century Economist*, a book that has achieved notable success in bringing heterodox economic ideas to a wider readership. Raworth is particularly interested in the images that are used to represent economic functioning and economic success. She describes how a highly influential textbook published by Paul Samuelson in 1948, *Economics*, established two profoundly consequential images. The first was the representation of the economy as an investment machine, with linear processes, inputs and outputs, depicting 'income flowing round the economy as if it were water flowing round plumbed pipes' (Raworth 2017: 20). This circular flow diagram 'turned out to be a bit of a hit for teaching the masses' and 'has since spawned a million imitations, with a variation of it in almost every economics textbook' (Raworth 2017: 63). The image second was the simple 'forwards and upwards' curve of GDP growth (Raworth 2017: 39).

Raworth's proposed paradigm, 'doughnut economics', offers an alternative image with which to represent the economy and economic success. The doughnut – a ring, rather than a jam doughnut – presents two thresholds. The outer boundary of the ring is the maximum limit of sustainable resource (ab) use. Its nine indicators are biodiversity loss, air pollution, ozone layer depletion, climate change, ocean acidification, chemical pollution, nitrogen and phosphorous loading, freshwater withdrawals and land conversion. The inner boundary is the minimum socio-economic requirements for a just society. Its 12 indicators are water, food, health, education, income and work, peace and justice, political voice, social equity, gender equality, housing, networks and energy. Between the doughnut's 'social foundation of human well-being and ecological ceiling of planetary pressure lies the safe and just space for humanity' (Raworth 2017: 44). Figure 14.1 illustrates a simplified model of the doughnut economy.

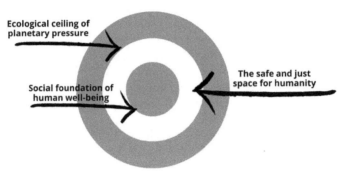

Source: Based on Raworth (2017: 44).

Figure 14.1   Simplified model of the doughnut economy

I am sympathetic to the doughnut. It makes a powerful contribution to challenging neoliberalism's naturalization of a very particular model of economy and prosperity. One of my reservations, however, is that the doughnut does not yet go far enough in telling a new story. Whilst 'progress' could be narrated against the 21 indicators of the doughnut's thresholds, the image risks being too static, and does not offer an overarching story of comparable dynamism to GDP growth. Establishing an alternative narrative able to make an effective challenge to the dominance of GDP is of course enormously difficult. Notwithstanding this difficulty, the need remains – to develop a simple story of complex prosperity; an account of prosperity that can rival the narrative power of GDP growth – a power born of GDP's capacity to aggregate 'the economy' into a single number, and to use this to tell a story of progress – whilst doing justice to what it actually means for humans to flourish together on Planet Earth. One candidate for an alternative economic narrative framework of this kind is the capability approach to human development, succinctly summarized by its originator, Amartya Sen, in the title of one of his most widely read books: *Development as Freedom* (Sen 1999).

Sen's work has spanned economics and philosophy, and the capability approach began life at this disciplinary intersection: at once a contribution to theorizing social justice and an intervention in development economics.

Sen's work on the Bengal famine, amongst other topics, led him to consider the need to conceptualize and measure poverty, prosperity and well-being in ways that 'extend the evaluative space' beyond whether people have particular resources, such as money or bread. Instead, he argues that what needs to be paid attention to is the range of beings and doings that people value (their 'functionings'), and their freedom to exercise these functionings (their 'capabilities'). It is in this sense that the capability approach offers a simple story of complex prosperity. Development is the expansion of human freedom. This provides a powerful framework for telling stories of progress, and perhaps for telling a new overarching story of collective prosperity. The notion of freedom here is materialist and pluralist. It takes human freedom to be contingent on material circumstances, and it recognizes that the freedoms people value – and how they choose to exercise those freedoms or not – is extremely diverse. As diverse as humanity itself.

And there's the rub. In seeking to do justice to the diversity of valued human freedoms, how can the capability approach achieve a coherence in telling a simple story of the expansion of complex prosperity? How can it keep hold of both the complexity and the simplicity? If the power and the problem of GDP is in part its stunning capacity for aggregation, how can the capability approach compete with that aggregative power whilst doing justice to the plurality of valuable human beings and doings? Moreover, how can it do so whilst fulfilling a commitment to the value of public deliberation in naming what is valuable? This commitment to 'public reason' is a key feature of Sen's thinking (Sen 2009), and of many who have employed and built upon his ideas.

These questions play out in relation to the practical task of measuring capabilities. As Alkire, Quizalbash and Comim observe, the worldly significance of the capability approach is by no means wholly dependent on the measurement of capabilities (Alkire et al. 2008). The approach has had notable success in changing the language and aims of leading development agencies, such as the United Nations Development Programme (UNDP). Nonetheless, as I have argued above, measurements can exercise considerable political power, and as Meyrick, Phiddian and Barnett suggest, it is the case in many evaluative processes that numbers and stories are both necessary, and, ideally, will complement, elucidate and enable each other (Meyrick et al. 2018). Indeed, it is surely in large part due to its contribution to the formulation of a metric – the Human Development Index (HDI) – that the capability approach has achieved the influence that it has within international development. The HDI is, precisely, one effort to expand the evaluative space beyond GDP to a composite index including income, health and education. The HDI, of course, does not go far in representing all of the potentially valued human freedoms that the capability approach invites people to name for themselves and their communities, and challenging questions of operationalizability remain. This is recognized even by researchers very committed to the approach. As Comim puts it, 'the "measurement challenge" is real' and 'the operational difficulties with the CA [capabilities approach] cannot be easily dismissed or ignored' (Comim 2008: 176). Some of the questions faced by those wishing to measure capabilities include those outlined in the passage from Alkire et al. below. They are articulated in relation to measures of poverty. But the same questions could just as easily be applied to capability measurements framed in terms of desired conditions such as wealth, well-being and flourishing, and they could be applied to capability measurements related to any conceivable area of public policy. Alkire et al. observe that, 'evaluation of capability raises a challenging array of issues of measurement, aggregation, comparison, vagueness, etc.' (Alkire et al. 2008: 7):

> Which are the *domains* or dimensions [functionings/capabilities] that will be included, and on what basis? Which *indicator(s)* best represent each domain or functioning, and on what grounds will these be selected? What is the poverty *threshold* for each indicator, or, if a fuzzy threshold is defined, what are the upper and lower boundaries of the fuzzy poverty band? How does one represent the *interaction* between different indicators and the interactions between dimensions of poverty and identify substitutes and complements? In those cases in which it is necessary to aggregate across domains, how is this achieved and what *relative weights* are set for various domains? And how does one *aggregate* across individuals? (Alkire et al. 2008: 9)

This may seem a daunting set of questions. Yet there are good examples of the effective measurement of capabilities (see Robeyns 2017), and the operationalization of the capability approach continues to be developed by researchers based in a wide range of academic disciplines, working across diverse geographic locations and policy domains.

14.5   NEW NARRATIVES FOR THE CREATIVE ECONOMY

What implications does this have for the creative economy? For several years I have been working with colleagues at King's College London to apply the capability approach to cultural policy (Wilson et al. 2017; Gross and Wilson 2018, 2019). We have used the capability approach to reconceptualize accounts of cultural opportunity (implicit and explicit) within existing cultural policy. In a Horizon2020 project, Developing Inclusive and Sustainable Creative Economies (DISCE), we brought these ideas to the study of the creative economy. A feature of our approach to cultural opportunity and creative economy is that we adopt an analytical perspective that is 'ecological' (De Barnard et al. 2021), paying attention to the 'interconnections and interdependencies' (Gross and Wilson 2019: 4) through which valued 'cultural capabilities'[5] are exercised. As we have shown in our empirical work, these interconnections and interdependencies cross the conventional boundaries of the creative industries, the publicly funded 'arts', and amateur or 'everyday' creative practice. In other words, we do not treat the creative economy as a 'sector' at all.[6] In DISCE we explicitly studied creative economy as ecological in this sense (Gross et al. 2019), treating forms of unpaid creative activity as part of the creative economy – creativity 'off the clock' (Gross 2018) – as well as remunerated 'creative work' in the more conventional sense.

One of the tasks we set ourselves within DISCE was the formulation of a Cultural Development Framework (CDF) and a Cultural Development Index (CDI). This composite index is organized in three broad categories: (1) capabilities of experiencing and reflecting; (2) capabilities of creating and enabling; and (3) capabilities of recognizing, legitimizing and governing (Wilson et al. 2020). Each of these three capability sets includes three indicators, giving nine in total, and these nine indicators constitute the evaluative space of cultural development as we are proposing it. Here we are drawing on our empirical and conceptual work to make an intervention in how 'success' for creative economies is understood and measured. In doing so, however, we share in Sen's commitment to the value of public deliberation. The idea is that the CDF/CDI provides a framework for discussion and deliberation of what cultural capabilities really matter to the people living in a particular location. This can take place at a local or municipal level, through processes comparable to citizens' assemblies. But we have also wanted to explore possibilities for establishing aggregated data in relation to the CDF/CDI's nine dimensions. We have therefore created a standardized survey instrument through which a town or city's 'progress' can be measured; holding together the plurality of valued beings and doings, and the possibility of meaningful aggregation and comparison across time and place.

In setting out to develop the CDF and CDI we set ourselves a challenging goal, but we think it is an important one. New narrative frameworks for the creative economy are needed. New backgrounds against which to tell simple stories of complex prosperity. We need these new frameworks for many different reasons: technical, environmental, conceptual and political, and for all these reasons at the same time. In a sense there are many reasons, and also just one: climate emergency. As Naomi Klein (2015) puts it, *This Changes Everything*. One of the things it must change is the stories we tell about creative economies, and why they matter.

Under what conditions could new narrative frameworks be developed? What are the enabling and constraining conditions of political and economic imagination? Parts of this chapter were written during the Covid-19 pandemic. The public health crisis raises fundamental questions about how governments manage economies. This includes the scope of governments' abilities to invest in jobs, and how 'social security' is conceived. These questions, and a range of answers – in Spain, for example, moves have been made to introduce Universal Basic Income – have not arisen from nowhere. Such questions and answers have been in the air for some time. The crisis, however, has created conditions in which these issues have greater political traction and public visibility, potentially opening up new space for political imagination (Gross 2021). What implications do these fundamental questions of political economy – and the answers being developed – have for the task of reframing narratives of creative economy?

Angela McRobbie suggests that creative labour is the canary in the coal mine of the neoliberal transformation of the economy as a whole (McRobbie 2016). The forms of precarity experienced by many people who work in 'creative' jobs is indicative of how working conditions are changing more widely, with reductions in job security, worker protections and union power. What makes this possible is, in part, that the work is enjoyable. Many people want to do these jobs, in which processes of meaning-making are central to what the work is. That these roles are often viewed as 'good work' is part of what makes it possible for large numbers of people to choose to live with the challenges of precarity that many such jobs entail. But what if, in post-Covid policymaking, we took seriously both the value of creative work as 'good work' and the value of 'social security'? This would open the space – and the need – for quite different approaches to policy for the creative economy.

One important intervention would be to rearticulate the value of public goods. Gaëtan Tremblay indicates that the shift in discourse from cultural industries to creative industries enabled a further erosion of the status of public goods within neoliberal public policymaking (Tremblay 2011). One of the likely policy implications of the replacement of GDP by doughnut economics or a capabilities approach as the primary narrative framework for the creative economy would be the need to make public goods central to the stories we tell of prosperity, and of the 'success' of policymaking. This could include support for, and measurement of, the growth of what Nick Wilson and I have referred to as 'cultural infrastructure': spaces in which 'opportunities for experiences of being-in-relation and storytelling are multiplied and democratized' (Gross and Wilson 2020: 148). This is an idea that we develop in the context of addressing the potential contribution of cultural policy to the Green New Deal. As will be clear by now, an implication of my argument in this chapter is that we can expect that changing the narrative framework within which the success of creative economy is narrated could have significant implications for the scope of 'creative economy policy': the range of questions, aims and resources that such policy concerns itself with.

In *A Planet to Win: Why We Need a Green New Deal*, Aronoff et al. (2019) reflect on the huge range of art that was made during the 1930s under Roosevelt's New Deal, by virtue of the large public commitment made to cultural production of many varied kinds. They write: now '[t]hat's what we call a creative economy' (Aronoff et al. 2019: 92). In this context they suggest that a reduction in working hours would be a hugely important part of the Green New Deal, giving people more time to learn new things, from surfing, to speaking a new language, to 'becoming an underground hip hop sensation' (Aronoff et al. 2019: 91). They are implying that a creative economy is one that gives people the time and space to be creative, supporting the flourishing of diverse cultural forms. It is a vision, we might say, of greater cultural and creative freedom, of expanded cultural capability. It indicates the kinds of growth that might be supported by 'successful' creative economy policy in the future, if alternative narrative frameworks enable new answers to the question: *growth of what?*

14.6   CONCLUSION

GDP is a measurement that was born during the 1930s with one set of aims and political commitments. It has since been harnessed to quite different goals. We are witnessing an upsurge of criticisms of GDP: in terms of its ability to measure what it purports to, its social and environmental consequences, and the neoliberal political projects it has increasingly been used to justify. In this chapter, I have linked those critical discussions of GDP to the creative economy, with a specific focus on what can be learned from the extraordinary extent to which this particular measure of economic activity has been established as a dominant narrative framework for public policy. The reason for doing so is, in part, to see what can be learned, by researchers and policymakers developing alternatives, from GDP's enormous power. How, then, can alternative narrative frameworks – and alternative measures – be established? In part this requires the kinds of empirical, conceptual and technical work that those developing the operationalizability of the capability approach are contributing. It is also a matter of iterative political communications: seeing, in practice, what ideas have the capacity to establish themselves in the vocabulary – and in the political imagination – of policymakers and publics.

When examining the need and possibilities for developing such large narrative frameworks, I am of course conscious of the scale of ambition this can represent. But I would hope that this kind of thinking may be useful, in part, for the new relationships it can encourage. For example, Kate Raworth has been actively involved in implementing doughnut economics at local and municipal levels, such as within the city of Amsterdam's post-Covid recovery plan (Boffrey 2020). How might heterodox creative economy thinking and practice be embedded within doughnut initiatives of this kind, or experiments in economic democracy such as the Preston Model (Manley and Whyman 2021)? And how might it align with political and environmental projects with international scope, such as the Green New Deal? Connecting to initiatives of this kind – real-world experiments in developing alternative narratives for public policy – will be important if research offering new ways to understand the 'success' of creative economies is going to make a sustained difference at scale. It needs to find its place – within broader collaborations – in helping to tell a new, simple story of complex prosperity. If, as Nesrine Malik puts it, *We Need New Stories* (Malik 2019), we need them not only to interpret the world, but also to change it.

NOTES

1. A sector or industry's contribution to GDP is measured by gross value added (GVA).
2. I have also explored the affordances of art in times of crisis – such as a global pandemic – in terms of its provision of material and immaterial resources with which to tell new collective stories, and to reactivate narratives that have been forgotten or suppressed (Gross 2020a).
3. The definition, famously, focuses on the production of intellectual property through acts of individual creativity, and identifies 13 sub-sectors as meeting this definition. The creative industries are:
    > those activities which have their origin in individual creativity, skill and talent and which have a potential for wealth and job creation through the generation and exploitation of intellectual property. These have been taken to include the following key sectors: advertising, architecture, the art and antiques market, crafts, design, designer fashion, film, interactive leisure software, music, the performing arts, publishing, software and television and radio. (DCMS 1998: 3)
4. National Endowment for the Sciences, Technology and the Arts. Nesta was set up by the Labour government in 1997, with David Puttnam as its first chair.
5. Cultural capability is 'the substantive freedom to give form and value (through storytelling and all forms of cultural expression) to our experiences of being-in-relation with each other, with the world, and with its possibilities' (Gross and Wilson 2020: 145).
6. For further theorization of what the creative economy is 'really', see Wilson, Chapter 16 in this book.

REFERENCES

Aldred, Jonathan (2009) *The Skeptical Economist: Revealing the Ethics Inside Economics*. Oxford and New York: Earthscan.

Alkire, Sabina; Qizilbash, Mozaffar; and Comim, Flavio (2008) 'Introduction', in Comim, Flavio; Quizilbash, Mozaffar; and Alkire, Sabina (eds), *The Capability Approach: Concepts, Measures and Applications*, 1–25. Cambridge: Cambridge University Press.

Aronoff, Kate; Battistoni, Alyssa; Cohen, Daniel Aldana; and Riofrancos, Thea (2019) *A Planet to Win: Why We Need a Green New Deal*. London: Verso.

Bakhshi, Hasan (2020) *Measuring the Creative Economy: A Guide for Policymakers*. London: Nesta.

Banks, Mark (2018) 'Creative Economies of Tomorrow? Limits to Growth and the Uncertain Future', *Cultural Trends*, 27(5), 367–380. https://doi.org/10.1080/09548963.2018.1534720.

Belfiore, Eleonora (2020) 'Whose cultural value? Representation, power and creative industries', *International Journal of Cultural Policy*, 26(3), 383–397. DOI: 10.1080/10286632.2018.1495713.

Beveridge, William Henry (1909) *Unemployment: A Problem of Industry*. London: Longmans & Co.

Bilton, Chris; and Soltero, Gonzalo (2020) 'Cultural Policy as Mythical Narrative', *International Journal of Cultural Policy*, 26(5), 681–696. DOI: 10.1080/10286632.2019.1624736.

Boffrey, Daniel (2020) 'Amsterdam to Embrace "Doughnut" Model to Mend Post-Coronavirus Economy', *The Guardian*. https://www.theguardian.com/world/2020/apr/08/amsterdam-doughnut-model-mend-post-coronavirus-economy (accessed 3 September 2021).

Chang, Ha-Joon (2014) *Economics: The User's Guide*. London: Penguin.

Comim, Flavio (2008) 'Measuring Capabilities', in Comim, Flavio; Quizilbash, Mozaffar; and Alkire, Sabina (eds), *The Capability Approach: Concepts, Measures and Applications*, 157–200. Cambridge: Cambridge University Press.

Coyle, Diane (2014) *GDP: A Brief but Affectionate History*. Princeton, NJ, USA and Oxford, UK: Princeton University Press.

Cunningham, Stuart (2009) 'Trojan Horse or Rorschach blot? Creative Industries Discourse Around the World', *International Journal of Cultural Policy*, 15(4), 375–386. DOI: 10.1080/10286630902977501.

Da Costa, Dia (2016) *Politicizing Creative Economy: Activism and a Hunger Called Theatre*. Urbana, Chicago, and Springfield, IL: University of Illinois Press.

DCMS (1998) *Creative Industries Mapping Document*. London: Department for Culture, Media and Sport.

De Barnard, Manfredi; Comunian, Roberta; and Gross, Jonathan (2021) 'Creative and Cultural Ecologies: A Review of Theories and Methods, Towards a Future Research Agenda', *Cultural Trends*. DOI: 10.1080/09548963.2021.2004073.

De Beukelaer, Christiaan; and Spence, Kim-Marie (2019) *Global Cultural Economy*. Oxford and New York: Routledge.

Galloway, Susan; and Dunlop, Stewart (2007) 'A Critique of Definitions of The Cultural And Creative Industries In Public Policy', *International Journal of Cultural Policy*, 13(1), 17–31. DOI: 10.1080/10286630701201657.

Garnham, Nicholas (2005) 'From Cultural to Creative Industries', *International Journal of Cultural Policy*, 11(1), 15–29. DOI: 10.1080/10286630500067606.

Gross, Jonathan (2018) 'Creativity Off the Clock: Re-Conceptualizing Creative Careers', in Martin, Lee; and Wilson, Nick (eds), *The Palgrave Handbook of Creativity at Work*, 209–217. Basingstoke: Palgrave.

Gross, Jonathan (2019) 'Practices of Hope: Care, Narrative and Cultural Democracy', *International Journal of Cultural Policy*, 27(1), 1–15. DOI: 10.1080/10286632.2019.1702032.

Gross, Jonathan (2020a) 'Holding Together Hope and Loss: Reflections on the Need for Art in Times of Crisis', *Journal of Psychosocial Studies*, 13(2), 448–457. doi.org/10.1332/147867320X15894731588869.

Gross, Jonathan (2020b) *The Birth of the Creative Industries Revisited: An Oral History of the 1998 DCMS Mapping Document*. London: King's College London. doi.org/10.18742/pub01-017.

Gross, Jonathan (2021) 'Hope Against Hope: COVID-19 and the Space for Political Imagination', *European Journal of Cultural Studies*, 25(2), 448–457. DOI:10.1177/13675494211004594.

Gross, Jonathan; Comunian, Roberta; Conor, Bridget; Dent, Tamsyn; Heinonen, Jarna; Hytti, Ulla; Hytönen, Kaisa; Pukkinen, Tommi; Stenholm, Pekka; Wilson, Nick. (2019) *DISCE Case Study Framework*. DISCE Publications. https://disce.eu/wp-content/uploads/2019/12/DISCE-Report-D3.1-D4.1-D5.1.pdf (accessed 25 May 2022).

Gross, Jonathan; and Wilson, Nick (2018) 'Cultural Democracy: An Ecological and Capabilities Approach', *International Journal of Cultural Policy*. DOI: 10.1080/10286632.2018.1538363.

Gross, Jonathan; and Wilson, Nick (2019) *Creating the Environment: The Cultural Eco-systems of Creative People and Places*. Creative People and Places https://kclpure.kcl.ac.uk/portal/en/publications/creating-the-environment-the-cultural-ecosystems-of-creative-people-and-places(7a85c020-f064-4d6e-973a-83b4be214d65).html (accessed 25 May 2022).

Gross, Jonathan; and Wilson, Nick (2020) 'The Green New Deal and Cultural Policy', in Oakley, K; and Banks, M. (eds), *Cultural Industries and the Environmental Crisis: New Approaches for Policy*. New York: Springer.

Higgs, Peter; Cunningham, Stuart; and Bakhshi, Hasan (2008) *Beyond the Creative Industries: Mapping the Creative Economy in the United Kingdom*. London: Nesta.

Jackson, Tim (2017) *Prosperity Without Growth: Foundations for the Economy of Tomorrow*, 2nd Edition. London and New York: Routledge.

Jones, Michael D.; and McBeth, Mark K. (2010) 'A Narrative Policy Framework: Clear Enough to Be Wrong?', *Policy Studies Journal*, 38(2), 329–353. https://doi.org/10.1111/j.1541-0072.2010.00364.x.

Jordan, Bill (2008) *Welfare and Well-Being: Social Value in Public Policy*. Bristol: Policy Press.

Klein, Naomi (2015) *This Changes Everything: Capitalism Vs the Climate*. London: Penguin.

Lee, Hye-Kyung (2016) 'Politics of the "Creative Industries" Discourse and its Variants', *International Journal of Cultural Policy*, 22(3), 438–455. DOI: 10.1080/10286632.2014.991783.

Lee, Hye-Kyung (2020) 'Making Creative Industries Policy in the Real World: Differing Configurations of the Culture–Market–State Nexus in the UK and South Korea', *International Journal of Cultural Policy*, 26(4), 544–560. DOI: 10.1080/10286632.2019.1577401.

Malik, Nesrine (2019) *We Need New Stories: Challenging the Toxic Myths Behind Our Age of Discontent*. London: Weidenfeld & Nicolson.

Manley, Julian; and Whyman, Philip B. (eds) (2021) *The Preston Model and Community Wealth Building Creating a Socio-Economic Democracy for the Future*. Oxford and New York: Routledge.

Mazzucato, Mariana (2018) *The Value of Everything: Making and Taking in the Global Economy*. London: Allen Lane.

McRobbie, Angela (2016) *Be Creative: Making a Living in the New Cultural Industries*. Cambridge: Polity Press.

Meyrick, Julian; Phiddian, Robert; and Barnett, Tully (2018) *What Matters? Talking Value In Australian Culture*. Clayton, Victoria: Monash University Publishing.

Oakley, Kate; and O'Connor, Justin (eds) (2015) *The Routledge Companion to the Cultural Industries*. Oxford and New York: Routledge.

O'Connor, Justin (2010) *The Cultural and Creative Industries: A Literature Review*, 2nd edition. Newcastle-Upon-Tyne: Creativity, Culture and Education.

O'Connor, Justin (2020) 'A Research Agenda for Creative Industries / A Research Agenda for Cultural Economics / Raymond Williams Cultural Analyst', *Cultural Trends*, 29(2), 166–170. DOI: 10.1080/09548963.2020.1767501.

Pilling, David (2018) *The Growth Delusion: The Wealth and Well-Being of Nations*. London: Bloomsbury.

Raworth, Kate (2017) *Doughnut Economics: Seven Ways to Think Like a 21st-Century Economist*. London: Random House Business.

Renwick, Chris (2018) *Bread for All: The Origins of the Welfare State*. London: Penguin.

Robeyns, Ingrid (2017) *Wellbeing, Freedom and Social Justice: The Capability Approach Re-Examined*. Cambridge: Open Book Publishers.

Roe, Emery (1994) *Narrative Policy Analysis: Theory and Practice*. Durham, NC: Duke University Press.

Samuelson, Paul Anthony (1948) *Economics: An Introductory Analysis*. New York: McGraw-Hill.

Schiller, Robert J. (2019) *Narrative Economics: How Stories Go Viral and Drive Major Economic Events*. Princeton, NJ: Princeton University Press.

Schlesinger, Philip (2017) 'The Creative Economy: Invention of a Global Orthodoxy', *Innovation: The European Journal of Social Science Research*, 30(1), 73–90. DOI: 10.1080/13511610.2016.1201651.

Sen, Amartya (1999) *Development as Freedom*. Oxford: Oxford University Press.

Sen, Amartya (2009) *The Idea of Justice*. London: Penguin Books.

Tremblay, Gaëtan (2011) 'Creative Statistics to Support Creative Economy Politics', *Media, Culture and Society*, 33(2), 289–298. DOI:10.1177/0163443710386519.

Tronto, Joan C. (2013) *Caring Democracy: Markets, Equality, and Justice*. New York and London: New York University Press.

Wilson, Nick; Gross, Jonathan; and Bull, Anna (2017) *Towards Cultural Democracy: Promoting Cultural Capabilities for Everyone*. London: King's College London. https://kclpure.kcl.ac.uk/portal/files/117457700/towards_cultural_democracy_2017_kcl.pdf (accessed 25 May 2022).

Wilson, Nick; Gross, Jonathan; Dent, Tamsyn; Conor, Bridget; and Comunian, Roberta (2020) *Re-thinking Inclusive and Sustainable Growth for the Creative Economy: A Literature Review*. DISCE Publications. chrome-extension://efaidnbmnnnibpcajpcglclefindmkaj/https://disce.eu/wp-content/uploads/2020/01/DISCE-Report-D5.2.pdf (accessed 25 May 2022).

Woolf, Virginia (2000 [1925]) *Mrs Dalloway*. Oxford: Oxford University Press.

15. Inclusive solidarity: emerging forms of resistance within the UK creative economy

Tamsyn Dent

15.1 INTRODUCTION

This chapter considers forms of resistance and solidarity that have emerged out of the neoliberal labour cultures that operate within the United Kingdom's (UK) creative economy. The chapter examines the evolution of a series of issue-based grassroots organisations/collectives, comprised of creative and cultural workers using social media and other internet-based technology, demonstrating their response to precarious labour and work-based inequality operating within the creative and cultural sectors. This collective mobilisation challenges previously understood models of creative workers as docile subjects of neoliberalism, internalising notions of individual entrepreneurialism and resilience as a form of self-exploitation and governmental control (McRobbie 2002; Banks 2007; Randle and Hardy 2016; Scharff 2016). This chapter argues that the existence of these forms of resistance represents a new form of creative work-based solidarity that has emerged in response to the labour conditions of the neoliberal economy. Issue-based collective action offers a 'practice of hope' (Gross 2020) in relation to solidarity communities that recognise the multiple, interconnected forms of exclusion and injustice, and who directly engage with questions of inclusivity. However, the research that informs this chapter acknowledges that many of these groups are operating on a voluntary basis and have limited access to funding. Their own precarious and undervalued position within their respective sectors presents potential challenges for their future sustainability and the visibility of the issues that they are working to change.

As discussed in the wider literature, the meaning of the term 'creative economy' is still uncertain (see Wilson et al. 2020). In addition, the terminology relating to the creative/cultural workforce is variable, with multiple distinctions at the national and international levels creating problems with how to identify workers across broader sectoral and industry-based definitions (see Dent et al. 2020 for a detailed summary). The data that informs this chapter is based on a series of face-to-face interviews with UK-based creative and/or cultural practitioners who had initiated an activity in response to their experience of inequality within their respective sectors, which included film, television, digital technology and the performing arts. I will use the term 'creative and cultural workforce' (CCW) to encapsulate the labour market they collectively belong to. The participants were initially contacted as part of a pan-European study, 'Developing Inclusive and Sustainable Creative Economies' (DISCE), and were selected to provide feedback on a draft survey questionnaire in relation to inclusivity and sustainability within creative work. All participants were already known to members of the DISCE research team through a shared interest in the relationship between inclusivity and creative work. Questions were asked in relation to their own work/creative practice, their respective campaign/organisation, and the issues or barriers to work and inclusivity in the creative sector that they were addressing.

At the time of the interviews, our purpose was to test the language around creative labour and activism, to get a sense of the types of work-based issues that were being publicly challenged. It was during the coding process that a concept which I term 'inclusive solidarity' emerged from within the data, along with the recognition that these organisations were funding and gathering valuable information on the CCW through their collaborations with external research partners. There was a uniform commitment to the issues that they were highlighting which included inequality in relation to gender, race and social class, but also an awareness of a wider perspective, a need to think inclusively and holistically about the questions of inequality that created barriers for all groups, not just those which they had personally experienced. This concept of 'inclusive solidarity' challenged individualised working conditions that have been promoted in the neoliberal paradigm. Inclusive solidarity was seen as a form of survival to remain 'creative' and continue with their practice, in resistance to structural barriers to being heard and valued in their particular sector. 'Activism' was a term largely rejected by these individuals. As will be discussed, they saw themselves as part of a wider creative ecosystem that connected to other actors, necessary for structural change.

This chapter first considers the literature on inequality in the creative economy and the development from precarious to harmful labour. Next, it looks at the literature around solidarity, activism and the emergence of new concepts of mutual aid and changemaking from below. The chapter then looks at the data in detail. It analyses interviewees' language in relation to their inspiration to seek change, the need to move beyond single causes and the wider relationship between these organisations/collectives and the creative economy, particularly in relation to their own sustainability following the outbreak of Covid-19.

15.2   INEQUALITY IN THE CREATIVE ECONOMY

In their 2008 article, 'In the social factory?', Gill and Pratt use Negri's concept of the 'factory without walls' to define the precarious labour conditions associated with creative and cultural work in the neoliberal era as:

> all forms of insecure, contingent, flexible work – from illegalized, casualized and temporary employment, to homeworking, piecework and freelancing. In turn, precarity signifies both the multiplication of precarious, unstable, insecure forms of living and, simultaneously, new forms of political struggle and solidarity that reach beyond the traditional models of the political party or trade union (Gill and Pratt 2008: 3).

A combination of both oppression but also opportunity for new political models of resistance and autonomy were linked to the working conditions for CCWs. It is interesting to question why, given that this article was published in 2008, it has taken so long for 'new forms of political struggle and solidarity' in relation to the CCW to emerge and/or be recognised? There is ample literature on precarious work and workforce inequality across the CCW. Studies on creative labour that emerged in the 1990s considered the state-driven deregulation of the broadcasting industry, which led to deteriorated working conditions (Ursell 2000; Antcliff 2005) and triggered the increase of flexible, project-based working contracts (see Dex et al. 2000 for a longitudinal study on working contracts in the UK television sector). A focus on individualised forms of finding work and the importance of self-reputation management has exposed the impact of closely tied networks that led to the exclusion of certain identities within the workforce (Blair 2001; Grugulis and Stoyanova 2012). Investigations on specific sectors within the CCW revealed examples of exploitative and unfair working conditions relating to unpaid early entrants in the television sector (Ross 2009); extreme working hours, for example the normalisation of 'crunch time', in the gaming sector (Dyer-Witherford and de Peuter 2006); and the impact of extreme individual responsibility and economic risk within the fashion industry (McRobbie 1998, 2002). The literature on precarious labour that emerged in the first decade of the twenty-first century challenged conceptions of the CCW as meritocratic (Florida 2002), to expose unfair and unlawful working practices that were producing traditional labour market divisions in relation to social demographics (Gill 2002; Dent 2020). Further empirical evidence concentrated on the CCW enabled an emerging realisation that the industry was dominated by a socially affluent, highly educated, able-bodied and white workforce, coupled with the knowledge that gendered restrictions meant that although some women could enter (as long as they fulfilled the characteristics already identified), their opportunities to develop and progress to senior creative or management roles were limited (Conor et al. 2015; Creative Skillset 2010; Dent 2020; Holgate and McKay 2009).

Within this literature was a critical interest in why creative workers accept such working conditions, and the absence of collective forms of activism or resistance. McRobbie's work on independent UK-based fashion designers identified commitment and love of the work as a rationale for accepting the long hours, bad pay and individualised risk associated with their work (McRobbie 1998, 2002). The 'do what you love' (DWYL) concept (Tokumitsu 2015) associated with creative production created an interest in the subjective relationship between the creative individual and their work (Taylor and Littleton 2013; O'Brien 2019). An interest in the 'new labouring subjectivities' (Gill 2014: 514), which internalised notions of resiliance and individualised entrepreneurialism in relation to the construction of a creative identity, rendered inequalities and injustice within creative labour markets as 'unspeakable' (Gill 2014). It also rationalised the absence of resistance and collective action, and in turn prompted an even more focused consideration of who the CCW actually are. A focus on creative identities has exposed the structural fragility of the labour market. Research that has considered the relationship between gender, care and creative work (Wreyford 2015; Dent 2019, 2020), disability (Randle and Hardy 2016), ethnicity (Nwonka 2015) and social class (Friedman and Laurison 2019), has exposed the dominance of actors who have the capabilities to participate within the labour market. The identity politics and structural barriers to inclusivity associated with the CCW challenged concepts of resilience and entrepreneurialism which were used to rationalise public funding cuts to the creative economy, as will be discussed below (Pratt 2017; Scharff 2016).

Following smaller, qualitative investigations on the CCW came larger investigations into workplace inequality, often commissioned by industry bodies, in relation to both off- and on-screen representation. In 2007, the UK Film Council (UKFC) commissioned Reena Bhavnani to write the report, *Barriers to Diversity in Film*. This comprehensive review, which identified workforce exclusion across demographics including gender, race, sexuality, disability and age, outlined the legal framework for employment in the UK and illustrated the normalisations of unfair employment practices that created barriers to a diverse and inclusive workforce. It made an ethical and business case for structural changes to ensure workforce diversity in the sector. Bhavnani died of cancer[1] shortly after the report's publication, and the timing of its release coincided with the global financial crisis of 2008. In this context, it is perhaps unsurprising that the Bhavnani report received limited attention. In 2010, the

UKFC was abolished by the Conservative and Liberal Democrat coalition government as part of an austerity policy that has re-modelled British society (Wilkinson and Pickett 2018), creating ongoing social disruption (The Care Collective, 2020). All the while, the UK's creative industries were politically heralded as the saviour of the economic downturn. In his first speech as the UK Prime Minister, Conservative leader David Cameron included the creative industries along with other knowledge-based 'growth' sectors as vital factors in 'rebalancing the economy', whilst outlining the government plans for austerity-driven cuts (Gov.uk 2010). A discourse of 'resilience' was attached to the post-crash economic bounce-back of creative-driven production, but this concept of resilience masked a shift towards private investment (which was already in operation but accelerated post-2010) and free not-for-profit labour (Pratt 2017). Resilience has also been exposed to be psychosocially fraught, and deeply political (Filion 2013; Gill and Orgad 2018), a concept that reinforces social divisions and further invisibilises the necessity of care and interdependence (The Care Collective 2020).

The dissonance between the politically celebrated economically resilient creative economy, and the precarious labour agenda previously summarised, not only challenges the reality and future sustainability of the creative economy but has also led to an awareness of 'harmful' creative labour (Banks 2017; Cobb and Horeck 2018; Brook et al. 2020). Following the Bhavnani report came a series of industry-commissioned research publications providing quantitative knowledge of the scale of workplace inequality across the CCW (Creative Skillset 2010; Follows et al. 2016; Creative Scotland 2017; Kreager and Follows 2018). Analysis of national employment data, for example, considered the relationship between socio-economic status and creative work (O'Brien et al. 2016), and larger pan-European comparisons of work-based inequality within certain sectors (EWA 2016) illustrated the broader extent of inequality, not just in the UK but also across Europe. In addition to large data analysis that identifies the sheer breadth of work-based inequality within the CCW, the exposure in 2017 of United States (US) film producer Harvey Weinstein and actor Kevin Spacey, among other significant gatekeepers, for gross sexual misconduct towards women and men provided a public manifestation of the scale of power imbalance within the industry. Reports of sexual misconduct came from creative workers located across the global film industry, including in the US, UK and Hong Kong. This revived the #MeToo digital activist movement, with significant participation from creative and cultural workers who were motivated to share their experiences publicly after, in many cases, years of silence (Cobb and Hoerck 2017). It is these mass 'moments' of resistance, as exemplified in digital forms of activism such as #MeToo and #Oscarssowhite, which illustrate the new forms of political struggle emerging and a shared language through which to identify harm within creative labour.

It would be interesting to consider how Bhavnani's paper would have been received today, following more than a decade of evidence that explores and exposes the complicated and psychologically charged relationship between the creative worker and their work. The next section considers some of the literature on work-based solidarity as a means to frame the emerging forms of resistance from the CCW.

15.3   NEW FORMS OF SOLIDARITY AND RESISTANCE

There is a rich body of literature on the relationship between the arts, creative practice and activism (Harold 2004; Harrebye 2015; Serafini 2019). However, the purpose of this chapter is not to consider the use of creativity or the arts as an aesthetic form of activism, but to consider forms of resistance emerging from within the CCW. Among the literature looking at resistance within the CCW are investigations into new forms of working practices; for example, physical creative co-operatives or maker spaces (Sandoval 2016; Boyle and Oakley 2018) that have formed in response to wider structural and spatial limitations. Greig de Peuter's (2014) work on creative labour movements considers the relationship between different co-working groups and activist movements. The identification of a 'new form of labour politics' (de Peuter and Cohen 2015) that considers the various forms of resistance and solidarity across what de Peuter and Cohen define as 'flexworkers' – freelancers, part-time workers, self-employed workers, interns, casual workers, contract workers and volunteers – links to wider work-based grievances in the growing gig economy, now including workplaces from services and social care (Beck and Brook 2020). Deuze predicted in 2007 that the new forms of fluid, individualised and risk labour embraced by 'media workers' were likely to be adopted by other industrial sectors. Austerity Britain's celebratory embrace of neoliberal forms of labour structure has led to increased cross-industrial solidarity; for example, the trade union United Voices of the World (UVW) was set up to support all 'migrant and precarious labourers'.[2] In response to these emerging forms of political engagement, de Peuter and Cohen (2015: 306) propose three concepts necessary to envision a new model of creative labour: mutual aid, policy from below and counter-interpellation. These three concepts are important factors when considering the emerging forms of resistance that I focus on in this chapter, and I frame them under the term 'inclusive solidarity', building on work by Morgan and Pulignano (2020), as a concept that highlights a developing bottom-up, changemaking agenda promoting discourses and practices of 'hope' (Gross 2020).

In the introductory paper to a special issue for the journal *Work, Economy and Society* (*WES*) titled 'Solidarities in and through work in an age of extremes', Beck and Brook (2020: 9) provide a definition of solidarity as: 'a form of identification which depends on individuals knowing, engaging with and, potentially, supporting other individuals around them'. The wording 'age of extremes' is used to contextualise the growth of populism and reactionary politics that has emerged against the background of austerity measures, conflict and individualisation. Solidarity is considered as a practice and experience to counter uncertainty, and shown to be an important element of the current workplace. Thus, they are interested in the multiple and new forms of solidarity that have emerged as part of the highly individualised, neoliberal gig economy. The gig economy has been productive of new forms of 'communities of coping' (Korcynski 2003, in Beck and Brook 2019), a concept that relates to Kropotkin's discourse of 'mutual aid' as applied to the CCW by de Peuter and Cohen (Krotpotkin 1902, in de Peuter and Cohen 2015). Mutual aid is not possible without solidarity; but solidarity, as discussed in the *WES* special issue, has multiple meanings. Beck and Brook apply the term 'solidarity' in relation to the idea of a common 'moral economy', applying E.P. Thompson's (1991, in Beck and Brook 2019: 6) understanding of the moral economy as a 'mentality'. A communal sense of injustice and the possibility of emancipation can be an important element of solidarity. But as Morgan and Pulignano (2019) note, solidarity can be either inclusive or exclusive, producing discourses of 'us and them', or, as in the early gendered trade union movements, prioritising the injustices of one group over another (ibid.). What is interesting in this body of literature, on the relationship between precarious labour, barriers and exclusions within the CCW with the growth of the gig-worker movement, is the emphasis on new forms of inclusive solidarity that have been produced out of the harm and injustice within much contemporary creative work. This is quite a conceptual break from the DWYL discourse inherent in policy from the late 1990s (Oakley et al. 2013). In their article on reconceptualising forms of solidarity in the context of creative precarious labour, Strauß and Fleischman (2020: 110) state:

> in contrast to institutionalised forms of organised labour, solidarity in the social factory is not linked to notions of stable community or homogeneity but is a temporary phenomenon between ever-changing actors who need to actively create the conditions for it.

That article is one example of how changemakers within the CCW use their own experiences to create conditions of change whilst acknowledging a wider relationship beyond the individual or the sector, to a wider population, embracing the language of inclusive solidarity as necessary for structural change.

15.4   EMERGING FORMS OF RESISTANCE

As stated, the data that informs this chapter is taken from a larger study on inclusivity and sustainability in the EU's creative economy. I conducted nine semi-structured interviews with another researcher from the DISCE consortium. The majority of interviews took place face-to-face with two interviewers, either in person or via the communication platform Skype. All participants were known to the research team and due to their public visibility all agreed to be identified within this research output.[3] The study participants had all founded, or were in the process of developing, organisations that related to a specific inequality-based issue in the CCW. We interviewed five of the founders from Raising Films,[4] a campaigning organisation and community for parents and carers in the UK film and television industry; two together and a further three on separate occasions. We also interviewed one of the two founders of Parents in Performing Arts[5] (PIPA), an organisation that also focuses on the issue of parents and carers across performing arts; the creator of COMMON,[6] an initiative to advocate for participants from low socio-economic backgrounds in theatre; and the two founders of The Offsite,[7] a leadership programme for women of colour within creative media and technology. Despite their specific issue-based focus in terms of engaging an audience or community, each interviewee subscribed to a strong value of inclusivity for all, in direct opposition to the model of individualised elitism that they identified as the current model of work in the creative and cultural industries (CCIs):

> I think its elitist. I think its closed. I think it's I think it's a boys club, I think that, you know, I mean, I think that you need to, the amount of people with degrees from Oxford or Cambridge, or, you know, I think …. I think it's elitist.

Elitism stood beyond factors of gender, race, disability, caregiving: all the issues that the interviewees publicly stood for as the driving forces for the inequality that necessitated their activity. It was summed up by David, founder of COMMON:

> Intersectional social economic inequality is, in my opinion, the biggest challenge that's facing the sector at this moment in time. And I deliberately use the term intersectional because I think, without getting into huge ideological debates, the term working-class or the term underclass has politically become very associated with white ethnicity … to the extent of excluding those from ethnically diverse backgrounds. So I really consciously use that framing of intersectionality, because in the research that I've done, and the work that I've done, and the companies and the organisations that I've worked for, I've increasingly discovered that you just can't talk about gender equality and isolation from class. And you can't talk about ethnic diversity in isolation from class, like, disability you absolutely cannot talk about in isolation from class, like, I think if you try and almost departmentalise,

these different areas of exceptional diversity, you just completely ignore such a significant structural part of where those issues stem from which is ultimately I think, class division. And so, I'd say, as a big, big banner. That's the big problem.

I later discuss David's and other participants' application of the term 'intersectionality', and their relationship with research. But in relation to 'elitism' specifically, it was identified as productive of the sort of self-disciplining discourse associated with the pleasure–pain axis in creative work. Nicky, a film producer and co-founder of Raising Films, responded;

> I think that one of the biggest issues that sort of seems to prevail across sort of all levels, is just this notion that we're kind of lucky to work in this kind of job.

So, a writer, film critic, bookseller and another co-founder of Raising Films who was interviewed along with Nicky, developed this point further:

> I think this relates to, to what Nicky is saying, which could also be called imposter syndrome, because I think not everyone is made to feel they're lucky and to work in the film industry, some people just feel entitled to be there ... which leads to people basically submitting to exploit themselves because of imposter syndrome. And often measures or policies that try and address one side of that, like trying to address diversity around issues of exclusion, that issue with class and race based class, don't necessarily think about the factory model and how that means to get in, you have to have confidence, you have to, you know, set aside all your issues or your problems or everything that's making you feel anxious, or meaning you can't join it, you have to become a perfect body.

There was a recognition that the industry was divided between those who felt entitled to be there, and those who felt they had been allowed to enter, and that divide created the space for the type of power imbalance, exploitation and self-disciplining subjectification that has been understood to operate almost silently within the labour market.

The operation of elitism and entitlement was linked to the problematic nature of defining value. Pamela, a producer and co-founder of The Offsite who worked within the creative and digital sector, described it as follows:

> But I also feel like the industry has a real challenge of being able to identify value and therefore be able to invest in the right areas. And I think that's a problem across the public and the private sectors. It's hard, it's like, where does creativity come from? And at what levels does it become something that becomes valuable to audiences?

She went on to connect this to an absence of strong leadership in the creative sector:

> Then linked to that is the idea of value there is certain parts of the industry, that are very unrecognised, so I think, the skills around management and leadership, which is so linked to not being able to identify value is, a huge problem, because it means that ... it just means that the sector as a whole is very slow to adapt and grow, because it can't reflect on itself and other things tangibly to realise what's working and what isn't working.

The intangibility of understanding creative value at a senior, leadership, structural level was then articulated as the problem, and not individual or certain demographic groups. That shifted the focus of defining and measuring value not onto the workforce, but onto its leadership and management structures, which as Pamela points out, are the group in most need of education.

15.5   INCLUSIVE SOLIDARITY AS A FORM OF SUSTAINABILITY

For many of them there was the idea that founding an organisation for change was a form of personal survival and a way to connect with others who had also experienced work-based barriers. Hope, who was the original founder of Raising Films, described in detail her experience of continuing to develop her career as a filmmaker alongside her caring responsibilities as a parent; the impetus to create Raising Films was a form of survival:

> I sort of felt a bit hopeless. And I thought, I'm never actually going to make a feature because I don't think there's a way this can happen ... The way I can stay in this industry is if I change it, you know?

It is the personal response to connect with others and desire to foster change that distinguishes this form of solidarity from discourses of 'resilience'. As discussed, the wider literature on the resilience agenda illustrates its interconnection with a neoliberal ideology of the individual ability to adapt to and accept risk (Gill and Orgad 2018), which in the case of marginalised workers, often leads to their exclusion. The participants in the study spoke of the need to connect with others who had had similar experiences of rejection, of perceptions of failure due to their class, their race, their caregiving responsibilities; and rather than internalise that perception, decided to create a community for change. It was only connecting with others that made this possible. As Cassie from PIPA explained:

> No, no I don't think I would have set it up because I didn't understand. There was no way I could have understood, and I suppose my lack of understanding is also, I understand other people's lack of understanding.

15.6   DESIRE FOR CHANGE

We're actually trying to bring about systemic change. (Hope)

Safri et al. (2018) suggest that reciprocity and 'mutual aid', are important aspects of solidarity: both as a labour market structure and as an economic model. The idea of sharing knowledge, resources and data with the wider communities that their organisations spoke to was another prominent theme that emerged across our interviews. An interest was shared in gathering empirical data and working with researchers as a means to understanding the impact of precarious labour on the CCW, and a desire for an intersectional understanding of inequality:

> I think what we've found through our research, is that more often than not, people aren't actually facing one barrier, that there are many. And so, whether there are socio-economic factors, or issues around ethnicity, background, that, that everything that people sort of experience in their kind of private life and their home life has become kind of a barrier to entry and sustainability. So, I think that the goal is to ultimately make it possible for more people, different kinds of people with different kinds of lives and backgrounds, to enter the industry and stay and be welcome in it. (Nicky)

There was a strong recognition that the work these organisations were providing fed into a wider nexus of individuals, campaigners, organisations and researchers all trying to bring about structural change. There has been a shift in the conceptual understanding of the creative economy towards an ecological framework (Holden 2015; Gross and Wilson 2020; de Barnard et al. 2021). The idea of a creative or cultural 'ecosystem' applies an 'ecological' perspective to cultural and creative activity, as interdependent among a number of different stakeholders, organisations and locations. Ecological perspectives of this kind strongly resonate with our interviewees' understandings that the issues they were campaigning for were beyond them individually, and that they contributed to a wider ecology of changemakers. Closely connected to that understanding was a strong desire to work with and generate academic research.

Beck and Brook, in their summary of 'solidarity', reference Bourdieu and Burawoy's concept of 'organic public sociology' which unites scholars with activists, as represented by the 'scholar activist' who acts as an educator, spokesperson or analyst for the group which they are connected to (Brook and Darlington 2013, in Beck and Brook 2020: 11). All the participants in this study spoke of their connection with academia, from fundraising and commissioning independent research, to providing information, angles, case studies and participants. They understand that research provides knowledge on what is known but also what is missing:

> I got the sense from the Breaking the Glass Ceiling inquiry as well, that, you know, so obviously, our guild report looked into gender inequality in the TV industries, but not into ethnic representation. So that was not covered. And that was a decision that we made, because to capture that would have taken a lot longer, because it's, it's a little bit more complicated in terms of how people identify and so on, and would have cost like them twice as much. And we had a certain amount of money it was funded by us. Yes. So that is still missing. But the other thing is the kind of also the intersection between classes not really representing, you know, obviously, you know, there's a lot of people kind of looking into that. Now, it's very tricky to identify class, because people leave out of the have a class label, then what do they identify with? They might come from working class roots, but, essentially, how they live now is, you know, middle class. (Line)

There was an acknowledgement that research did not cover the multiple forms of exclusion linked to the identity politics operating across the CCW. 'Intersectionality' was originally developed as a term and a theory in response to the 'vexed dynamics of difference and solidarities of sameness' that had emerged in anti-discrimination legislation from the late 1970s, which excluded African American women's experiences of injustice (Cho et al. 2013), but has now evolved into a field of study that incorporates academic and political interpellation (ibid.). Notably, it was a term adopted across the interviews. There was a recognition by interviewees that particular voices and particular kinds of data are missing from existing research. They identified how their connection with a community within the workforce could generate resources relevant for establishing new knowledge and, thereby, for the development of new approaches to challenging structural inequalities, with new possibilities for 'accountability', as this example from Pamela demonstrates:

> And I think the first thing that is useful, which kind of goes back to I was talking about earlier around the accountability is having kind of like that stake in the grass and being like, this is what the current situation is actually like. So, I don't think anyone really knows. So, I think that's the first thing, which is that kind of field research of, you know, people's personal experiences, but also their personal experiences within organisations. That kind of makes it really clear, like what isn't working. And then I think the other benefit of research is, again, it creates kind of some kind of benchmark from which things can become better or worse, which answers a little bit of that question around intangibility, and not being able to quite

like define value. And so, I think those two things like the benchmark and the accountability, would be useful, from my perspective.

This drive to generate knowledge and work, in partnership with both academic and industry stakeholders, visibilises the bridging functionality of these organisations within this ecosystem. This is something that David articulates:

> Despite increasingly over the last, I'd say specifically, kind of 12 months, two years, many research studies have been published, which evidence ... statistically, what the inequalities are surrounding social economic disadvantage, and yet, no practical changes [have] been implemented.

What frustrated many of these organisers was their absence from policy. There was a desire not simply to generate evidence-based research, but to use it to question, hold stakeholders to account and then push for implementational change at the industry and in some cases the policy level. This drive linked to a tension in how they articulated their position. When asked if they would define themselves as an activist, many – although they would acknowledge that on a personal level they could be identified as a type of activist – did not relate activism to the work that they did:

> Like there's a difference between being an activist and organiser, I guess, like anyone can be an activist, but an organiser is, that's huge levels of skill and wisdom. (So)

> When you think of activism, you think of marches ... you have to be very active about being an activist. (Amy)

> whereas permanent change maker feels a bit more, yeah ... Someone makes change. It's like quite tangible. (Pamela)

So, the idea of being an activist was rejected in favour of this position of changemaker, a body of grassroots-based initiatives who were able to position themselves, partly through their own social and cultural capital as in between academic and industry: as a force to drive research, to develop a new evidence base, with the aim to develop structural change.

15.7   SUSTAINABLE CHANGEMAKING

Another prominent theme that emerged from the data was an awareness of the participants' own temporal position within the broader ecosystem:

> When we started Raising Films, we didn't want to exist in decades. We wanted the film industry bodies to have taken on the work we were doing, and have incorporated it into how they were, you know, mandating how gatekeepers were mandating

the industry. So, we weren't seeing this as like a long-term platform for ourselves, or that it was going to develop into a larger campaigning organisation. And the idea was to hand it on to the people who could take our research, take our ideas. (So)

With systemic change as a goal, these organisations flagged up the hope that through their work there would be a future where their existence would no longer be necessary. Alongside this concept of temporality was a commitment that the organisations they founded embodied the values that they highlighted. All, for example, spoke of the importance of paying anyone who undertook work for them:

> We also have a paid comms manager and we've had things like paid web designers PR [public relations], and some people who've given us pro bono assistance as well. So, we are we're a community business, and the project managers manage that aspect and then manage the different projects that we decide on as by consensus as a team of founders, with the part time very part time staff whose wages come from crowdfunding. (Cassie)

For many of these founders, that meant working for free themselves:

> because of an unwillingness to bring anybody into the team who isn't paid, you know a more than reasonable living wage because of the values that I am Common hold, and it's run as a one-person band. It's one it's just me. (David)

Although the founders and changemakers interviewed were still participating within their industry, they were not in stable positions and were still struggling with the reality of precarious labour themselves:

> It also, without question, every week involves at least one, at least one sometimes four meetings where I am either having a general meeting or I'm pitching for a job that I'm not, you know that I've had to do work for that I haven't been paid for. (Hope)

There was a recognition that these organisations provided some form of value to the industry, linked in part to the wider acknowledgement of the diversity and inclusion agenda from industry bodies. There was a realisation that by creating these communities, generating research, devising training and networking support platforms, this group of changemakers were fulfilling a role that should be undertaken on a larger, more structural level. So, whilst they would be invited to share their knowledge, their contribution was not necessarily economically valued or supported:

> What people don't understand, like, at a time when inclusion is becoming really visible, and really important, we're asked to be on many more panels, and, you know, we're suddenly our presence is requested and yet, you know, we're not being

paid, there's this complete lack of recognition, that activism is unpaid work. And that if you want us to talk about it, it would be really like the most supportive thing you could do is to pay us because we're spending so much time already, you know? (Hope)

There was also the question of the financial sustainability of these organisations. Although some had received project-based grants from a state-supported funding source – for example, Arts Council England or the British Film Institute – most survived financially on crowd-funding, either online or through local fundraising events. David from COMMON pointed to the class-based assumptions of fundraising applications, and the amount of unrecognised free labour that goes into the process of fundraising. As stated, whilst their labour was largely donated for free, the commitment to paying others meant that many of these organisations had a precarious business model, and yet the work that they did was recognised to create value, not just for the creative economy, but for those in higher education and research as well.

15.8 CONCLUSION: WHAT IS THEIR ROLE AND FUTURE IN THE CREATIVE ECONOMY?

You know, it has been two years of the Time's Up movement. I think soon we can start looking at, like, a mini longitudinal study of what impact has this actually had not just like scare stories in the newspapers about "Is this the end of sex scenes in cinema?" Because I think it will, there will be some backlash to it as well, in terms of renewed conservatism and status quo and, and risk management, as well as exciting projects. And it's the question of where is the level? Like, is all of the exciting stuff just happening at the grassroots? And then at a certain level it's like, okay, but we're not making any change. Where is the change going all the way through? And I feel like often with these big research projects that happen, that set up the conditions for change, there's not necessarily the follow up to see well, what actually got done? (So)

This is how these participants differ from other forms of activism, resistance or resilience. First, they are not process-oriented as defined by Harrebye's (2015) concept of 'creative activism' art or aesthetic-based cultural jamming initiatives, although there are similarities in their structural organisation and strategic use of new media. They have a clear agenda, to achieve structural change, by engaging a number of different stakeholders from within the creative ecosystem and both driving and sharing knowledge. Second, they identify as organisers, not activists. The reluctance to apply the term 'activist' to their organisation or work, even if they apply it to themselves in a personal capacity, relates to their positionality as 'inside' the ecosystem and working with stakeholders to create change, rather than agitating on the outside. Third, they themselves are precariously positioned, and although critically valued within the communities they represent, their value, the work and research they generate are largely ignored or responded to superficially by the gatekeepers able to provide sustainable funding and/or promote structural, policy change. Despite holding strong values in relation to how they employ and pay people who are working for the organisation, they themselves are largely working for free, or devoting a significant amount of unpaid labour.

This chapter was written during the early months of the Covid-19 pandemic, when questions of the economic stability of the creative economy were being addressed across the globe. At this moment, it is too early to comprehend what the long-term repercussions of the pandemic will be on the creative economy, or indeed on the organisations interviewed in relation to this research, although one of the organisations included in this research project has announced its closure. As already identified, many were operating a precarious funding model themselves, positioned at a level of superficial value in relation to the wider industries that their work spoke to, lacking significant financial support to ensure their sustainability, and without the political capital to have their research widely recognised and responded to. There was a reluctance to define themselves as 'activists' and a preference to frame their position as 'change-makers', with a goal to research, organise and mobilise for structural change to improve the conditions for everyone in the CCW. There was an awareness that issues could not be addressed singularly, that they spoke to wider concerns related to structural injustices and cultures that legitimised exploitation and inequality. Their existence points to a shift in how the creative and cultural workers are cognizant of their position within broader socio-economic systems, and their engagement with the wider literature providing evidence of the harms caused by precarious creative labour. The values that frame this part of the creative ecosystem can be characterised, as I put it, as 'inclusive solidarity'. As our understanding of the creative economy develops, the place of resistance, solidarity and change from within the workforce will be an important part of determining how inclusive and sustainable creative economies are.

NOTES

1. https://www.theguardian.com/theguardian/2008/sep/09/1.
2. https://www.uvwunion.org.uk/.
3. We acknowledge and thank the participants to the project: Hope Dickson Leach (filmmaker, Raising Films founder); Nicky Bentham (producer, Raising Films founder); So Mayer (freelance writer and bookseller, Raising Films founder); Jess Levick (producer, Raising Films founder); Line Langbek, (screenwriter, lecturer, Raising Films founder); David Loumgair (theatre director, dramaturge, COMMON founder); Cassie Raine (actor, director, Parents in Performing Arts founder); Amy Dick (multidisciplinary producer, The Offsite founder); Pamela Peter-Agbia (producer, The Offsite founder).

4.   https://www.raisingfilms.com/.
5.   http://www.pipacampaign.com/.
6.   https://commontheatre.co.uk/.
7.   'About – The Offsite' (the-offsite.com).

BIBLIOGRAPHY

Antcliff, V. (2005), 'Broadcasting in the 1990s: competition, choice and inequality?' *Media, Culture and Society* 27, pp. 841–859.

Banks, M. (2007), *The Politics of Cultural Work*. London: Palgrave Macmillan.

Banks, M. (2017), *Creative Justice. Cultural Industries, Work and Inequality*. London: Rowman & Littlefield International.

Beck, U., Giddens, A. and Lash, S. (1994), *Reflexive Modernization: Politics, Tradition and Aesthetics in the Modern Social Order*. Cambridge: Polity Press.

Beck, V. and Brook, P. (2020), 'Solidarities in and through work in an age of extremes'. *Work, Employment and Society* 34(1), pp. 3–17.

Bhavnani, R. (2007), *Barriers to Diversity in Film A Research Review*. London: UK Film Council.

Blair, H. (2001), 'You're only as good as your last job: the labour process and labour market in the British film industry'. *Work, Employment and Society* 15(1), pp. 149–169.

Borén, T. and Young, C. (2017), 'Artists and creative city policy: resistance, the mundane and engagement in Stockholm, Sweden'. *City, Culture and Society* 8, pp. 21–26.

Boyle, D. and Oakley, K. (2018), 'Co-operatives in the creative industries'. Available at: https://www.uk.coop/sites/default/files/uploads/attachments/coop_creative _industries_final.pdf (accessed 6 April 2020).

Brook, O., O'Brien, D. and Taylor, M. (2020), *Culture is Bad for You: Inequality and the Cultural and Creative Industries*. Manchester: Manchester University Press.

The Care Collective (2020), *The Care Manifesto: The Politics of Interdependence*. London and New York: Verso.

Cho, S., Crenshaw, K.W. and Mccall, L. (2013), 'Toward a field of intersectionality studies: theory, applications, and praxis'. *Signs: Journal of Women in Culture and Society* 38(4), pp. 785–810.

Cobb, S. and Horeck, T. (2018), 'Post Weinstein: gendered power and harassment in the media industries'. *Feminist Media Studies* 18(3), pp. 489–491.

Comunian, R. and England, L. (2020), 'Creative and cultural work without filters: Covid-19 and exposed precarity in the creative economy'. *Cultural Trends*, 29(2), pp. 112–128. https://doi.org/10.1080/09548963.2020.1770577.

Conor, B., Gill, R. and Taylor, S. (2015), 'Gender and creative labour'. *Sociological Review* 63, pp. 1–22.

Creative Scotland (2017), 'Equality matters: a review of equalities, diversity and inclusion in Scotland's screen sector'. Available at: http://www.creativescotland.com/ what-we-do/latest-news/archive/2017/01/screen-equalities-diversity-and-inclusion -review-published (accessed 16 July 2018).

Creative Skillset (2010), 'Women in the creative media industries'. Available at: http:// www.creativeskillset.org/uploads/pdf/asset_15343.pdf?3 (accessed 10 January 2011).

de Barnard, M., Comunian, R. and Gross, J. (2021), 'Cultural and creative ecosystems: a review of theories and methods, towards a new research agenda'. *Cultural Trends*, pp. 1–22. https://doi.org/10.1080/09548963.2021.2004073.

Dent, T. (2019), 'We need to talk about caring'. London: Raising Films. Available at: https://www.raisingfilms.com/wpcontent/uploads/2019/06/RaisingFilms_CarersReport_June2019.pdf (accessed 24 June 2019).

Dent, T. (2020), 'Devalued women, valued men: motherhood, class and neoliberal feminism in the creative media industries'. *Media, Culture and Society* 42(2), 537–553.

Dent, T., Comunian, R., Conor, B., Burlina, C., Pica, V. and Wilson, N. (2020), *Creative Workforce in Europe Statistics Report*. DISCE Publications. Available at: https://disce.eu/wp-content/uploads/2020/05/DISCE-Report-D3.2.b.pdf (accessed 7 September 2020).

de Peuter, G.S. (2014), 'Confronting precarity in the Warhol economy: notes from New York City', *Journal of Cultural Economy*, 7(1), pp. 31–47. https://doi.org/10.1080/17530350.2013.856337.

de Peuter, G. and Cohen, N. (2015), 'Emerging labour politics in creative industries'. In Oakley, K. and O'Connor J. (eds), *The Routledge Companion to the Cultural Industries*. Abingdon: Routledge, pp. 305–318.

Deuze, M. (2007), *Media Work*. Cambridge: Polity Press.

Dex, S., Willis, J., Paterson, R. and Sheppard, E. (2000), 'Freelance workers and contract uncertainty: the effects of contractual changes in the television industry'. *Work, Employment and Society* 14(2), pp. 283–305.

Directors UK (2014), 'Women directors – who's calling the shots? Women directors in British television production'. London: Directors UK. Available at: https://www.directors.uk.com/news/who-s-calling-the-shots (accessed 21 December 2015).

Dyer-Witherford, N. and de Peuter, G.S. (2006), '"EA Spouse" and the crisis of video game labour: enjoyment, exclusion, exploitation, and exodus'. *Canadian Journal of Communication*. Graduate Program in Communication Studies, University of Calgary, 31(3), pp. 599–617.

European Women's Audiovisual (EWA) Network (2016), 'Where are the women directors? Full report'. Available at: http://www.ewawomen.com/uploads/files/MERGED_Press-2016.pdf (accessed 12 December 2016).

Filion, P. (2013), 'Fading resilience? Creative destruction, neoliberalism and mounting risks'. *Sapiens. Copernicus* 6(1), pp. 1–10.

Florida, R. (2002), *The Rise of the Creative Class and How It's Transforming Work, Leisure, Community and Everyday Life*. New York: Basic Books.

Follows, S., Kreager, A. and Gomes, E. (2016), 'Cut out of the picture. A study of gender inequality amongst film directors in the UK film industry'. London: Directors UK. Available at: https://www.directors.uk.com/press/cut-out-of-the-picture-a-study-of-gender-inequality-among-film-directors-within-the-uk-film-industry (accessed 15 August 2016).

Friedman, S. and Laurison, D. (2019), *The Class Ceiling: Why it Pays to be Privileged*. Bristol: Policy Press.

Friedman, S., O'Brien, D. and Laurison, D. (2017), '"Like skydiving without a parachute": how class origin shapes occupational trajectories in British acting'. *Sociology* 51(5), pp. 992–1010.

Gill R. (2002), 'Cool, creative and egalitarian? Explaining gender in project based new media work in Europe'. *Information, Communication and Society* 5(1), pp. 70–89.

Gill, R. (2014), 'Unspeakable inequalities: post feminism, entrepreneurial subjectivity, and the repudiation of sexism among cultural workers'. *Social Politics: International Studies in Gender, State and Society* 21, pp. 509–528.

Gill, R. and Orgad, S. (2018), 'The amazing bounce-backable woman: resilience and the psychological turn in neoliberalism'. *Sociological Research Online* 23(2), pp. 477–495.

Gill, R. and Pratt, A. (2008), 'In the social factory? Immaterial labour, precariousness and cultural work'. *Theory, Culture and Society* 25, pp. 1–30.

Gov.uk (2010), 'Transforming the British economy: coalition strategy for economic growth'. Available at: https://www.gov.uk/government/speeches/transforming-the -british-economy-coalition-strategy-for-economic-growth (accessed 22 May 2020).

Gross, J. (2020), 'Holding together loss and hope: reflections on the need for art in times of crisis'. *Journal of Psychosocial Studies* 13(2), pp. 209–217. https://doi.org/ 10.1332/147867320x15894731588869.

Gross, J. (2021), 'Practices of hope: care, narrative and cultural democracy'. *International Journal of Cultural Policy* 27(1), pp. 1–15. https://doi.org/10.1080/ 10286632.2019.1702032.

Gross, J. and Wilson, N. (2020), 'Cultural democracy: an ecological and capabilities approach'. *International Journal of Cultural Policy* 26(3), pp. 1–16. https://doi.org/ 10.1080/10286632.2018.1538363.

Grugulis, I. and Stoyanova, D. (2012), 'Social capital and networks in film and TV: jobs for the boys?' *Organization Studies* 33(10), pp. 1311–1331.

The Guardian (2008), Reena Bhavnani Obituary. Available at: https://www.theguardian .com/theguardian/2008/sep/09/1 (accessed 1 March 2020).

Harold, C. (2004), 'Pranking rhetoric: "Culture jamming" as media activism'. *Critical Studies in Media Communication* 21(3), pp. 189–211.

Harrebye, S.F. (2015), 'The ambivalence of creative activism as a reorganization of critique'. *Culture and Organization* 21(2), pp. 126–146.

Holden, J. (2015), *The Ecology of Culture*. Swindon: Arts and Humanities Research Council.

Holgate, J. and McKay, S. (2009), 'Equal opportunities policies: How effective are they in increasing diversity in the audio-visual industries' freelance labour market?' *Media, Culture and Society* 31(1), pp. 151–163.

Kreager, A. and Follows, S. (2018), 'Gender inequality and screenwriters. A study of the impact of gender on equality of opportunity for screenwriters and key creatives in the UK film and television industries'. London: Writers Guild of Great Britain. Available at: https://writersguild.org.uk/wp-content/uploads/2018/05/WGGB -Gender-Inequality-and-Screenwriters-Report.pdf (accessed 21 August 2018).

McRobbie, A. (1998), *British Fashion Design: Rag Trade or Image Industry?* London and New York: Routledge.

McRobbie, A. (2002), 'Fashion culture: creative work, female individualization'. *Feminist Review* 71(1), pp. 52–62.

McRobbie, A. (2010), 'Clubs to companies: notes on the decline of political culture in speeded up creative'. *Cultural Studies* 16(4), pp. 516–531.

Morgan, G. and Pulignano, V. (2020), 'Solidarity at work: concepts, levels and challenges'. *Work, Employment and Society* 34(1), pp. 18–34.

Nwonka, C.J. (2015), 'Diversity pie: rethinking social exclusion and diversity policy in the British film industry'. *Journal of Media Practice* 16(1), pp. 73–90.

Oakley, K., O'Brien, D. and Lee, D. (2013), 'Happy now? Well-being and cultural policy'. *Philosophy and Public Policy Quarterly* 31(2), pp. 18–26.

O'Brien, A. (2019), *Women, Inequality and Media Work*. Abingdon: Routledge.

O'Brien, D., Laurison, D., Miles, A. and Friedman, S. (2016), 'Are the creative industries meritocratic? An analysis of the 2014 British Labour Force Survey'. *Cultural Trends* 25(2), pp. 116–131.

Pratt, A.C. (2017), 'Beyond resilience: learning from the cultural economy'. *European Planning Studies* 25(1), pp. 127–139.

Randle, K. and Hardy, K. (2016), 'Macho, mobile and resilient? How workers with impairments are doubly disabled in project-based film and television work'. *Work, Employment and Society* 31(3), pp. 447–464.

Ross, A. (2009), *Nice Work If You Can Get It: Life and Labor in Precarious Times*. New York and London: NYU Press.

Safri, M., Borowiak, B., Healy, S. and Pavlovskaya, M. (2018), 'Putting the solidarity economy on the map'. *Community Economies* (January). Available at: https://www.communityeconomies.org/publications/articles/putting-solidarity-economy-map (accessed 9 April 2020).

Sandoval, M. (2016), 'Fighting precarity with co-operation? Worker co-operatives in the cultural sector'. *New Formations* 88(88), pp. 51–68.

Scharff, C. (2016), 'The Psychic Life of Neoliberalism: Mapping the Contours of Entrepreneurial Subjectivity', *Theory, Culture and Society*. SAGE Publications Ltd, 33(6), pp. 107–122. https://doi.org/10.1177/0263276415590164.

Serafini, P. (2019), *Performance Action: The Politics of Art Activism*. London: Routledge.

Strauß, A. and Fleischmann, A. (2020), 'Reconceptualising solidarity in the social factory: cultural work between economic needs and political desires'. *Work, Employment and Society* 34(1), pp. 109–125.

Taylor, S. and Littleton, K. (2013), 'Negotiating a contemporary creative identity'. In Ashton, D. and Noonan, C. (eds), *Cultural Work and Higher Education*. London: Palgrave Macmillan UK, pp. 154–171.

Tokumitsu, M. (2015), *Do What You Love: And Other Lies about Success and Happiness*. New York: Regan Arts.

Ursell, G. (2000), 'Television production: issues of exploitation, commodification and subjectivity in UK television labour markets'. *Media, Culture & Society* 22(6), pp. 805–825. https://doi.org/10.1177/016344300022006006.

Wilkinson, R. and Pickett, K. (2018), *The Inner Level: How More Equal Societies Reduce Stress, Restore Sanity and Improve Everyone's Well-Being*. London: Penguin Random House.

Wilson, N., Gross, J., Dent, T., Conor, B. and Comunian, R. (2020), *Re-thinking Inclusive and Sustainable Growth for the Creative Economy: A Literature Review*. DISCE Publications. Available at: https://disce.eu/wp-content/uploads/2020/01/DISCE-Report-D5.2.pdf (accessed 14 September 2020).

Wreyford, N. (2015), 'Birds of a feather: informal recruitment practices and gendered outcomes for screenwriting work in the UK film industry'. *Sociological Review* 63, pp. 84–96.

16. What is the creative economy – really?

Nick Wilson

INTRODUCTION

We do not really know what the 'creative economy' is. And yet, all too often, policymakers and commentators treat it as a given. My purpose in this chapter is to challenge this theory–practice inconsistency, and to suggest a radical way of overcoming it. In keeping with this book's title, I consider the *longue durée* rather than short-term *événements* and situate the 'actually existing' creative economy within a cultural self-understanding of modernity, or what Habermas (1985 [1987]) termed *The Philosophical Discourse of Modernity*. Instead of continuing to advocate for the creative economy on behalf of either a poorly theorized taxonomic classification, or the blanket assertion that creativity (a necessarily 'open' phenomenon) can be treated as a systematic (hence 'closed') driver of the economy, I focus instead on the freedoms we have (or lack) to undertake processes of valuing, which are pivotal to making human creativity possible. Drawing on the capability approach (Sen 1999; Nussbaum 2011), the philosophical framework of aesthetic critical realism (Wilson 2019), and research from the European Union (EU)-funded project 'Developing Inclusive and Sustainable Creative Economies' (DISCE), the chapter highlights the central importance of 'cultural capability'; namely, our being able to experience, discover, connect with, give sharable form to and participate in recognizing what we have reason to value. I re-imagine the creative economy as 'a social domain that emphasizes the practices, discourses, and material expressions associated with the production, use, and management of [the] resources'[1] required to enable cultural capability.

Creative economies are (or should be) more than particular domains of industrial activity. At stake is the management of resources required to motivate and enable projects of human flourishing. Such an assertion directly challenges the prevailing 'value neutrality' of discourses of human creativity (see Wilson 2018), where currently the 'ends to which creativity is put are not seen as significant' (Craft et al. 2008: 3). 'Blending creativity with its consequences makes the generation of novel and effective solutions more than merely a question of what we could do, and turns it as much into an issue of what we should do' (Cropley et al. 2014: 299). Rather than framing the creative economy as merely an invented 'global orthodoxy' (Schlesinger 2017), or 'versatile policy script' (Vlassis and De Beukelaer 2019), the chapter presents an alternative vision of creative economies as social systems of value recognition focused on supporting and expanding the resources and infrastructures needed for people to recognize what they have reason to value.

THE (ACTUALLY EXISTING) CREATIVE ECONOMY

Christiaan De Beukelaer and Justin O'Connor argue that the 'creative economy' is an example of 'fast policy'. Such policy is easily available to politicians and policymakers and can be adopted as a quick fix, adopted without extensive scrutiny. As they put it, fast policy 'often has the virtue of touching the zeitgeist, no matter how fleeting and insubstantial'.[2] John Howkins was surely getting in touch with the zeitgeist of the new millennium when in his 2001 book, *Creative Economy*, he argued that this is where people make money from ideas. Seven years later, the United Nations published its first 'creative economy' report.[3] This consolidated a view of the creative economy as being broader than the creative industries (often confined to those industries involved in generating intellectual property), including 'not-for profits, informal and public funded activities, as well as for-profit, formal and private sector activities [and] the production systems and value chains necessary to sustain such products' (Pratt and Hutton 2013: 3). Twelve years later, launching its *Manifesto for the Creative Economy*, the National Endowment for the Sciences, Technology and the Arts (Nesta) recommended the government to adopt its definition as 'those economic activities which involve the use of creative talent for commercial purposes'.[4] As Mark Banks (2017) observes, today in the United Kingdom (UK), 'the "creative economy" is officially defined … as all the people employed in the officially designated "creative industries" (whether these people have creative jobs or not) plus all the people working in creative occupations employed in "non-creative" industries'.[5] According to this 'creative trident' model,[6] the creative economy includes 'all creative areas of the economy', where 'creative' means 'having or showing an ability to make new things or think of new ideas';[7] that is, it refers both to creative industries and to creative work.[8] Contributing to the British Council's *Creative Economy* website, former special advisor to the UK's Minister for Culture, John Newbigin, reflects more widely on the significance of the term:

> It is sometimes said that where oil was the primary fuel of the 20th century economy, creativity is the fuel of the 21st century. In the same way that energy

policy and access to energy was a determinant of geopolitics throughout the 20th century, it may be that policies to promote and protect creativity will be the crucial determinants of success in the 21st.[9]

Taking all this into account, it might be countered that we do, in fact, have a good working knowledge of what a creative economy is; albeit one that separates into two distinctive viewpoints. The first, following the logic of the creative trident model, maintains that the creative economy is an attempt to capture a sectoral perspective on who is doing creative work that contributes to the overall economy. It is, in effect, a taxonomic label that captures a particular kind of economic industrial input. The second, mirroring changes that have taken place in post-industrial society, casts the creative economy as representing and accounting for the 'new' role of creativity in fostering economic growth and prosperity. Individually, both views are open to critique. The implication that there are 'creative' and therefore 'non-creative' jobs and workers is not just hard to vouch for, but exclusionary. Indeed, the causality of creativity as a driver of growth cannot be defended without much clearer definition, explanation and contextualization.

Current understandings of creative economy are reproducing a situation under which 'creativity' is being diminished. I am by no means the first person to advance a critical view. Arguing that we are in need of a new political economy of culture, Justin O'Connor notes that 'creation ex nihilo has Faustian overtones resonant with a global capitalism in which endless growth at the expense of nature is a central defining feature of human endeavour' (O'Connor 2019: 10). The development of a 'creativity agenda' and its associated 'economic imaginary' (Campbell 2014, 2019), under which the role of 'creativity' in the economy has been continually re-assessed, has come under fire from an increasingly wide range of commentators. As much as the creative economy represents an exciting opportunity to re-imagine and re-position our collective social futures, it also raises profound questions as to whether an obsession with creativity overlooks, or indeed exacerbates, systemic inequality and injustice.[10]

We need to step back and ask some serious questions; most centrally: What is the creative economy – really? This is the task that I undertake here. Rather than focusing my attention 'inwards' on matters of detailed statistical mapping (which have been the usual starting position for re-analysis), my task begins by casting the field of vision 'outwards' in a deliberate act of expansion. I seek to understand the (actually existing) creative economy across the broad temporal sweep of modernity. Over and above providing a telling historical context for this enquiry, the approach taken challenges us to bring some much-needed clarity to the ontology of the creative economy, including its underlying normative project. In the process, I hope to establish not just what a creative economy is, but what it should be.

THE CREATIVE ECONOMY AND THE PHILOSOPHICAL DISCOURSE OF MODERNITY

Up until the rise and consolidation of a capitalist system in the sixteenth and seventeenth centuries, the prevailing philosophical discourse was one 'in which [by and large] people defined themselves in relation to a cosmic order viewed as intrinsically meaningful, valuable and sacred'.[11] The philosophical discourse of modernity (PDM), on the other hand, is the revolutionary (Western) philosophical discourse that displaced this earlier one, with a central focus on 'the self-defining subject'.[12] As Roy Bhaskar[13] observes:

> the real force underpinning [the dichotomies and dualisms of the PDM] was nothing else than the remorseless logic of the nascent capitalist mode of production and exploitation of nature and human beings alike, a dynamic and self-expanding form of exploitation without precedent in human history, in which an unconstrained and unconscious conatus or drive to accumulation is hurtling humanity (and with it the planet) into crisis.[14]

It is against this backdrop that the DISCE project is endeavouring to 're-think inclusive and sustainable growth'; see Wilson et al. 2020 for discussion of 'growth beyond GDP [gross domestic product]'. In the years since the birth of capitalism, the PDM has undergone a number of phases, associated with socio-political revolution. Taking the broad sweep of the PDM as my starting point, Table 16.1 includes reflections on the particular implications for creativity, art(s) and culture (note that these do not always follow a strict chronological order; new ideas or approaches often emerge in non-linear ways). The table points towards there being a very close association between the PDM (that is, its 'modern' commitment to 'the self-defining subject') and to our relationship with, and collective management of, creativity.

My overall discussion of the actually existing creative economy has reached the fifth phase (above). Here, the underlying error of triumphalism/endism and market fundamentalism is described by Bhaskar as that of 'ontological monovalence'; that is, 'the view, underpinned ultimately by fear of change on the part of ruling elites, that Being is purely positive, devoid of the negativity that is transcendentally necessary for change to occur' (Hartwig 2011: 495). The actually existing creative economy's teleological drive towards the commodification of creativity constitutes a 'high point' of this phase of the PDM. We see this in neoliberalism's fetishization of creativity, and by extension of creatives, creative industries and the creative economy. Of course, we all know that human creativity is not the sole domain of 'special' people who call creatives,

Table 16.1   Phases of the philosophical discourse of modernity

Phase of modernity	Description of phase
1. Classical modernism	The moment of the birth and consolidation of the capitalist world system, involving the global colonial expansion of Europe and the accompanying socio-cultural-political revolutions of the sixteenth, seventeenth and eighteenth centuries (see Bhaskar 2002c: 103). *This also sees the birth of the 'work concept' (see for example Goehr 2007) – opening the way to the commodification of artworks, the reification of artists, and the concomitant 'absenting' of art and care (as universal human practices).*
2. High modernism	The revolutions of 1848 and 1917. *An increasingly static conception of 'high culture' facilitates comparison and measurement between cultures. The seeds of 'ideology critique*[a] *are later taken up in the Frankfurt School's critical analysis of the 'culture industry'.*
3. Modernization	The defeat of fascism, the Chinese revolution of 1949 and the onset of the Cold War and of formal decolonization. *In the 21st century, 'developing' countries undergoing modernization are attracted by the increasingly global logic and reach of the (technologically enabled) cultural and creative industries. Alternative modes of modernity begin to emerge – e.g., those founded on 'capabilities' (see Sen 1999).*
4. Postmodernism	The revolutionary upheavals of 1968 and the early 1970s in Western Europe, and revolution and counterrevolution in the South, beginning with the Vietnam War. *A new politics of identity and difference underpins increasingly prominent artistic responses to 'dis-enchantment'.*
5. Bourgeois triumphalism/ endism and fundamentalism	The collapse of the Soviet bloc and the intensification of the second phase of globalization of capital; *the 'actually existing' creative economy, premised on the commodification of creativity in the service of economic growth, represents a high point of market fundamentalism.*[b]
6. Long revolution…?[c]	*What next? The replacing of the 'actually existing' creative economy with an 'imagined future' creative economy, dedicated to resourcing people's substantive freedoms to experience, discover, give sharable form to, and participate in recognizing, value (i.e., cultural capability).*

Notes:
a. 'Ideology critique exposes, first, "the representation of sectional interests as universal ones", revealing the "tacit dependence of the excluding on the excluded" captured in the figure of the intrinsic exterior; and this has been built on by feminism, dependency theory and other movements representing the excluded' (Hartwig 2011: 499).
b. 'Fundamentalism (or foundationalism) … is the view that one's knowledge is incorrigible or certain because it is based on indubitable principles'. It 'inevitably splits reality into two (viz. that which conforms to its criterion and that which does not)' (Bhaskar 1993 [2008]: 300, in Hartwig 2011: 505, n. 97).
c. See Williams (1961).
Source: After Hartwig (2011: 494); author's adaptions and extensions in italics.

or indeed the domain of the creative industries, but we nonetheless choose to go along with it. Perhaps it is reassuring for citizens and policymakers alike to think that it is happening 'over there', and therefore to some extent, at least, it is 'under control'. But really, it is hard to imagine any more consequential and self-destructive act of human power – as a 'self-defining subject' – than the commodification of human creativity; both reifying creativity and making it subservient to individual wealth accumulation.

THE CREATIVE ECONOMY AS A TINA FORMATION

Some readers may find my willingness to write off our actually existing approach to the creative economy as rash. After all, on the surface at least, encouraging more creativity looks like a 'no-brainer'. But this is precisely why the creative economy is so appealing and so resistant to penetrating critical analysis. To be clear, I am not dismissing the centrality and importance of human creativity per se; far from it. I share the aim of enabling creativity, and my re-imagining of the creative economy has this purpose fully in mind. What I am doing, on the contrary, is challenging the assertion that the actually existing creative economy can deliver on its implicit promise to advance this creativity for the benefit of individuals and society alike. At the heart of my critique is the diagnosis of a TINA ('there is no alternative') formation, that is, 'the suppression by the false of the truth on which it depends and which sustains it' (Bhaskar 2002a: 219). Put simply, the falsity in theory is that human creativity per se is a thing that can be commodified; the truth in practice is that we are behaving as if human creativity is a thing that can be commodified. In this section I briefly highlight two forms of conceptual obfuscation, which I suggest play an integral role in sustaining and buttressing this TINA stance and which, in turn, are themselves sustained by it: conceptual conflation and conceptual absenting.

Conceptual Conflation

In asking 'What is the creative economy – really?' I seek to draw attention to a deeply entrenched, even systemic, vagueness. Conceptual conflation refers to treating terms as synonymous when they are not. In simple rhetorical terms, it is like treating apples as oranges. There are many relevant examples to choose from, but what I have in mind here is when people ask questions or discuss 'creativity', 'the arts' or 'culture' as if they are the same. Policy and research documents are full of implicit (sometimes explicit) conflations relating to the creative economy: creativity is culture; creativity is creative goods; culture is creative goods; creativity is creative expression; creativity is art; art is culture; art is the arts; art is artworks; the aesthetic is the arts; the arts is culture; culture is the non-economic; and so on and so forth. In asserting that these are false conflations I am making a series of ontological claims. Some commentators, and critics of my position, would respond that what is being referred to here are social constructions, and so we should be cautious of any 'objectifying' truth-claims. Whilst it is the case, of course, that all knowledge is conceptually mediated, and therefore all our observations of the world are 'theory-laden', this does not determine what reality is like; rather, reality exists independently of our knowledge of it (Danermark et al. 2002). The ensuing problem is that if we act on the basis of false beliefs (for example, limiting creativity to a certain 'cultural' sector, or treating creativity as a thing that can be commodified) we perpetuate unsustainable situations, at odds with the way the world is: the 'natural necessity' of the world (Wilson 2019: 29).

Conceptual Absenting

Closely allied to the entrenched conceptual conflation just referred to, I iden-tify a further source of ongoing obfuscation, which is conceptual absenting. This concerns the gradual disappearance of key terms from both policy and commentary, as other concepts ('creative economy' amongst them) gain favour (see earlier remarks about 'fast policy'). Such change, of course, evi-dences the ideological transformations associated with the PDM (as in Table 16.1). Most centrally, I have in mind here the relatively recent absenting of 'art' (to be distinguished from 'the arts' or 'artworks' and its intrinsic value).[15] If we take it here that 'art' is synonymous with the production of (institution-ally recognized) 'artworks', and therefore the actually existing 'arts' – which are indeed subject to forms of elitism, inequalities, class privilege and suchlike – there are clear grounds for preferring instead to talk in terms of, say, culture, creativity and the creative economy. This also has the advantage of speaking a language (the hegemonic language of the market) that politicians understand. Such conceptual absenting plays an important role in continuing to legitimate the creative economy, and the cultural and creative industries, as the location where culture and creativity happen. But in the process, culture and creativity (properly conceived) are effectively absented from areas of society not seen as directly connected to this sector, and this includes education, where the increasingly instrumental goal is to educate for the creative economy (currently conceived). As such, the actually existing creative economy is, paradoxically, though wholly in keeping with the PDM, complicit in a closed system that is reproducing inequality and, by its own standards, is not fit for purpose: it is not enabling creativity for everyone in society, which is its discursive promise.

Taken together, these forms of conceptual obfuscation perpetuate a situation in which leading commentators are saying one set of things about the creative economy, and then going on to contradict those things. There is a high level of path dependency and vested interest, with arts and cultural organizations, industry representatives, academics and policymakers (so-called 'corporate agents') all committed, in various (and, as we have seen, sometimes paradoxical) ways, to the status quo continuing.[16] It is against this context that I now introduce an alternative approach.

RE-IMAGINING THE CREATIVE ECONOMY

To be clear, just as I am not 'against' creativity, so I am not 'anti-modern' or 'against' modernity in any regressive or undialectical sense. Rather, the problem lies with how this is undertaken. For critical realists, 'the PDM is fundamentally inimical to universal free flourishing' (Hartwig 2011: 494). Our economic and environmental crises have at their root 'a triple disembedding: of money from the real economy; of the real economy from society; and of society from its spiritual infrastructure', allied to a 'four-fold alienation of people from nature, each other, their social relations and their essential selves' (Hartwig 2011: 507). Whilst reference to the 'spiritual' is undoubtedly off-putting for many (critical realists included), I suggest that the types of alienations outlined are, in fact, buttressed by a more immanent problem: the progressive marginalization of embodied human experience. It is to this that we need turn if we are to fully understand, and then transform, our creative practices in line with human flourishing.

Aesthetic critical realism (ACR) is a branch of critical realism that is premised on a depth ontology of experience.[17] ACR opens up our understanding of experience as a form of emergent practice and work.[18] Beginning with a definition of experience as our cognitive conscious and non-conscious (thought and unthought) knowledge gained through interaction with our environment, ACR offers explanatory accounts of different types and levels of emergent experience. Far from being limited to the domain of the arts, this emergentist approach offers insights for a wide range of topics, including value, culture, truth, beauty and good. It also promises some important new directions for how we theorize creativity. Whilst there is still no definitional consensus within the academy as to precisely what creativity is, it is generally taken to involve novelty and value: 'the ability to produce work that is both novel (i.e., original, unexpected) and appropriate (i.e., useful, adaptive concerning task constraints)'.[19] My critical realist definition holds that creativity is 'the capability to discover and bring into being new possibilities' (Martin and Wilson 2014: 37). Furthermore, 'human creativity *may (or may not)* gain individual, group, organizational, community or global recognition and this process of recognition can be influenced by many factors including psychological, economic, political and power processes' (ibid.). Building on the insights of ACR, I suggest that this process of creativity is dependent upon three interrelated freedoms that together constitute people's opportunities to recognize what they have reason to value: (1) the freedom to have experiences of being-in-relation with the world – aesthetic experience; (2) the freedom to undertake creative and artful projects; and (3) the axiological freedom to participate in value recognition.

The Freedom to Have Aesthetic Experience

I define experience as the human capacity for cognitive conscious and non-conscious, that is, thought and unthought, knowledge gained through interaction with our environment. Experience is a form of work, meaning (contrary to popular belief) that it does not all come naturally; we can be more or less experienced in experiencing the world. Whilst of course our experiences are infinitely diverse, thereby defying any easy categorization, at an analytical level at least we can distinguish between experience and aesthetic experience. I define aesthetic experience as our emergent experience of being-in-relation with the 'natural necessity' of the world; that is to say, with the way the world is. This meta-cognition is a form of reflexive, second-order knowing that both embraces and transcends direct observation. It takes in our (thought and unthought) knowledge of our knowledge of our relations, structures, mechanisms, powers, processes, systems, forces, values and energies, and indeed possibilities; none of which we can 'see'. To elaborate, this type of experiential knowledge has been discussed at some length within the domain of psychoanalytic aesthetics (Glover 2009). Christopher Bollas, for example, introduces 'unthought knowns' (Bollas 2018) as when we 'know' something perhaps as a feeling, a hunch, an intuition or suchlike, rather than as a conscious thought or fully cognized idea. This is highly relevant to creativity (for example, Richards on intimation), which, as I have argued, is centrally about our discovery and bringing into being of new and valued 'possibilities': things we cannot actually see, hear or sense directly.

The Freedom to Undertake Creative and Artful Projects

Aesthetic experiences are ours alone. We cannot share them with others. But it is here where come into play our practices of creativity, as the discovery and bringing into being of possibilities we value; and of art, as the skilled practice of giving sharable form to our aesthetic experience, i.e. where we care 'about' and 'for' experience. Such practices of care (see Tronto 2013 for discussion of caring about and caring for) be they in the doing, making and sharing of stories, dances, pictures, landscapes, performances, models, encounters and so on, are not exhausted by activities undertaken solely within the 'creative industries' or 'the arts'. They are not limited to those individuals who we call 'creatives' or 'artists'. Nor, indeed, should they be reduced to focusing alone on 'creative products' or 'artworks': collectively (more or less) valued forms given to our aesthetic experience. By the same token, what is being argued here should not be misconstrued as calling for the many and varied creative and artful practices that people do to be somehow legitimized as 'artworks'. This would be to miss the point.

From a policy perspective, the freedom to undertake creative and artful projects is the most obvious area of potential intervention in the context of 'developing inclusive and sustainable creative economies'. This is where attention is readily directed to the tangible and intangible resources, opportunities for encounters and interactions, training, education and cultural infrastructures that support people doing creativity (within or outside of the subsidized cultural sector or the commercial creative industries). The conceptualization being advanced here challenges this focus as being overly limited, however. More attention needs to be given to aesthetic experience, on the one hand (as introduced above), and to the ways in which we collectively recognize value, on the other (as discussed next).

The Freedom to Participate in Recognizing Value

Crucially, whether or not people consider the sharing of aesthetic experience through their creative and artful projects to be valuable is contingent upon culture, which I define as our systems of value recognition.[20] Culture is comprised of multiple systems operating with different logics and at different scales. One such system is 'the arts';[21] another is education, and another – indeed, the dominant culture of our age – is the 'economic' market-driven system. Such systems are constituted by, emergent from, but irreducible to clusters of axiological phenomena that are consciously and/or unconsciously reproduced or transformed through people's creative practice. Under my ACR definition, culture does not denote shared 'cultural values', but rather shared systems of value recognition. This is a fundamental distinction (and one that too often appears to have been overlooked within cultural sociology and cultural studies more broadly). Systems of value recognition are reproduced and transformed through a wide variety of structures, institutions and ideologies; including, for example, those discussed by Terry Eagleton (1990) under the 'ideology of the aesthetic'. When understood in this way, we can now see how actually existing creative economies reproduce institutions, structures and ideologies that both constrain and enable who gets to be involved in the process of value recognition in more or less democratic ways.

Each of the three freedoms outlined in this section are capabilities: that is, 'real [opportunities] that we have to accomplish what we value'.[22] We can now say more about how these capabilities directly impact upon human creativity.

First, 'aesthetic' capability (as our freedom to have aesthetic experience) is a prerequisite for 'discovering' possibility (possibilities being beyond our direct observation). Second, 'artful' capability (our freedom to give sharable form to our aesthetic experience) is a prerequisite of 'bringing into being' any new possibility. Arguably, there is no creativity without this stage of communication, which creative projects provide. Third, 'axiological' capability (our freedom to participate in value recognition[23]) is a necessary requirement if the 'value' of projects undertaken is to be recognized. Another way of thinking about this in the particular context of the arts is whether and how art is seen as 'art'. More widely, I suggest that doing creativity is always and necessarily dependent upon this capability set – what I term 'cultural capability' – being in place. The upshot of this, and where this chapter has been headed, is the claim that the overarching objective of any 'managed' social system of value recognition (culture) focused on expanding the material and immaterial resources needed for creativity for its citizens (creative economy), must be on cultural capability (the freedom to experience, discover, connect with, give sharable form to, and participate in recognizing what we have reason to value) rather than the commodification of creativity.

DISCUSSION

I have presented an explanatory critique of the actually existing creative economy. This was based on the 'long view' of the PDM, and it identified a series of conceptual practices that support the TINA stance that we can, and should, commodify human creativity. As a form of triumphalist 'endism' the actually existing creative economy is certainly much less obvious or explicit than other fundamentalisms that dominate the political landscape, such as Trumpism (the 'wall'), Brexitism ('Take Back Control') and a tide of national populisms driven by cultural closure. But perhaps it is just this 'going unnoticed' that makes it all the more worrying, and urgently in need of transformation.

We are now at a crossroads. Contrary to the prevailing TINA stance, there is an alternative, and this has to re-focus on providing the kind of supportive resources and infrastructure (that is, creative economy), that enables cultural capability. This is a normative project worth supporting. But actually, we need to go further still. At the beginning of this chapter, I referenced the EU-funded research project 'Developing Inclusive and Sustainable Creative Economies' (DISCE) as providing an important vantage point from which to consider the subject of this book. Taking the argument presented here to its conclusion, developing 'inclusive and sustainable creative economies' is worth doing not only on account of their promise for developing more inclusive and sustainable (more valuable) cultural and creative industries. Inclusive and sustainable creative economies are, in effect, the means to, and end of, recognizing what is valuable. Inclusive and sustainable creative economies are comprised of structures, practices and institutions that enable valuing; an infinitely diverse human process that, whilst individually experienced, is collectively achieved. It follows that inclusive and sustainable creative economies are neither limited to a discrete section of the wider economy, nor are they separate from 'the economy': they are what makes thriving economies possible. Furthermore, to the extent that they put human needs at their very centre, they are not just 'creative', they are 'caring'.

If policymakers are serious about developing inclusive and sustainable creative economies, their focus can no longer be limited to the arts, heritage, and cultural and creative industries (important though these are). A more inclusive ecological perspective is needed. The task of cultural development outlined here challenges us to fundamentally reconsider the relationship between culture and (sustainable) development for everyone.[24] This is about cultural democracy. There is a double irony here. First, looking back at cultural policy from the 1990s (before the 'cultural and creative industries' discourse really exploded on the international stage) we can see a very central interest in just this idea: for example, the 1995 UNESCO report *Our Creative Diversity* frames its approach towards culture and development by observing that 'cultural freedom leaves us free to meet one of the most basic needs, the need to define our own basic needs' (UNESCO 1995: 15). Second, in order to 'see' the potential of this alternative perspective, one needs the very structures, institutions and practices being advocated to be available to the policymaker right now. Within DISCE we are seeking to offer a modest first step in breaking the cycle, developing a policy tool that re-directs attention towards the aesthetic, artful and axiological dimensions of cultural development (a Cultural Development Index). We are starting with where people are now; but the question is: Do we have time for a 'long revolution'? At stake is cultural development – the expansion of cultural capability; and cultural development must surely be what cultural policy strives for and manages with care. Such is the premise and the promise of the creative economy – really.

NOTES

1.   James et al.'s (2015: 53) definition of 'economy'.
2.   De Beukelaer and O'Connor (2016: 27).
3.   UNCTAD et al. (2008); followed up by UNCTAD et al. (2010) and UNESCO and UNDP (2013).
4.   Bakshi et al. (2013: 34). The authors further argue that a defining characteristic [of creative industries] is their especially 'intensive use of creative talent' (ibid.: 28). Nesta was originally established by New Labour in 1998, and has operated

as a charity – now an 'investment foundation' – since 2012. See also Nesta (2017).

5. Banks (2017: 10, n. 2).
6. See Higgs et al. (2008).
7. Definition of 'creative' by Merriam-Webster.
8. David Throsby defines 'creative workers' as:

> those engaged in producing primary creative output; those engaged in interpretive activity; and those supplying creative services to support arts and cultural production. Those in the first group could be stratified according to the nature of the object or service produced: text, sound, fixed image, moving image, three-dimensional objects, etc allowing the identification, respectively, of writers (for all media); musicians; visual artists; film, television and video makers; sculptors and craftspeople; and so on. Those in the second group could also be classified according to the end-product, i.e. as performers interpreting works of drama, dance, music etc in a wide variety of media from live performance to digital transmission via the internet. The third group, comprising those supplying creative services in support of arts and cultural production, would include workers such as book editors, lighting designers, music producers and so on, in all of whose work some creative input is required. (Throsby 2003: 175)

9. Newbigin (n.d.), available at https://creativeconomy.britishcouncil.org/guide/what-creative-economy/ (accessed 22 July 2019).
10. See, for example, Oakley and O'Connor (2015), McRobbie (2016), Banks (2017), Reckwitz (2017), Mould (2018), Campbell (2014, 2019). Campbell identifies three stages in the 'persistence' of the 'creativity agenda': (a) the creative industries are shown to be economically important (1998–2011); (b) changing definitions (2011–14); and (c) the persistent economic success of creativity (2014–).
11. Hartwig (2011: 486). The phrase 'philosophical discourse of modernity' was introduced by Habermas (1985) in his book of that title.
12. Ibid. 'Modernity can and will no longer borrow the criteria by which it takes its orientation from the models supplied by another epoch; *it has to create its normativity out of itself*' (Habermas (1985 [1987]: 7).
13. Roy Bhaskar is the founder of the philosophy of critical realism, and this review of the PDM is based on his analysis.
14. Bhaskar (2002b: 172, n. 7, quoted in Hartwig 2011: 486, n. 5).
15. Mark Banks, for example, writes:

> certainly, in sociology, especially, claims that cultural objects might contain their own 'intrinsic' value have come to be regarded as partial, elitist or otherwise politically suspect – and much less significant than theorising either the social origins of value judgement, or the (non-aesthetic) economic or social benefits that culture might usefully provide. (Banks 2017: 3)

16. See Margaret Archer's discussion of corporate and primary agents (whether or not one is in a social position enabling active strategic change), vested interests and change in the context of her morphogenetic approach (Archer 1995: 259).
17. A 'depth ontology' recognizes the 'stratified' nature of the world and its being comprised of difference; this is contrasted with a 'flat ontology' (the implicit ontology of actualism) that is prone to the epistemic fallacy: 'the analysis of definition of statements about being in terms of statements about our knowledge (of being)' (Bhaskar 1993 [2008]: 397).
18. Emergence refers to when a whole possesses a property that is 'not possessed by any of the parts individually and that would not be possessed by the full set of

parts in the absence of a structuring set of relations between them' (Elder-Vass 2010: 17).

19.   Sternberg and Lubart (1999 [2007]: 3); see also Kaufman and Baer (2012), Runco and Jaeger (2012). Despite 70 years of research on creativity, fundamental issues remain concerning the nature of novelty, the role of effectiveness, whether recognition is necessary to the existence of creativity, and the nature of the value created (see Adarves-Yorno et al. 2008; Boden 2004; Kasof 1995; Kaufman and Baer 2012; Martin and Wilson 2017; Runco and Jaeger 2012).

20.   For a detailed discussion of definitional issues concerning 'culture', see Wilson (2019, Ch. 7).

21.   See, for example, Dickie (1974) and Danto (2013) on the 'institutional theory' of the 'artworld'.

22.   Sen (1992: 31); see also Sen (1999: 74).

23.   See Donati and Archer (2015) for a related discussion of 'relational subjects' and 'relational goods'; Wilson et al. (2017) and Gross and Wilson (2018) on 'cultural democracy'.

24.   See Clammer (2019), Isar (2017), Kangas et al. (2017); and Comunian et al. (2020) who in an editorial declaring 'The creative economy is dead' argue for 'creative-social economies' instead; and Pratt (2021) who suggests that the United Nations' designation of 2021 as the International Year of Creative Economy and Sustainable Development is the creative economy's 'coming of age'.

REFERENCES

Adarves-Yorno, I., Haslam, S.A., and Postmes, T. (2008), 'And now for something completely different? The impact of group membership on perceptions of creativity', *Social Influence*, 3, 248–266.

Archer, M.S. (1995), *Realist Social Theory: The Morphogenetic Approach*, Cambridge: Cambridge University Press.

Bakhshi, H., Hargreaves, I., and Mateos-Garcia, J. (2013), *A Manifesto for the Creative Economy*, London: Nesta.

Banks, M. (2017), *Creative Justice: Cultural Industries, Work and Inequality*, London: Rowman & Littlefield.

Bhaskar, R. (1993 [2008]), *Dialectic: The Pulse of Freedom*, with an introduction by M. Hartwig, London: Routledge.

Bhaskar, R. (2002a), *From Science to Emancipation: Alienation and the Actuality of Enlightenment*, New Delhi, India; Thousand Oaks, CA, USA; London, UK: SAGE Publications.

Bhaskar, R. (2002b), *Reflections on Meta-Reality: Transcendence, Emancipation and Everyday Life*, New Delhi, India; Thousand Oaks, CA, USA; London, UK: SAGE Publications.

Bhaskar, R. (2002c), *The Philosophy of meta-Reality, Volume I, Meta-Reality: Creativity, Love and Freedom*, New Delhi, India; Thousand Oaks, CA, USA; London, UK: SAGE Publications.

Boden, M.A. (2004), *The Creative Mind: Myths and mechanisms*, 2nd edition, London: Routledge.

Bollas, C. (2018), *The Shadow of the Object. Psychoanalysis of the Unthought Known*, 30th Anniversary edition, Abingdon: Routledge.

Campbell, P. (2014), 'Imaginary success? The contentious ascendance of creativity', *European Planning Studies*, 22 (5), 995–1009.

Campbell, P. (2019), *Persistent Creativity. Making the Case for Art, Culture and the Creative Industries*, London: Palgrave Macmillan.

Clammer, J. (2019), *Cultural Rights and Justice. Sustainable Development, The Arts and the Body*, London: Palgrave Macmillan.

Comunian, R., Rickmers, D., and Nanetti, A. (2020), 'Guest editorial', *Social Enterprise Journal*, 16 (2), 101–119.

Craft, A., Gardner, H., and Claxton, G. (2008), *Creativity, Wisdom, and Trusteeship: Exploring the Role of Education*, Thousand Oaks, CA: Corwin Press.

Cropley, D., Kaufman, J.C., Murphy, M., and Moran, S. (2014), 'Summary. Creativity and ethics – two golden eggs', in S. Moran, D. Cropley and J.C. Kaufman (eds), *The Ethics of Creativity*, Basingstoke: Palgrave Macmillan, pp. 299–307.

Danermark, B., Ekström, M., Jakobsen, L., and Karlsson, J. (2002), *Explaining Society: Critical Realism in the Social Sciences*, London: Routledge.

Danto, A.C. (2013), *What Art Is*, New Haven, CT: Yale University Press.

De Beukelaer, C., and O'Connor, J. (2016), 'The creative economy and the development agenda: the use and abuse of "fast policy"', in P. Stupples and K. Teaiwa (eds), *Contemporary Perspectives on Art and International Development*, London: Routledge, pp. 27–47.

Dickie, G. (1974), *Art and the Aesthetic: An Institutional Analysis*, Ithaca, NY: Cornell University Press.

Donati, P., and Archer, M.S. (2015), *The Relational Subject*, Cambridge: Cambridge University Press.

Eagleton, T. (1990), *The Ideology of the Aesthetic*, Oxford: Blackwell.

Elder-Vass, D. (2010), *The Causal Power of Social Structures: Emergence, Structure and Agency*, Cambridge: Cambridge University Press.

Glover, N. (2009), *Psychoanalytic Aesthetics: An Introduction to the British School*, London: Karnac.

Goehr, L. (2007), *The Imaginary Museum of Musical Works: An Essay in the Philosophy of Music*, Oxford: Oxford University Press.

Gross, J., and Wilson, N. (2018), 'Cultural democracy: an ecological and capabilities approach', *International Journal of Cultural Policy*, 26 (3), 328–343.

Habermas, J. (1985 [1987]), *The Philosophical Discourse of Modernity*, F. Lawrence (transl.), Cambridge, MA: MIT Press.

Hartwig, M. (2011), 'Bhaskar's critique of the philosophical discourse of modernity', *Journal of Critical Realism*, 10 (4), 485–510.

Higgs, P., Cunningham, S., and Bakhshi, H. (2008), *Beyond the Creative Industries: Mapping the Creative Economy in the United Kingdom*, London: Nesta.

Howkins, J. (2001), *Creative Economy: How People Make Money From Ideas*, London: Penguin.

Isar, Y.R. (2017), '"Culture", "sustainable development" and cultural policy: a contrarian view', *International Journal of Cultural Policy*, 23 (2), 148–158.

James, P., Magee, L., Scerri, A., and Steger, M.B. (2015), *Urban Sustainability in Theory and Practice: Circles of Sustainability*, London: Routledge.

Kangas, A., Duxbury, N., and De Beukelaer, C. (2017), 'Introduction: cultural policies for sustainable development', *International Journal of Cultural Policy*, 23 (2), 129–132.

Kasof, J. (1995), 'Explaining creativity: the attributional perspective', *Creativity Research Journal*, 8, 311–366.

Kaufman, J.C., and Baer, J. (2012), 'Beyond new and appropriate: who decides what is creative?', *Creativity Research Journal*, 24, 83–91.

Martin, L., and Wilson, N. (2014), 'Re-discovering creativity: why theory–practice consistency matters', *International Journal for Talent Development and Creativity*, 2 (1), 31–42.

Martin, L., and Wilson, N. (2017), 'Defining creativity with discovery', *Journal of Creativity Research*, 29, 417–425.

McRobbie, A. (2016), *Be Creative*, Cambridge: Polity Press.

Mould, O. (2018), *Against Creativity*, London: Verso.

Nesta (2017), *Nesta's Work in the Creative Economy, Arts and Culture*, London: Nesta.

Nussbaum, M. (2011), *Creating Capabilities: The Human Development Approach*. Cambridge, MA: Belknap Press of Harvard University Press.

Oakley, K., and O'Connor, J. (2015), *Routledge Companion to the Cultural Industries*, London: Routledge.

O'Connor, J. (2019), *Resources of Hope? Creative Economy and Development in the Global South*, ifa Input 02/19, ad hoc Expert Meeting on Creative Economy and Sustainable Development, 28 October 2019, Stuttgart: Institut für Auslandsbeziehungen.

Pratt, A.C. (2021), 'The creative economy and sustainable development', *City, Culture and Society*, 25, 100393.

Pratt, A.C., and Hutton, T. (2013), 'Reconceptualising the relationship between the creative economy and the recession: learning from the financial crisis', *Cities*, 33, 86–95.

Reckwitz, A. (2017), *The Invention of Creativity*, Cambridge: Polity Press.

Runco, M.A., and Jaeger, G.J. (2012), 'The standard definition of creativity', *Creativity Research Journal*, 24, 92–96.

Schlesinger, P. (2017), 'The creative economy: invention of a global orthodoxy', *Innovation: The European Journal of Social Science Research*, 30 (1), 73–90.

Sen, A. (1992), *Inequality Reexamined*, Cambridge, MA: Harvard University Press.

Sen, A. (1999), *Development as Freedom*, New York: Knopf.

Sternberg, R.J., and Lubart, T.I. (1999 [2007]), 'The concept of creativity: prospects and paradigms', in R.J. Sternberg (ed.), *Handbook of Creativity*, Cambridge: Cambridge University Press, pp. 3–15.

Throsby, D. (2003), 'The cultural workforce: issues of definition and measurement', in S. Bernier and D. Lievesley (eds), *Proceedings of the International Symposium on Culture Statistics*, Montreal, Canada: UNESCO Institute for Statistics, pp. 173–187.

Tronto, J.C. (2013), *Caring Democracy. Markets, Equality, and Justice*, New York: New York University Press.

UNCTAD, UNDP, UNESCO, WIPO, and ITC (2008), *Creative Economy Report 2008: The Challenge of Assessing the Creative Economy Towards Informed Policy-Making*, New York: UNDP and UNCTAD.

UNCTAD, UNDP, UNESCO, WIPO, and ITC (2010), *Creative Economy Report 2010: A Feasible Development Option*, New York: UNDP and UNCTAD.

UNESCO (1995), *Our Creative Diversity. Report of the World Commission on Culture and Development*, World Commission on Culture and Development.

UNESCO and UNDP (2013), *Creative Economy Report 2013 Special Edition: Widening Local Development Pathways*, New York: United Nations Development Programme and UNESCO.

Vlassis, A., and De Beukelaer, C. (2019), 'The creative economy as a versatile policy script: exploring the role of competing intergovernmental organizations', *Media, Culture and Society*, 41 (4), 502–519.

Williams, R. (1961), *The Long Revolution*, London: Chatto & Windus Ltd.

Wilson, N. (2018), 'Creativity at work: who cares? Towards an ethics of creativity as a structured practice of care', in L. Martin and N. Wilson (eds), *The Palgrave Handbook of Creativity at Work*, London: Palgrave Macmillan, pp. 621–647.

Wilson, N. (2019), *The Space that Separates: A Realist Theory of Art*, Abingdon: Routledge.

Wilson, N., Gross, J., and Bull, A. (2017), *Towards Cultural Democracy: Promoting Cultural Capabilities for Everyone*, London: King's Cultural Institute.

Wilson, N., Gross, J., Dent, T., Conor, B., and Comunian, R. (2020), *Re-thinking Inclusive and Sustainable Growth for the Creative Economy: A Literature Review*, DISCE Publications. https://disce.eu/wp-content/uploads/2020/01/DISCE-Report-D5.2.pdf.

Index